Also by Megan Kate Nelson

Ruin Nation:
Destruction and the American Civil War

Trembling Earth:
A Cultural History of the Okefenokee Swamp

THE THREE-CORNERED WAR

The Union, the Confederacy,
and Native Peoples in
the Fight for the West

Megan Kate Nelson

SCRIBNER

New York   London   Toronto   Sydney   New Delhi

SCRIBNER
An Imprint of Simon & Schuster, Inc.
1230 Avenue of the Americas
New York, NY 10020

First Scribner hardcover edition February 2020

SCRIBNER and design are registered trademarks of The Gale Group, Inc.,
used under license by Simon & Schuster, Inc., the publisher of this work.

For information about special discounts for bulk purchases, please
contact Simon & Schuster Special Sales at 1-866-506-1949
or business@simonandschuster.com.

The Simon & Schuster Speakers Bureau can bring authors to your live
event. For more information or to book an event, contact the
Simon & Schuster Speakers Bureau at 1-866-248-3049 or visit
our website at www.simonspeakers.com.

Interior design by Laura Levatino

Manufactured in the United States of America

1   3   5   7   9   10   8   6   4   2

Library of Congress Cataloging-in-Publication Data is available.

ISBN 978-1-5011-5254-2
ISBN 978-1-5011-5256-6 (ebook)

For Mathilde Bodensieck Fritschel and Genevieve Miles Riddle

and all of the grandmothers

Contents

Prologue   xiii

PART ONE

Those Whom
the Gods Would Destroy

Chapter 1   Baylor   5
Chapter 2   Mangas Coloradas   15
Chapter 3   Canby   24
Chapter 4   Davidson   33
Chapter 5   Juanita   42
Chapter 6   Ickis   50
Chapter 7   Valverde   57

PART TWO

Trail Men

Chapter 8   Baylor   79
Chapter 9   Clark   90
Chapter 10   Glorieta   99
Chapter 11   Davidson   115
Chapter 12   Carleton   124

Chapter 13 Mangas Coloradas   136
Chapter 14 Canby   144
Chapter 15 Ickis   152

PART THREE

—

Land of Suffering

Chapter 16 Mangas Coloradas   165
Chapter 17 Clark   176
Chapter 18 Tséyi'   185
Chapter 19 Carleton   200
Chapter 20 Juanita   214
Chapter 21 Clark   224
Chapter 22 Juanita   232

Epilogue   247
Acknowledgments   253
Abbreviations   257
Notes   259
Bibliography   293
Index   315

THE
THREE-
CORNERED
WAR

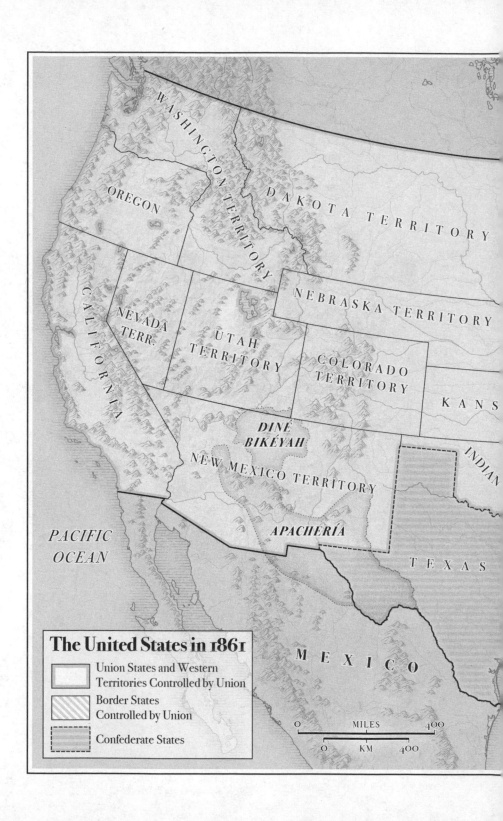

WASHINGTON TERRITORY

OREGON

DAKOTA TERRITORY

NEBRASKA TERRITORY

NEVADA TERR.

UTAH TERRITORY

CALIFORNIA

COLORADO TERRITORY

KANS

DINÉ BIKÉYAH

NEW MEXICO TERRITORY

INDIAN

APACHERÍA

PACIFIC OCEAN

TEXAS

MEXICO

The United States in 1861

Union States and Western Territories Controlled by Union

Border States Controlled by Union

Confederate States

0   MILES   400

0   KM   400

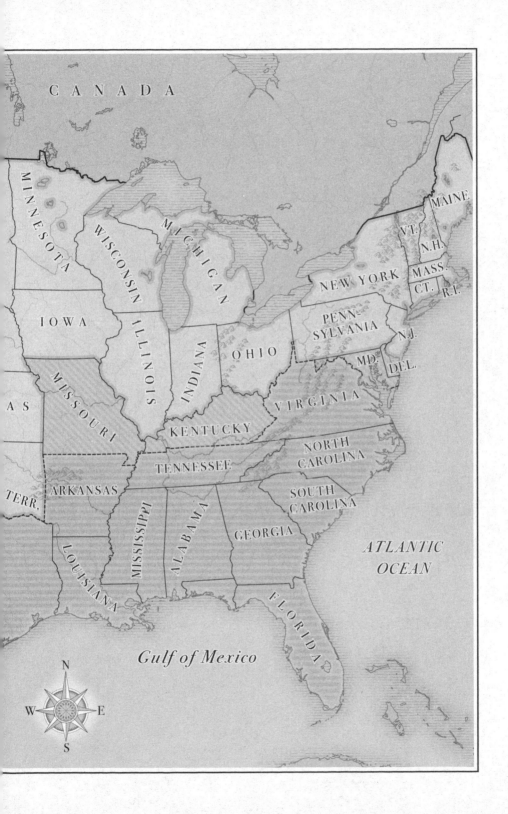

Prologue

I t was the first summer of the Civil War, and everyone thought it would be the last. Hundreds of thousands of Americans converged on train platforms and along country roads, waving handkerchiefs and shouting goodbyes as their men went off to military camps. Most of these men were civilian volunteers: farmers and laborers, doctors and lawyers who had never fought in any sort of battle. Some were professional soldiers: army regulars who were recruited into service in the 1840s and '50s, paid to fight first against Indians in Florida and then Mexicans across the border, and afterward, to garrison frontier forts from the Mississippi River to the Pacific.

In those first warm days of June 1861, there had been only a few skirmishes in the steep, stony mountains of western Virginia, but large armies of Union and Confederate soldiers were coalescing along the Potomac River. A major battle was coming, and it would be fought somewhere between Washington, D.C., and Richmond.

As the war was beginning in Virginia, the struggle over lands west of the Mississippi was also getting under way. In the Union War Department a few steps from the White House, clerks wrote out dispatches to commanders in California, Oregon, and the western territories. The federal government needed army regulars currently garrisoned at frontier forts to fight in the eastern theater. These soldiers should be sent immediately to the camps around Washington, D.C.

In New Mexico Territory, however, some regulars would have to remain at their posts. The political loyalties of the local population—large numbers of Hispano laborers, farmers, ranchers, and merchants; a small number of Anglo businessmen and territorial officials; and thousands of Apaches and Navajos—were far from certain. New Mexico Territory, which in 1861 extended from the Rio Grande to the California border, had come into the Union in 1850 as part of a congressional compromise regarding the extension of slavery into the West. California was admitted to the Union as a free state while New Mexico, which was south of the Mason-Dixon Line, remained a territory. Under a policy of popular sovereignty, its residents would decide for themselves if slavery would be legal. Mexico had abolished black slavery in 1829, but Hispanos in New Mexico had long embraced a forced labor system that enslaved Apaches and Navajos. In 1859 the territorial legislature, made up of predominantly wealthy Hispano merchants and ranchers with Native slaves in their households, passed a Slave Code to protect all slave property in the Territory.

In order to ensure that this pro-slavery stance did not drive New Mexico into the arms of the Confederacy, the commander of the Department of New Mexico would have to keep most of his regulars in place to defend the Territory from a secessionist overthrow. Louisa Canby's husband, Edward R. S. Canby (his wife and family members called him by his middle name, Richard), a colonel in the Union Army who had assumed command in Santa Fe after his superior officer resigned to join the Confederacy, was in his headquarters until all hours during the summer of 1861, organizing his troops and making defensive plans. Louisa was used to being alone at such busy times. She and Richard had been married for more than twenty years, and they had moved together with their daughter Mary to frontier posts in Florida, Pennsylvania, New York, California, and Utah Territory. Living in Santa Fe at this moment, however, was different. Everyone was talking not only of a secessionist insurrection, but also a possible Confederate invasion of New Mexico. If that came to pass, Louisa would do whatever she could to help the Union win the fight.

The Lincoln administration had to retain control of the West in order to win the war. It was an immense region, making up more than 40 percent of the United States landmass. The U.S. government had purchased most of it from England, Spain, and France early in the nineteenth century and acquired the rest after defeating Mexico in 1848. New Mexico Territory was the gateway to southern California, and to much of the rest of the West. In 1861 it was also the only far western territory to share a border with the Confederacy. It was therefore vulnerable to invasion.

To move large armies through New Mexico Territory would be a challenge. It was a forbidding landscape, with rolling deserts breaking suddenly into volcanic ranges and mesas. Its lands averaged 5,700 feet above sea level. Newcomers immediately felt the effects of the elevation, and of the semi-aridity of the climate. Towns, farms, and ranches were clustered along three major rivers (the Rio Grande, the Colorado, and the Gila) and trails that led to other water sources: springs and wells, small creeks and arroyos. Bright green fields edged these waterways and were themselves crossed by acequias, irrigation ditches that brought water to the plants. The fields were a vivid contrast to the brown desert sands that surrounded them.

Like the region's scrub plants, the people who lived in New Mexico Territory had developed strategies of survival. They scattered across the landscape in order to use the region's scarce resources without depleting them. Those who were able to move quickly through the desert, and knew where there were steady supplies of meat, plants, and water, were those who endured in New Mexico. They hunted, farmed, staked claims in silver and copper mines, traded goods and sold slaves, and regularly raided one another's horse and cattle herds.

Union officials wanted more Anglo-Americans to settle in New Mexico Territory at some point in the future, in order to colonize its lands and integrate the Territory more firmly into the nation. As the Civil War began, however, they wanted to control it as a thoroughfare, a way to access the gold in the mountains of the West and California's deep-water ports. They needed the money from the mines and from international trade to fund their war effort. The Confederates wanted these same resources, of course. In the summer of 1861, Richard Canby's forces had to defend New Mexico Territory in order to protect California, and the entire West.

Colonel James Henry Carleton had the security of California in mind as he walked down the streets of San Bernardino in July 1861. It was a small but growing town with 1,500 residents, who hailed from every state across the nation. Would they side with the North or the South? Carleton believed that the people of San Bernardino would identify more with their comrades in the mines than with the communities they had left behind. He felt he knew towns like this well, after more than twenty years posted at U.S. Army forts in the West. Carleton soon discovered, however, that large groups of secessionists were gathering in secret in San Bernardino, hatching plans to overthrow the state government. As he boarded a stage to take him back to Los Angeles, Carleton wrote out requests to send two more companies of soldiers to that town. They would help to keep the peace and represent the power of the Union. And if the Confederates should invade New Mexico and then march toward southern California, these Union soldiers would be perfectly positioned to defend it.

Mining communities throughout the West mirrored San Bernardino's diversity, and its volatility. Although Colorado Territory had thrown in with the Union after its organization in February 1861, there had been fist-fights and gunfire in the streets of Denver as northerners and southerners fought for control of the town. Twenty-four-year-old Alonzo Ickis had not participated in those brawls. He had been up in the Rocky Mountain gold mines for the previous two years, trying to find a vein that he could work for a profit. In the summer of 1861 he moved to Breckenridge, a small town filled with Midwestern miners like him. They voted to change the spelling of the town's name so that it no longer honored John C. Breckin-ridge, who had run for president as a pro-slavery Democrat in 1860. It was a small gesture of their fealty to the Union. Ickis had been reading the war news in the papers—months old, but to him still news—and the conflict seemed very far away. He was not sure what he would do after that sum-mer in the mines, whether he would go back home to Iowa and muster into the Union Army or stay in Colorado and wait for the war to come to him. That decision was still ahead of him, Ickis reckoned. The days were bright and warm, and he had digging to do.

Union military officials in New Mexico were not yet recruiting Colo-rado soldiers for their defense of the Territory. Richard Canby hoped that in addition to his army regulars, he could enlist enough Hispano soldiers to fight off an invading Confederate Army. To recruit, train, and lead these soldiers the Union Army needed charismatic officers, men who could speak Spanish and who had experience fighting in the rolling prairies, parched deserts, and high mountain passes of the Southwest. Several such men volunteered for the Union Army in the summer of 1861, including Christopher "Kit" Carson, the famed frontiersman. Carson had been born in Kentucky but had lived and traveled throughout New Mexico for more than thirty years, working as a hunter, trapper, and occasional U.S. Army guide. He volunteered for the army when the Civil War began, accepting a commission as a lieutenant colonel. In June 1861, Richard Canby sent him to Fort Union to take command of the 1st New Mexico Volunteers, a regiment of Hispano soldiers who had come into camp from all over the Territory. Carson knew that most of New Mexico's Anglos were skeptical about these men and their soldiering abilities. The frontiersman believed, however, that the soldiers of the 1st New Mexico would fight well once the battles began. His job was to get them ready.

Some of Carson's men came with experience, having served in New Mexican militias that rode out to attack Navajos and Apaches in response to raids on their towns and ranches. It was a cycle of violence with a long history, one that predated the arrival of Americans in New Mexico. That summer, however, as soldiers gathered in Union military camps, there had been few raids into Diné Bikéyah, the Navajo homeland in northwestern New Mexico. The calm was unusual, but welcome. In the valley between the Defiance Plateau and the Chuska Mountains in the center of Diné Bikéyah, Juanita gathered the first of the wild plants pushing up through the dirt, looked to her cornfields, and tended the large sheep herd that belonged to her and her husband, a Navajo headman named Manuelito. The herd had grown over the spring, after Navajos raided Hispano ranches and towns and brought back hundreds of animals. There had been no reprisals from the Hispanos or the Americans for these attacks, and several U.S. military posts had been abandoned. Hopefully this meant that the Navajos would have a peaceful harvest season, and a winter of comfort and plenty.

The Navajos were not the only ones who noticed a shift in the balance of power in the summer of 1861. In the southern reaches of New Mexico Territory, the Chiricahua Apache chief Mangas Coloradas watched Americans move through Apachería, his people's territory. This was the latest in a series of Anglo migrations through Apachería over the past thirty years. First the trappers and traders arrived and then, in 1846, U.S. soldiers under Stephen Watts Kearny, on their way to fight the Mexicans in California. Long wagon trains filled with Anglo families followed, on the hunt for gold in the Sierras. U.S. soldiers came again in the 1850s, and this time they stayed. Mail stage drivers and miners flooded in. They began to build towns in Mangas Coloradas's lands, cutting his trees and killing the mule deer that sustained the Chiricahuas during harsh high desert winters. Mangas decided that these incursions would not stand. In June 1861, sensing that the U.S. Army was distracted, he decided that this was the time to drive all of the Americans from Apachería.

Navajos and Chiricahua Apaches were a serious challenge to the Union Army's campaign to gain control of New Mexico at the beginning of the American Civil War. If Richard Canby could secure the Territory against the Union's Confederate and Native enemies, he would achieve more than Republicans had thought possible after ten years of constant, angry debates about the introduction of slavery into the West, and the significance of that region in the future of the nation. Would the West become a patchwork of plantations, worked by black slaves? Southern Democrats, led by

Mississippi senator (and future Confederate president) Jefferson Davis, had argued that the acquisitions from Mexico, particularly New Mexico Territory, "can only be developed by slave labor in some of its forms." The amount of food and cotton that New Mexico plantations would produce, Davis imagined, would make that Territory a part of "the great mission of the United States, to feed the hungry, to clothe the naked, and to establish peace and free trade with all mankind."[1]

Members of the Republican Party disagreed. A relatively new political organization born out of disputes over slavery in 1854, Republicans considered slavery to be a "relic of barbarism" and argued that it should not be expanded into the western territories. "The normal condition of all the territory of the United States is that of freedom," their 1860 party platform asserted. The western lands should be reserved for free laborers who would "enjoy all of the rights and privileges to which they are entitled" by the Constitution.[2] Preventing Confederate occupation of New Mexico Territory and clearing it of Navajos and Apaches were twin goals of the Union Army's Civil War campaign in New Mexico, an operation that sought not only military victory but also the creation of an empire of liberty: a nation of free laborers extending from coast to coast.

To make this vision a reality, New Mexico had to be both militarily secure and politically stable. The appointment of Republican officials to territorial posts would ensure that in the wake of the Union Army's successes, the conquest of the region would continue. In late July 1861, the Union Department of the Interior sent a certificate to John A. Clark, an Illinois lawyer and landowner, appointing him surveyor general of New Mexico Territory. Clark was pleased. He had experience surveying public lands in his home state, and in this new position he would have the opportunity to examine and map the Southwest. The knowledge he produced would be essential to the Anglo settlement of New Mexico, and its cultivation by free farmers. This was also a chance for Clark to serve his country in a time of crisis. At forty-five, he was too old to be shouldering a rifle in the field of battle. His service would take him far away from his wife, Anna, and their seven children, but perhaps he would send for them after he settled into his quarters and put his office in order. In early August John Clark began to pack his bags for the journey to Santa Fe. His role was an essential one in the Lincoln administration's plan to extend its political influence and power to the Pacific.

As Union soldiers, civilians, and politicians began to mobilize in New Mexico Territory, word spread across Texas: the Confederate Army needed soldiers to march to war on the well-worn trade route from San Antonio to the Mexican trading town of El Paso. They needed men who could bring their own horses and gear. Men who were not afraid of a hard fight in rough places. Men who would help their new nation claim what had always been rightfully theirs.

Jefferson Davis himself had approved the plan. New Mexico Territory, he believed, would be an ideal location for a transcontinental railroad, the center of a network of iron rails that would bind the Atlantic and Pacific coasts of the Confederacy together. Davis also hoped that the Southwest could become the heart of a Confederate empire of slavery, extending from Georgia to California and perhaps even southward into Mexico. For now, though, Davis wanted New Mexico for the same reason Lincoln did: for its access to gold and Pacific ports, which would help the Confederacy win the war to come.

In June 1861 the Confederate president gave former U.S. Army officer Henry Hopkins Sibley permission to raise troops in Texas, for a campaign to take New Mexico. At almost the same moment, a thirty-eight-year-old rancher rode into San Antonio with three hundred men in tow. Throughout the spring, John Robert Baylor had traveled through the western counties of the state, making impassioned speeches about the southern cause, the northern menace, and the fun that Texas men would have on their "buffalo hunt." Baylor was as charismatic as he was physically imposing: six-foot-three and broad-shouldered, with flashing blue eyes and long, dark hair swept back from a receding hairline. His recruiting success so impressed his superiors that Baylor was given command of the 2nd Texas Mounted Rifles, a regiment that grew to almost a thousand men in the next few weeks. Baylor soon received orders to take his soldiers and occupy several abandoned federal forts strung out along the road between San Antonio and El Paso. The 2nd Texas would then halt at Fort Bliss, an installation built near the border of Texas and Mexico. From there it was a short forty-mile march to New Mexico Territory. Baylor and the 2nd Texas left a few days later.

When Baylor's men vacated their camps outside San Antonio, hundreds of other soldiers moved in. Texans from all over the state were answering Henry Sibley's call for troops. William Lott Davidson (Bill to his friends), twenty-three years old and Mississippi-born, read the notices in the papers and decided to enlist. A lawyer living in a small town outside Houston, Davidson had no military training but he did have some experience fighting

Indians, and bore the mark of those fights: a ragged scar along his jawbone where a local surgeon had sawed a Comanche arrow out of his face. In late July 1861, Bill Davidson began to load up his gear for the ride to San Antonio, determined to do all he could to win the West for the Confederacy.

———

It was the first summer of the Civil War and all of these people—Canby, the army wife; Carleton, the Union colonel; Ickis, the gold miner; Carson, the frontiersman; Juanita, the Navajo woman; Mangas Coloradas, the Apache war chief; Clark, the surveyor general; Baylor, the ambitious rancher; and Davidson, the young lawyer—were moving toward the Rio Grande, and toward one another.

Some had met before. Others would meet on battlefields: Valverde, Glorieta, and Tséyi' (Canyon de Chelly). Most would cross paths obliquely, never realizing how much their actions altered each other's lives. Together, their stories help to explain how the conflict in New Mexico, as one soldier put it, was a "three-cornered war" involving Union soldiers, Confederates, and Native peoples fighting for power over the region's natural resources. In the summer of 1861, it remained to be seen if any one community could fully win New Mexico and, with it, the greater West. The battles that followed took place across the entire Territory, from the Rio Grande to the California border, up toward Colorado and across the border in Mexico. They illuminate the ways that New Mexico became a pivotal theater of the Civil War, the center of a larger struggle for the future of the nation, of Native peoples, and of the West.

———

As these nine people converged in New Mexico Territory in 1861, a comet appeared overhead, burning through the desert sky. Astronomers speculated about its origins. It could be the Great Comet of 1264, the huge and brilliant orb that had presaged the death of the pope. Or it might be the comet of 1556, whose tail resembled a wind-whipped torch, and whose splendor had convinced Charles V that a dire calamity awaited him. In either case, the editors of the *Santa Fe Gazette* found the appearance of this "new and unexpected stranger" in the skies to be ominous.

"Inasmuch as bloody [conflicts] were the order of the day in those times," their report read, "it is easy to see that each comet was the harbinger of a fearful and devastating war."[3]

PART ONE

Those Whom
the Gods Would Destroy

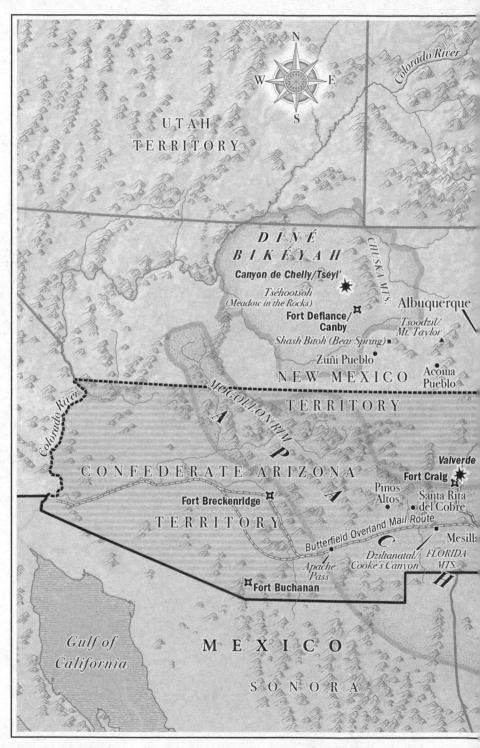

The Southwestern Theater, Summer 1861–Winter 1862

1

=

Baylor

When Texas seceded from the Union in February 1861 and the Civil War began in earnest two months later, John Baylor had not thought he would end up in the deserts of southern New Mexico. He had first volunteered for the Confederate Army in May, hoping to defend Texas from invasion or to take the fight to the Yankees in Virginia. He had come to Texas from Kentucky as a teenager, part of a flood of migrants who poured into the newly established republic after it secured independence from Mexico in 1836. His family had been lured by its rich, loamy bottomlands, the promise of booming cotton crops, and the right to own slaves.[1] By the 1850s Baylor and his wife, Emy, were living near the south-central town of LaGrange, with some acreage in crops and a growing herd of cattle.[2]

Baylor liked the work, but he was a man on the make, always interested in new ways to make money and to gain the respect of his peers.[3] In 1851, he ran for the Texas legislature and was easily elected. He also began to read the law and was admitted to the state bar in 1853.[4] He was proud of all he had achieved and saw his success as part of a family effort.

"Them Baylors," he wrote to his sister Fanny in 1857, "may they never cease to have good luck until the poorest among them is worth millions."[5]

Baylor saw his service in the Confederate Army as another opportunity to make his mark. He was ecstatic about his appointment as lieutenant colonel of the 2nd Texas Mounted Rifles, and about their orders to secure the Union's abandoned military installations in West Texas.[6] In June 1861, Baylor and his men had traveled quickly along the San Antonio–El Paso Road. Whenever they arrived at a fort, they left a company of soldiers behind to defend it before moving on.[7] This process, along with a high rate of desertion, left Baylor with only about 350 soldiers when he finally arrived at Fort Bliss, on the far western edge of Texas, on July 5.[8]

According to his orders, Baylor was supposed to stay at Fort Bliss. But after he had rested his men for two weeks, the Texans received word that a detachment of Union troops had left Albuquerque and was moving south along the Rio Grande. Baylor was alarmed. It looked like the Yankees were planning to invade Texas, and his men were the only force positioned to defend it. He pondered his options. The road from San Antonio was not yet strung with telegraph wires, and he did not have time to send a letter to headquarters asking for orders. He did not know that at that moment, a dispatch was already on its way to Fort Bliss, instructing Baylor to make no attempt to move into New Mexico Territory until a senior officer arrived to take command.[9] By the time that letter reached Fort Bliss, Baylor had already crossed the border. He had decided that moving forward was better than standing still. He would take responsibility for whatever resulted.[10]

———

Riding quietly through the desert on the night of July 24, 1861, John Baylor and three hundred men approached Fort Fillmore, the Union's southernmost military installation in New Mexico Territory. The fort was full of medicine, weapons, and food that Baylor and the 2nd Texas would need for the invasion of the Territory. The plan was to surround the fort and then attack as the sun rose over the jagged peaks of the Organ Mountains. They crept close to the fort in the early-morning darkness, but then Baylor heard Fillmore's buglers begin to play the long roll, summoning the Union soldiers within to take up their arms. He found out later that a deserter from his ranks had slipped away to warn the federals, and so the 2nd Texas had lost the advantage of surprise. Disgruntled, Baylor abandoned his original plan and ordered his men to march toward the small trading town of Mesilla.[11]

A few miles north of Fort Fillmore, Mesilla was at the crossroads of the Southwest's two most well-trafficked thoroughfares: *El Camino Real de Tierra Adentro* ("the Royal Road of the Interior Lands"), moving people north and south between Mexico and Santa Fe along the Rio Grande, and the Butterfield overland mail route, an east-west road linking Missouri and Los Angeles. Mesilla was also the gateway to the region's silver, gold, and copper mines. Some had been worked for years by Hispano miners, while others, deep in Chiricahua Apache country, had just been discovered by Anglos. If John Baylor could occupy Mesilla, the Confederates could control access to these mines, as well as traffic in and out of southern New Mexico.

As the 2nd Texas rode northward, they passed lush fields of corn and wheat, a pleasing sight to soldiers who had spent the past month traveling through the dusty brown tablelands of western Texas. On the outskirts of Mesilla, the regiment turned onto the town's main road, guiding their horses around deep holes dug out by Hispano artisans to make adobe bricks. News of their arrival spread ahead of them, and by the time the Texans reached Mesilla's central plaza, a crowd had gathered. The Confederates halted.

"Viva!" someone shouted. And then a chorus: "Hurrah!"[12]

The 2nd Texas dismounted, pleased with all of the "manifestations of joy" that greeted them on the streets of Mesilla. Although the New Mexico legislature had declared for the Union, most of Mesilla's Anglo residents had come from the states of the Confederacy, looking for their fortunes in the mines and finding other opportunities in frontier businesses.[13] In November 1860, a handful of these citizens had held a mock election in the town plaza, voting overwhelmingly for Kentucky's John C. Breckinridge rather than the Republican Abraham Lincoln or the northern Democrat Stephen Douglas. After the secession of Texas, Anglo miners, teamsters, and businessmen from southern New Mexico issued their own proclamation of secession. They wanted to create a newly independent territory they called "Arizona," with Mesilla as its capital. The area was already so decidedly pro-Confederate by the time Baylor arrived that, as one Unionist reported, "this country is now as much in the possession of the enemy as Charleston is."[14]

While the officers of the 2nd Texas sought out lodging and supplies for their men, John Baylor looked for a good place to establish his headquarters. In the center of Mesilla plaza, the U.S. flag came down and the Confederate flag went up. The crowd cheered again.

When he occupied Mesilla on July 25, 1861, John Baylor became the first Confederate to lead a successful invasion of Union territory in the Civil War. He did not have time to revel in this distinction, however. Rising dust clouds to the east told him that Union soldiers from Fort Fillmore were on the move. Baylor figured that even if the Texans were outnumbered, they had the advantage of a defensive position. He ordered most of the 2nd Texas to leave their horses and move on foot to the southern edge of town. He placed some of them along the road, others on the flat roofs of surrounding adobe houses, and the rest in corrals and cornfields. Then they waited.

In the late afternoon, two riders came into view, carrying a flag of truce. Baylor sent two of his most trusted officers to meet them, and soon they came galloping back.

"Major [Isaac] Lynde of the Union Army," they informed him, "demands the unconditional and immediate surrender of the Texan forces."

Baylor knew that his position was too strong to give in to such a demand.

"Tell Lynde," he said to his officers, "that if he wants the town he must come and take it." Turning to the soldiers gathered around him on the road, he added, "We will fight first, and surrender afterward."[15]

Lynde's couriers disappeared down the road. Within a matter of minutes, two cannon shots hurtled toward Baylor's line. One exploded on the roof of a building and the other struck a tree, sending limbs and shards of bark flying. Then the Texans turned to see a regiment of Union cavalry pounding down the road toward them. Baylor waited until the federals were in range of his men's shotguns and pistols before giving the order to fire. The bullets ripped through the Union ranks, and in the ensuing chaos the Yankees wheeled their horses and rode back toward their own lines.

Baylor's men fired at the retreating soldiers and then waited for another charge. It did not come. The scouts Baylor sent out reported that Lynde had taken his soldiers and his artillery back to Fort Fillmore. Should the Texans follow? Baylor considered it, but then decided that the Union retreat might be a trap. Better to return to Mesilla and prepare for a Union assault, which he was sure would come the next day. When the Confederates marched back to the plaza, the townspeople once again emerged from their houses and stores to cheer them. As his men celebrated throughout the night, Baylor reviewed the events of the day with satisfaction. The Battle of Mesilla was not long, nor was it costly. But the Texans had won. The Confederate conquest of the West had begun.[16]

The day after the Battle of Mesilla, Baylor scanned the skies to the east, looking for a sign that the federals were marching toward him. There was no movement in that direction. He sent scouts out to see what the federals were up to, and they returned to report that Lynde's soldiers were digging entrenchments around Fort Fillmore. Baylor saw a chance to put his original plan back into action and sent for his artillerists, who were still at

Fort Bliss. The next day, the Texans would march again on Fillmore, and pound it into submission from the high sand hills between the fort and the Rio Grande.[17]

Once again, Baylor's plans were frustrated. On July 27, his scouts woke him at daybreak, reporting dust rising up fifteen miles away. Baylor leapt out of bed, grabbed his field glasses, and climbed onto the flat dirt roof of his headquarters. What he saw confirmed the scouts' account: a large column of soldiers was making its way slowly toward the Organ Mountains to the east. They were on a military road that led up and over the mountains and then north to Fort Stanton, another federal installation filled with valuable supplies. The federals had to cross twenty miles of desert and then summit San Augustin Pass, which towered almost two thousand feet above the valley floor. There was a silver-mining town called San Augustin Springs a few miles past the pass on the east side of the range; the troops would likely stop there to rest. Baylor climbed down from the roof and ordered his command to prepare their horses and fill their canteens. Instead of assaulting Fort Fillmore, they would chase down and intercept the enemy in the middle of the desert road. They would force the retreating Yankees to fight or surrender.[18]

The 2nd Texas pounded out of the town and splashed through the Rio Grande. A scout joined them on the eastern bank and informed Baylor that the federals had abandoned and partially burned Fort Fillmore, but its storehouse was still intact. Baylor was delighted. He sent a detachment of soldiers to occupy the fort and gather its supplies.[19]

Baylor led the 2nd Texas along the riverbank and then turned east onto the road to San Augustin Springs, lined with dark green creosote bushes. As the sun rose up over the dark edges of the mountaintops, the Texans gained on the federals. The sky was a nearly cloudless, vast expanse of blue and the temperature was climbing. By noon it would be nearly ninety degrees.[20]

When the road reached the foot of the mountains, it pitched upward into a more extreme grade. The federals' wagon trains, at the rear of the column, slowed to a crawl, and Baylor passed them. Farther on, Baylor halted his lathered horse and looked down from the saddle on a group of Union soldiers who had collapsed along the road. Some were trying to crawl along a trail that led into a narrow cut in the mountains. When they saw Baylor, they called to him through parched lips.

"Water," they begged. "Please. Water."

It was hard to believe that these U.S. Army regulars, who were seasoned frontier soldiers, had succumbed to the most common of desert maladies: thirst. The federals had carried only small canteens with them, and their water wagons lagged far behind, their wheels mired in desert sand. They had been on the march for only ten hours, but they were already suffering from extreme dehydration. Baylor had no love for Yankees, but he and his men dismounted and gave the collapsed men all of the water they had. Then they declared them prisoners of war.[21]

Galloping to the top of the pass, Baylor and his men reined in as a breathtaking view opened up in front of them: miles of undulating foot-hills, dotted with brown and green desert scrub, easing down into the broad, bright white gypsum flats of the Tularosa Valley. The Confederates turned away from the view and toward San Augustin Springs, which lay a few miles down the winding road. What they saw here was just as aston-ishing as the valley vista. The road, Baylor reported, "was lined with the fainting, famishing soldiers, who threw down their arms as we passed."[22] Baylor could also see, in the distance, two hundred Union soldiers form-ing into a ragged line of battle on the edge of town. He gave the order to charge and the Texans dashed down the road. The federals scattered. Baylor pulled up, and as he did, he received a message that the Union commander wanted to meet with him.

Baylor walked into San Augustin Springs with a few of his officers and sat with Major Isaac Lynde. The Union officer was disoriented, his white hair and beard matted with sweat.

"[I was] so much exhausted from fatigue and excessive heat," Lynde wrote later, "that I could sit on my horse no longer, and I had to stop and dismount." The pain in his head was so intense that he could barely open his eyes. He had mismanaged the retreat from the start, ordering his soldiers to leave Fort Fillmore without preparing enough water supplies, and issuing a series of increasingly contradictory orders that resulted in chaos on the road. The choice to head into the mountains rather than retreat northward along *El Camino Real* to Albuquerque was the wrong one. Lynde had made all of the decisions. He was clearly the one to blame for this disaster. As he sat hunched in pain, it was Baylor who now demanded an unconditional surrender. Lynde, convinced that "it was worse than useless to resist; that honor did not demand the sacrifice of blood after the terrible suffering that our troops had already undergone," agreed.[23] The two men—one a profes-sional U.S. Army soldier with years of experience in desert warfare, the other a Texas rancher in command of a regiment for the first time—signed the articles of capitulation.[24]

Baylor and his men were forced to stay in San Augustin Springs for two days, until their prisoners (around four hundred soldiers and several civilians, most of them the families of officers) recovered from their dehydration and exhaustion. Feeling magnanimous, Baylor offered the federals a chance to switch sides.

"All who take service with us in the C.S.A.," he announced, "will be given $26 per month, a horse, saddle, and bridle, and all each can make besides."[25]

A few of the Union soldiers took Baylor up on this offer, but most of them did not, and all of the officers refused. What to do with his prisoners, then? While he would have relished the cheers that would greet him as he marched into Mesilla with his captives, Baylor did not have enough men to guard them. And although the Texans now had Fort Fillmore's salvaged supplies, the food and fodder would not last long. The Mesilla Valley was fertile, but its crops could not sustain both the 2nd Texas Mounted Rifles *and* the Union prisoners.

"Being desirous . . . to afflict the enemy in every way," Baylor took his prisoners to the Rio Grande and then let most of them go. "It was much better for [the Yankees] to bear the expense of feeding [them], than for me to do so."[26]

Baylor confiscated the federals' weapons and horses and ordered them to march to Fort Craig, a Union installation 125 miles north of Mesilla. From there they would head to Fort Leavenworth in Kansas, where they would muster out of the Union Army and never bear arms against the Confederates again, however long the Civil War should last.[27] The Union parolees had two choices for their journey to Fort Craig: travel along the Rio Grande, which twisted in broad arcs through a narrow valley, or take the more direct route through the Jornada del Muerto ("Path of the Dead Man"), a ninety-mile stretch of scrubby desert with no springs, creeks, or sinks to sustain men or animals. The Yankees, still reeling from their experiences on the Fort Stanton Road, chose the Rio Grande route. It might be longer but at least they would have water. As the federals turned northward, Baylor and the 2nd Texas turned to the southwest, toward Mesilla, which was now the headquarters of the Confederate campaign for the West.[28]

Three days later, Baylor sat down at a wooden table in his headquarters, placed a piece of paper in front of him, and dipped his pen in ink.

"I, John Baylor, lieutenant-colonel, commanding the Confederate Army in the Territory of Arizona," he wrote, "hereby take possession of the said Territory in the name and behalf of the Confederate States of America."

Arizona's northern border was the 34th parallel and its western border was the Colorado River. With this proclamation, the Confederacy now stretched from the Atlantic Ocean to California.

Baylor organized the new territorial government into executive and judicial departments and declared that the executive authority "shall be vested in the commandant of the Confederate Army in Arizona." Baylor had contemplated running for governor of Texas in 1861 before the war broke out. Taking up this post in Arizona seemed an even better opportunity for fame and fortune. He would establish his government offices in Mesilla, which was now designated the territorial capital. From there, Baylor would be able to see both friends and enemies coming for miles.[29]

Baylor sent one copy of his proclamation to Richmond and another to the *Mesilla Times*, a local newspaper founded by pro-Confederate Anglos in 1860. He then penned a letter to General Earl Van Dorn, commander of the Confederate Department of Texas, describing the events of the previous week in New Mexico Territory.

"I have acted in all matters relating to the acquisition of Arizona entirely upon my own responsibility," he wrote, "and can only refer the matter, through you, for the approval of the Government."

Baylor assumed that President Jefferson Davis and the Confederate Congress would not object to his actions because, he noted, "the vast mineral resources of Arizona, in addition to its affording an outlet to the Pacific, make its acquisition a matter of some importance to our Government."[30] There was no question that Arizona Territory was essential to the Confederacy's plans to reach California, and John Baylor had just cleared the way. He was the vanguard of Confederate manifest destiny.

———————

Word of the Battle of Mesilla, the Union surrender at San Augustin Springs, and the creation of Arizona Territory reached Texas a week later, and then spread throughout the Confederacy in the summer and fall of 1861. Although he had acted without orders, Baylor's victories pleased his superiors in San Antonio and Richmond. Van Dorn immediately notified the War Department about Baylor's "complete success" in his expedition, boasting of the prisoners and supplies that the Texas officer had taken.[31] Confederate Secretary of War Judah Benjamin lauded Baylor's success in his report to President Davis on the progress of the war in 1861.

"All the proceedings of Lieutenant-Colonel Baylor appear to have been marked by prudence, energy, and sagacity," Benjamin wrote, "and to be deserving of high praise. The result of his action has been the securing to the Confederacy a portion of the territory formerly common to all the States but now forming a natural appendage to our Confederate States, opening a pathway to the Pacific."[32]

It was glorious news for the South. Their empire of slavery appeared to be growing in the West, at the same moment that they had won the first major battle outside the town of Manassas, Virginia, in the East.

When John Baylor's family heard about his victories, they were beside themselves.

"I can't pretend to tell you all the compliments I have had on your brilliant success," wrote his sister Fanny. Their mother, she reported, had been campaigning among the local families in San Antonio to have "a report of the Missilla [sic] Battle published."[33]

The residents of Mesilla reacted similarly, complimenting Baylor at every opportunity. Robert P. Kelley, the editor of the Mesilla Times, wrote on the day of the San Augustin surrender that the 2nd Texas had "changed our position from one of fear and anxiety to wild enthusiasm—the dread of armed oppression and outrage give place to the brightest hopes and most confident security." Baylor's victories had liberated southern New Mexico from the "Abolition despot," the editor crowed, "the transition from darkness to light has been sudden, skillful, and glorious."[34]

Baylor basked in the praise. He worried, however, that his small force was not strong enough to occupy Confederate Arizona for very long.

"Now that I have taken possession of the Territory," Baylor wrote to Van Dorn, "I trust a force sufficient to occupy and hold it will be sent by the Government, under some competent man."[35]

While Baylor waited for an experienced soldier to take his place, he became fretful. Yes, he had captured southern New Mexico and declared it the Confederate Territory of Arizona without much difficulty. There were still innumerable threats to his position, however, from all directions.[36] His scouts confirmed that thousands of Union Army troops were concentrating at Fort Craig. Mexicans from Sonora, hearing of the chaos in New Mexico and sensing weakness on their northern border, were threatening to retake Tucson, which they had lost to the United States in the Gadsden Purchase in 1854. Mescalero Apaches had attacked the small detachment of soldiers Baylor had sent to Fort Stanton, a former Union Army post nestled in the mountains in central New Mexico. And

Chiricahua Apaches were raiding wagon trains and mining camps along the Butterfield mail route in western Arizona.

Baylor became desperate for men to help him fight what he was sure would become a multi-front Civil War against Yankees, Mexicans, and Apaches. Until these reinforcements arrived, the future of the Confederate West was uncertain. Shaking off visions of disaster, Baylor wrote to Confederate officials in San Antonio, promising that "I will do all in my power to hold the country, against all odds."[37] He could not do much about the Yankees or the Mexicans without more Texas soldiers. What he could do, however, was launch a successful campaign against Arizona's Apaches. John Baylor was a farmer, lawyer, legislator, military commander, and now a governor. He had one other area of expertise: finding and killing Indians.

2

Mangas Coloradas

Eighty miles west of Mesilla in the Mimbres Mountains, flames crackled and threw shadows onto the rocky hillsides. Four men sitting around the fire beat stretched rawhides with a steady rhythm. Their songs grew louder, more urgent. A large group of Chiricahua Apaches stood behind the drummers, swaying, listening.

"*Kan-da-zis-tlishishen!*" the drummers called.

Mangas Coloradas stepped toward the fire and began to walk around it. At six-foot-four, he towered above most of his people. He moved slowly, his head bowed toward the flames and his long hair swaying. He was seventy years old and had been a leader of the Chihenne and Bedonkohe bands of the Chiricahua Apaches for more than forty years. Mangas's people lived between the Mimbres and the Mogollon Mountains to the west, verdant woodlands with elk and deer to hunt and agave plants to harvest for mescal. His Mexican enemies had initially called him Fuerte ("the Strong One"), but in the 1830s he had worn a red-sleeved coat into battle and had been given the name Mangas Coloradas. The drummers sang of his legendary attacks on towns in northern Mexico, the way he rode straight at his enemies with a lance held high in one hand and a musket in the other. As Mangas Coloradas walked around the fire, his fighting men joined him, tracing his footsteps as a sign of their loyalty.

"*Goci!*" the drummers called.

Mangas Coloradas's son-in-law stepped forward. Cochise was shorter than Mangas, five-foot-nine, with a stout frame and broad shoulders. He had long been a war chief of the Chokonen band of the Chiricahuas, who lived in the Dragoon and Chiricahua Mountains near Tucson. He had married one of Mangas Coloradas's daughters, cementing their bands' alliance.[1] Now he joined Mangas in his father-in-law's stronghold, bringing all of his people with him. Cochise's warriors moved into the light behind him.

After the two war chiefs had circled once around the fire, they and their fighters formed a line, pausing briefly before leaping toward the drummers with their weapons in their hands. It was both a reenactment and a foretelling. As they had in the past, the Chiricahuas would launch themselves at their enemies with aggression and bravery.[2]

After the war dance, the Chiricahuas dispersed to their camps. Several months before, Mangas Coloradas and Cochise had brought their people to this mountain valley in southern New Mexico. Above them, Dzilta-natal ("Mountain Holds Up Its Head Proudly") towered more than three thousand feet above the valley floor. The mountain was a beacon within Apachería, the Chiricahuas' homeland. It was a massive territory that extended from the Rio Grande in the east to the Dragoon Mountains in the west, northward to the Navajo homeland and southward into Mexico.

In one of the deep-cut canyons below Dziltanatal, the ancient ones had recorded their history in carvings on red and gray stone: petroglyphs of hunters, snakes, antelopes, and elks. They had come here, as the Chiricahuas did, for game but also for water. On the southeastern slope of the mountain, one of the few perennial water sources in the area bubbled up in the foothills. The spring drew both men and animals, and it had been a way station for Chiricahuas for centuries.

At Mangas Coloradas's camp on the north side of the mountain, the Chiricahuas' horses, sheep, and cattle browsed shrubs between the wickiups that women had built out of oak and willow branches. From a distance, the shelters were almost indistinguishable from the piñon pines and mesquite that dotted the hills: blooms of green against the bright white rock. Women climbed the hillsides, gathering plants and nuts, or sat bent over pairs of moccasins, pulling tanned deerskin pieces together with firm tugs on strings made of sinew.

The men sat nearby, smoothing and sharpening their mulberry bows and attaching turkey feathers to arrows made of carrizo wood. They secured the knife blades to the ends of their lances, while those with guns and pistols gathered ammunition.[3] Unlike the campaigns they had undertaken against Mexican towns during the previous fifty years, the Chiricahuas would not have to go far to make war upon their new enemies. Just a few miles to the south of the camp, crossing near the vital spring, was the Americans' central road through Apachería, the Butterfield overland mail route.[4]

The Butterfield route had not been blazed by Americans. The Chiricahuas' ancestors had created it long before the Anglos arrived. It was one of hundreds of trails connecting hunting grounds, piñon pine groves, and patches of agave with Chiricahua, Navajo, Comanche, and Mexican communities. These paths marked the large extent of Apachería and demonstrated the Chiricahuas' power as the dominant raiders and traders in the Southwest.[5]

In 1846, the first U.S. soldiers appeared on the eastern edge of Apachería, led by Brigadier General Stephen Watts Kearny. The Americans were at war with Mexico, and this large army was one part of a two-pronged overland invasion of Mexico's northern states. Kearny's men were moving west to California while General Zachary Taylor was moving south from Texas toward Mexico City.[6] No one traveled through their territory without the Chiricahuas' permission, however. Mangas Coloradas sent emissaries to notify Kearny that he would meet with him. In late October 1846, Mangas arrived with several of his warriors at Santa Rita del Cobre, a former Mexican mining town north of the road.[7] He entered Kearny's tent, which had been pitched among the red adobe ruins. Kearny told Mangas that the Americans were crossing Apachería not to fight Indians, but to make war on Mexicans. This pleased the chief immensely.

"*Nuestra gente tiene un odio eterno de los mexicanos,*" he told Kearny. Spanish was the language of trade and diplomacy across the Southwest, and Mangas Coloradas spoke it well. Kearny, however, spoke only English.

"'Our people have an everlasting hatred of the Mexicans,'" the general's translator explained.[8]

The Chiricahuas had raided in the northern Mexican states of Sonora and Chihuahua for as long as Mangas Coloradas could remember, riding south on a well-worn trail that was named after them, attacking towns and presidios and stealing horses, sheep, and cattle. Mexican civilians and soldiers retaliated, riding into Apachería and striking Chiricahua camps, killing as many men as they could and taking the women and children to work as slaves in their fields or households. In response, the Apaches went on the warpath, killing hundreds of Mexicans in sharp strikes on frontier towns and taking Hispano slaves of their own. Chiricahua warriors came back from these campaigns wearing crosses and medals seized from the bodies of their enemies as talismans, with saddles decorated by silver ornaments taken from Mexican horses. By the 1840s, this era of violence had created ghost towns across southern Apachería, as Mexicans fled the northern frontier for the safety of the midlands.[9]

As long as the Americans joined them in their long-standing fight against their mutual enemy, Mangas Coloradas told Kearny, the Apaches pledged "eternal friendship to the whites. You might now pass in safety through our country."[10]

Kearny gave Mangas Coloradas papers to show that the Chiricahuas had talked with him, and "that they had promised perpetual friendship with the Americans."[11] After a few hours of brisk trading—the Apaches offered mules, ropes, whips, and mescal in exchange for American shirts, blankets, knives, needles, thread, and handkerchiefs—Kearny's army moved off to the west toward Tucson and California.[12]

For several years after this first meeting, only Anglo traders and a few American soldiers traveled the roads through Apachería. Then in 1849 wagon trains began to appear on the eastern horizon, creaking slowly over sand-drifted ruts from Mesilla to Tucson. They were filled with the families and belongings of American gold seekers, intent on making their way to California along the southern route. Sometimes the Chiricahuas would descend upon caravans, get between the animals and the wagons, and herd the cattle, sheep, and horses back into the hills. Other times they would surround the encampment and Mangas Coloradas would meet with the migrants. If it appeared that they were merely passing through Apachería, the chief let them go, though not before charging a toll: a loaf of white sugar, perhaps, or a particularly fine horse.[13]

In the summer of 1851, a large party of three hundred well-armed American soldiers and civilians passed under the shadow of Dziltanatal and camped in the same place that Kearny had, among the ruins of Santa Rita del Cobre. It was a surveying party led by John Russell Bartlett, who was there to mark the newly negotiated international boundary between Mexico and the United States.

When Mangas Coloradas met with Bartlett, the surveyor explained to him the particulars of the Americans' treaty with Mexico. Mangas was alarmed to hear that American soldiers had promised to protect the Mexicans from Apache raids, and to return any enslaved Mexicans they found in Apache camps.[14] When Bartlett took two of Mangas Coloradas's own slaves into custody during their talks, the Chiricahua chief was incensed.

"You came to our country," he said to the surveyor. "You were well received by us. Your lives, your property, your animals, were safe. You passed by ones, by twos, and by threes, through our country; you went and came in peace."

Mangas Coloradas began to shout. "We were friends! We were brothers! . . . We believed your assurances of friendship and we trusted them. Why did you take our captives from us?"[15]

Bartlett tried to explain that the United States and Mexico were now allies rather than enemies. To Mangas Coloradas, and to all Chiricahuas who believed in the power and significance of "the will and the word," this was nonsensical. It was just more evidence of traits that all whites, both Mexican and American, shared with one another: a tendency to lie and to betray even their own allies. Clearly, the Americans could no longer be trusted.

Mangas Coloradas left Santa Rita del Cobre that day in July 1851 and did not return to meet with Bartlett again. His suspicions of the Americans' motives were proven right when later that fall, his scouts reported to him that U.S. Army soldiers had encamped and started building adobe forts along the southern Rio Grande, and along the road to Tucson. Miners and farmers had followed, constructing houses and towns, digging out their fields for crops, and defending their settlements with armed guards.[16] It seemed that the Americans were no longer content to merely move through Apachería. Instead, they were attempting to colonize Chiricahua territory through a combination of military force and settlement.

Mangas Coloradas was a war chief, but he did not believe in warfare as the first and only course of action. The Americans had come in force to Santa Rita del Cobre, and he did not like to attack an enemy with greater numbers than his and a strong defensive position. He decided to negotiate. In 1852 he met with an American general, Edwin Vose Sumner. The Chiricahua chief ultimately agreed to recognize the jurisdiction of the United States and to allow the army to build forts in Apachería. In return, the Americans would not launch military campaigns against the Chiricahuas, and would distribute rations at regular intervals. Again the sticking point came, however, when Sumner asked Mangas to prohibit the Chiricahuas from raiding in Mexico.

"Are we to stand by with our arms folded," Mangas Coloradas protested, "while our women and children are being murdered in cold blood? . . . Are we to be the victims of treachery and not be revenged? Are we not to have the privilege of protecting ourselves?"

Sumner caved on this provision, and Mangas Coloradas left this first treaty negotiation with the Americans satisfied with his diplomatic achievement. He had ceded no land, and he could now concentrate on his own campaigns into Mexico. By adhering to the treaty's stipulations, he could show the Americans the importance of his word.

"If we say we will keep peace," Mangas told his people afterward, "we will do so. We keep our agreements."[17]

————

During the 1850s, however, a series of clashes with Americans convinced Mangas Coloradas that peace was no longer an option. First, the U.S. Army had built three more installations in Apachería: Forts Breckenridge and Buchanan protecting Tucson, and Fort McLane south of Santa Rita del Cobre. Then the Butterfield mail route workers arrived in 1858. The U.S. Congress had appropriated $600,000 for the road, which they hoped would offer a safe and rapid route from the Mississippi River to the Pacific Ocean. This transcontinental transportation scheme, like so many in the 1850s, became mired in sectional rancor, but ultimately the contract was awarded to John Butterfield, a New York entrepreneur. The road workers built stone-and-adobe mail stations every twenty miles along the road, and stashed provisions and crates of Sharps rifles in the storerooms.[18] In 1860, thousands of American and Mexican miners came to Apachería, spurred by news of gold strikes at the center of Mangas Coloradas's stronghold.

The Chiricahua chief was enraged when miners began digging out the creeks and rivers, killing all of the elk, deer, and antelope, and cutting down trees to build makeshift towns, the largest of which was called Pinos Altos.[19] Chiricahuas began raiding the camps for stock and provisions, and the miners retaliated by attacking Chiricahua *rancherías*. By December 1860, the situation had devolved and Mangas Coloradas was forced to make another decision. Again he chose to avoid war for the moment, and left his stronghold. He joined his son-in-law Cochise and his band of Chokonens at Apache Pass, in the Chiricahua Mountains in western Apachería. Before he left, he told the miners to get out.

"We do not want peace with the Americans," Mangas declared. "If the settlers on the Mimbres [River] do not leave we will kill them all."[20]

Mangas Coloradas expected to return to the Mogollons and find the Americans gone. Then there would be peace. But just a few months after he arrived at Apache Pass, an event occurred that made amity with the Americans impossible.

In February 1861, a U.S. Army officer appeared near the western summit of the pass, with seventy soldiers in tow. The road made its way across a rolling plateau dotted with juniper and scrub oak trees. The soldiers could see the rocky peaks of the Chiricahua Mountains in the distance, their highest points dusted with snow. The soldiers stopped at the Butterfield stage station, then moved on to water their horses at Apache Spring, the only water source within a sixty-mile radius. Anyone moving through that part of the region had to stop at the spring if they wanted to survive.

The soldiers had come from Fort Buchanan, near Tucson. Their commander, Second Lieutenant George Bascom of the 7th U.S. Infantry, invited Cochise to talk in his tent under a flag of truce. Cochise agreed, and the two men sat down together.

The soldiers were looking for a boy, Bascom said. It was unclear who exactly the child was: a captive who had escaped from an Apache band with his Mexican mother and fled to the ranch of a U.S. government beef contractor named John Ward, or the son of Ward and his Mexican wife. A band of Apaches had raided Ward's ranch a few days before, Bascom said, taking the boy and most of Ward's cattle herd off with them.

Cochise conferred with several of his fighting men.

Neither his nor Mangas Coloradas's warriors had any part in this raid, he told Bascom. He had seen nothing of the boy. It seemed reasonable to conclude that the Coyoteros (a band of Western Apaches, distantly related to the Chiricahuas, who lived near Ward's ranch) had taken him. Cochise offered to send emissaries to the Coyoteros and negotiate for the boy's release. Bascom seemed amenable to this plan and the two leaders settled in to eat dinner. As they ate, Bascom's soldiers quietly surrounded the tent.

When they finished their meal, Bascom informed Cochise that he would hold him and his men hostage until the boy was found. Cochise was initially surprised, and then enraged. He jumped up, drew a knife from one of his leggings, and leapt for the back of the tent, cutting his way through it. Several of his men made it out with him, but Cochise's brother Coyuntera and four other Chiricahuas were captured, taken back to Bascom's tent, and secured.[21]

While Cochise ran back to his camp to gather his warriors, the soldiers withdrew to the Butterfield stage station, maneuvering their wagons along one edge and packing the empty spaces between the wooden slats with grain sacks. They dug a trench and sent men up to Apache Spring to fill all of the kegs and canteens. Cochise captured the Butterfield station agent and several stagecoach passengers unlucky enough to arrive in the midst of the battle. An attempt at a parlay and exchange of prisoners failed. Bascom continued to insist that he would not let Coyuntera and the others go until the Ward boy was recovered.[22]

When the U.S. soldiers tried to take their parched stock to Apache Spring for water, Cochise's men rode swiftly toward the herd, driving all of the animals into the hills. For several days, the Chiricahuas rained gunfire down on the soldiers from the high ridges around the station. They killed and injured several Americans before Cochise decided to withdraw. Before they left the pass, the Chiricahuas killed their captives, stabbing them multiple times with lances and burning their bodies, leaving their charred remains in a gulch.

It took some time for Bascom and his men to emerge from the stage station after Cochise and Mangas Coloradas had gone. Scouts found the bodies of the Americans and Mexicans and buried them under a cluster of oak trees at the western edge of Apache Pass. In retaliation for these deaths, Bascom placed ropes around the necks of Coyuntera and the other Chiricahua captives and ordered his men to winch them up toward the branches of the same oak trees. When the Chiricahuas returned to Apache Pass a few months later, they found the desiccated bodies of their kinsmen still hanging there. They had been "hoisted so high by the infantry that even the wolves could not touch them."[23]

It was this event, which the Chiricahuas remembered as "Cut the Tent" and the U.S. soldiers reported as "the Bascom Affair," that led Mangas Coloradas to Dziltanatal in July 1861 and to a declaration of war on the Americans.

In the summer of 1861, the memory of Cut the Tent was still strong. For weeks Mangas Coloradas, Cochise, and their men had been attacking wagon trains on the road south of Dziltanatal, establishing their positions behind the jutting granite rocks and piñon pines along a wide turn in the canyon road. In late August, Mangas Coloradas's scouts came to tell him of a large party on the move, coming from the west: nine wagons in all, and almost forty men, women, and children, with four hundred head of cattle and nine hundred sheep in tow. They were ranchers and miners from Tubac, a mining town south of Tucson, who had finally decided to leave their homes after U.S. soldiers had abandoned Fort Buchanan. The Ake party (named after their captain, fifty-five-year-old Felix Grundy Ake) had made it to Tucson unscathed, and the Chiricahuas had not attacked them at Apache Pass, and so they figured their luck might just hold out on this one last push through the canyon toward Mesilla.[24]

The day after their war dance, Mangas Coloradas and Cochise lay in wait on the western slopes of the canyon. When the Ake party entered a wide turn on their approach, the lead wagon rolled over the body of a Mexican cowboy, killed on the road a few weeks before. The wagon train halted and the Chiricahuas swarmed out of the rocks. They stampeded the miners' herds of cattle and sheep and drove the animals away. The American teamsters managed to arrange some of the wagons into a breastwork across the road, while those in the rear took the women and children back toward the mining town of Pinos Altos. The Apaches and the party exchanged gunfire for several hours, and then the Chiricahuas withdrew, riding back up the canyon and dispersing into the hills. Mangas Coloradas and Cochise met up and agreed to split the captured herd. Mangas would return to the war camp near Dziltanatal and then take the animals back to his stronghold in the Mogollons. Cochise would drive the rest into Mexico on a road through the Florida Mountains and sell them at Corralitos, a busy trading town in Chihuahua.[25]

Cochise and his warriors celebrated their victory as they rode southward, reenacting their attack for one another and telling stories of their brave deeds. As they approached the boundary between Apachería and Mexico, forty Americans jumped out of a draw and began firing on them. They were a group of miners and adventurers from Pinos Altos (most of them, ardent Confederate secessionists) who had banded together to protect their community when U.S. soldiers abandoned nearby Fort McLane. They called themselves the Arizona Guards. After members of the Ake party had come rushing into Pinos Altos and reported the attack, the Guards' captain guessed that the Chiricahuas would ride for Mexico through the Florida Mountains, and they lathered their horses getting there before Cochise.

When the Americans attacked, the cattle and sheep herds bolted and Cochise's men scattered, dragging their wounded and dead men with them. The Chiricahuas turned their horses and rode hard for Dziltanatal. When they came into Mangas Coloradas's camp, the older chief was shocked to see them. Their campaign against the Americans had been going well and this was their first setback. But no matter. The Chiricahuas were familiar with the fortunes of war. For fifteen years they had engaged with the Americans in various ways: treaties, tolls, avoidance, and attacks. Now they were on war footing, and this was Apachería. The Chiricahuas knew this high desert landscape better than anyone, and they would show the Americans that it would always belong to them. When Mangas Coloradas heard that it was the Arizona Guards who attacked Cochise and took half of the Ake party's animals, he began to plan his revenge on the miners at Pinos Altos.[26]

3

=

Canby

In mid-October 1861, weeks-old copies of the *Mesilla Times* appeared in Santa Fe, detailing the Chiricahuas' assault on Pinos Altos. On September 27, Mangas Coloradas and Cochise had divided their men, striking simultaneously at multiple mining camps in the hills above the town. After dispatching or driving off the miners, the Apaches moved down into Pinos Altos and set fire to many of its wooden houses and stores.

"In such formidable numbers they have never assembled before on a war scout," the *Times* reported, "and never before have they, in all time, evinced such boldness and daring as to attack a town of two or three hundred houses in open daylight."[1]

The Arizona Guards managed to put out some of the fires and mount a defense of the town.

"A desperate fight was kept up," noted the *Times*, "for several hours, from the houses and corrals."

Chiricahuas killed two Arizona Guards and three civilians before a group of women managed to drag a twelve-pound howitzer into the middle of town. They loaded it with nails and buckshot and fired it at an oncoming group of Chiricahuas. This took the riders by surprise and they bolted. The miners took advantage of this pause in the attack and charged, and Mangas Coloradas and Cochise were "finally compelled to raise the siege with loss of many of their braves." Despite this outcome, the *Times* noted with alarm, the Apaches were still in control of "nineteen-twentieths of the Territory of Arizona."[2]

The editors of the *Santa Fe Gazette* reprinted parts of this account with horror, but also with relish. If nineteen-twentieths of Arizona belonged to the Chiricahuas, then it followed that only "one-twentieth of the Territory, therefore, remains in the possession of the Texans. That leaves a small field for the army of occupation to operate in," the *Gazette* crowed, "and proves the Indians quite as good, if not better, at conquest than the Texans."[3]

Despite the paper's scoffing, the Texan invasion of New Mexico was a serious threat to Union control of the Territory in the fall of 1861.[4] Santa Fe was full of soldiers moving in and out, and civilians spreading rumors about the size and strength of the oncoming Confederates. For Louisa Canby, the bustle of Santa Fe, which at the moment was both a frontier city and a growing army garrison, was like nothing she had ever experienced, even after a life spent in military camps across the nation.

Louisa had not been born into the military life. Her father had been a merchant and a farmer in Crawfordsville, Indiana, where she first met Richard in the summer of 1837. He was home from West Point and she was about to leave for Georgetown Female Collegiate Institute in Kentucky. He was impressed by her long, dark hair and the strength he heard in her quiet voice. She found his calm, earnest demeanor pleasing. Louisa was serious about her studies and determined to finish them, so they did not marry until she had completed her courses at the Institute, in the summer of 1839.[5] After the wedding, they left almost immediately for Florida, where Richard plunged into the swamps with the 2nd U.S. Infantry, trying in vain to track down and defeat Seminoles who refused to be removed to reservations west of the Mississippi. The Canbys honeymooned in cramped army quarters built of decaying logs. After a few months they were able to move into a small house on the banks of the St. Johns River.[6]

In those days the U.S. Army was small and spread out over the continent. In the 1850s there were fewer than fifteen thousand army regulars living and fighting and policing international boundaries from the Atlantic to the Pacific.[7] Many of the forts they lived in were hastily constructed and in a constant state of disrepair. Soldiering was a hard life for men who enlisted, and for the women who sometimes came with them. The army did allow officers to live with their wives wherever they were stationed, but they made no special provisions for them or for their growing families. Some rules were unwritten, most of them tied to the military's hierarchies. The best quarters went to the highest-ranking officers' families, and on long marches officers with seniority placed their family wagons up

front. Otherwise, it was up to army wives like Louisa Canby to manipulate
military bureaucracies to get what they needed, to cook and clean, or hire
servants to do that work for them, and to create their own social connections within the insular world of the U.S. military.

It could be a lonely life. Sometimes there were only a handful of officers' wives at a fort, and socializing with the laundresses and cooks who
worked there was out of the question. Army life could also be dangerous.
Most garrisons were hundreds of miles from the nearest town. Doctors
were hard to come by, and even the most minor of illnesses or a complicated pregnancy could mean a painful death.

Louisa, like many army wives, recognized the dangers. But she also
delighted in the constant changes of scenery and the opportunity to travel
widely across the United States.[8] One of her childhood friends recognized
this spirit in her.

"I wish sometimes I could be with you to share in and witness (to me)
your strange mode of life," her friend wrote to Louisa in 1858. "Were you
here surrounded by friends and all else to make life desirable, you would
still have a more isolated feeling than you can probably have situated as
you are."[9]

As much as she took to army life, Louisa did not always accompany
Richard to his postings. In 1841, when he fell ill in the Florida swamps,
she brought him back to Crawfordsville to recover and then decided to
stay rather than return with him to the battlefield. In the summer of 1842,
they reunited in upstate New York, where their daughter Mary was born.
Their lives were relatively tranquil for the next few years, but soon the
United States was embroiled in another war effort.[10]

The rebellion of Texas in 1835–36 had angered Mexico and provoked a
series of conflicts along the border in the years afterward. President James
Polk, who saw an opportunity to expand the nation's boundaries and assert its power over the western hemisphere, used a skirmish along the
Nueces River as an excuse to declare war on Mexico in 1846. In March
1847, when Richard left to join troops heading to Mexico City, Louisa and
Mary did not go with him. When he returned to Indiana more than a year
later, he came back with a promotion and a persistent fever. Louisa nursed
him back to health and vowed that they would never be separated again,
no matter the circumstances.[11]

For the next ten years, the Canbys traveled back and forth between
forts and garrisons across the West and army headquarters in the East.
They were in Monterey, California, in the midst of the Gold Rush and the

California statehood fight. In 1851, they returned to the east coast, living in Washington, D.C., until June 1857, when Richard received orders to join a large army of American soldiers launching a campaign against the Mormons in Utah Territory.

There had been turmoil in Utah since the Mormons had settled along the shores of the Great Salt Lake in 1847. Brigham Young and his followers wanted to control their own territory, but Congress insisted on appointing outside judges and other government officials in order to monitor the religious sect's actions. Clashes between the Latter-Day Saints and these federal appointees, and Mormon attacks on Anglo emigrants on the Oregon Trail, ensued. President James Buchanan, who had already faced a series of bloody disputes over slavery in Kansas during his first years in office, decided that a show of military force was necessary to stamp out this nascent Mormon rebellion before it could gain strength.[12]

In June 1857, the Canbys arrived at the U.S. Army camp at Fort Leavenworth, Kansas. The fort, crouching on a bluff above a sweeping bend in the Missouri River, was swarming with people: soldiers marching and riding in with their regiments; sutlers unpacking their wares for sale; women setting up their washtubs and hiring out their cooking services; and teamsters whipping their oxen as they strained to pull fully loaded wagons into the corral. In a matter of days, a city of white shelter tents sprouted on the rolling plains. Louisa, Richard, and fourteen-year-old Mary stayed in a large tent outside Fort Leavenworth's walls, among towering shade trees. Some of their neighbors also constructed bowers over their tents, making porches for shade and visiting.

"A more beautiful and picturesque spectacle one could not well behold," remarked Jesse Gove, an army captain and one of the Canbys' family friends.[13]

Within three weeks, this canvas city had disappeared, packed into more than two hundred wagons for the journey to Utah. Louisa and Mary rode in a wagon while Richard traveled on horseback, directing the march. Louisa was one of the few officers' wives in the column.

"It does one good to see her amiable countenance beaming with goodness and graciousness of heart," Captain Gove wrote to his wife. "A truer and more amiable woman God never created, always a kind word for everyone."[14]

In the first months of the march, Louisa and Mary were either hot and dusty or drenched with freezing rain. The vivid green hills of Kansas gave way to the burned-out browns and chalky white plains of Nebraska and

Wyoming.[15] As the army moved westward, Louisa saw the sights made famous in written accounts and illustrations of the Oregon Trail, sandstone bluffs carved by wind and water to resemble "stupendous churches or other buildings in various styles of architecture."[16] They also passed the wreckage of American migration strewn about the trail: abandoned mail stations; remnants of handcarts that Mormons had used during their journeys to Salt Lake; whitening bones of cattle that had given out or frozen over the winter; and graves of migrants, marked with rough boards. Death was never far from the roadside in the mid-nineteenth-century American West.[17]

In early October 1857, the U.S. Army pulled into a broad tableland in the Rockies, west of the Continental Divide and seven thousand feet above the sea. The ruins of Fort Bridger were in the distance; the Mormons had burned it to the ground a few weeks before. The valley was spread before the army, with ridges and bluffs running along its edges and the Uinta Mountains, four feet deep in snow, in the distance.[18]

The Canbys set up their tent near one of the two streams south of the Bridger ruins, an area named Camp Scott after Winfield Scott, a hero of the Mexican-American War and a commanding general of the U.S. Army. Winter storms set in almost immediately, frustrating the army's plan to launch a surprise attack on the Mormons. While Richard and the other officers began to plan for a spring campaign, Louisa put the tent in order, mended their clothes, and visited soldiers who had fallen ill with the onset of cold weather.[19]

In November, Louisa received a letter in camp from an unexpected correspondent. Brigham Young himself had heard that the Canbys had no other protection from the elements than a thin canvas tent, and the thought alarmed him. He invited the family to lodge in a house in Salt Lake City for the winter. Louisa declined. Young also sent a number of newspapers, one of them the most recent issue of the *Deseret News*. It contained a poem by a young Mormon woman named "Miss Snow" entitled, "The Ladies of Utah, to the Ladies of the United States Camp in a Crusade against the 'Mormons.'"[20] Miss Snow had a question for Louisa Canby and the handful of other officers' wives at Camp Scott:

> "Why are you in these mountains,
> Expos'd to frosts and snows,
> Far from your shelt'ring houses—
> From comfort and repose?"

Unlike Mormon women, who had been "driven to these distant valleys / By cruel, murd'rous foes," Louisa and the other U.S. Army wives had not been forced to join the Utah Expedition. Miss Snow could not understand why they were participating in a crusade against an innocent people. She went on to warn Louisa and the other American ladies that if they stayed at Camp Scott through the winter, they would become sick, their children would starve, and their husbands would be defeated in battle. The Mormon scriptures had foretold it. The Ladies of the U.S. Army would come to regret their decision to accompany their husbands into the field and to encourage their violent actions against a peaceful people.[21]

Miss Snow's predictions did not come to pass. Over the winter the soldiers drilled on the parade ground, the officers held dinner parties in their tents, and the enlisted men put on theatricals to pass the time. In the end, there were no bloody battles in the fight for Utah. Brigham Young accepted President Buchanan's offer of a pardon in exchange for submission to federal laws. In June 1858, the U.S. Army moved out of Camp Scott toward Salt Lake. The Canbys marched with the soldiers down the city's main thoroughfare, and then set up housekeeping in a camp between Salt Lake and Provo.[22] The family returned in August to Fort Bridger, where Richard took command and supervised the fort's reconstruction.

For two years, the Canbys remained at the rebuilt Fort Bridger, which became an epicenter of trade and military protection for emigrants moving west. In the summer of 1859, Louisa's sister Fannie traveled from Kentucky by herself to visit the Canbys. When she arrived, she was ill and Louisa nursed her back to health.[23] It was a comfort to have Fannie to talk to, not only because the female society at Fort Bridger had not grown any larger or more sophisticated since the U.S. Army's arrival, but also because the Canbys were suffering the loss of their daughter Mary. It is unclear what happened, but after that summer, the family ceased to speak of her.[24] Mary was their only child, and had been with them almost constantly on their journeys from fort to fort across the country. Louisa eased her own pain by tending to Fannie and to the soldiers at Fort Bridger.

"Mrs. Canby is the idol of the army," the sutler at Fort Bridger wrote to his wife. "She devotes her time to the happiness and good of others."[25]

One year later, in the summer of 1860, Richard received orders to report to New Mexico Territory. Louisa packed up their belongings and took her seat in the middle of a large wagon train. It took them two months to make their way out of the northern Rockies, down the Front Range through Denver City, into Santa Fe, and then on to Fort Defiance, the army's westernmost post in New Mexico. Richard was there to direct another campaign, this one against the Navajos.

In September, Richard led one of two large columns of troops into the heart of the Navajo homeland, but could not force them into battle. The Navajos launched swift raids on the army's columns and then disappeared into the hills and canyons. Richard's army did have some successes, killing a handful of warriors and confiscating thousands of sheep, but after just a few weeks their supply lines were depleted and their animals were jaded. A two-year drought in western New Mexico had burned out the grasses and dried up the arroyos, making it difficult to sustain the campaign.

Over the next few months, Richard sent out smaller units into Navajo territory, and those soldiers skirmished with warriors and confiscated whatever sheep herds they could find. This strategy was successful, and the Navajos came to the negotiating table over the winter of 1860–61. Richard traveled to sites throughout New Mexico to parlay with Navajo leaders, including a headman of growing power named Manuelito.[26]

Soon, however, the "Indian Problem" in the Department of New Mexico was overshadowed with talk of another, different kind of war. Louisa read in the papers about the secession of southern states, and every day afterward, U.S. Army officers resigned their commissions in order to join the Confederacy. One of these men was Colonel William Loring, who had been in command of the Department of New Mexico; Richard replaced him after his departure.[27] The new commander had to see to the defense of New Mexico but also potential treason among the citizens of Santa Fe. Mesilla was not the only town in which secessionists lurked about. Many of them in Santa Fe were prominent Anglo men and wealthy Hispano merchants and ranchers. In August 1861, a convention of territorial delegates met in the city to declare their "faith, lives, property, and most sacred honor" to the Union, but the threat of a secessionist overthrow from within Santa Fe was ever present.[28]

By the summer of 1861, city residents were already feeling the effects of the war in the eastern theater. The armed struggles taking place in Missouri—the battles of Carthage and Wilson's Creek and attacks by Confederate guerrillas on Union rail lines—had disrupted railroad traffic into Kansas. As a result, the mail coaches arriving in Santa Fe had a "very light paper mail," and Louisa and the other residents could only rarely buy coffee, sugar, bacon, and butter.[29] The Canbys could find out very little about what was happening in the battlefields and army camps of Virginia.

"Every report is met with correction, explanation, or contradiction," the *Santa Fe Gazette* lamented. This left Santa Fe residents anxious and unsure about what to believe. The editors of the paper advised any reader "to make the most of [the dispatches] that he can; to believe and disbelieve as suits his pleasure or inclination and form his own opinion in reference to all things therein contained."[30]

Richard Canby was similarly flummoxed regarding the intentions of the Texan armies rumored to be on the move toward New Mexico. He did not know for sure that John Baylor was even in the Territory until the paroled soldiers formerly garrisoned at Fort Fillmore began to appear in Santa Fe in early August. With them were Lieutenant William Lane and his family, who had left Fort Fillmore just a few days before Baylor arrived, with a wagon train of supplies bound for Fort Craig. Louisa offered to give Mrs. Lane and her children several rooms in the Canbys' quarters for as long as they might need them. The adobe house Richard had rented for him and Louisa was large, and for the next few months, the Canbys enjoyed the company of the Lane family.[31] In the fall, the Lanes left for the East, joining an army column of soldiers who surrendered at Fort Fillmore, including the disgraced Major Isaac Lynde and his wife.[32]

Throughout the fall Louisa continued to busy herself with housekeeping and social calls. In October 1861, just as the news of Mangas Coloradas's attack on Pinos Altos reached Santa Fe, the new surveyor general of New Mexico Territory arrived in town and was sworn in to office. John Clark was a charming, educated man and a friend of Abraham Lincoln's. Louisa welcomed him into the Canbys' social circle, which included army officers in addition to territorial officials, merchants and other local businessmen, and their wives.

At dinner parties, Louisa and the others talked of the situation in Santa Fe and lamented the events of the Civil War so far. They had read about the Union disasters in Virginia, first at Bull Run (Manassas) and then Ball's Bluff. In the latter fight, the Confederates had pushed the federals down a riverbank, shooting them as they struggled through the current. In late November, intelligence arrived that was more encouraging. Union troops had landed at Port Royal in South Carolina and were planning to advance toward Charleston. This, at last, was gratifying news.[33]

The Canbys and their friends continued to speculate about the war that might come to New Mexico. Throughout the fall and winter of 1861, Union fighting men arrived every day in Santa Fe. Hispano militiamen, recruited by Kit Carson, rode through town on their way to be mustered into the army at Fort Union or Albuquerque. Increasing numbers of U.S. Army regulars, transferred from their now abandoned posts in southern New Mexico and along the Navajo frontier, arrived and bivouacked outside the walls of Fort Marcy, high up on a hill north of the city. These soldiers, weathered men with experience fighting in high desert conditions, were Richard's great hope for the defense of the Territory. Their example would help the inexperienced soldiers of the 1st New Mexico Volunteers, and the recruits from Colorado whom Richard had requested from that Territory's governor. Many of these army regulars brought their wives with them to Santa Fe. These women joined Louisa in forming a central core of civilians who had valuable experience as nurses and "domestic quartermasters," providing supplies and aid for their husbands in the army. This was important work, and would become even more so if their home front became a battlefield when the Civil War came to Santa Fe.[34]

4

=

Davidson

As Union forces gathered around Santa Fe in the fall of 1861, Bill Davidson reclined on his blanket on the banks of Salado Creek, a few miles northeast of San Antonio. In July, Davidson had galloped into that city filled with southern pride and optimism. He and his family had lived in Mississippi until they moved to Texas in 1853, when he was fifteen. Davidson was not a slaveholder, but he believed in the Confederate cause, and he expected that Henry Hopkins Sibley's campaign to take the West would be successful. They would march from San Antonio to Fort Bliss, join up with John Baylor's men in Mesilla, and then fight their way north along the Rio Grande. After they conquered New Mexico, they would take Colorado and Utah, and then move west to California. It seemed to him that the Confederates could "whip the whole United States in time to be home for Christmas dinner."[1]

These future plans were not yet a reality, however. It was October 1861 and the Sibley Brigade had been idling along the Salado, at a camp they called "Manassas" in honor of the Confederacy's first great victory, for more than three months. Davidson had mustered into Company A of the 5th Regiment Texas Mounted Volunteers, which was under the command of a man he knew well from home, John Shropshire. After forming a "mess" with a few friends, Davidson gathered with them on the camp's parade ground every day to learn how to march in unison with his comrades, form battle lines, follow Shropshire's commands, and maneuver in combat. When they were not drilling, Company A occupied themselves with the usual camp activities, and they visited San Antonio.

They especially delighted in seeing the Alamo, the storied building that had sheltered Texas rebels in the spring of 1836, as a much larger Mexican army led by Antonio López de Santa Anna laid siege to the compound.[2] Although the Alamo was a site of slaughter and defeat, the men of the Sibley Brigade saw it as the Shrine of Texas Liberty, a symbol of the ultimate sacrifice made for the cause of independence. The Texans' compatriots in Virginia had Mount Vernon to gaze upon as inspiration for their war service. The men of the Sibley Brigade walked through San Antonio and were animated by the spirit of '36.[3]

Soon, Davidson and his comrades believed, they would have a chance to engage in their own fight for freedom. But when? This was the question every soldier at Camp Manassas was asking themselves and one another in the fall of 1861. As the days passed Davidson became increasingly frustrated. The 5th Texas, along with two other regiments of Texas Mounted Volunteers deemed the 4th and the 7th, were whiling away their time in camp, doing nothing while Union forces were undoubtedly amassing large numbers of troops at their forts along the Rio Grande. Why hadn't they left yet for New Mexico? What was Sibley's plan for them?

———

Henry Hopkins Sibley had arrived in San Antonio just two weeks after Bill Davidson rode in. A career U.S. Army officer, Sibley had coveted command all of his life, but his quick temper and aversion to paperwork undermined his ambitions. Convincing Jefferson Davis to let him lead the campaign for New Mexico had been easy, perhaps because Sibley had professed that he did not need much financial help from the Confederate War Department. He would arm and provision his Texas troops himself. But organizing his brigade and getting it on the road would prove more challenging than Sibley had anticipated.

Neither Earl Van Dorn (in command of the Department of Texas) nor Texas government officials would help him equip his men, and so Sibley bought firearms on the open market. By the late fall, the Sibley Brigade was armed with "squirrel-guns, bear guns, sportsman's guns, shot-guns, both single and double barrels, in fact, guns of all sorts," according to one 4th Texas soldier.[4] In addition, Sibley had procured an unusual set of weapons: two hundred lances, to be carried by one of the Brigade's companies. Nine feet long with three- by twelve-inch blades, they were topped by large red pennants with a white star in the middle: the original Texas flag. Sibley had first seen lancers in battle during the Mexican-American War, as Mexican forces wielding them charged U.S. positions.

The aesthetic splendor of that vision stayed with him. It would be difficult
to train the men to fight with the lances, and with their motley collection
of guns. There was no help for it, however. Sibley's brigade would just
have to do the best they could with what they had.[5]

Finding enough food for the men and hay for the horses and mules
was as difficult as procuring weapons. It was vital to the campaign's success that his men have enough rations and the animals enough fodder to
sustain them on the seven-hundred-mile march to New Mexico. There
were few towns or farms along the way, and the brigade had to take everything with them. Once they reached New Mexico, where the locals
grew wheat, corn, and fruit along the banks of the Rio Grande, the Sibley
Brigade would live off the land. This was a central element of Sibley's campaign plan, which he had laid out for Jefferson Davis during their meeting
in Richmond. Davis had promoted Sibley to brigadier general in the Confederate Army, and informed him that given the length of the march and
the lack of telegraph wires along the route, he would be in command of
the entire campaign. Sibley should be, as Davis put it, "guided by circumstances and your own good judgment."[6]

For his part, Bill Davidson believed in Sibley and his plan. Most of
all, he believed in the men of the Sibley Brigade. It was among the finest
armies in the nation, he thought. The Texas boys were "inbred from their
earliest boyhood to hardships, used to camping out," and they were certainly braver than any Yank in the field of battle.[7]

The delays that fall, however, were maddening. It was outrageous, Davidson thought, to be "kept in idleness . . . all the while the Confederacy
was needing our services."[8] He was not the only impatient one. On October 24, 1861, John Baylor wrote to Henry Sibley that twenty-five hundred
Union soldiers were on their way to Mesilla.

"Hurry up," Baylor urged, "if you want a fight."[9]

———————

On a dreary morning at the end of October, Davidson and Company A
were called to the parade ground at Camp Manassas. Almost three thousand men gathered together, their boots sinking into the trampled mud.
An officer read the order. They were to take up the line of the march to
New Mexico.

"Such a cheer as rent the air was never heard before along the Salado,"
wrote Davidson.[10]

The men of the 4th Texas would leave first, while Davidson and the rest of the 5th would leave two weeks after that. The 7th would depart last, in mid-November. The reason for this seemed mysterious, until the officers explained. Once the Texans marched west of the Pecos River in West Texas, water would become harder to find. A drought had reduced most creeks in the region to crooked lines of damp sand. There were wells and water holes, but they were unpredictable. Some might be brimming, fed by the fall's massive thunderstorms. Others would just be pits of dirt. So the Texans would be staggered along the road. This would allow water holes time to refill.[11] It was a smart strategy, and one that revealed how well Henry Sibley knew the vagaries of the desert and the challenges of moving so many men through it. He had been posted at garrisons across the West in the 1850s, and was in command of Fort Burgwin in Taos when the Civil War began.

While Davidson appreciated this approach, he was disappointed not to be on the move quite yet. And he was anxious. The days were getting colder, and the three thousand animals that had been corralled for months in San Antonio were already thin and sickly. There were rumors of Union troops gathering in Albuquerque under Kit Carson, arming themselves for a definitive battle along the Rio Grande. But the orders to march "carried joy and gladness to the hearts of the members of the Sibley Brigade." Soon Davidson and the 5th Texas would be on their way at last, to "contribute our share in covering the Confederate arms with glory."[12]

In early November 1861, the bugler sounded "boots and saddles," and Company A lined up to have their baggage weighed and loaded into wagons. The notes of "assembly" rang through Camp Manassas, creating "a scene of bustle and confusion," and then they were off.[13] Their first stop was San Antonio, where women lined the streets, waving handkerchiefs and cheering for the boys. The regiment received battle flags from well-wishers and stood at attention while the 5th Texas commander, Colonel Tom Green, spoke to each company individually.

"The Confederacy is counting on you," he said, "and I, personally, am depending on you."[14] After more fanfare and some additional inspiring words from the officers, Davidson and his comrades turned to the northwest, and stepped onto the San Antonio–El Paso Road. The road was in good shape, pounded into smooth ruts by wagon trains and stagecoaches traveling along it for more than ten years. It had been the brainchild of San Antonio merchants, who had seen in the shifting international boundaries of 1848 an opportunity to trade with the mining regions of northern Mexico. Military surveyors improved the road in the early 1850s, and after that vehicles carrying passengers, mail, cargo, and soldiers began to travel on it, between the southern regions of Texas and a spot where the Rio Grande cut a pass through the Franklin Mountains: El Paso. When John Baylor had marched his 2nd Texas Mounted Rifles over it the previous summer, the San Antonio–El Paso Road became a thoroughfare of military invasion.[15]

Just a few miles out from San Antonio, Davidson and the others were surprised to find General Sibley sitting on his horse at the crest of a nearby hill. Sibley did not speak as they passed but saluted them by lifting his hat, and watched as they marched out of sight over the flat blackland prairies. He would continue to oversee the mobilization from San Antonio until the 7th Texas departed. Only then would he board a carriage that would take him to Fort Bliss quickly, and in comfort.[16]

For the next week, Davidson and the others marched steadily westward, crossing rivers and creeks and passing small towns. They traded with locals, adding butter, cheese, and milk to their packs filled with meager rations. One week into the march, storms gathered over the horizon and came at the 5th Texas with incomprehensible speed. They were blue northers, fast-moving cold fronts characterized by rapid drops in temperature. Sleet pricked the soldiers' skin and drenched their clothes as they shivered in the cold. There were no trees to protect them from the sweeping winds, and the soldiers struggled to make campfires. Any man serving in the Sibley Brigade who had looked upon this march as a lark was disabused of his notion that night.

"We were tasting the bitter delights and mournful realities of the soldier's life," Davidson lamented. "We are now for the first time beginning to find out that we are engaged in no child's play."[17]

The Sibley Brigade's morale was still high, but for many men the rigors of army life were already taking their toll. Tempers flared and jokes turned quickly to insults and fights. One private in the 5th, who struck his captain in a dispute, was court-martialed and sentenced to wear irons for one month and to travel on foot for the rest of the march, "tied to the hind end of a baggage wagon." This was a severe punishment indeed for a Texan, who viewed his ability to ride a horse as proof of his manhood.[18]

Another week of marching brought the Sibley Brigade into Texas brush country, the southern plains in which mesquite and thorn scrub predominated. One night they lay over at San Felipe Springs, a large and deep water hole that was a crossroads of trade in West Texas. In order to manage water supplies even more effectively, their officers divided the regiment into three squadrons that would leave San Felipe Springs in waves.[19]

Company A waited their turn, and as they did, General Sibley's carriage overtook them and then disappeared into the western horizon. Davidson and the others jumped off a few days later, marching northwest toward Devil's River, where the country grew rougher and rockier, with steep hillsides descending to the water's edge. The path along the riverbanks was crushed into dust, and the horses and wagon wheels churned through it, the clouds of fine particles choking the men.[20]

The 5th Texas struggled on, and soon they passed by Painted Cave, a rock shelter that was "in the early days of Texas a real resort for Indians, who have left upon the walls in the different compartments of the cave many of their crude paintings." The soldiers explored the cave and then ransacked it for souvenirs. "This seemed to be a peculiar characteristic of the Confederate soldier," Davidson noted.[21] The men had little else except mere survival to keep them occupied.

From Painted Cave they had a long haul through a waterless track to Howard Spring. When they arrived, they found a twelve-foot-deep hole with the promise of water only at the very bottom. They pulled it up in buckets. It was a slow, wearying task, and this meant that only the soldiers and their horses quenched their thirst. The beef herd and the oxen and mules had to go without.[22]

It was another waterless slog to the Pecos River, one of the region's major waterways that, like the Rio Grande, was born in the mountains of New Mexico Territory and flowed southeastward into the arid plains of West Texas.[23] The road here was difficult to navigate. It meandered up and down steep riverbanks, gaining elevation every day. Mesas and small mountains began to jut up out of the desert floor. One energetic soldier climbed to the top of a mesa along the Pecos, and up on that promontory he "bethought myself standing upon the top of Mount Blanc with Europe lying before me." He imagined that perhaps the Sibley Brigade would soon come across "the crude castle of some baron or knight."[24]

Davidson found it difficult to find beauty in this parched landscape. The desert was a place of hardship and danger. They were halfway through the march and already their food supplies were dwindling. Most men only had beef and wormy crackers for meals. Dying of thirst was a real possibility. And there were no barons or knights in their path, only Apaches.

In the lands west of the Pecos, Mescalero and Lipan Apaches descended on every detachment of Texans that rolled past. When they raided Company A's horses at Leon Holes, "the boys gave them a charge," Davidson reported, "but the only result was that the boys ran their horses down." By that point, in early December 1861, the 5th Texas had been on the road for one month. They were still three hundred miles from Fort Bliss.[25]

There was some relief ahead, however. Limpia Canyon rose up out of the undulating plain and brought the 5th into the Davis Mountains. Vertical tubes of dark red volcanic rock towered overhead as the soldiers made their way up Wild Rose Pass. As they descended the western side toward Fort Davis, the scrub brush, yucca, and grasses gave way to a canyon floor lined with live oak trees. The soldiers were refreshed by the change in the landscape. Even better was the sight of several supply wagons, sent by John Baylor's troops stationed at Fort Davis. After eating their fill of sop and biscuit, Davidson and the others traded with the sutler, mailed letters home, and bought new clothes. Some of them bought liquor and "got tight." They regretted this the next day, when they had to march forty miles to Barrel Springs.[26]

Two days later, Davidson and Company A arrived at Ojo del Muerto ("Dead Man's Hole"). It was a large spring on the western edge of the Davis Mountains, and 120 miles from the Rio Grande. Here, the 5th Texas guide, a man named Dunn, recruited Davidson and twenty others to scout a shortcut through several canyons. After some wrong turns and an Apache attack on their horse herd, Dunn's group found a shorter trail that the wagons could get through. A few days later, they were kneeling on the bank of the Rio Grande, drinking their fill.[27]

From "Dunn's Cutoff" to Fort Quitman on the Rio Grande was another long haul, but Davidson and Company A made it there a few days later. Then they proceeded up the river by easy marches to Fort Bliss, arriving on December 24, 1861. Davidson had thought that the Confederates would have whipped the Yankees by Christmas dinner, but on that day the Sibley Brigade was still in Texas, and Davidson had not yet even seen a Yankee in person. He was relieved, however, to have finished the long march along the San Antonio–El Paso Road, and to have corn for his horse and a roof over his head.[28]

When Davidson's company trudged into Fort Bliss, Henry Sibley was already there. He had set up his departmental headquarters and sent word to John Baylor in Mesilla that he was taking military command in Arizona Territory and absorbing Baylor's men into the Sibley Brigade.[29]

When Davidson heard about this reorganization, he was excited. "We were united with Baylor's Regiment . . . who were already here when we were ordered to be organized," he wrote. "These are a glorious set of boys. The bravest of all brave soldiers and truest of all true friends."[30]

After restructuring his army, Sibley issued a proclamation. It was written in both English and Spanish and distributed throughout Arizona and southern New Mexico. In it Sibley announced his intentions to the residents of the territories.

"An army under my command enters New Mexico," he declared, "to take possession of it in the name and for the benefit of the Confederate States."

Sibley reassured residents that he did not intend to wage war on peaceful civilians but to "liberate them from the yoke of military despotism erected by usurpers upon the ruins of the former free institutions of the United States." He felt sure that Hispano New Mexicans would volunteer to fight for the Sibley Brigade and donate wheat, corn, and animals to the Confederate cause. Surely they were as much the enemies of the federal government in Washington, D.C., as the Texans were.

"By geographical position, by similarity of institutions, by commercial interests, and by future destinies New Mexico pertains to the Confederacy," Sibley insisted.[31]

———

Davidson and Company A were less concerned about recruiting New Mexicans than recovering from the long march to Fort Bliss. Davidson found the fort a pleasing place to spend a few weeks. Even in winter the river valley was lush with green grass. The boys set up their shelter tents outside the adobe walls of the fort and made forays across the Rio Grande to look around the Mexican town of El Paso. There they feasted on the tamales, fresh fruit, and vegetables they bought in the town markets. Some of them kept a sharp lookout for Colonel Green's enslaved man, who had escaped across the Rio Grande on the colonel's horse as the regiment neared Fort Bliss. A few of the Sibley Brigade officers, like Green, had brought enslaved men along on the campaign, a common practice in the Confederate Army in all theaters of the Civil War. Some of these camp slaves exploited the chaos of wartime to escape from bondage. Davidson and his friends looked for Green's man every time they were in El Paso, but they never did find him.[32]

Meanwhile, the Sibley Brigade waited for their orders to leave Fort Bliss, cross into Confederate Arizona, and from there, invade New Mexico. Davidson huddled near the campfire in whatever blankets he could scrounge up, and thought back on the Brigade's long and harrowing journey from San Antonio, marveling that they had survived.

In early January 1862, Henry Sibley commended all of the Texans for their conduct on the march, expressing "his high appreciation of the patience, fortitude, and good conduct, with which, in spite of great deficiencies in their supplies, they have made a successful and rapid march of seven hundred miles in mid-winter, and through a country entirely devoid of resources."[33]

It was the longest single march that a Confederate army had undertaken during the Civil War, and the conditions had been unlike any that their comrades in the eastern theater had faced. The Texans, like their commander, were proud of their achievement, but it had taken a toll on them and their animals. Would they recover enough by the time Sibley called them into battle? Would they be able to sustain themselves on the way to Santa Fe? Bill Davidson could only guess at the answers to these questions, and worry about how the long delays and immense distances they had to travel would affect the rest of the Confederate campaign for the West.

5

=

Juanita

The harshness of the high desert winter might have come as a surprise to Bill Davidson, but it was a way of life for the Diné—or "the people," as the Navajos called themselves. In Diné Bikéyah, the Navajo homeland that lay in the northwest reaches of New Mexico Territory, the heart of January was ice. It was the month to prepare for corn planting, perform sacred healing ceremonies, and tell the stories of how the Diné had come to be.[1]

Juanita, her husband, Manuelito, and their two children, Manuelito Segundo and the baby girl Shizie, had come to the foothills of the Chuska Mountains a few months before. They made the short trip from their summer fields, which were tucked into a narrow valley called Tséhootsoh ("Meadow in the Rocks"), in the center of Diné Bikéyah. When they arrived they joined their band, an informal kin group of several hundred men, women, and children, related through matrilineal clans. There were more than forty bands of varying sizes scattered all over Diné Bikéyah, each led by a headman: a warrior skilled in battle and in possession of large herds of sheep. Juanita and Manuelito brought most of their belongings with them to this winter camp, and placed them in their hogan, a circular structure with a domed roof that had been constructed of wooden poles, its crevices patched with mud. The hogan would shelter them from the winter's vicious storms, which brought stinging snow and sleet, and driving wind.[2]

The Navajos had been moving from higher valleys to southern grasslands in Diné Bikéyah every fall since the mid-eighteenth century, in order to provide fresh pasturage for their sheep herds.[3] The sheep were short and stubby churros, hardy descendants of the first sheep to come to North

America from Spain. They were well adapted to the high desert scrub-lands, able to root out edible plants from the sandy, rocky soil and survive on very little water. The Diné had obtained the first of these churros from Spanish traders, and they immediately understood their value: their wool could be spun and then woven into blankets and clothing, and in lean times they could be butchered for meat. Over time, Navajos built large flocks and grazed them on lands adjacent to their fields of corn, wheat, and melons. Juanita and the other women took most of the responsibility for maintaining the herds, shearing the sheep, weaving, and butchering.[4]

Every family in the band needed at least two hundred animals for their herd to flourish. Juanita and Manuelito had many thousands of sheep, but even their herd required replenishing every spring. For the Diné and the Hispano sheep ranchers who lived along the Rio Puerco and Rio Grande to the southeast, rebuilding flocks meant raiding the enemy. For genera-tions, Hispano raiders had ridden into Diné Bikéyah, taking animals and stealing Navajo women and children to sell as slaves in the markets of Santa Fe. The Diné struck back in reprisal raids, driving hundreds and sometimes thousands of sheep from Hispano ranches back to the Navajo homeland. The Diné took slaves as well, integrating Hispano women and children into their bands as family members or trading them for goods at nearby towns or pueblos. In both Navajo and Hispano communities in New Mexico Territory, sheep and slaves created wealth, and required ter-ritorial conquest. They also fueled a cycle of violence in the southwestern tablelands.[5]

———

The Americans had tried to dismantle this trading and raiding network when they first came to Diné Bikéyah in 1846, just a few years after Jua-nita was born. That fall, U.S. soldiers had appeared on the eastern bor-der of the homeland and sent messengers to let the headmen know they wanted to talk at one of the Navajos' most sacred sites, Shash Bitoh ("Bear Spring"). A bubbling spring on the road to Albuquerque, it was a place where Navajos rested and filled their water casks. Up in the Zuni Moun-tains south of the spring, tucked inside smooth sandstone caves, were the adobe ruins of the ancient ones. The shards of wall, made of earthen bricks of different shapes and sizes, were crumbling and jagged. But they remained, silent sentinels surrounding and protecting Shash Bitoh.[6]

In November 1846, the headmen, accompanied by five hundred Diné warriors on horseback, sat down with an American Army officer named

Alexander Doniphan, who spoke on behalf of General Stephen Watts Kearny. Kearny's army was marching through the region, taking possession of it on their way to California. He had sent Doniphan northward to the Navajos, to make a treaty. Doniphan had 350 soldiers with him, all impressively mounted and armed. The Navajos, like their Chiricahua neighbors to the south, were gratified to hear that the Americans were at war with the Mexicans. Then Doniphan told them the same thing that Kearny had said to Mangas Coloradas:

"Attacks on New Mexicans must cease," he warned, "or the Navajos would face war with the United States."

Like the Chiricahuas, the Navajos found this assertion befuddling.

"Americans! You have a strange cause of war against the Navajos," protested one of the headmen. "You now turn on us for attempting to do what you have done yourselves. We cannot see why you have cause of quarrel with us for fighting New Mexicans on the west, while you do the same on the east."

This was the Navajos' war, the headman reminded Doniphan, and "we have more right to complain of you for interfering in our war, than you have to quarrel with us for continuing a war we had begun long before you got here."[7]

Doniphan insisted that if the Navajos attacked Hispanos, American soldiers would retaliate. The treaty the Americans wanted the Navajos to sign that day included this stipulation, among others that required the Diné to give up Hispano slaves and any other property they had taken in raids on New Mexican settlements in the previous three months. The treaty also declared that the U.S. Army would prevent Hispano raiders from riding into Diné Bikéyah, and that a "firm and lasting peace and amity shall henceforth exist between the American people and the Navajo tribe of Indians."

The headmen had conferred and agreed that it made sense to be cautious and sign the treaty, for the Americans' military strength was obvious to all.[8] Doniphan and his soldiers left Shash Bitoh believing that they had secured a "lasting peace" with the entire Navajo tribe in this, the first treaty they had made with them. The Americans did not understand that even those headmen who had signed the treaty could not control all the Navajos in Diné Bikéyah. While some Navajos attempted to abide by the terms of the treaty in the years after its signing, most continued to raid Hispano ranches, and to wage the war they had been fighting long before the Americans arrived.[9]

One of the headmen who signed Doniphan's Treaty, and who subsequently ignored most of its stipulations, was Juanita's husband, Manuelito. By 1846, Manuelito had already established himself as a war leader and man of property. He was in his late twenties then and had fought in several wars against Mexican soldiers in his youth. Leading bands of raiders, he had attacked Mexican towns and ranches, building up a large sheep herd.

Manuelito's first two marriages reflected his standing. Initially he wed the daughter of the legendary Navajo headman Narbona. Later he married one of the daughters of Chiricahua chief Mangas Coloradas, creating a strong tie between those two communities. With these women and a third wife, Manuelito gathered a large band that moved between Tséhootsoh and the Chuska Mountains, exploiting their rich grasslands and plentiful wood and water supplies. Juanita had grown up in this part of Diné Bikéyah and met Manuelito when she was a teenager. She was petite, with delicate features and long black hair tied back and folded over at the base of her neck in the traditional style. He was broad-shouldered and towered over her. In the late 1850s, after her Kinaaldá, a weeklong celebration of her first menstruation, Juanita became Manuelito's fourth wife.[10]

The first few years of Juanita's marriage to Manuelito were turbulent times for the Diné. For their band, most of the trouble was focused on a fort that the Americans had built at Tséhootsoh in 1851. The American officers had named it Fort Defiance, although the soldiers who built it named it Hell's Gate. Like other forts that the U.S. Army had built on Native lands in the West, Defiance was meant to provide protection for Anglos who would be migrating to the region. It was also the first material marker of the American Army's determination to colonize Navajo country.

Fort Defiance's twenty unbarked log buildings, huddled together around a large, rectangular parade ground, were built not on the eastern border but in the heart of Diné Bikéyah. Manuelito found the fort especially galling, for it sat at the center of his lands.[11] Throughout the 1850s, Manuelito continually argued with the fort's commanders over grazing rights.

"All of that land has belonged to me since I was a boy," Manuelito told one Defiance officer in the late 1850s. The Americans could send as many of their soldiers against the Navajos as they liked. "I am a powerful war leader," Manuelito declared, "and I could quickly call about me one thousand warriors."[12]

After a series of clashes with Defiance soldiers in the late 1850s, tensions escalated. In the summer of 1859, at an annual gathering of the Navajos, Manuelito appeared with his torso painted white and his legs painted black, and snakes on the soles of his moccasins.

"We will stop this suffering!" he shouted. "I will lead the Navajos. We will make war and drive the white men from our land!"[13]

Manuelito's plan was to attack and lay siege to Fort Defiance. At dawn on August 30, 1860, he and one thousand warriors approached the fort from three sides. The Navajos were successful for the first few hours of the engagement, before being driven back by cannon fire.[14] The reprisals were swift. Hispano New Mexican militias, empowered by U.S. Army support, launched slave raids into Diné Bikéyah. The Navajos' historic enemies the Utes joined in, attacking *rancherías* in the Chuska Mountains. And in late September 1860, sizeable numbers of U.S. troops under the command of Richard Canby began to mass at Fort Defiance. The next month, two large columns of soldiers approached Tséyi' (Canyon de Chelly) from different directions, trying to force the Navajos into a large-scale battle. They did not succeed. But this military campaign into Diné Bikéyah, the first that the Americans had undertaken, was the beginning of a period that the Diné came to call *Nahondzod* ("the Fearing Time").[15]

For more than a year, Manuelito's band was constantly on the move as they evaded Hispanos, Utes, and American soldiers. Their fields did not fare well. The patrols that Canby sent out to Diné Bikéyah in January 1861 destroyed the crops that Juanita had laid by to stave off hunger during the winter. In February, Manuelito consulted with many of his fellow headmen and they decided to ask for terms. Once again, he found himself traveling to Shash Bitoh to negotiate with the Americans.[16] They met not at the spring itself but at Fort Fauntleroy, a new Army installation that had been constructed nearby.[17]

The treaty stipulations were harsh but familiar. The Navajos were to "submit themselves unconditionally to the Government of the United States." They were to restrain their young men who had been raiding Hispano towns and ranches, and deliver the worst of the offenders to the U.S. Army. They were to return all property taken in those raids, including Hispano slaves. They were not to graze their sheep, cattle, or horses east of Fort Fauntleroy, or raid beyond its gates. This meant that some of the best grasslands in Diné Bikéyah, the valleys between the Chuskas and the Zuni Mountains, would no longer belong to the Navajos. They would also lose access to Tsoodzil ("Blue Bead"), the sacred mountain that marked the eastern edge of the homeland. Richard Canby told Manuelito and the others that the Navajos would have to settle farther west in their territory and build pueblos for themselves. By ceasing their regular migrations within their territory and living in one place, Canby argued, the Navajos would become civilized people.[18]

Manuelito and the other headmen signed the treaty. Once again, they did not abide by it. After February 1861, the Diné grazed their animals wherever they liked and continued to raid Hispano ranches. They did not build pueblos, but kept living in the traditional way, in bands scattered across Diné Bikéyah. This way they could plant their fields, graze their herds, and manage the meager supply of water in the tablelands. All of the bands would have enough resources, and all would survive.

During the summer of 1861, as the American Civil War began in New Mexico Territory, it appeared that the Fearing Time might be over. Hispanos were no longer riding into Diné Bikéyah, even after Navajos siphoned sheep from their herds. The American soldiers disappeared from Fort Defiance, taking their horses and weapons and Manuelito's hay with them. In December, Navajo horsemen had ridden into Fort Fauntleroy to find that its officers' quarters, soldiers' barracks, storehouses, and sutler's shop were empty. So were the corrals and the hay camps.

Did this mean that the army had gone off on a campaign and would return in the spring? They had done such things before. Or did it mean that the Americans had given up their conquest of Diné Bikéyah? In January 1862, many Navajos pondered these questions, and the future.

They also looked toward their own survival. Juanita buried bags of dried watermelons, squash, berries, and parched corn outside their winter hogan. These, along with the deer and antelope meat that Manuelito and their kinsmen could kill in the forests, would sustain them until spring.[19] There were also plenty of wagons on the roads near the Rio Grande these days, long trains belonging to the U.S. Army and its suppliers, filled with grain, hay, and weapons. It might be time, Manuelito thought, to resume his warlike habits.[20]

While her husband strategized, Juanita turned to her upright loom. She was known as Asdzáá Tł'ógi ("Lady Weaver"), a talented artisan who, along with many other Diné women, made long-lasting, watertight blankets for which Navajos were renowned.[21] Kneeling in front of the loom, she wove between vertical "warps" the wool strands sheared from her sheep, tamping each strand down with her batten stick. She had dyed the wool with colors squeezed from local plants, and as she wove them together, designs emerged: horizontal stripes in black and white, small triangles and zigzag patterns in vibrant reds and greens.[22]

Some of the blankets that Juanita and other Navajo weavers made were added to stacks in their hogans, to be used as protection against the winter's freezing temperatures and howling winds. Others were fashioned into *biil'éé'*, one-piece dresses cinched at the waist with a concho belt, silver disks fastened together with leather cords. The rest were sent with riders bound for nearby pueblos and for Santa Fe, Taos, and Socorro, to trade for goods the Navajos could not make themselves.

Juanita's name acknowledged her skill in weaving. There were some who believed that Tł'ógi referred not to her individually but to her maternal clan, prolific weavers of grass and yucca mats who originally came from Zia Pueblo, a large complex of adobe structures one hundred miles east of Diné Bikéyah.[23] Navajos visited Zia Pueblo regularly to trade rabbits, deerskins, and blankets for vegetables and cotton textiles. The two peoples also raided, traded, and bought slaves from one another.[24] There were rumors that Juanita may have been part of this regional slave trade, taken from a Zia or a Hispano community in the Rio Grande Valley as a young child and adopted into a Navajo clan. Regardless of her origins, when Juanita wed Manuelito in the late 1850s she was considered by all who knew her to be a Navajo woman. If she was not Diné, she would not have been taught to weave.[25]

In their winter hogans in January 1862, after the herding and the weaving and cooking and eating were done, the Diné gathered around their fires and Juanita and the other mothers told their children how the people came to be. In addition to taking care of sheep, Navajo women also narrated the history of the Diné.

The mothers took baskets made of sumac fibers from the walls of their hogans and traced the coils from the center outward while they talked, moving in a clockwise direction. In the knot and the light brown coils at the center of the basket was the First World, a "floating island in a sea of water mist." Here mothers told their children about the creation of the

First Man and First Woman and the other beings of the First World. Tracing their fingers along the spirals, they described the disorder and chaos
of that world, and the quarrels among these beings that forced migrations
upward. Where the light tan sections pushed out into a band of black, the
Navajos emerged into the Glittering World, the earth's surface. Working
their way along the next band of coils, made bright red with dye made
from the roots of mountain mahogany, the mothers talked about how the
First Man and First Woman had constructed the Navajo homeland. They
had planted four mountains in each direction to mark out a sacred geography, affixing each of them to the earth with natural forces. Tsoodzil
was closest to their winter camp. If the children rode out eastward toward
Acoma Pueblo, they would see it.[26]

It was into the Glittering World that Changing Woman was born in the
center of Diné Bikéyah. She became a woman and then gave birth to twin
boys. After raising the twins, Changing Woman made the Diné out of
her own skin. The Navajos could see her continual presence in their lives
through the changes of the seasons. During the winter of 1862, Changing
Woman was preparing for her rebirth. They would see her again soon
during the time of little leaves, as the green shoots of the wild plants and
grasses pushed up through the soil.[27]

Telling these stories, Juanita and the other mothers spoke the past into
being and hoped that the histories of the Diné would help their children
learn to be brave. They would all need to remember these lessons when
the snows melted and the Americans and the Hispanos returned, as they
most certainly would. The Navajos would not let their enemies take their
sheep, their women and children, or their land. Changing Woman had
given them Diné Bikéyah. The land was central to their understanding of
who the Diné were, and who they would become. They would defend it
in order to survive.[28]

6

=

Ickis

Hundreds of miles east of Diné Bikéyah, the Union soldiers at Fort Garland in Colorado Territory were telling their own stories around winter fires. Tales about their time up in the Rocky Mountain gold camps, how they spent months panning streams and staking claims that never paid out. Anecdotes about their families back home, who never wrote them enough letters to stave off their loneliness. These stories made Alonzo Ickis gloomy.

"Thought more of home within the last month than ever before," he confessed. "O! how I should [have] loved to sit down to a Christmas dinner in the States . . . but here I am and cannot be in more than one place at a time so here is <u>the</u> place."[1]

The boys in Ickis's company also talked about the future, about what might happen to them when they finally got the call to leave Fort Garland and march south into New Mexico.

"We're getting tired of this kind of soldiering," Ickis sighed, "and long for active service. [We] hope to go to Santa Fe soon."[2]

———

When the Civil War began, Ickis had been in the Colorado gold mines for more than two years, having made his way there in the spring of '59 with his oldest brother, Johnathan. On their Iowa farm, they had heard about the gold strikes in the gullies west of Denver, and figured this was their chance to make their fortune. Ickis and the other young gold seekers from the Midwest searching for a new life in the Rockies were not so different from the southerners like John Baylor and Bill Davidson striking out for

Texas in the 1840s and '50s. They were all restless and moving down the road toward a different future.

In the fall of 1861, Ickis and the others pored over papers for bits of news that trickled in from the East. Mostly it was bad news for the Union. Ickis felt sure that his younger brother George was thinking of enlisting, although he was only twenty. He speculated that his older brother Thomas was also "deeply absorbed in the war," and this was why "he cannot take time to write to his brother in the wilderness."[3] In early October, Johnathan went back to Iowa, and Alonzo was considering following him and enlisting in an Iowa company. Later that month, however, a notice appeared in a local newspaper.

"VOLUNTEERS WANTED! For C.D. Hendren's Company of Colorado Volunteers, to serve for three years, or during the war."

The governor of Colorado Territory, at Richard Canby's request, had authorized the creation of several companies, to be recruited from Denver and the gold mines. He sent officers and equipment to Cañon City, a thriving town just off the road that led from Denver to Santa Fe.[4] It did not take long for Alonzo and several of his friends to pack up and leave their claims and head to the rendezvous.

In Cañon City they met a lot of other miners they knew, all of them coming off of disappointing prospecting seasons and facing a winter of deep snows and inactivity. Like Ickis, they were all young and able-bodied, and had grown out their hair and beards in the frontier style. Their sense of adventure and the ability to adapt to variable conditions helped them survive in the camps. The gold rush had brought thousands of these young men of military age into the West, and the federal government's desire to protect the mineral wealth of the region brought hundreds of these Colorado men into the Union Army. They were perfectly suited to endure it.

For Ickis and the other Colorado miners who volunteered at Cañon City in the fall of 1861, soldiering seemed like a fine way to spend the winter. They would have plenty of grub and earn regular wages, and maybe they would get to fight a few Confederates.

"I hope you will not think I have done wrong," Ickis wrote to his family after he signed up. "For I do think it is the duty of every single man to enlist and do all in his power to end this war."[5]

For more than a month, Ickis lived in a hotel in Cañon City and received weapons, uniforms, and training. He spent some time drilling but most of his time carousing, tossing back glasses of a local brew called Taos

Lightning and running around town, "determined to spend the time as pleasantly as possible."[6]

In early December 1861 Ickis and the others left Cañon City for Fort Garland. The march had started off well enough. They had moved southward along the Front Range trail, through rolling prairies full of bounding antelopes. Then the company and their wagon train had turned toward the mountains, to make their way up and over Sangre de Cristo Pass. The road was covered with a thin layer of ice. The cattle lunged up the slope but backslid into the wagons, their hooves scraping the surface. The train halted, the wagons piled up on one another. The soldiers unhitched the cattle, took the ropes in their hands, tied them to the wagon tongues, and began to pull. They heaved and swore and heaved again. It took them until dusk to reach the summit, but they did it with the wagons all right side up.[7]

A few days later they were at Fort Garland, drinking their fill of Taos Lightning to celebrate. Then they were mustered into the United States service, and introduced to their new captain, Theodore Dodd, who had an impressive beard and mustache, and dark eyebrows that arched upward so that he looked perpetually surprised. Dodd was a Buckeye, a graduate of West Point, and a clever man. Ickis was sure he would lead their company to glory. From that point on, they were known as "Dodd's Independents."

As they settled into their quarters at Fort Garland, the boys got their hands on some recent newspapers from the east. One story attracted their attention: President Lincoln had relieved John C. Frémont of his command in Missouri. The Great Pathfinder was a man like themselves, an explorer and soldier unafraid to launch himself into the wilderness. Frémont had been out in California when the war with Mexico began and had captured several of its cities on behalf of the United States. Now he was a general in the Union Army, and in trouble.

Some said Frémont had been skimming from suppliers and overcharging his own soldiers for goods they needed. Others said he had issued an emancipation proclamation, ordering that all slaves of proven secessionists and Confederate guerrillas in Missouri were henceforth free, and that the president was enraged. Lincoln needed Missouri, a slave state with a divided populace on the northwest border of the Confederacy, and Frémont's proclamation imperiled its relationship with the Union. If Frémont's actions caused Missouri to go with the Confederacy, it would be a problem for Lincoln and for Ickis and the other Union soldiers in Colorado and New Mexico. They would be cut off from Independence, the eastern terminus of the Santa Fe Trail, and their supply line would be disrupted or severed altogether.

Otherwise, the Civil War was progressing slowly. Union and Confederate troops continued their skirmishing in Virginia and Kentucky, and the Union Navy was making inroads in coastal South Carolina. As Ickis got comfortable at Fort Garland, the armies of the East settled into winter quarters in Virginia with a frustrated sigh, hunkering down and speculating about the spring campaigns to come.[8]

Ickis thought that Dodd's Independents would be staying at Fort Garland until the aspen trees leafed out in glorious green, but on New Year's Day 1862, they received orders to pack up their gear and put on their boots: they were going to Santa Fe. On January 2 the company left the cozy confines of Fort Garland and marched onto a road that moved south along the floor of the San Luis Valley. The trail was one of the great trading and raiding roads that crisscrossed southern Colorado, blazed by Utes and Hispanos, tying the communities of the Southwest together.[9] Up ahead and to the east, the highest peaks of the Sangre de Cristo range stuck up like knots on a curving spine. To the west were the remote and ragged San Juans, where there had been a brief gold rush during the winter of 1860.[10]

Now snow blanketed the tops of the peaks. Soon, the flakes were coming down fast upon Dodd's company. Ickis limped along the trail, blisters blooming on his heels and toes from hard marching in his stiff boots. They finally halted outside the small town of Culebra, just north of the New Mexico border. Ickis slept on the frozen ground with just one blanket for warmth.[11] It was a little uncomfortable, but he was used to such conditions. For the two years he was in the mines, Ickis had slept in lean-tos made of pine branches and under overlapping blankets held aloft by pickaxes jammed into the ground. Every now and again he and the other miners had built themselves wooden stockades, but that was only if they had found a quartz vein worth working. Otherwise, they kept moving. On to another gulch, tracing another stream back up into a rocky crevasse, looking for "some ledge upheaved edgewise." No sense putting down roots when you had prospecting to do.[12]

His first, adventurous days in the West seemed long past to Ickis, who now found himself crossing the border into New Mexico Territory. Dodd's Independents passed town after town on the march, small squares of one-story buildings organized around central plazas.

"All the towns in this Territory are alike," Ickis noted in his diary, all of them constructed with adobe, a combination of dirt, hay, and water. For hundreds of years, Pueblos had used adobe to build their houses. When the Spanish came to the region in the sixteenth century, they adapted this material to make uniform bricks, and laid out towns around plazas in their traditional style. The towns were evidence of New Mexico's long history of cultural conflict and adaptation.[13]

Ickis appreciated these towns, partly for their unusual architecture but mostly for their fandangos. Ickis had heard rumors about these New Mexican social assemblies, which attracted soldiers, trappers, traders, military officials, and westward-traveling migrants, in addition to locals. Attendees could buy liquor and food, and dance until the wee hours of the morning.[14] After experiencing their first fandango, Ickis and his friends vowed to attend as many as possible during their march to Santa Fe. They made good on their promise, stumbling out of most towns on the route, slowed by injuries sustained in drunken brawls.

The first long stretch of the road in New Mexico Territory was well marked and pounded smooth. It crossed several acequias, ditches that carried water from streams to nearby fields. Ickis had not seen irrigation canals before. The cornfields on his family farm in Iowa were watered by steady, seasonal rainfall. In the high desert, however, it rained fewer than twenty inches a year. Even in the mountains, where snow was more plentiful and long lasting, creeks and streams often ran dry. Pueblos had dug out the first networks of acequias throughout northern New Mexico, moving water from rivers to fields in order to raise beans, corn, and squash. Now, in the dead of winter, the acequias were crusted over with ice, and crossing them was perilous. Ickis slipped while he was picking his way across one, and fell with a thud. He bruised his hip, and it was rough going for him after that.[15]

Over the next week, Dodd's Independents continued their march through a widening valley filled with small farms, passing through the pueblo and town of Taos.[16] The snow began to fall more thickly and the company's ox teams began to give out. Ickis and his comrades took the ropes into their hands once again and pulled wagons up mountainsides three feet deep in drifts.

"We are cursing the Service this day," Ickis wrote in his diary. The Union recruiters at Cañon City had clearly lied to them about how being in the army was "nothing like hard work." If the boys had known then what they knew now, Ickis thought, they would have stayed in the mines.[17]

On January 16, 1862, Dodd's Independents arrived at Fort Marcy, a military installation perched on a high hill north of Santa Fe. They pitched their tents outside its walls and received their Union uniforms: blue frock coats, pants, overcoats, forage caps, blouses, shirts, shoes, and blankets. The kits and good grub lifted their spirits. The company certainly looked better than they had in previous weeks, and some of the men strutted like peacocks. Ickis was amused that even Captain Dodd, the icicles melting off of his beard and mustache, "steps around as proud as [Don] Juan."[18]

The company stayed in Santa Fe for eight days, drilling every morning and marching on the parade ground of Fort Marcy every evening. When he had time and could secure a pass, Ickis walked through Santa Fe.[19] He thought the town was beautiful, with its plazas that "will compare very well with the Squares of many towns in the States."[20] As for the residents, well, that was another matter.

"There are about 15,000 inhabitants," he judged, "out of that No. perhaps 400 'Americans.'" Ickis, like many Anglo-Americans in the mid-nineteenth century, believed that race and nationality were synonymous. To him, true Americans were white. The Hispanos who lived in New Mexico Territory, despite the fact that they had been living within the borders of the United States for fifteen years, were "Mexican." And in his racist view, all of the Hispanos living in Santa Fe were either peons (laborers) or criminals.[21]

Ickis did not think much of the Anglo residents of Santa Fe, either. He found it a "slow town by daylight but a fast town by moonlight." The whole place, he wrote to his brother Thomas, was nothing but a giant brothel. "Licentiousness is deemed a virtue, and gambling is carried on in this city on a large scale."[22]

Not that Alonzo necessarily disapproved of living in a fast town. There was a fandango every night in Santa Fe and Ickis tried to attend as often as he could. When they were not drilling or on guard duty, Dodd's men lived as they had in Cañon City, drinking, dancing, and gambling.

At Fort Marcy, rumors swirled like dust devils. The Texans were approaching, closer every day! Marching up the Rio Grande from Fort Bliss! Sneaking up the Pecos River from central Texas with their Apache and Comanche allies! Coming down the Santa Fe Trail in order to cut off the Union Army from their supply route!

On January 23, Ickis and the boys finally found out the real state of things. The Confederates were in southern New Mexico in force. Dodd's Independents had orders to gather up their kits, yoke up the cattle, load the wagons, and move south. They were going to join Richard Canby and the rest of the Union Army of New Mexico at Fort Craig.[23]

Like Bill Davidson, Ickis had faith in the men around him. Dodd's men would fight well, for their company was "the best that was ever raised in any country," he judged. "All large, strong men and the most of them damn sharp."[24]

On January 24, 1862, Alonzo Ickis left Santa Fe, following a road down the Rio Grande. Dodd's Independents marched toward wide expanses of the New Mexico desert, and the Civil War that had finally come to the West.

7

=

Valverde

By the time Dodd's Independents left Santa Fe, Colonel Kit Carson and his New Mexico Volunteers were already encamped around Fort Craig, 175 miles to the south. In early January 1862, Richard Canby sent Carson orders to bring the 1st New Mexico from Albuquerque to Fort Craig to help defend it against a Confederate attack. Carson had listened carefully to these instructions—although he had picked up a working knowledge of Spanish and several Native languages during the thirty years he had lived in the Southwest, he had never learned to read—and then dictated orders to his men. Then he went to see his wife, Josefa, who was living with him and their three small children at his headquarters in Albuquerque. He told her that the war was coming, and she must return to their house in Taos. Once he had seen them safely on the way north, Carson and his soldiers left for Fort Craig.[1]

When he arrived the next week, Richard Canby informed Carson that he had named the encampment around Fort Craig after him. It seemed an odd choice, given that Carson was not a professional military man and had not yet distinguished himself in battle. But he was famous in New Mexico, and across the nation. Ever since the explorer and politician John C. Frémont had written about him in his 1840s exploration reports, Carson had become a mythical figure, an Anglo man who personified American manifest destiny. Those who met him for the first time were surprised at his small stature and his quiet demeanor, but most were also impressed by how quickly he moved even in his fifties, and his reputation for bravery. Surveyor General John Clark met Carson soon after arriving in New Mexico, and confessed that he "would go further to see him & do him honor, than I would to see any Prince on the globe."[2] This kind of reaction befuddled Carson whenever he was confronted with it, but his fame inspired the men in the ranks.

As the New Mexico Volunteers settled into Camp Carson, Kit met with the other officers to work out battle plans. Carson was in command of the 1st New Mexico as well as several militia units, companies of forty to a hundred men who enlisted for three months' service. All of these soldiers were Hispanos born in New Mexico Territory or Anglos who had married into Hispano families. The 1st New Mexico had been training since the summer of 1861. Carson, who was more practiced in the guerrilla fighting tactics of the frontier than in military maneuvers, had learned alongside his men. By the time they arrived at Fort Craig, he was pleased with their progress. The militias, however, still needed instruction. Most of them had experience riding out to pursue Navajo and Apache warriors who had raided their ranches. They did not, however, bend naturally to military discipline. Both Carson and Richard Canby hoped there was enough time to prepare them before the Texans arrived.[3]

———

Alonzo Ickis and Dodd's Independents made good time from Santa Fe to Fort Craig, marching an average of twenty miles a day. They arrived on January 31, 1862, and were ordered to set up their tents at Camp Carson.

"Kit is here," Ickis wrote excitedly. With him, he added with derision, was "his regiment of Greasers."[4]

Ickis thought that the New Mexico Volunteers would probably be all right as scouts and spies, but he did not trust them to stand and fight on the field of battle. He believed that the only useful outcome of an engagement with the enemy would be if the Texans managed to shoot all the Mexicans.

"The more of them are killed the better the country is off," Ickis groused.[5]

The fighting force that was gathering at Fort Craig in January 1862 was the first multiracial army to fight in the American Civil War, but it was not an integrated one. Its Anglo and Hispano volunteers and Pueblo and Ute scouts served in different units, spoke several languages, and looked upon one another with suspicion rather than respect.

For the next two weeks Ickis tried his best to ignore the New Mexico Volunteers while Dodd's Independents spent their days "knocking rust off our guns," and visiting Fort Craig.

"It is a good post," Ickis judged. "But a poor fort."[6]

Built in 1854 on a high bluff above the Rio Grande, Fort Craig gave soldiers a view of the broken tableland of black basaltic lava across the river and the wide valley of sandbanks extending northward to Mesa de la Contadera. The fort was a large square enclosure with seven-foot walls built mostly of adobe and a tall, arched gateway constructed out of lava rock. Anticipating a Confederate attack, Union troops had built trenches outside of the fort's walls, and a battery platform in the southeast corner, on which they mounted four cannons that could rake the valley and the riverbank to the south. When it was first constructed, Fort Craig could comfortably house about two hundred men. By mid-February 1862, there were more than 3,800 Union soldiers encamped within and outside of its walls.[7]

On February 15, 1862, Bill Davidson and the 5th Texas marched through a howling snowstorm and halted one mile south of Fort Craig. The winds blew "so hard as to almost pull the face off a man." Gathering around their campfires, they cracked jokes and sang "as merrily as if they were at home," trying to make the best of things. But the truth was, they were in bad shape.[8]

They had been encamped around Fort Thorn, a former U.S. Army installation forty miles north of Mesilla, for more than a month. After their long march from San Antonio, the rest had done them good. But the camp quickly became a hotbed of disease, like others across the nation during the Civil War. Measles and smallpox outbreaks had ripped through the camp, and most of the men were suffering from exposure-related illnesses like pneumonia. The Texans did not have much to do but take care of their sick friends and worry about the future.

"The thought naturally presented itself," mused Bill Davidson, "how many of these noble men, now so full of life and hope, will ever live to see Texas soil again." Everyone knew that "toil and suffering and danger is ahead of us. We know that hard blows are going to be given and received. We know that some will be killed, but how many and who, time will tell."[9]

Early in the morning of February 16, the Texans marched in force on Fort Craig. As they formed a line of battle, Richard Canby's Union Army of New Mexico came out to meet them. Alonzo Ickis and thousands of soldiers dressed in blue assembled on the plain south of the fort, and the Texans watched them come. A private broke the silence.

"Gee whilikens captain I ain't half as mad at them fellows as I was before they showed up so many men," he cried out. "Let's go home to mother!"[10]

The Texans roared with laughter.

Bill Davidson had to admit that the Union forces made an impressive picture. The Yankees "did not seem scared a bit. They ran up their flag on the mast within the fort and cheered like they were trying to split their throats."

Not to be outdone, Davidson and his comrades "waved our flag and gave them a round yell" back.[11]

The Texans, like most Confederate armies in the field during the Civil War, were outnumbered. They did not see this as a problem. They believed their 2,500 men were more than a match for Canby's 3,800. Both of these armies were small, however, compared to those in the eastern theater, where more than 100,000 men had been fighting against one another on the battlefields of Virginia and Tennessee. But Richard Canby's army and Henry Sibley's brigade were the largest fighting forces that the desert Southwest had ever seen in one place. New Mexico had a long history of violent conflict, but these battles were usually waged between small groups of armed raiders and soldiers using guerrilla tactics. The scarcity of food and water in the high desert meant that sustaining large armies for long periods was a challenge. Both Canby and Sibley were aware of this potential problem, and both wanted to defeat the enemy as quickly as possible because of it.

For two hours, the Union and Confederate armies maneuvered in front of each other.

"It looked to me," said Davidson, "like two boys in my school days, daring each other to knock the chip off the other's shoulder and each afraid to do so."[12]

Canby had a strong defensive position on high ground, and he knew it would be folly to give it up. He might have thousands of men, but many of them were "green" militiamen and volunteers. He had little confidence in either Kit Carson's New Mexico Volunteers or the gold miners in Dodd's company. So Canby stayed put and dared the Texans to come at him.[13]

Sibley recognized Canby's advantage and realized he could not make a charge on the federals with any hope of success. While he, like Canby, did not believe that the Union volunteers would fight, Sibley knew that the U.S. Army regulars would. A few of them had been under his command at Fort Burgwin, near Taos, before he had resigned his commission in the U.S. Army. They were professional soldiers, all of them "reared in camps of instruction and trained to deeds of war and not peace."[14] The Texans were skilled with their rifles and full of enthusiasm, but Sibley knew that familiarity with the ways of war usually won the day on a battlefield like this.

As night fell, therefore, both armies withdrew.

Ickis, Carson, and the Union Army retreated behind the adobe walls of Fort Craig and returned to Camp Carson. Ickis settled into his tent and pulled out his diary and a pencil.

"Almost had a battle today," he wrote.

Davidson and his comrades marched back to their camps along the Rio Grande.

"We thought the ball was about to open," Davidson lamented.[15]

Later that night Henry Sibley called his officers to his tent. The Confederate general was disappointed that Canby had not taken the bait.

"Battle [was] offered on the open plain," he wrote to the Confederate War Department. "The challenge was disregarded."[16]

Sibley had known Richard Canby and his wife, Louisa, quite well, from U.S. Army campaigns in Utah and New Mexico in the late 1850s and early 1860s. He anticipated that Canby would defend his fort and fight according to established military practice, even in a desert landscape not particularly suited to large scale, long term battles. The Texans needed to make another plan, one that would confound Canby with its boldness.

Sibley and his officers discussed the options and decided to cross the Rio Grande east of their camp, putting the river between them and the Union artillery at Fort Craig. Then they would move northward, following ridges of drifting sand, parallel to the river. This route would give them several advantages, by "concealing [their] movements and securing [them] from attack by the impracticable character of the country."[17] When they passed Mesa de la Contadera, they would cross back over the Rio Grande and get between the Yankees and their supply base at Santa Fe. This would force Canby out of Fort Craig and bring on a battle on a field of Sibley's choosing.[18]

But where to ford the river north of the Mesa? Sibley had traveled along *El Camino Real* several times. He thought he knew just the place to cross, a broad plain marked by the ruins of a pueblo and a hacienda. The Rio Grande here had changed its course several times as it ran up against the Mesa, creating a broad basin of low sand hills where the riverbanks used to be. The place went by several names. Some Hispanos called it Contadero, but most Anglos in New Mexico knew it as Valverde.[19]

—————

Two days later, the Texans began to cross their men and wagons to the east side of the Rio Grande.[20] The next morning, they started to move northward. On the hard surface of the black lava rock, they made good time. The path gained elevation as they progressed, until it crested at a shard of lava jutting out toward the river. Here, the Texans could see Fort Craig below them, across the river to the west.[21] As they looked, several hundred Union troops poured out of its gates toward the Rio Grande. Canby had sent them to cross the river and get between it and the Texans, cutting the Confederates off from their water supply. Some were soldiers in Kit Carson's 1st New Mexico Volunteers, and they were joined by Alonzo Ickis and Dodd's men, as well as a company of militia who had been mustered into the Union Army only a few days before. All of them splashed through the frigid Rio Grande and then labored through the sand hills on the eastern bank, their feet sinking into the soft surface.

The Confederates lobbed some shells toward the federals and, as Ickis noted with frustration, "We [could not] return fire as we [were] far below them."[22] As the shots continued to rain down, the militiamen broke and ran. Canby ordered Carson's Volunteers and Dodd's company to follow them and retreat back to Fort Craig. But he left some men in the sand hills to defend the river.[23]

As they watched these developments from up on the lava ridge, Bill Davidson and his comrades cheered. It was the rebel yell, a full-throated scream that the Texans always claimed had originated during the Rangers' wars with Comanches in the 1840s and '50s. As it echoed over the valley, Davidson felt sure that "the yell must have sent a chill to the hearts of the boys in blue."[24]

As it was late in the day, Sibley ordered the men to camp where they were. The next day, February 21, they would march toward Valverde and bring the fight to the Yankees. They needed to rest and eat. Davidson and the others burned mesquite and sat around the fire, casting bullets from melted lead bars.[25] Later that evening, the commander of the 5th Texas, Colonel Tom Green, came around to see the men of Company A.

"Boys, you've come too far from home hunting a fight to lose," he told Davidson and his comrades. "You must win tomorrow, or die on the battlefield."[26]

Davidson ate a dinner of dried meat and drank the last drops from his canteen.[27] The Sibley Brigade had been without water since they had crossed the Rio Grande the day before. After most of the brigade had turned in, Davidson and a few others crept out of their blankets and grabbed as many canteens as they could carry. They made their way down the lava field to the plain, crawled by the Yankee camps to the river, filled their canteens with water, and brought them back to their comrades. Davidson was happy to have helped stave off their thirst, at least for a little while.[28]

That night, in his headquarters at Fort Craig, Richard Canby tried to anticipate Henry Sibley's next move. The Texans might continue marching northward and attempt to cross the Rio Grande at the Valverde ford. They might countermarch and re-cross the river to charge Fort Craig from the south. Or they might attempt an assault on the fort from their current position on the lava ridge across the way.

It was paramount to protect Fort Craig. The Union Army could withstand a siege, if it came to that. A large wagon train had arrived from Santa Fe that day, and its seventy wagons would provide enough food, weapons, and forage for several weeks. Canby knew, however, that he could not let Sibley trap him in the fort and cut off his communications with Santa Fe. Also, his soldiers were restless and eager to fight. He could not keep them from the battlefield much longer.

A few hours after dawn on February 21, 1862, Canby made his decision. He would stay at Fort Craig to oversee its defense. His second in command, Benjamin Roberts, would take a mixed regiment of Army regulars, New Mexico Volunteers, and artillerists northward to Valverde, to occupy and hold the ford.[29] Kit Carson would take the 1st New Mexico, the militia, and Dodd's Independents back across the Rio Grande in front of the fort. If it became clear that Sibley was turning south or charging across the river, Carson's forces would "impede his movements as much as possible."[30]

Alonzo Ickis was none too happy to be posted with Carson's men again. There was not much he could do about it, though. Orders were orders, and he was just a private. So Ickis hunkered down in the sand hills and tightened his grip on his rifle, watching the Confederate camp for any signs of movement. The early-morning light did not reveal much, except Texans making cook fires and dust clouds rising to the northeast.

Bill Davidson and Company A were going about "our usual morning duties—some digging roots, others moving their horses, and others cooking
breakfast," when they saw about two hundred of their compatriots riding
out of camp, northward toward Valverde.[31] It was John Baylor's former
regiment, the 2nd Texas Mounted Rifles, with Major Charles Pyron in
command. They were moving swiftly, eager to reach the ford and get "a
square drink of water."

"If one of us coughed," a 2nd Texas private wrote, "you could see the
dust fly."[32]

Soon Pyron's men disappeared, descending into a ravine that passed
to the east of Mesa de la Contadera, and then turned west toward the river
at Valverde. Davidson went back to his breakfast, and tried to make the
best of things. Company A sat around, "some telling yarns, some playing
cards, though cards were very scarce, they, like our clothing, being worn
out." Some of the men got out a piece of tin and held it over their cook fire
with sticks, and then picked lice out of their clothes and dropped them on
the metal. The men gathered around, placing bets "on which one got off
that hot tin first." In this way, they passed two pleasurable hours.[33]

The sun was up over the mountains and just beginning to warm the
chill air when Davidson heard it. The pop pop pop of rifle fire. Faint but
distinct, coming from somewhere past the Mesa. The Confederates' camp
snapped to attention. "Every fellow sprang to arms and for his horse," but
their officers told them to stand down. They would receive orders when
Sibley wanted them to move.

"By god!" objected one of the Texans. "Are you going to let Pyron whip
them before we get there?"[34]

Down on the sandbank, Ickis could not be sure what he was hearing. Your
ears played strange tricks on you in the desert, and the Mesa had a way of
bending sound. But there it was again. The boom of artillery shells, fired
from cannons and arcing toward their targets.

The federals in the sand looked up at the Texan camp and saw a flurry
of activity. Soldiers were leaping on their horses and riding hard for Mesa
de la Contadera. Kit Carson sent a courier back across the water with this
intelligence, advising Richard Canby that the Texans were on the move
toward Valverde. Soon the courier came riding back, with orders for Car-

son to leave a contingent of soldiers along the bank and march with the rest of the 1st New Mexico and Dodd's Independents to the battlefield. Ickis was delighted. Finally, the ball was to begin in earnest.[35]

A few hours passed in the Texan camp, and then a courier came and handed one of their officers orders to hasten with most of the 5th Texas to the field. Company A cheered and mounted their horses. With them were two companies under the command of Captain Willis Lang, holding aloft the lances that Henry Sibley had made for them back in San Antonio.

The 5th Texas and Lang's Lancers passed Mesa de la Contadera and moved down into a narrow canyon, which funneled them into the northern edge of the plains of Valverde. They poured out of the ravine and found themselves on the far right of the Confederate line, facing the Rio Grande and more than one thousand Union troops. Davidson had barely registered their position before several of his comrades were shot off their horses.[36]

At the same moment, Alonzo Ickis arrived on the west bank of the Rio Grande across from the battlefield.[37] He could not see much. A large number of cottonwood trees were clustered between Dodd's Independents and the enemy, and their flat, spreading branches obscured most of the battlefield. Smoke from the gunfire drifted through the trees, making it even harder to see. The Union artillerists had been doing hot work for the previous two hours, and had driven the Texans behind the sand embankments that formed a natural trench on the east side of the river.[38]

"It did look awhile as if the 'Yanks' had taken a contract to bark and limb all the cottonwood trees in our vicinity," remarked one Texan. "The ping and spud of their bullets, the roll and thunder of their bursting bombs and the crash of falling timber about us, had no comfort in them."[39]

Soon Dodd's men were wading across the river, "selecting step by step their foothold among quick sands and against the strong current of the Rio Grande up to their arms in its water."[40] Once he had come through, Ickis pressed his back against the dark red bark of a cottonwood tree and fixed a bayonet onto the end of his rifle. Then Dodd's company began to move through the woods toward the Confederate line.

Behind the sandbank four hundred yards away, the 4th Texas waited.

Their colonel, William Scurry, divided his command to meet the threat, ordering those with minié rifles to pick off the Union officers while the rest of the men waited behind the sandbank until the soldiers came within range of their shotguns. If one of the sharpshooters was wounded or killed, his rifle "was given to one of the shotgun men, who was put in his place."[41]

As Ickis and Dodd's company advanced, they fired, sending hundreds of bullets thunking into the sandbank, and into the bodies of the 4th Texas sharpshooters. They caught one as he leaned out too far from behind a tree, and he fell to the ground "with heart-rending groans." Bright red drops of blood spattered the sand as another Texan was "shot through the mouth and his tongue nearly shot out." He impressed his fellow soldiers by pulling out a part of his tongue "which was hanging ragged to the edge," and cutting it off with his knife.[42]

Ickis and the others continued on toward the Texans. As they came, the Confederates speculated about them. They did not move or dress in the manner of professional soldiers.

"They thought us Mexicans," Ickis said scornfully. Because of that, the Texans "thought they had the soft snap."[43]

Through the smoke of their gunfire, Ickis and the others saw something that seemed hard to believe: fifty horsemen, riding at a gallop and holding long spears with gleaming metal blades, bearing down on them.

When Theodore Dodd saw Lang's Lancers coming, he worked quickly, remembering his West Point training on cavalry charges. He organized Ickis and the other men into a small hollow square. The men stood two deep, the first rank kneeling with their bayonets and the second rank behind them standing up, waiting with their guns, ready to shoot.

"Steady there my brave mountaineers!" Dodd yelled. "Waste not a single shot. Do not let your passions run off with your judgment."

The Lancers sped toward them, closing the gap.

"Steady men steady, do not fire until I command."

Ickis stared at the oncoming horsemen and their lances, "each tipped with a small Secesh flag" from Texas: red with a white star.

There was not a sound in the company ranks. Ickis could hear his own heartbeat.

"Steady men," ordered Dodd. "Guns to faces but wait for the command to fire."

The horsemen came within forty yards of the Coloradans and it was then that Dodd gave the command.

"Fire!" he yelled. "They're Texans! Give 'em Hell!"

Ickis, in the second row, fired his gun. Then came the dull thud of the impact of bullets in flesh, the terrified bleats of horses, the screams of men. When the smoke dissipated, Ickis could see that "many brave Texans [had] bit the dust, many horses were riderless." The rest of the Lancers wavered for a few moments and then "on they came and fierce fellows they were with their long lances raised."

The Coloradans had reloaded their guns and "we gave them a second volley." Then they rushed upon the Lancers with their bayonets.

"They appeared bewildered, did not appear to know how or what to do," he said. Ickis and the boys took advantage of the Texans' confusion and leapt upon them, stabbing and bludgeoning the Confederates with their bayonets. One of Ickis's comrades ran his bayonet through one Texan "and then shot the top of his head off" for good measure.

The Lancers "were soon butchered," Ickis wrote. "I cannot call it else."[44]

Captain Lang staggered back to the Confederate lines, mortally wounded. He did not know how many soldiers he had lost. Half of them at least, maybe more, and almost all of the horses. The men of the 4th and 5th Texas looked on, temporarily stunned. It had been a gallant charge, but a doomed one.[45]

Dodd's company had little time to revel in their victory. The hand-to-hand fight with the Lancers had brought them close to the Texan lines, and within range of the Confederates' double-barreled shotguns. The 4th and 5th Texas rose up onto the lip of the sand hill and took aim at the federals.[46] Ickis and the others backed away slowly, picking up abandoned guns and dragging wounded men with them.[47] When they arrived back at the Union line, Dodd's company threw themselves on the sand behind a battery of six cannons commanded by a seasoned artillerist named Alexander McRae. They ate some of their rations and replenished their ammunition pouches. Soon, McRae put his guns into action and a cannonade began. The noise was deafening.

"Away went the shot shell Grape & Canister," Ickis wrote, and "the ball kept rolling."[48] Snow flurries swirled around them and on the battlefield, flakes coming to rest and then melting on the torn bodies of men and horses.

Behind the sandbanks in the center of the Confederate line, Bill Davidson clutched his shotgun and lay down as flat as he could, shivering in the cold. He had discharged his last bullet at the retreating Coloradans, and at some point he had lost his hat. One of Lang's lances was lying nearby. He crawled to it, picked it up, untied the red–and–white flag from its tip, and secured it around his head. This kept him slightly warmer, but he knew the red kerchief would now be a target for the Yankee gunners. Davidson "squeezed the ground" and pondered the Sibley Brigade's situation.

"Under all military rules and science we were whipped," Davidson admitted. "Out flanked on our right, outnumbered more than two to one in the center and an enfilading fire on our left that threatened our entire line." It seemed to him that the Confederates had little choice. They had to retreat or surrender.[49]

Farther down the Confederate line, the 5th Texas commander, Colonel Tom Green, called the other officers of the Sibley Brigade together. Henry Sibley was sick, Green informed them, and had chosen to stay behind in the camp on the lava ridge. The officers looked at one another knowingly. It was an open secret that Sibley was a drunk, and that his frequent bouts of "illness" were due to his fondness for the whiskey keg. The general's incapacitation meant that Colonel Green was now in command of the field of battle. The Texans did not have a path of retreat, and Green had no thoughts of surrendering. As he had told the men of the 5th the day before, they had come too far not to fight until the end.[50]

On the eastern bank of the Rio Grande, Richard Canby arrived. He had received reports from Benjamin Roberts that the battle had intensified, so he left a small group of soldiers to defend Fort Craig and brought the rest of his men with him. When they came around the north side of Mesa de la Contadera, Canby could see the flashes of artillery fire and smoke billowing up at the ford. He urged his horse through the river and joined Roberts behind the federal line. Surveying the scene, he became worried about the Confederate batteries facing the Union right, and the fact that the top of Mesa de la Contadera was unoccupied. He turned to his aide and dispatched an order to Kit Carson, telling him to take the New Mexico Volunteers, a regiment of Army regulars, and two heavy guns to hold that side of the line.

Carson left immediately, marching his men southward through a grove of cottonwood trees. Canby seemed unaware, however, that Carson's departure had just weakened his center. McRae's guns were there, firing shot and shell at the Confederates, but now there were only about three hundred men, including Dodd's Independents, to defend the battery.[51]

Across the sandy plain, Tom Green looked through a pair of field glasses and realized that a gap had just opened up at the center of the Union line. Quickly, he issued two sets of orders. First, he sent men to engage with Kit Carson's soldiers, who looked to be headed for the Mesa. Then he sent a man galloping down the line to inform all of the company commanders to prepare for a charge. The goal was McRae's battery, which had been pummeling them for more than two hours. Take those cannons, Green ordered, and break the Union line.[52]

The messenger rode up to Company A's captain, John Shropshire, leaned down and gave him the order, and then galloped off. The news reverberated through the ranks. Davidson rose to his knees, buckled his Colt six-shooter around his waist, stuffed ammunition into his pockets, and grabbed his shotgun. Then he and the rest of Company A gathered around Shropshire, turned toward the enemy, and waited for the command to charge.

From the Confederate side of the line, a cannon started roaring.[53] Soon after, one of Davidson's comrades saw a company of Texans on their right bolt into the battlefield. Shropshire turned to his men and yelled, "Come on, my boys!"

Davidson jumped up, leapt over the edge of the sand hill, and began running toward the Union guns. There was "one yell as they started and then an ominous silence, broken only by our gallant officers as they cheer their men onward."[54] In front of them, a mostly level plain extended seven hundred yards toward the federal lines, dotted here and there with cottonwoods. Smoke was drifting across it, some of it from the muzzles of cannons but most from the grass, which was on fire. Davidson ran, the small flames licking at his heels.

All of McRae's guns swiveled toward them and shots and shells began exploding all around, shrapnel ricocheting across the sand. Davidson ran on while all around him men were "falling, bleeding, dying at every step." The rest were racing for the cannons. When they drew within fifty yards of the battery, Davidson aimed his shotgun at the nearest Yankee and fired.[55]

─────────

Alonzo Ickis had just been ordered to lie down behind McRae's battery when he heard the yell resounding across the battlefield in front of them. Dodd's men stood and readied themselves for the onslaught. As they did, they felt a shift in the lines behind them.

"At the first sight of such a very large body of Texans," Ickis complained bitterly, the militia were running toward the river, "leaving us white men only to hold the section or let it go."[56]

Ickis did not see that some Army regulars had also fallen back, joining the militia in their flight. He and Dodd's Independents turned and began to fire at the Texans, again and again. McRae's gunners turned their cannons upon the rapidly advancing brigade. "At every shot you could see their ranks open and pieces of men flying in the air," Ickis said. But "they still came down upon us."[57] There was no time to pull the battery back across the Rio Grande, and McRae's boys could only spike a few of the cannons before the Texans were upon them. McRae took two bullets and kept firing at the Texans. Another shot killed him where he stood.

"It was not in human power to stop or resist that wave," Davidson reported.

Ickis could only watch as the Texans swarmed over the cannons. Then he, too, turned and fled.[58]

One of the Union artillerists, realizing that the Texans had overwhelming numbers, jumped up on a magazine that stood at the side of the guns, and drew his pistol.

"Victory or death!" he cried. Then he fired into the ammunition.

The explosion was one "loud crash" and "all was over with that brave boy," said Ickis. "The explosion must have killed several of the enemy, [who] were thick as they could stand."[59]

─────────

Davidson and Company A had just recovered from the shock of this blast when they heard the now familiar sound of rifle fire, but from an unexpected direction. They turned to the left and saw a company of soldiers coming toward them. At first the Texans thought that these were their own men, coming to support them. Davidson and the others ceased firing, but soon learned of their mistake as Kit Carson's soldiers poured flanking fire into the Confederates gathered around the cannons.[60]

———

Carson was proud of his men. They had scattered the Confederate left after the charge, and could still win the day. After this, the Anglos at Fort Craig would have to admit that the Hispanos could fight, and that they were just as brave and committed in their defense of the Union as the Army regulars, and the volunteers from Colorado.

Richard Canby saw the work that Carson's men had done and he "for some moments entertained the confident hope that the battery, and with it the fortunes of the day, would yet be saved." But then he decided that even Carson's men could not disperse the charging Texans and "that to prolong the contest would only add to the number of our casualties without changing the result." He turned to his aide and asked for paper, wrote a few lines, then sent a courier to find Carson. When the courier handed the note to him, Carson unfolded it and asked an officer to read it to him. It was an order to retreat from the field.[61]

———

When Davidson realized the Union troops were heading back toward the Rio Grande, he and Company A turned to the cannons and tried to figure out how to work them. But they had not been trained as artillerists, and did not know where to start.

"Oh hell," said Davidson, "we don't know which end of the thing goes foremost." He turned to the others and waved at them. "Let's [go] cut them fellows off."[62]

He dashed toward the riverbank. The Texans could see the Union infantry splashing through the water, the cavalry on their horses overtaking and riding over some of them, artillerists trying to lug guns through the bottoms and then giving up and abandoning them mid-stream. Davidson began shooting at the Yanks as fast as he could load and fire. Finally, the Confederate gunners arrived at McRae's battery. They turned the guns around, loading them with ammunition, and poured a "perfect shower of shot" at Dodd's Independents, Carson's New Mexico Volunteers, and the rest of the Union men trying to cross the river. Soldiers were hit and went facedown into the water, spinning off into the current.[63]

Soldiers from the 4th Texas urged their horses into the river in pursuit but were stopped short by a Union rider galloping up to the bank, holding a white flag aloft. Davidson cheered, believing it to be a flag of surrender. Instead, as the note the rider bore informed Tom Green, it was a flag of truce. Richard Canby wanted a period of cease-fire, to gather the wounded and the dead from the battlefield.

Green looked across the Rio Grande in the fading light. The Sibley Brigade was exhausted. After the charge, many of them had dropped their guns and waded into the river, drinking their fill after two days without water. After some discussion among the officers, "the flag was respected and the firing ceased." The 4th Texas had just reached the west bank of the river when they heard the buglers sounding "halt." Frustrated, they turned back. There was a smattering of gunfire, and then silence.[64]

Davidson went to the captured battery, where he found John Shropshire speaking "a few words to us complimenting and congratulating us."[65] The Texans walked back to the battlefield, searching for a place to set up camp for the night. Their officers turned to the writing of reports. Tom Green sent word to Henry Sibley that the Texans had won the day. The road to Albuquerque and Santa Fe was now open to the Confederates.

There was one problem, however. The capture of Fort Craig had been a central component of Sibley's plan to conquer New Mexico Territory. The Sibley Brigade needed its supplies and weapons to sustain them on the march to Santa Fe. Although the Texans had proven they could win a battle in the high desert, they had lost their best chance to take the fort. The officers were concerned about what this would mean for their men in the days to come.

———

The night of February 21, 1862, both the Texans and the Union troops moved slowly through the plains of Valverde, following the sounds of groans to the bodies of men. They carried the wounded to their respective field hospitals and heaved the dead into wagons, "as many as could lay side by side." Davidson heard a faint call and followed it, finding a friend of his who had been shot through both thighs and waited all night for help.

"How we missed finding him so long is a mystery to me," Davidson noted sadly, "as I had passed several times within ten feet of him, hunting specially for him."[66]

———

After retreating across the Rio Grande, a despondent Alonzo Ickis marched back to Fort Craig. In his tent at Camp Carson, he tallied the company's losses. He guessed that there were forty men dead, wounded, or missing from Dodd's Independents alone. Added to those who had fallen to illness before Valverde, the "Brave Mountaineers" had lost more than half of the men they had started with from Cañon City. This was a very high casualty rate for one company, across all theaters of the Civil War, and almost 10 percent of the total Union casualties at Valverde.

"Many of the boys with whom I was acquainted in the mountains are dead and wounded," Alonzo wrote sadly to his brother Tom. "These were trying times if I have seen any."[67]

———

At dawn on February 22, the men of the Sibley Brigade gathered more than seventy bodies together, side by side. They had selected a burial ground near the site of their greatest achievement during the battle: the capture of McRae's battery. At 10 a.m. the entire army gathered there, the chaplain said the funeral service, and Bill Davidson offered up a heart-felt prayer. Then they buried their comrades, wrapping them tightly in blankets and coats and laying them in three long trenches. They shoveled the dirt over the piles and left no other markers. They reckoned that the cottonwood trees that clustered all around would have to do. These "grand shapely old monarchs of the plains" would stand as sentinels, protecting the Confederate dead in the deserts of New Mexico.[68]

———

While the Texans buried their men, Alonzo Ickis walked toward one of Fort Craig's storehouses, which had been converted into a dead room. He had seen the wagon teams as they brought the bodies back to Fort Craig the day before, heard the "shrieks of the wounded and dying together" as the ambulance men carried them to the field hospitals hastily erected outside the fort's walls. And he had seen "the ghastly appearance of the dead" as they were taken to the storehouse. Ickis went there to look for several friends. He had lost track of them during the retreat and they were nowhere to be found at Camp Carson.

He opened the door and walked in. The bodies were heaped upon one another. Ickis climbed around them, peering into their faces. One of the bodies he clambered over was Lieutenant George Bascom, the U.S. Army officer whose fight with Cochise and Mangas Coloradas at Apache Pass in 1861 had provoked the Chiricahuas into a campaign of revenge. He had been shot in the retreat and caught in an eddy in the Rio Grande. The state of the bodies in the dead room was a shock. Ickis had never seen so much blood or so many mangled limbs.

"Never did I expect to witness a scene like this," Ickis confessed. "But such is <u>War</u>."[69]

On February 23, Union soldiers buried fifty men in Fort Craig's graveyard, "<u>each in a separate coffin</u>, an act seldom seen in a time of war." The artillerymen fired three volleys over the dead, which echoed across the valley.

"Their bodies will there rest in peace," Ickis was sure, "but their names and acts will live to form one of the brightest pages in the history of the war against Infamous Rebellion [and] deep double-dyed treason."[70]

Later that afternoon, Kit Carson's scouts reported that the Texans were on the move, crossing over to the western side of the Rio Grande and marching toward Albuquerque. They had McRae's six cannons with them, mementos of their victory that they henceforth referred to as "the Valverde Guns." Richard Canby's army was trapped between Henry Sibley's men to the north and John Baylor's to the south, and their supply line was severed. Canby immediately sent couriers racing toward Albuquerque and Santa Fe to warn the citizens that the Union Army had failed, and that the Texans were coming.

PART TWO

Trail Men

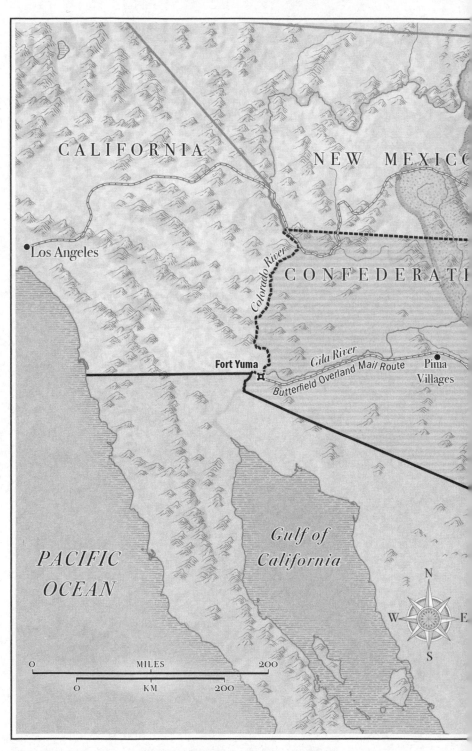

The Southwestern Theater, Winter–Summer 1862

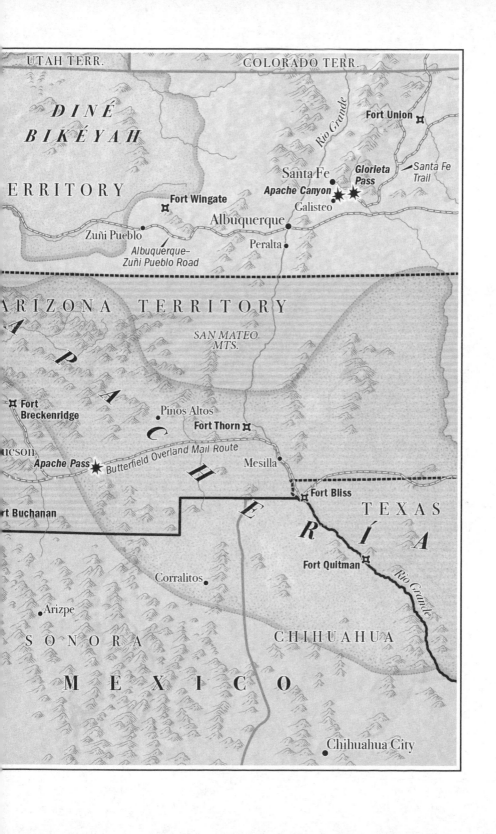

8

=

Baylor

A few days after the Sibley Brigade's victory over the Yankees at Valverde, an express rider galloped into Mesilla with reports of the battle.

"This glorious news creates a glow in this Valley," crowed the *Mesilla Times.* "The armies of the South will ever fight bravely, but they will never achieve a more brilliant victory than this." It was, as the *Times* argued, "memorable in our country's history, [and] replete in potent results for the present and future of our new Confederacy."[1]

John Baylor had given three cheers for the Sibley Brigade like everyone else in Mesilla. But he was resentful that he missed what would probably turn out to be the most pivotal battle in Civil War New Mexico. When Henry Sibley had arrived at Fort Bliss in December 1861, he had taken command of the campaign, absorbed Baylor's men into his army, and then sent William Steele, a career military man, to hold Mesilla with the 7th Texas.[2]

Baylor had offered his resignation, but Sibley refused to accept it.

"I don't see what Sibl[e]y wants with me," Baylor wrote to his wife Emy. He guessed that the general might want to "learn all the ropes" from him, to exploit Baylor's knowledge of Confederate Arizona and the contacts he had made among local Anglo communities. Before Sibley's officers left for Valverde, they often came to Mesilla to consult with him.

"I am [al]most too popular," he had bragged.[3]

But then Sibley had left him behind. Perhaps Baylor would be useful when the brigade returned to Mesilla and launched their campaign for California. But Baylor knew that the Confederates' march to Los Angeles would not be possible unless they exterminated or expelled the Chiricahua Apaches living in Arizona. To this end, Baylor had asked for the authority to recruit a militia to pursue the Chiricahuas and attempt to force them into battle, and Sibley had approved his request. As the Sibley Brigade left for Fort Craig, Baylor began to seek out bandits and thieves for his militia. As he well knew, men who loved risk and had no regard for rules made good Indian fighters.[4]

In the fall of 1840, soon after he arrived in Texas as a teenager, Baylor had joined a group of Texas Rangers heading northwest from the town of LaGrange (midway between Houston and Austin) into Comanche country. In those early years, most men who called themselves Rangers were loosely affiliated Anglo Texans propelled into action by proclamations in brochures or newspapers. They volunteered for a three-month enlistment and their campaigns were led by men with military experience. Other Texans came together in a more spontaneous fashion, reacting to news of local Comanche raids by riding out with their brothers and neighbors and engaging in running fights that lasted a few weeks at most.[5]

Baylor's first fight was a retributive attack in which the Rangers killed more than 130 Comanche men, women, and children and looted their village.[6] On their return trip to LaGrange, Baylor and the other Rangers carved their names into the ruined walls of San Sabá Presidio, one of Spain's northernmost colonial outposts in Texas.[7] Fifteen years after this first foray into Comanche country, Baylor returned in a different capacity. In September 1855, he was appointed as Indian agent at the Clear Fork Agency northwest of Dallas.

Baylor left Emy and their five children on a ranch they had just bought in central Texas, and moved to Clear Fork alone. As part of what had become a widespread American Indian policy by the 1850s, the state of Texas had removed more than three hundred Penateka Comanches from their territory to Clear Fork in an attempt to "civilize" them through agriculture and education.[8] Within a few months, Baylor became suspicious that the reservation Comanches were aiding and abetting their northern relatives in strikes against local ranches. He wanted to make war on these off-reservation Comanches, but his superiors preferred a more diplomatic approach. The ensuing arguments led, in 1857, to Baylor's dismissal as Indian agent.[9]

Baylor was embittered, but also inspired. During his time at the agency he had seen the ranching possibilities in the tablelands and prairies of West Texas. He began to buy up cattle and ultimately purchased land along the Brazos River south of the Clear Fork reservation, near the town of Weatherford. Emy and the children joined him, and by 1858 Baylor had 150 cows grazing on their land.

"If I can get as many more," he figured, "I will have enough to live on and do well with them." He knew of nothing better than ranching for making the land pay in Texas.[10]

Over the next year, Baylor's ranch was the target of several Comanche raids. He felt a keen sense of betrayal. In his view, as Indian agent he had done nothing but help the Comanches try to survive. In the spring of 1859 Baylor began traveling through West Texas, making fiery speeches about the "savage acts" of the "red devils."[11] He found he liked this new role as frontier agitator. He joined the editorial staff of a Weatherford newspaper called the *White Man*, which published lurid tales of Indian raids and murders on the frontier, and called for violent reprisals.

In June 1860, after Comanches attacked two of Baylor's neighbors while they were out herding cattle, Baylor gathered four friends and his younger brother George at his ranch. They spent two days "cleaning our arms thoroughly, molding bullets, cutting and greasing [and] sharpening our knives, baking bread, and grinding coffee."[12] They struck out from Baylor's ranch and "cut for sign," catching a trail moving northwest. Three days later they found a small Comanche camp in the brush and attacked. In a running fight over several days, Baylor's party killed eight men, scalping them with a hunting knife that Baylor claimed to have also used to kill mountain lions.

"We had no qualms of conscience about serving them in such a way," remembered George Baylor, "as we were not in the missionary business."[13]

When they returned, their neighbors threw Baylor's Rangers a grand ball in Weatherford. They stretched a rope from pillar to pillar in the town courthouse and strung up "the shields of the chiefs and the scalps . . . above the heads of the dancers," George remembered. "And so we had a regular scalp dance."[14]

As a memento of the fight, John Baylor took a silver hair clasp from the body of one of the Comanches. That fall, he had it melted and re-formed as a belt buckle, stamped with a Lone Star. Baylor was wearing it when he rode into Mesilla in the summer of 1861.

———

In February 1862 Baylor recruited enough local men to launch his campaign against the Chiricahuas in Arizona. He mustered them into the

Confederate Army as Company A, Arizona Rangers, and selected a man named Sherod Hunter to command them.

Hunter had arrived in Mesilla a few years before the Civil War, when he was twenty-five years old. He had plowed out a farm along the Mimbres River, which was within the borders of Apachería. During his first harvest in 1860, Mangas Coloradas's Chiricahuas raided his farm and several others. Over the next year, Hunter sent multiple letters to the U.S. Army commanders at Fort Fillmore, demanding assistance in defending his homestead. When his pleas came to nothing, Hunter abandoned his farm and moved to Mesilla. He arrived there just a few weeks before Baylor occupied the town in July 1861. Hunter joined Baylor and the 2nd Texas in their pursuit of the federal troops retreating to San Augustin Springs, and distinguished himself as a natural leader.[15] As the commander of Company A, Arizona Rangers, he would oversee what the *Mesilla Times* judged to be a "crack company of the service," an enviable unit of men "inured to the hardships of frontier life and conversant with all of its details."[16]

The Arizona Rangers began to prepare for their march westward just as the Sibley Brigade arrived at Fort Craig. Baylor gave Hunter his orders. He was to move along the Butterfield mail route and fight any Chiricahuas who might appear along the way. When he arrived in Tucson, he was to raise the Confederate flag above the town and declare martial law, then send out troops as far west as possible. There had been rumors that Union soldiers were on the way to Tucson from Los Angeles. If Hunter saw any movement along those lines, he should dispatch an express rider to bring this news to Baylor in Mesilla.

Baylor also wanted Hunter to begin laying the groundwork for the invasion of California. To this end, Hunter should send emissaries out to the Pimas and Maricopas, whom Baylor had heard might be amenable to a peace treaty with the Confederates. These two tribes grew many of the crops that fed military personnel stationed at Fort Yuma on the Colorado River, California's eastern border. If they agreed to help the Texans, these Native peoples would become the Confederate Army's quartermasters on their march to the Pacific.[17] Once Hunter had accomplished this alliance, Baylor wanted him to send riders across the Colorado River to recruit secessionist Californians, mustering them into the Arizona Rangers.

The day before the Rangers left Mesilla for Tucson, Jefferson Davis signed a proclamation recognizing Arizona as a Confederate Territory, designating Mesilla its capital. Davis also appointed John Baylor the territorial governor for a term of six years. Because Arizona would henceforth be part of the Confederacy, "the institution of slavery in said Territory shall receive all necessary protection, both from the Territorial Legislature and the Congress of the Confederate States." There were only a handful of black slaves in Confederate Arizona in 1862. Most of them were the property of officers in the Sibley Brigade. In writing this provision, Jefferson Davis and the Confederate Congress were looking toward the future. Arizona would be the center of their growing empire of slavery after the war's end.[18]

When the Arizona Rangers left Mesilla, they took with them three wagonloads of supplies. One wagon carried casks that would transport water for the company across the parched deserts of western Arizona. Joining them on the road was James Reily, a legendary Texan who was setting out on another mission on behalf of the Confederacy.

Reily had been a soldier in the war to free Texas from Mexico in 1835–36, a diplomat sent to negotiate the Republic's entry into the United States in 1842, an officer in the U.S. Army in the war against Mexico in 1846, and now, a colonel in the 4th Texas Mounted Volunteers.[19] When Reily arrived at Fort Bliss in late December 1861, Henry Sibley informed him that like John Baylor, he would not be joining the Sibley Brigade on their march to Santa Fe. Sibley had another, equally vital task for him.

"In view of the importance of establishing satisfactory relations with the adjacent Mexican States of Chihuahua and Sonora," Sibley explained, Reily would "proceed to the capitals of those States, for the purpose of delivering to their respective governors the communications which I have addressed to them."[20]

The journeys would be risky. Reily's traveling cohort would have to ride more than two hundred miles from Fort Bliss to Chihuahua City in Chihuahua, and then from Tucson to Arizpe in Sonora. Along the way, they would be vulnerable to Chiricahua and Comanche attacks. If Reily made it to the capitals and could convince the Mexican governors to officially recognize the Confederacy, the dangers would be more than worth it.

The plea for recognition would be a hard sell, however. Most foreign countries had been watching the events of the American Civil War and waiting to declare their allegiance until it became clear who would win. Early in the war, both Abraham Lincoln and Jefferson Davis had sent diplomats to Europe. Lincoln urged the heads of state there to see the Confederacy as a rebellion rather than a lawful act of secession, while Davis argued that under the Declaration of Independence, the Confederate states had a right to separate themselves from a tyrannical government trying to take away their property in slaves. Lincoln and Davis had also sent emissaries to Mexico, making the same arguments. For the Confederacy, Mexican allegiance would provide both political recognition and economic viability. Southerners could ship their cotton out of Mexican ports, and evade the Union blockade. An alliance with Mexico would also benefit Texas.

"We must have Sonora and Chihuahua," James Reily wrote to a friend. "With [them] we gain Southern California, and by a railroad to Guaymas render our State of Texas the great highway of nations."[21]

Reily carried several letters with him into Mexico, written by Henry Sibley and addressed to Chihuahua governor Luis Terrazas and Sonora governor Ignacio Pesqueira. In them, Sibley presented himself as an envoy of the Confederate States of America and described the Sibley Brigade's intentions to conquer New Mexico and California. He then proposed an agreement that, to Sibley's mind, would benefit both the Confederacy and Mexico. The governors would allow only the Confederacy to transport military supplies over land and through the port of Guaymas on the Gulf of California. And the governors would sell supplies only to the Confederate Army.

In exchange the Confederates would pour money and cotton into northern Mexico, enriching its merchants and politicians. And if the governors would allow it, the Confederates would launch coordinated, border-crossing military assaults on Apaches and Comanches. In so doing, they would make good on the promises that the U.S. government had failed to keep after the Treaty of Guadalupe Hidalgo, and rid northern Mexico of Indians once and for all.[22]

Although army officers were traditionally empowered to negotiate treaties with Native peoples, James Reily's diplomatic missions to Chihuahua and Sonora in 1862 were unsanctioned. Jefferson Davis and his cabinet were very interested in securing a Mexican alliance, but they wanted to pursue it through their own diplomatic channels, not through army personnel. Henry Sibley, however, saw his proximity to Mexico as an opportunity, and figured he would ask for forgiveness rather than permission. After all, President Davis had ordered Sibley to act on his own authority in all matters in the campaign. And so Sibley had called James Reily into his headquarters at Fort Bliss and informed him of his new status as a Confederate diplomat.

By the time Reily joined Sherod Hunter's wagon train to Tucson in February 1862, he had already been to Chihuahua and held talks with Governor Luis Terrazas. They had discussed terms, and then Terrazas had sent Reily back to Mesilla with a reply. After reassuring Sibley that he was eager to cultivate a productive trade relationship with the Confederates, Terrazas confessed that he did not have the power to dictate Mexican policies concerning right of transit. However, he vowed that he would never allow Union troops to cross Chihuahua in order to invade Texas. And while he appreciated the offer for Confederate help in defending Chihuahuan citizens against Apaches, Terrazas could not allow southern troops to cross into his state. This would be a violation of the Treaty of Guadalupe Hidalgo, even if soldiers were in "hot pursuit" of Apache raiders.[23]

Despite Terrazas's somewhat measured response, Reily believed that his visit had been an unqualified success. And now he would ride to Tucson with the Arizona Rangers. From there, Reily and his guard would turn southward toward the capital of Sonora to present terms that would produce, hopefully, a similarly happy result.

———————

John Baylor watched James Reily and the Arizona Rangers disappear into the western horizon with some satisfaction. He had had a hand in every part of the Confederate campaign for the West so far, and in his view he had done more for Arizona than anyone else.

Mesilla's residents, however, did not always see it that way. Back in December, Robert Kelley, the editor of the *Mesilla Times*, had begun to criticize Baylor's military and political leadership, accusing him of "incapacity for the duties of the position he held, and probable cowardice and corruption." Baylor's mismanagement of the Territory of Arizona, Kelley argued, was delivering its people into the hands of their Chiricahua enemies.[24]

Initially, Baylor ignored Kelley's columns. After joining the masthead of the *White Man* in 1860, he had developed "pretty liberal views about the liberty of the press." But his officers and his brother George took Kelley's accusations personally, and confronted Baylor after the *Times* had printed an especially abusive editorial.

"If you don't notice this article," the officers warned Baylor, "we will."

A few days later, Baylor ran into Kelley on the plaza in Mesilla. What happened next depended on who was telling the story.

According to John Baylor's brother George, the governor happened to be in a store when Kelley walked in.

"Mr. Kelley," Baylor said, "if you don't stop your abuse of me in the paper I shall make it a personal matter between us." Kelley swore at him and drew a knife.

According to Kelley, he was walking up Main Street at 2 a.m. on December 12 and "I saw Col. Baylor talking with two gentlemen in front of his quarters . . . when opposite and within two or three feet of the door, I received a severe blow over the head, from a gun in the hands of Col. Baylor, accompanied with the exclamation, 'Now I've got you, my 'jewlarkey'!'"[25]

Witnesses reported that Baylor and Kelley ended up on the ground, with Baylor gaining the advantage easily. There were not many men in Arizona Territory who could take the Texan down in hand-to-hand combat. Baylor spied a Springfield rifle leaning up against the wall, grabbed it, and hit Kelley over the head. The editor was jabbing at the Texan with his knife but to no avail. When Kelley refused to yield, Baylor held him down with his right hand, drew his pistol with his left, and shot the editor in the jaw. The bullet tore through Kelley's carotid artery. Baylor got to his feet, re-holstered his pistol, and left Kelley on the floor in a growing pool of blood.

Kelley lingered for two weeks, mustering enough energy to write several editorials castigating Baylor. After Kelley died, Baylor was brought to trial for murder, but a panel of men from Mesilla acquitted him.[26]

Baylor reported his fight with Kelley to his sister Fan with some regret. She reassured him that although it was a lamentable situation, "I can only say you were in the right." All of his friends at home felt so, she said, and understood why he was provoked. "I feel my face glow with anger even yet," Fan wrote, "when I think of his insulting slanders." Baylor's mother, too, defended him. "She is sorry it was necessary for you to shoot Kell[e]y," Fan reported, "but she does not blame you."[27]

Feeling cheered by these reassurances, Baylor became more optimistic about his future in Confederate Arizona, and about his family joining him there someday.

"The climate is lovely," he wrote to Emy. "Cool dry beautiful weather all the time. I never saw such a mild winter anywhere." He thought maybe they could make a life here, after the Texans had conquered the Hispanos and federals in New Mexico, and the Chiricahuas in Arizona. They would build a house and buy some land. He would start preparing for their arrival in a few months.

"I intend to have a fine vegetable garden planted," Baylor daydreamed, "and mostly in summer vegetables so that I can have them put up for winter. I want you when you come to have plenty to eat for I know you will like that part of my new home."[28]

———————

For a man like Baylor, however, it did not take long to become discontented. By late February 1862 he had grown bored sitting in his gubernatorial office, signing stacks of papers, with only a street fight or a court case in Mesilla for entertainment. He wrote to Fan, expressing his frustration. She tried to encourage him.

"Occasional skirmishes keep up the men's [sic] spirits," she wrote, "and you know how discontented men grow under inaction."[29]

Galvanized by his sister's letter, Baylor decided that this was his moment. He would strike out on the kind of campaign that got his blood up. He gathered more than one hundred men, whipped them up with generalized tales of Chiricahua raiders who had attacked farms and roads in Arizona, and headed south. They rode first to Fort Bliss, and then crossed the Rio Grande into Mexico.

Four days later, after a ride of almost two hundred miles, Baylor's band entered the mining town of Corralitos, in Chihuahua. When they arrived, Baylor and his men dismounted and began to break into houses, searching rooms and knocking over furniture. They told the townspeople they were looking for Chiricahuas, a group of raiders who had attacked farms, emigrant wagon trains, and Confederate Army camps along the Rio Grande. In the end, Baylor found only three Apaches in Corralitos, two women and one man who were hiding in a mine owner's house. The owner protested that these Apaches were his house slaves, converted to Catholicism and at peace with the community. Baylor waved off the man's protestations, dragging the Apaches out from their hiding places and into the street. By this time, a crowd had gathered in the plaza. Baylor executed the women and man with his pistol, then strode out into the midst of the crowd.

"If you continue to harbor Apaches," he warned them, "we will return and raid Corralitos again."[30]

Baylor believed he was justified in pursuing any Apache across international lines and punishing individuals for the crimes of the entire tribe. Governor Terrazas disagreed.[31]

"The unwelcome and vituperative behavior of Colonel Baylor and all the forces of his command," Terrazas seethed in a subsequent letter to Henry Sibley, was an insult to the Mexican nation. Baylor did not have the right or the authority to "violate the territory that he chose as the theater of operations." To make matters worse, the Confederate was not actually in "hot pursuit" of Apache raiders. The three people he had killed were not Chiricahua warriors in Corralitos to trade sheep and horses they had stolen from Confederate wagon trains in Arizona. They were slaves in a Mexican household, Apaches who had been sold to the mine owner years ago by Comanches.[32] When they killed these Apache slaves, Baylor and his men had disgraced the rights and honor of Mexico. These were not the acts of honorable soldiers, but of cowards.

Terrazas expected that Henry Sibley would punish John Baylor and all of the men who participated in the Corralitos Raid, along with any Confederate soldier who "may intend to follow such a pernicious example." In any event, Terrazas promised Sibley that he would apprehend Baylor or any other Confederate soldier if they ever crossed the border into Chihuahua again.[33]

———

Baylor and his men had already returned to Mesilla by the time Terrazas's letter arrived at Fort Bliss, where it was filed in a stack of correspondence awaiting Henry Sibley's return to that post. Baylor was unbothered by the notion that his Corralitos Raid threatened to dislodge the foothold that he himself had secured for the Confederacy in the West. Happy with his short campaign, his lust for violence and adventure temporarily sated, Baylor returned to his work as the governor of Arizona Territory. He waited for dispatches from Sherod Hunter and James Reily, but there was silence from the West. In March 1862, Baylor once again grew restless.

He began to dream of recruiting again. This time, he would build his own company of Texans, real frontier men, trained to fight in the guerrilla style in the deserts of Arizona. In order to do this, Baylor could not just send a letter to the Confederate War Department. He needed "to see the president and get matters arranged" in Richmond.

"If I sit still and wait for others to attend to my interests," Baylor told Emy, "I will be forgotten at head Quarters."[34]

In mid-March, as he began to pack for his journey, Baylor received a letter from the new captain of the militia in Pinos Altos, the mining town that Mangas Coloradas and his men had attacked the previous September. The captain informed him that Mangas was back and had sent word that he wanted to discuss a peace treaty.[35]

Baylor was suspicious. He did not believe that Mangas Coloradas wanted peace with any Americans, Union or Confederate.[36] He sat down and wrote out the final order he would issue as an officer in the 2nd Texas, and the governor of Confederate Arizona.

"You will use all means to persuade the Apaches or any tribe to come in for the purpose of making peace," he instructed the captain. "And when you get them together kill all the grown Indians and take the Children prisoners and sell them to defray the expense of killing the Indians." If the soldiers had to purchase whiskey in order to get the Apaches to the parlay, Baylor noted, the Confederate Army would pay for the barrels. He signed the order and sent it off with an express rider to Pinos Altos. It seemed to him only reasonable to murder Chiricahua men and women and enslave their children, given that the "cursed pests" had "already murdered over one hundred men in this Territory."[37]

———————

A few days later, John Baylor folded and sealed his letter of resignation and left it on his desk, addressed to Henry Sibley. At first he had written only a brief sentence, indicating how honored he had been to serve as colonel of the 2nd Texas Mounted Rifles and governor of the Confederate Territory of Arizona. But he could not resist adding another line, complaining about how Henry Sibley had treated him.

"I should be wanting in self respect," he wrote, "were I to serve or hold a Commission under an Officer who has shown so palpable a want of confidence in my courage or ability."[38]

Soon Baylor was on his way to Fort Bliss, where he caught a stagecoach that would take him through northern Texas and back to his ranch. He would spend as much time with Emy and the children as possible and then travel by stage to the Mississippi River. From there it was just a few boat rides on the river and then at sea, and he would be in Virginia. When he left Arizona, John Baylor believed he was still engaged in the fight for the Confederacy, and for its future interests in New Mexico.

"I know I can get something and yet hold on to the Government position if I can get Mr. D[avis] fixed on my notion," he wrote to Emy. "We will be all right yet."[39]

9

=

Clark

As John Baylor was gathering men to ride to Corralitos, residents in Santa Fe were waiting for news from Fort Craig. Residents had heard that the Confederate and Union armies had clashed near the fort, but after the arrival of those reports there had been only silence.

It was difficult for John Clark to concentrate on his work as surveyor general of New Mexico Territory. He was supposed to be reviewing documents in a case involving lands along the Jornada del Muerto. The Mexican government had given the tract in that massive desert to two Hispano petitioners in 1846, but the grant conflicted with an earlier concession. Ownership had been disputed in the territorial courts since then.[1] In 1854, the office of the surveyor general in New Mexico had been established, in part, to weigh in on such disagreements and to "ascertain the origin, nature, character, and extent of all claims to lands under the laws, usages, and customs of Spain and Mexico." The appointees who preceded Clark as surveyor general had not made much headway.[2] Hispano land grantees had to be able to prove their ownership of these grants, or they could fall into the public domain. Selling these and other lands in New Mexico would help support the Union's war effort. It would also help to stabilize the Territory by attracting Anglo (and hopefully, Republican) settlers.[3]

Since his arrival in New Mexico in October 1861, Clark had been learning Spanish in order to read original land grants and petitions, but he found it slow going. In mid-February 1862, the anxiety of waiting to hear from Fort Craig did not help. Each day after work he went to army headquarters at the Palace of the Governors in Santa Fe Plaza to inquire about the news. There were no dispatches.

"We are all deeply interested in the issue," Clark wrote, "for it will decide for a time the destiny of this country."[4]

While he worried and waited, Clark tried to distract himself. He went for long walks up into the hills above Santa Fe, and daydreamed about home and the future. On February 21, the night of the Battle of Valverde, he accepted a dinner invitation from the wife of a prominent lawyer. After they ate, Clark and the other guests, including Louisa Canby, sat perfectly still around the table, with their hands placed flat upon it. They all stared silently at a man who had placed himself in front of a dial (a circular plate with the alphabet printed upon it) fastened to the surface. Slowly, the table began to pitch, and the hand of the dial pointed to the letters, spelling out words.[5]

Clark was familiar with spirit rappings. Most Americans were, after the furor they created in New York in the spring of 1848. The news had been all over the papers. Two teen girls named Margaret and Kate Fox had received mysterious communications from the beyond, in the form of sharp sounds emanating from the furniture and the walls in their house. The girls would ask a question and with one knock for yes, two knocks for no, the spirits would answer.[6]

Séances had been all the rage in Santa Fe that winter, as the nights grew longer and the snow fell in thick white flakes. Clark had attended several of them with Louisa Canby, who was gazing intently at the dial. Perhaps she would receive a message from Mary, or from one of the soldiers she had sat vigil over in army forts across the West. John Clark also found himself staring, fascinated with the dial and its effects.

"What is the agency that moves the table?" he wondered. "It is certainly independent of the will & of all physical force—What is it?"[7]

Pondering such existential questions helped Clark and the others avoid thinking about Fort Craig, at least for a few days. Then on February 23, a letter from Valverde arrived, written by New Mexico governor Henry Connelly. It was a hastily written note, brought by an express rider, reporting "a battle & defeat—but no particulars." In the afternoon more reports arrived and they learned the awful truth. Union troops, led by Richard Canby, had lost the Battle of Valverde and had retreated to Fort Craig, with more than two hundred casualties.[8]

It was a day of intense disquiet in Santa Fe, and the people could talk about nothing else. Clark walked to his office in a daze. Again he took out the Jornada del Muerto grant documents but did not work on them. Instead he sought out his friends in the army and talked with them about the battle, and how it could have possibly gone the way it did.

"The general opinion of the officers here," Clark discovered, "is that Col Canby should have renewed the battle on the 22d but whether he did so or not we do not know."[9] Now that the Texans were between the fort and Santa Fe, all communications were cut off.

Over the next few days, the tension mounted in the city.

"Matters do not brighten," Clark wrote in his diary. "Our prospects are gloomy enough but I hope for the best."[10] He did not know what the future would bring. But he would continue to do the work the Lincoln administration had sent him to New Mexico to do, for as long as he could.

———

John Clark had lived most of his life in the upper Midwest, after moving there from New York when he was nine years old. His father had been hired to work for Michigan's General Land Office, and Clark had followed in his footsteps, becoming a civil engineer and surveyor, measuring lines and setting boundary markers in the 1830s. In 1835, he moved to Freeport, Illinois, and helped to lay out that flourishing town. By that time, he had met and married Jane Kyle, and like John Baylor, he subsequently tried his hand at all kinds of work in order to support his growing family.

Clark became a lawyer and a speculator in real estate. The Panic of 1857 forced him to return to surveying to supplement his income as an attorney, but by 1860 he had recovered financially. Clark owned $30,000 worth of real estate and employed three servants to help Jane run their busy household. Many of their friends were prominent lawyers and local and national politicians. It was these friends who had orchestrated his appointment as surveyor general of New Mexico Territory in the summer of 1861.[11]

Clark was one part of a large network of Republican officials sent to the western territories and states at the beginning of the war. They were there to establish political and civil control of the region, where secessionist sentiment was still percolating.[12] President Lincoln had reason to worry about New Mexico's loyalty, and to be judicious in his appointments there. The Territory had come into the Union in 1850 with a long history of enslavement of Apaches and Navajos, and had protected their right to own property in people in 1859. American political party organizations were almost nonexistent, and local officials continued to govern based on Mexican tradition and precedents.[13] Lincoln appointed several Unionist Democrats to posts in New Mexico to appease the pro-slavery contingent

there. He was hoping that John Clark, a staunch Republican and abolitionist, would bring some balance to the leadership ranks.[14]

———

In the days after Valverde, Clark tried to work, reviewing both Mexican
land grants and surveys of New Mexico's public lands. Then on March 2,
the residents of Santa Fe received devastating news. The Union Army had
abandoned Albuquerque, and the Texans were on their way to occupy that
city, and march on Santa Fe. Major James Donaldson, the Union Army
officer in command of Santa Fe, decided that he did not have enough
manpower to defend the city against the more than two thousand Texans
who would soon arrive. He began to load wagons with military stores and
government documents and send them off to Fort Union, eighty miles
northeast. The streets were thronged with military men and government
officials hurling trunks and boxes into wagons. Smoke billowed from two
military storehouses north of the plaza, in which the army had been keeping a large supply of flour. Luckily, Hispano and Anglo residents were able
to extinguish the conflagrations before they leapt to nearby buildings, and
they took the flour for themselves.[15]

John Clark stayed up until 3 a.m. the morning of March 3, packing
"all the field books, plats . . . the papers filed by claimants of Mexican
grants . . . & the records of the office."[16] Later that morning he went to
Louisa Canby's house to say goodbye. She had been a particular friend to
him in the months since he came to Santa Fe. Louisa told him that she had
decided to stay in the city and wait for Richard to arrive with his troops.
Clark did not try to convince her to go, but bid her farewell and then went
back to his office. He and his clerks carried the surveyor general's archive
out to a wagon that Donaldson had commandeered for him.[17]

Clark's wagon joined a large train to Fort Union, and he followed in
a stage, feeling despondent. The Union Army had abandoned Santa Fe
to the rebels! It had seemed impossible, even just a few weeks before.[18] It
was a disgrace. The mules pulling Clark's stage began to slow, straining
to move up and over the first stretch of the Santa Fe Trail, which wound
through the foothills of the southern Sangre de Cristos. Clark remained
watchful as they passed through Apache Canyon and Glorieta Pass. With
their steep hills on either side of the road, these were perfect sites for ambush, according to his military friends. Only when they arrived at Kozlowsky's ranch, a stage station on the other side of the pass, did Clark
breathe more easily.[19]

The stage made good time the next day, skirting the southern tip of the mountain range and then heading north alongside it toward a junction of the Santa Fe Trail's Mountain and Cimarron routes. There, the eight parapets of Fort Union's earthwork loomed up out of the rippling prairie.[20] On March 4, as Clark's stage arrived outside of the fort's sloped walls, hundreds of soldiers and civilians were pitching tents wherever they found space. Clark had made no arrangements for accommodations and had little hope of finding shelter that night. He was in luck, however. While walking through the fort, he happened upon the sutler, a genial man who ran a general store on the grounds. The sutler offered him a place to sleep and Clark gladly accepted.[21]

The next day, a mail coach from the States arrived, bringing bundles of eastern newspapers and glorious news. At the same time that the Texans were marching up the Rio Grande toward Fort Craig, Union troops under Ulysses S. Grant had taken Forts Henry and Donelson on the Tennessee River, forcing the surrender of thousands of Confederate troops. In so doing, Grant's army had secured Kentucky for the Union, and cleared the way for an invasion of Tennessee. Along the south Atlantic coast, there was also good news. Ambrose Burnside's troops had successfully stormed Roanoke Island in North Carolina, aided by a flotilla of gunboats that pounded several Outer Banks forts into submission. This would help to tighten the blockade against Confederate ports, making it more difficult for southerners to bring trade goods in and ship cotton out of North Carolina's harbors. It also appeared that Union troops were making gains in Missouri, after their disastrous loss at Wilson's Creek over the summer.

Clark was amazed. There did not seem to be a single item of bad news about the Civil War in the East.

"If our affairs were a little more prosperous here," he lamented, "I could enjoy [this] good news better."[22]

On March 7, Major Donaldson arrived from Santa Fe, along with Governor Connelly and several other territorial officials. At that point Fort Union became the temporary seat of New Mexico Territory's government.[23] Clark went to see Donaldson, who told him that he had been forced to set fire to more government storehouses in Santa Fe as he retreated. They could not let any supplies fall into the hands of the Confederates. The Texans' major weakness was their reliance on the provisions confiscated along the road. If the Union troops could scorch the earth in front of the enemy's soldiers and their animals, the Confederate invasion of New Mexico would slow to a crawl. Beyond this policy of defensive burning, however, Donaldson had no other strategies in place. He had no orders from Richard Canby. Clark was outraged.

"I am beginning to think that military men do not after all <u>monopolize</u> all the wisdom in the world," he wrote. "The management of affairs in this department for the past six months has been a <u>blunder</u> from beginning to end—beginning with the imbecility & treason of Lynde & continuing up to the present time."[24]

Clark did not understand why a seasoned officer like Richard Canby, with the most experienced army in the field, could not defeat a half-starved army of Texan volunteers armed mostly with double-barreled shotguns. Why hadn't Canby been more aggressive? Why had he not renewed the battle on the day after Valverde? Why had he let Sibley slip by him and reach Albuquerque? Over the next few days Clark, Donaldson, and the other New Mexico officials discussed all of these matters over meals at Fort Union. They recounted everything they had heard about the battle, and tried to figure out why the Union had lost. Most of them ultimately blamed the army's Hispano soldiers.

Clark had initially championed the recruitment of the 1st New Mexico Volunteers, going so far as to give a toast to them at a supper that Governor Connelly had hosted at Santa Fe's famous hotel La Fonda on New Year's Eve 1861.

"To the volunteers of New Mexico," he had intoned while raising his glass, "as in their patriotic response to the call of their country, they have not been excelled by their brethren in any of the States—so will they be found equal to them in defending the flag of our country on the field of battle!"[25]

Now, after all that he had heard about Valverde, how the Hispano militias had fled twice during that conflict, Clark no longer believed in their ability to fight for the Union. He conveniently ignored the fact that Anglo soldiers, both volunteers and Army regulars, had also cut and run. He was also more paternalistic than Alonzo Ickis, believing that their cowardice was not necessarily their fault. Most Hispanos were illiterate and so "only know what they see or what is told them by others." They were vulnerable to the persuasions of Anglo secessionists, who likely pressured Hispanos into thinking they should save themselves rather than the Union. The 1st New Mexico Volunteers were hardly better than their comrades in the militias. They were "like children," Clark thought. "Ignorant, weak, with no fixed principle of actions."

"They have now been tried & will be set aside," he wrote in his diary on a chilly night in his quarters at Fort Union. "<u>We must have Americans to fight against Americans</u>."[26]

―――――――

Having come to this bitter conclusion, Clark was delighted when, on March 11, a regiment of more than nine hundred Colorado Volunteers appeared north of Fort Union, marching down on the road from Denver. Like Dodd's Independents, they were Anglos recruited from the Rocky Mountain mining camps. They had responded to a plea from Richard Canby, which he had sent after the Battle of Valverde. It was clear from one glance at their long beards and ruddy faces that this regiment had long ago shed the niceties of eastern society, adopting instead a "free-and-easy border" style.

"They are a magnificent body of men," Clark reported.[27]

The 1st Colorado had left Denver less than two weeks before. As they neared the top of Raton Pass, one hundred miles north of Fort Union, a stage met them and its passengers gave their commander some "jumbled intelligence" about the Texans marching up the Rio Grande toward Santa Fe. After hearing this, the Coloradans abandoned everything but their weapons and two blankets for each man, and marched on the double-quick to Fort Union. When they arrived, they had come more than 350 miles, and made the final stretch from Raton Pass in two days.[28]

"This, for an infantry regiment, astonishes everybody," said John Clark.

The Coloradans marched inside the gates and around the parade ground of Fort Union, and despite their weariness their steps were "as elastic & rapid as if they were on dress parade." After a welcoming speech from the commander of the fort and Governor Connelly, the 1st Colorado (nicknamed the "Pikes Peakers") cheered heartily and went into camp, commandeering six boxes of champagne, a wheel of cheese, and a box of crackers from the sutler.[29]

"If we had but one more such regiment we could start back to Santa Fe," Clark judged, and "they would drive the Texans out of the Territory."[30]

―――――――

God willing, this would happen. John Clark would not stay to see it, however. After his discussions with Donaldson, he had decided that the threat of a Confederate victory in New Mexico was too great. Clark did not want to be captured and placed under arrest, or held as a prisoner to exchange.

He decided to leave New Mexico Territory until the Civil War in the West was over. He would travel to Washington, D.C., and meet with James Edmunds, the commissioner of the General Land Office.

Clark had been sending Edmunds letters every week from Santa Fe, reporting on all matters pertaining to his work. The General Land Office, which was part of the Department of the Interior, oversaw the survey and sale of public lands across the nation. In the spring of 1862, Edmunds had a particular interest in New Mexico Territory, and whether or not the Sibley Brigade's invasion might disrupt land claim and sale processes across the West. The Union Congress, shed of southerners who had objected to land distribution legislation that northerners had tried to push through in the 1850s, was ready to pass the Homestead Act, which would give Americans "who had never borne arms against the U.S. Government" the opportunity to claim 160 acres of surveyed public lands. If the Texans occupied Santa Fe and succeeded in taking the West, however, the Republicans would not be able to fulfill their vision of a nation of free laborers, spread across the continent. Passage of the Homestead Act was delayed, therefore, until the outcome of the Civil War in New Mexico was determined. Given these developments, no doubt Edmunds was eager to know how John Clark's work had progressed before the Texans arrived, and how and when he thought the conflict there might end.[31]

Clark also hoped to meet with President Lincoln, whom he had known during their lawyering days in Illinois and considered a friend. Clark had even grown his beard in the same style as the president's. Lincoln would be focused on the spring campaigns to come in Virginia and Tennessee, of course. General George McClellan, now in command of the Union's Army of the Potomac, had already begun his preparations for an assault on Richmond, moving his soldiers to Fortress Monroe, at the tip of the Virginia Peninsula. The slowness of his movements had given the Confederate Army under Joe Johnston more than enough time to establish a network of defenses around Richmond, however, and the word was that Lincoln was aggrieved.[32]

Clark was wary of delivering more bad news to Lincoln and to Secretary of War Edwin Stanton about how Richard Canby's army was faring in the battles for New Mexico. Reports of the disaster at Valverde had been delayed by bad weather and the lack of telegraph lines on the Santa Fe Trail. The administration and Congress would want to know the details. New Mexico Territory was vital to the federal government's plans, both during the war and afterward. If Richard Canby's soldiers could push the

Confederates back to Texas and John Clark could resume his work preparing lands for sale, the Lincoln administration could redraw the national map, marking the West as Union territory reserved for the settlement of patriotic Anglo farmers and miners.

On March 12, 1862, John Clark loaded his black trunk into a stagecoach and set out once again on the Santa Fe Trail. He and his fellow passengers would take the mountain route north over Raton Pass and then east to Kansas City.[33] It would take Clark two weeks to make his way to Washington, D.C. Perhaps by that time there would be news of a final battle with the Texans, and the fate of the desert Southwest.

10

Glorieta

The Confederates were encamped in the Sandia Mountains east of Albuquerque when they heard the Yankees had abandoned Santa Fe and withdrawn to Fort Union. The city would be theirs without firing a gun. Hopefully, they would also find food and fodder there to sustain them on their campaign. When they had arrived in Albuquerque the week before, they found most of the Union Army's storehouses on fire, the smell of burning bacon wafting through the air.[1] They had lingered at Valverde for too long, they realized.

On March 7, 1862, Henry Sibley sent the Brigands, a company made up of prominent New Mexico secessionists, to take possession of Santa Fe on behalf of the Confederacy. Bill Davidson followed with a command led by Major Pyron, and they were trailed by Company A and the 5th Texas. Once Pyron's men occupied Santa Fe, the rest of the Sibley Brigade would move up. Then they would follow the Yankees to Fort Union and lay siege to it. Sibley himself would remain in Albuquerque, ensconced in a luxurious house owned by merchants Rafaél and Manuel Armijo. The Armijo brothers had been coy about their allegiances at the beginning of the Civil War. They saw the conflict in New Mexico Territory as a business opportunity. When Sibley arrived, they offered their house to him, and it was here that the Confederate general would map out the rest of his campaign for the West.[2]

As the Texans began their march toward Santa Fe, Louisa Canby watched the last of the Union Army wagons disappear on the road to Fort Union.

Major Donaldson had offered her safe passage eastward, but she had refused. She was sure that Richard would be pursuing the Texans, and she wanted to wait for his arrival. In the days after Donaldson left, the people of Santa Fe hurried through the streets, liberating whatever they could from Union storehouses. They took hay and firewood that had been stacked in the army's stable yards, and boxes filled with candles, pickles, soap, rice, vinegar, hominy, and dried vegetables.[3]

The town was half-empty. Many civilians had gone to their families' homes outside of Santa Fe, while others had fled into the hills. Most of those who remained were army wives like Louisa and their families, and Anglo and Hispano residents who chose to stay and defend their homes and businesses. Many of them went out into the courtyards of their adobe houses and dug holes in the ground, filling them with sacks of flour and other provisions. They heaved dirt back into the holes and scattered it around to try and cover the evidence of their digging.[4]

On March 10, the Brigands appeared in Santa Fe. The residents recognized many of them, men who had lived in Santa Fe for years, doing business and socializing with politicians and military officials. When Sibley had arrived at Fort Bliss these secret secessionists rode southward to volunteer for the Confederate Army. Returning now as conquerors, the Brigands claimed the Palace of the Governors as the Texans' headquarters and occupied La Fonda. Seeing that Union troops had cut down the flagpole in the plaza, they felled a tree to make their own.

Four days later, Bill Davidson arrived, and by the next week the rest of Pyron's men, including all of Company A, had marched into town. When they raised the Confederate flag above the Union Army's former headquarters in New Mexico, they became the first and only Confederate Army to occupy a capital city in Union territory during the American Civil War.[5]

The next week Pyron sent a note to the editor of the Santa Fe Gazette, with orders to surrender the keys to the printing office. The Texans set the type and ran the press, then walked through town, handing out broadsides to the residents.

"To the people of New Mexico," Henry Sibley had written from Albuquerque, "the signal victory which crowned our arms at Valverde on the 21st of February proves the truth of the assertions contained in my first Proclamation in regard to our powers and ability to accomplish the purposes therein declared." He went on to promise "complete and absolute amnesty to all citizens who have or may within ten days lay aside their arms and return to their homes and avocations." Santa Fe residents like Louisa Canby could be sure that the men of the Sibley Brigade would treat them with honesty and integrity, and would protect them from injury while the Texans occupied the city.[6]

It took some doing, but Bill Davidson and his comrades found places to sleep. A few of them discovered John Clark's surveyor general office and bedded down among its remaining papers and surveyors' tools. Company A of the 5th spent the next two weeks breaking into buildings, searching for food and weapons that the federals had forgotten to send away or destroy. They rested their horses and mules and readied themselves for the march to Fort Union.[7]

The sixty-mile journey from Albuquerque had been relatively short but strenuous. The road gained almost two thousand feet of elevation in that distance, moving from the sandy, fertile plains of the Rio Grande Valley to an undulating landscape of brown hills and mesas, covered with dark green piñon pines and junipers. The Texans were now familiar with the toll that this kind of march took on their bodies: the shortness of breath, the constant thirst, the rapid onset of physical exhaustion.

Compounding their problems was the fact that while Santa Fe was the largest city they had seen since they left San Antonio, it was not an ideal location in which to house a sizeable army. Its water supplies were meager. Only one small river meandered through town, and much of its water was diverted through acequias to fields on the city's edges. Although they had rations to last for another month or so (thanks to the discovery of a stash of supplies at Cubero, a Union post west of Albuquerque), the lack of provisions in Santa Fe meant that Davidson and the others could not stay there for very long.[8]

While the Texans waited for the rest of the Sibley Brigade to march up from Albuquerque, a few travelers arrived from the east. When Pyron questioned them, he discovered that the 1st Colorado Volunteers had arrived at Fort Union, and were likely on the move toward Santa Fe. Pyron was an aggressive commander, and had learned from Valverde that it often paid to make the first move. On March 24, 1862, Davidson and Company A received orders to be ready to march the next morning. They would set out along the Santa Fe Trail and fight the federals wherever they found them.[9]

The trail would take them south and then east, moving up into the foothills of the Sangre de Cristos before turning northeast toward Fort

Union. They would need to be vigilant during their march through Apache Canyon, which was just fifteen miles from Santa Fe. There the trail wound through rocky terrain, edged by steep slopes covered with stunted pines and cedars. The soils were light and shallow, and eroded easily during thunderstorms. Parts of the trail were cut through with deep ravines and gullies. Apache Canyon was, as one traveler through the region put it, "one of those grim and dangerous passes common in New Mexico."[10]

After Pyron's men left for Apache Canyon, Louisa Canby got to work. She made up beds in her house off the plaza and boiled large batches of soup. She located all of the linen cloth available in the city, and she and some of the other army wives tore it into pieces, scraping the fabric with knives to make soft, cotton-like lint bandages. Union troops had taken most of their medical supplies to Fort Union; Louisa collected the medicines and blankets that remained. In the twenty years she had lived with Richard in forts across the nation, Louisa had accrued plenty of experience nursing soldiers at garrison hospitals. During the dreadful first winter camped outside of Fort Bridger in Utah in 1858, she had been a nearly constant presence at the bedsides of sick and wounded men.

"A good many of those rough old soldiers," one of her former patients attested, "who had not seen the smiling face of a mother, sister or any kindred, for a number of years, showered blessings on that excellent lady."[11]

Although most American women did not have Louisa's frontier medical experience, many spent significant time tending to sick family and community members. Nursing was one of the many domestic responsibilities that daughters, sisters, wives, and mothers took on. In the mid-nineteenth century, being a woman meant being a nurse.[12] Now that the Civil War had come to Santa Fe, Louisa and the other women who remained in town, including many other wives of Anglo and Hispano soldiers in the Union Army, had to prepare to receive the soldiers who might end up in the city after the battles to come. Louisa Canby brought together the women of Santa Fe, urging them to contribute everything they had that might be useful, to provide for the injured soldiers. Her recruits listened, and some objected.

"Might not the wounded be rebels?" one asked.

Louisa bridled at this. Although her own husband was leading the fight against the Texans, she had met enough soldiers from all over the nation to believe in their inherent humanity.

"No matter whether friend or foe," she retorted, "our wounded must be cared for and their lives saved if it is possible. They are sons of some dear mother."[13]

The four hundred Texans marching along the Santa Fe Trail expected an easy victory over the Yanks. Their experience at Valverde suggested that they could take on a larger army and defeat it without much effort. After camping on the road the night of March 25, Pyron's men were up again the next morning and moving into Apache Canyon, crossing several wooden bridges over deep ravines. About a mile into the chasm, Pyron could not see much beyond the next bend, so he ordered his men to halt. They established scattered camps and the artillerists brought up cannons to face east toward the enemy. Pyron sent the Brigands to scout up the road and return with haste if they spotted any federals.

It was around noon, and Bill Davidson figured he had time to take a short nap. The sun had finally come out and it was warm. He curled up on the ground, wrapped in a Union coat he had taken from the Valverde battlefield, and drifted off to the sound of his friends engaged in a "learned discussion, the question being, 'Which traveled the fastest, the top or bottom of the wagon wheel?'"[14]

Soon he and others were "rudely awakened from our slumbers by a volley of musketry fired into camp."

Davidson leapt up, grabbed his shotgun, and looked around for Company A's officer, John Shropshire. He found him in the middle of the road with Pyron, "calm, cool, and deliberately restoring order and forming us in a line to meet the foe." As they came together across the canyon, Union soldiers appeared on the road. The Confederate gunners started throwing shells at them, "preaching to [the enemy] in true war-like style." Over the next hour, Davidson and his comrades were able to push the federals back into the canyon.[15]

Soon, however, bullets began to rain down on the Confederates and ricochet off the dirt. Davidson and his comrades looked up to see Union soldiers jumping from rock to rock on the steep inclines, shooting the Texans down like sheep. The Confederates pulled back more than a mile down the road, dragging their cannons and burning one of the wooden bridges behind them. Then they stopped and established their line again, turning to face the federals in pursuit. One of the Texas horsemen held the Lone Star flag, a five-pointed white star on a red field, and it whipped in the wind. Pyron sent some of his own men up into the hillsides to pour flanking fire into the enemy.[16]

The federals came, having leapt their horses across the bridgeless ra-vine, and the battle raged for another hour. The Texans retreated once, and then again as the bullets flew all around them. There was so much smoke and dust that neither the Texans nor the 1st Colorado could see much. Pyron pulled his men back to the western end of Apache Canyon, near a ranch whose owners, the Johnsons, had abandoned it when the Texans first rode into Santa Fe. Although the fight was exhausting, David-son suddenly found that his feet could fly.

"All I have to say," he wrote, "is that I was leading the retreating. That is the only time I could lead Company A. The Yankee bullets were playing 'Yankee doodle' behind me, but did not travel quite fast enough to over-take me."[17]

The Texans threw themselves down on the Santa Fe Trail, gathering dirt and rocks in front of them in protective mounds.

"We wanted night to come and we wanted it mighty bad," Davidson wrote, "but the sun seemed to hang in the heavens and would not go down. . . . I almost believe that evening made my hair turn gray."

Finally, night did come and the Texans stood down. "When it became too dark for 'Mr. Yank' to see what he was doing," Davidson guessed, "he withdrew and the fight ceased."[18]

In the Texans' camp on the night of March 26, Davidson and his friends discussed the Battle of Apache Canyon. It was not a *clear* victory, they thought. But by standing their ground they believed they had won the day. It was vital, however, that they be reinforced to defend against the Yankee attack everyone felt sure was coming. The major sent off an express rider to find William Scurry, who was encamped with eight hundred men of the 4th and 7th Texas sixteen miles south of Johnson's Ranch. The rider carried a note from Pyron detailing the sharp fight at Apache Canyon and urging Scurry to "hasten to his relief."[19]

Back at Johnson's Ranch, Davidson and his messmates bedded down by a fire, with their shotguns at their sides, eyes wide open. At 3 a.m., Davidson heard a faint sound. Placing his ear to the ground, he heard it more clearly.

"It was the tramp tramp tramp of soldiers on the march," he deter-mined, "not the regular step but the 'rout' step." He knew that the men were Texans and not Yankees because he heard "not the clear ringing of men well shod striking the cold frozen earth, but the clear ringing sound of sandals or bare feet." A few minutes later, Scurry and his men marched into camp.

"I tell you I was glad to see them," Davidson said. "I thought they were the finest looking men I ever saw in my life."[20]

In an instant, the camp was abuzz with activity. Scurry's men threw down their packs and guns and lay down by the fires, or went to Pyron's supply wagons for something to eat. Some set off into the canyon to get more wood, and others wandered into Johnson's Ranch to find a place to sleep. While ransacking the house, some soldiers found armfuls of women's skirts and dresses. They had no bedding, so they draped themselves in the ladies' finery and snuggled down to sleep.

Davidson was wide awake, however, animated by the excitement of the battle and the arrival of his comrades, whom he had not seen since encamping with them in the Sandias outside Albuquerque several weeks before. For hours, he and Company A regaled any Texans who would listen with stories about how they had "set to the Yanks" in Apache Canyon, and how "we would have 'whaled' them if the 4th and 7th had only been with us."[21]

———

The next morning, March 27, William Scurry walked around the Texans' camp and down the Santa Fe Trail in both directions, surveying the ground. He was now the ranking officer in the field and in command of the 1,250 Texans huddled around Johnson's Ranch. Scurry had seen his fair share of battlefields as a soldier in the Mexican War. He understood immediately that the western end of the canyon was a strong natural position, and that with just a few earthworks it would be an ideal place to stop a federal assault. He wrote out orders and his men got to work, digging out rudimentary earthworks and preparing for battle. In their front, the Santa Fe Trail disappeared into Apache Canyon. Behind them, Scurry placed the army's cannons on a high hill. Then he ordered sharpshooters to climb up the mountains on either side of the road ahead and take shelter behind trees and rocks.[22]

They waited all day, remaining in line under arms, expecting an attack at any moment. When night fell, they were finally able to relax. The Yankees had not come. To add to the Texans' relief, Scurry's wagon train, delayed on the rough road from the south, arrived in camp that night. For the first time in many days Bill Davidson relished the taste of meat.

"The officers said it was dried buffalo. The boys said it was mule steak," he wrote. "No matter what it was, it was the best our officers could do and it really tasted well to hungry men."[23]

The next morning, March 28, the orders came to march. Colonel Scurry, who was as aggressive a soldier as Pyron, had concluded that if the Yankees did not come to them, they would go to the Yankees. Leaving only a handful of men, with one cannon, behind to guard the train of eighty wagons and the field hospital, Scurry and the Texans started up the road to Apache Canyon and, beyond it, Glorieta Pass.[24]

———

The Texan advance guard rode quietly around a big bend in the Santa Fe Trail that arced north and then straight back south again before turning east and descending through Glorieta Pass toward a group of adobe buildings known as Pigeon's Ranch. The ground on either side of the road was a "densely wooded pine country," wrote one Texan, "where you cannot see a man 20 steps unless he is moving." The hills sloped up away from the road, "rising more abruptly as they near the mountains. Heavy masses of rock, too, crown most of these hills, and the timber is low and dense."[25] As they came around the curve, the Texans saw a group of Union cavalry ambling toward them. All of the soldiers reined up, grabbing for their pistols. Shots rang out and the men began to yell.

"Get out of our way you damned sons of bitches!" shouted one of the Coloradans.

"You'll take dinner in hell!" replied a Texan.[26]

Both groups wheeled their horses around and galloped back the way they had come. The Texans did not have far to go to report their initial engagement with the enemy. Scurry's troops were close behind them, their steps quickening as the trail began to narrow and run more steadily downhill. With confirmation that the Yankees were close, Scurry halted. He ordered the cannons unlimbered, and sent the men to gather among the thick groves of trees on both sides of the road. Union troops appeared in front of them a few minutes later. Scurry's artillerists lobbed a cannonball into the trees above the Yankees' heads. The federals scattered into the rocky hillsides and took cover.[27]

Bill Davidson, who was with Company A on the right side of the Texan line, saw that unlike Valverde, this battle would be the bushwhacking kind: fought in the forest, face-to-face, by small groups of soldiers. He dismounted, tied his horse to a tree, and ran forward on foot. His comrades were already trading rifle and shotgun fire with the Yanks. They moved forward, pushing the federals back. The country was so rough and the smoke was becoming so thick, however, that the Texan companies "got all mixed up before we had been fighting very long." They did not see the palisade fence before they ran up on it, a long row of vertical tree limbs jammed into the earth. They tore the fence down as quickly as they could and ran through the muddy field that it had protected, heading for a hill looming up out of the smoke.[28]

As the Texans reached the slope, Davidson felt a hard ping in his leg and was left behind, limping through the pines toward the road. He sat down and took off his coat, and then his pants. He removed his shirt and began tearing it up, all the while "cursing the world and the Yankees." He was tying a strip of his shirt around his leg wound when one of the officers in the 7th Texas found him.

"What is the matter?" the captain asked.

"The Yankees have ruined my breeches!" Davidson complained. "They tore two big holes in them!"

The captain asked him where his company had gone, and Davidson gestured over to the hill, where he had last seen Company A. He figured they had already crested it and taken the enemy's cannon that had been placed on top. The captain left Davidson there by the side of the road and disappeared into the forest. Davidson did the best he could to stop the bleeding in his leg, and waited for someone else to find him.[29]

—————

The sounds of the battle—the popping of pistols, echoing shots of rifles, reverberating thunder of cannons—receded as Davidson made his way to the field hospital. Five miles to the west, other wounded Texans and a handful of Union prisoners of war arrived at another hospital at Johnson's Ranch. The regimental surgeons had set up a tent along the creek south of the Santa Fe Trail and were evaluating and dressing the Texans' wounds.

In the afternoon, a sergeant who had been left in charge of Johnson's Ranch's single cannon noticed a few small rocks tumbling down a high mesa across the creek. He looked up and saw that the steep hillside was alive with Union soldiers, some of them sliding and some running down the slope toward the Confederate camp. One of them skidded to a stop on a narrow ledge and yelled down at the sergeant.

"Who are you below there?"

"Texans, god damn you!" the sergeant yelled back.

"We want you!" the Union soldier shouted.

As the Texan ran toward the cannon to swing it toward the mesa, he hollered over his shoulder, "Come and get us god damn you, if you can!"[30]

A contingent of Union soldiers stayed on the ledge and trained their rifles on the Confederate camp and hospital while hundreds of their compatriots began to run down through the trees and rocks, following mule trails that were used to bring wood to Johnson's Ranch. The Texan sergeant made it to the cannon but was only able to fire two rounds at the mesa before Union soldiers overran his position. The Texans guarding the wagon train scattered into the woods, some of them leaping on horses and riding hard for Glorieta Pass. During the melee the 4th Regiment's chaplain emerged from a hospital tent waving a white flag. He was caught in the cross fire and shot. The skirmish was over in a matter of minutes.[31]

The Union soldiers cheered. They were a mixed group of Army regulars and 1st Colorado Volunteers, led by the officer who had commanded the fight in Apache Canyon, a Methodist minister from Denver named John Chivington. There were also several 1st New Mexico soldiers and guides, led by Lieutenant Colonel Manuel Antonio Chaves. They had been marching since early that morning, following a narrow path that ascended Glorieta Mesa south of the Santa Fe Trail and wound westward along its mostly flat top. Their flanking maneuver was part of a plan developed by John Slough, the officer in command at Fort Union. Slough was a lawyer who admired Napoleonic tactics and had decided to send one-third of his total forces under Chivington to get behind the Confederates' line. Slough would lead the rest of the 1st Colorado in a frontal assault against Scurry's troops.[32]

Chivington's and Chaves's commands had picked their way slowly through the pine and juniper woods on top of the mesa. Early in the afternoon, they found themselves five hundred feet above the Texan camp. At first they had waited for Slough to appear, as they expected that the Union Army would be driving the Texans back. After an hour it became clear that Slough and his men were having a harder time of it than anticipated, and Chivington had decided to act.[33]

The wounded Texans could do nothing but watch as the Union soldiers secured the field hospital, liberated several of their Union prisoners of war, and drove off around five hundred horses and mules that had been staked in the corral. The Texans were particularly outraged when they saw the Yankees rifling through their wagons, which contained "a great deal of fine officers clothing, fine Mexican blankets and all kinds of military stores, wines, Brandies, pickles, candied fruit, oysters & Navy revolvers, double-barrel shot-guns," and soldiers' knapsacks stuffed with letters and diaries. The Yankees took some items as souvenirs of the attack and then grabbed the wagons' tongues, dragging them around so that each wagon touched another. Having distributed kegs of powder among the train, they applied torches to the wagons' wooden planks. The fires spread rapidly.[34]

As the Union soldiers climbed back up to the ledge on Glorieta Mesa, the wagons in the Texan train exploded, one by one. "Sitting to rest upon the top," one Coloradan noted, "we witnessed every wagon, with its contents, a smoldering heap of ruins."[35]

Chivington's and Chaves's men then resumed their climb to the top of the mesa and began to march on the double-quick in the fading light. The Union prisoners of war they had freed at Johnson's Ranch had told them about the battle of Glorieta Pass. The Texans had been winning, pushing Slough's men past Pigeon's Ranch and then back to Kozlowsky's, another stage stop on the Santa Fe Trail. Their successful flanking maneuver would be for naught if the Texans had defeated Slough and the 1st Colorado, and were on their way to Fort Union.

As the Union soldiers disappeared, the wounded Texans and those who had stayed with them ventured out of their tents to survey the damage. When Bill Davidson arrived later that evening and heard what had happened, he was disgusted.

"Those men sent in our rear . . . were a set of miscreants," he complained. "They are certainly no part or parcel of the brave men we have been confronting and fighting for the past six weeks. . . . Oh! Wouldn't I have liked to have come on that crowd with Company A."[36]

At Pigeon's Ranch, Scurry's Confederate Army had been jubilant. At the end of the day they were in control of the field. Just as Scurry sent a white flag to Slough asking for a cease-fire to bury the dead, however, a small group of Texans came galloping in from Johnson's Ranch and informed him of the destruction of the wagon train.

"Flushed with the joy of winning the battle," one Texan soldier lamented, "we were suddenly confronted with the fact that after all we had lost the victory."[37]

That night, temperatures plummeted and a spring snowstorm rolled into the Sangre de Cristos, covering the charred remains of the Confederate wagon train in a thick layer of white flakes. All of the brigade's tents, wool blankets, horse and buffalo hides, and extra clothing had been burned to ash in the conflagration. Bill Davidson, who could move around on his patched-up leg, helped his fellow wounded Texans as much as he could.

"We took off our coats and piled them upon them. We built the best fires we could. We rubbed their limbs and bodies," he wrote, "but all to no avail."

Several of his injured comrades died of exposure in the night, and Davidson and the others buried them the next morning, piling them two-deep in shallow graves with whatever belongings they had tucked into their pockets when they died: "combs, pipes, tintypes, needles, tobacco, pencils, etc."

"It was bad," one of the Texans lamented, "but it was the best we could do."[38]

Later that morning on March 29, the first companies of Scurry's men marched into Johnson's Ranch. From them, Davidson found out that Company A's captain, John Shropshire, had fallen in battle. This news made the suffering of the previous day even worse.

"We were his old company, his boys, upon whom his whole affections centered," Davidson cried. "I was a wild, wayward boy . . . and he was my friend. I see him now around the camp fire, his smile, dark-blue eyes beaming in love upon us."[39]

William Scurry, who had not slept for forty-eight hours and whose face was bloody after being grazed by two bullets during the Battle of Glorieta Pass, rode into camp and established a hasty headquarters. When he saw the smoking ruins of the train for himself, the colonel determined that the Sibley Brigade could not march toward Fort Union. They would return to Santa Fe, "to procure supplies and transportation to replace those destroyed by the enemy."[40]

Davidson gathered what few personal effects he had left and readied himself for the journey. It was not a long march, but the first part of it was a steady ascent through tall pine forests. The surgeons had not yet been able to do much for him and his leg, and there were no conveyances to transport him or any of the other wounded Texans.

"1,000 miles from home, not a wagon nor a dust of flour, not a pound of meat," he moaned.

One of his comrades, a soldier in the 2nd Texas, leaned in close to Davidson.

"We're in a hell of a fix," he whispered.[41]

In the mid-afternoon on March 29, 1862, dust clouds appeared in the air south of Santa Fe. Soon the Texans began to arrive in the city, some wrapped in coats or blankets, many without shoes and hats. Some rode jaded mules or horses while others walked.

"Their appearance clearly manifested the severe usage to which they had been subjected," noted the *Santa Fe Gazette*, and "all were in the most destitute condition in regard to the most common necessities of life."[42]

As the men streamed by Louisa Canby's house and collapsed in doorways and courtyards, they informed her that the most desperately injured Texans were still up in the mountains, at the field hospitals at Johnson's Ranch and Glorieta Pass.[43] Louisa commandeered several wagons and then found a supply of canvas, which she stretched across the beds, creating cots on which the wounded soldiers could lie. She sent these wagons up the road to the Texans' field hospitals, and they began to make a series of forty-mile round-trips between Santa Fe and Glorieta Pass. Bill Davidson was a passenger on one of these medical wagons. His life, like "the life of many a poor fellow, was saved by [Mrs. Canby's] invention," one of his fellow soldiers attested.[44]

Over the next few days, Louisa helped to direct the Confederate wounded to the hospitals and houses of Santa Fe residents, including her own. Others bivouacked in the burned-out shells of government storehouses on the north end of town or among piles of hay that they found in Union Army corrals.[45]

On March 30, William Scurry arrived and sent men through the city, scouring it for hidden supplies. Some managed to scrounge up food hidden in nooks and crannies, while others found merchants willing to trade with them, providing bread and whiskey in exchange for whatever the Texans had left in their knapsacks.[46]

Scurry then went to the office of the *Santa Fe Gazette*, and set some soldiers to work printing an address he had written to his men while on the battlefield at Glorieta.[47]

"*Soldiers*," the address began. "You have added another victory, to the long list of the triumphs won by the Confederate armies. By your conduct you have given another evidence of the daring courage and heroic endurance which actuate you in this great struggle for the independence of your country."

The Texans' achievement at Glorieta Pass—the fact that Scurry's men "drove before you a foe of twice your numbers over a field chosen by themselves, and deemed impregnable"—gave them the right to "stand by the side of those who fought and conquered on the red field of *San Jacinto*." Glorieta had been a victory in the spirit of '36, proof of the Sibley Brigade's patriotic inheritance and their particularly Texan brand of martial bravery. Despite the fact that the destruction of their wagon train forced them into retreat, Scurry hoped to inspire in his troops the conviction that Glorieta, like San Jacinto, would be a decisive battle in a Texan war for independence.

"It will not be long," he concluded confidently, "until not a single soldier of the United States will be left upon the soil of New Mexico."[48]

Davidson and the boys in Company A suspected the truth. The Battle of Glorieta Pass *would* be decisive, but not in the way that Scurry meant. Without supplies, they could never hope to march back up the Santa Fe Trail and take Fort Union. The lives that had been lost in the effort to conquer New Mexico had been wasted.

"There is a sort of gloom resting on the company," one Texan wrote. "We seldom sing now save when liquor abounds, and the sound of a violin makes me sad."[49]

The Texans became even more despondent as they watched wagons leave the hospital and roll toward Fort Marcy. The Confederates had converted it into a cemetery, and the wagons were bearing their dead comrades to their final resting places.[50]

Over the next week, the Texans tried to amuse themselves by visiting the Cathedral of St. Francis of Assisi and the local steam mill, and reading the most recent newspapers they could find, all of them published in early March 1862. From them they learned of the Union occupation of Nashville. It was the first Confederate capital city to fall to the federals, at almost the exact moment that the Texans had occupied Santa Fe. The papers also printed rumors that twelve thousand Union troops were on their way to Aransas Bay on the Gulf Coast, and that the Union hoped to launch an invasion of Texas from there. If this was true, one of Sibley's soldiers smugly noted, the federals "will have a merry time of it."[51]

While he was "'laid-up' undergoing repairs," Bill Davidson noted, "Mrs. Canby won the hearts of all our boys through her kindness to our sick and wounded. She spent several hours every day . . . bringing them delicacies and cheering their drooping spirits with kind words."[52]

Louisa chatted with the Confederates about their lives, and about their desperate lack of blankets, tents, and food. William Scurry came to her to ask about other supply depots in the city. Soon after these discussions, Confederate foragers broke into the office of the superintendent of Indian affairs. In it they found stacks of thick wool Mackinaw blankets in white, red, and blue; more than one hundred New Mexican blankets with their distinctive patterns of interlocking red diamonds; white handkerchiefs and blue denim shirts; hunting knives; and plows and farming implements. These items had been promised to the Navajos after the treaty Richard Canby had signed with Manuelito and the other headmen in February 1861. When the Civil War began, they were never distributed. The *Santa Fe Gazette* estimated that the supplies were worth more than $30,000.[53]

Many of Santa Fe's Unionist residents thought that the "sudden" discovery of the Navajo annuities was suspicious.

"The location of the room, together with the precautions which were taken to prevent the doors from being visible," the editor of the *Gazette* noted, "would have secured the existence of the goods from the knowledge of the Texans and saved them to the government—had it not been that some treacherous person betrayed a confidence that had been placed in him."

Davidson and the rest of the Confederate wounded were convinced that this "treacherous person" was Louisa Canby. One Texan reported that he had overheard her tell Scurry that "there are a large number of government blankets where you never could find them, but I will tell you where they are."[54]

On April 4, Henry Sibley arrived in Santa Fe. He found that the "sick and wounded had been comfortably quartered and attended; the loss of clothing and transportation had been made up from the enemy's stores and confiscations; and indeed everything was done which should have been done."[55] Much of this was due to Louisa Canby's efforts on behalf of soldiers she knew were enemies, but whom she could only see as army boys. After he settled into his new headquarters in Santa Fe, Sibley called on Louisa, to thank her for her work on behalf of the injured Confederates, and to talk about old times in Utah in '58 and during the Navajo campaign in '60.[56]

This conversation, and the cheerful concerts that Sibley ordered his brass band to put on in the plaza, could not improve the general's dark mood. When he had received dispatches in Albuquerque reporting on the battles at Apache Canyon and Glorieta Pass, he had believed that the Texans had once again been victorious. Only after he arrived in Santa Fe did it become clear how dire their situation was. The loss of the wagons was catastrophic.

Initially, Sibley thought he might take his army into the mountains south of Santa Fe to regroup. Soon he received reports that Richard Canby had left Fort Craig and was marching toward Albuquerque. Believing that Canby would not stir, Sibley had left only a few companies of soldiers in that city to defend his base of operations. The Brigade would now have to march back and defend it. On April 7, 1862, the Sibley Brigade abandoned its plan to take Fort Union and move on to Denver. Instead, they marched southward to face Canby's Union Army once again.[57]

———————

Louisa Canby watched them leave. The Texans ripped the canvas cots from her ambulance wagons and loaded them with whatever provisions they could carry, and soon they disappeared down the road to Albuquerque. With them, acting as wagon master, was Bill Davidson. He had decided that although his leg was still healing, he preferred to go along with the boys rather than stay in Santa Fe to become a prisoner of war.[58]

Henry Sibley left behind more than two hundred sick and wounded men in Santa Fe, all of whom still needed the attention of Louisa and the other army wives and women of the city.[59] Louisa would tend to them, and would wait for Richard's soldiers to appear. Then the residents could once again raise the stars and stripes above Santa Fe, taking back that town for the Union.

11

=

Davidson

What began as a sixty-mile march ended almost a month later in Mesilla as one of the longest retreats a Confederate army would undertake during the American Civil War. When the Texans hobbled into Albuquerque, the federals were amassing near the base of the Sandia Mountains. It was a combined force of Richard Canby's troops from Fort Craig (including Dodd's Independents) and the 1st Colorado, who had marched on the double-quick on the eastern side of the Sandias, from Glorieta. The Union troops did not attack, however. Women and children had not been evacuated from Albuquerque, and the accepted rules of warfare stipulated that Canby refrain from lobbing shells into the town, or charging the Confederates behind its adobe walls.

Henry Sibley took advantage of the pause in the action to withdraw, taking the Brigade down the Rio Grande to Peralta. Here there was a skirmish on April 15, and Bill Davidson was almost shot out of the church tower he was using as a lookout. But once again, the federals did not charge. Peralta was a small farming town crisscrossed with acequias and low adobe walls, and the Texans had the defensive advantage. Again, Sibley pulled back, crossing his men over the Rio Grande and marching southward. The Yankees remained on the eastern side of the river, and shadowed the Texans' every move.[1]

"A novel sight was here presented," Bill Davidson noted, "of two hostile armies marching down a river valley in plain view of each other with only a narrow river between them."[2] When the Texans halted, the federals halted. "Neither [seemed] anxious to bring on a battle, yet neither [tried] to avoid it." Many of the men on both sides were perplexed. One Texan, attempting to get to the bottom of this strategy, broke from the march and went to the riverbank.

"Say," he called across the water, "I want to know whether you fellows have gone crazy, or whether you are a set of damned fools, naturally!"

The Union troops answered with "a piece or two of lead."

The Texan "took the advice kindly and lovingly administered" and hastened back to his companions.[3]

On the night of April 17, 1862, the Sibley Brigade halted near the confluence of the Rio Puerco and the Rio Grande, having marched 120 miles in ten days. Soon after nightfall, the wind blew with great fury. Sand pelted the sides of the Texans' tents and found its way through the seams, covering the men and all of their belongings with a layer of grayish-white silt.[4] The Brigade's officers struggled through the storm to Henry Sibley's tent, where the general sought their counsel. If they continued southward, perhaps they could beat Canby's men to Fort Craig, where only a small contingent of 1st New Mexico Volunteers led by Kit Carson was defending the walls. It was more probable that Canby would cross the Rio Grande just south of their current camp and a battle would ensue. It would be a gallant fight, most likely, and an honorable surrender.

After listening to the officers debate these options, Bethel Coopwood, the commander of a Confederate spy company, offered an alternative. He knew of a narrow track that wound along the slopes of the San Mateo Mountains to the west. He believed the Brigade could take this route to Mesilla, using the mountains to shield them from the Union Army's view. They would bypass Fort Craig, avoid a fight with Carson's and Canby's men, and emerge from the mountains near Fort Thorn, and then return to Mesilla. There they could recuperate and defend Arizona Territory from a Union assault.

Coopwood "swore by all that was holy," Davidson noted, "that he could take us through."[5]

Before setting out just after midnight on April 18, Bill Davidson and Company A shoved ammunition into their pockets, grabbed their shotguns and pistols, and jettisoned most of their belongings. They set fire to the majority of the Brigade's remaining wagons and loaded the rest with extra provisions and hospital supplies. On that first day of the march, the wagons became mired in deep, heavy sand. Davidson's men unpacked them and stuffed the smaller items into bags they slung over the backs of the mules. The rest of it (feather beds, bottles of medicines, old harnesses) they left strewn across the road.[6]

A few days later, when they saw the narrow paths they would have to navigate through the steep and rocky San Mateo Mountains, the Texans realized they would also have to abandon their cannons. To keep them out of the hands of the Yankees, they buried three of them deep in the sand.[7] There was also some talk of leaving the Valverde Guns, the six cannons of McRae's battery, which the Texans had taken on that battlefield. But William Scurry, who had led his regiment at Valverde and the entire army at Glorieta, would not hear of it. Most of their other battle souvenirs, proof of the Texans' valor and mementos of their wartime experiences, had been destroyed at Johnson's Ranch. The Valverde Guns "were the only trophies we have been able to keep of our victories."[8] As the Brigade moved into the San Mateos, Scurry's men dragged the Valverde cannons up and down the rocky cliffs, in the shadows of vast peaks that "rise up so high as to make one giddy to look up at them."[9]

Every day that they marched, the Sibley Brigade left behind soldiers who were too sick or weak or dehydrated to go on. Mules and horses fell by the wayside, the edges of their ragged bodies soon blurred with drifts of sand. The Texans who managed to stagger into camp at dusk every day did so in no particular order. Soldiers from different companies mingled on the road, thinking of nothing but putting one foot in front of the other and making it to water. When their comrades informed them that they were drawing close to a cool creek or a tumbling river, they quickened their steps.[10]

"With lips black and parched, and throats swelled and dry, and breath hot and voice husky," wrote one Texan, "on we rushed till we reached the water." They threw themselves down upon the creek banks, "regardless of the crowding horses and mules, regardless of the swearing men, regardless of everything, and drank the cool clear soft water; drank until we sank back completely satiated."[11]

On April 24, 1862, when the Texans emerged from the mountains into a giant desert basin of salt flats, dunes, and windblown sand, they found wagons loaded with provisions and mail that the commander of the 7th Texas (in charge of Mesilla now that Baylor was gone) had sent them. Davidson and his comrades forgot their fatigue and their hunger, and "sat up late reading letters and discussing their contents and talking with the men who had come in." There was a "great and general stir in camp which did not calm down till 10 o'clock that night." It was a "grand hallelujah of a time."[12] The next morning, the Texans tramped a bit more quickly, spurred on by the knowledge that "once more we were in the valley of the

Rio Grande with no enemy between us and home, and no more suffering for water."[13] They could see the end of their trials.

The men of the Sibley Brigade talked of many things in the final days of their 350-mile retreat from Santa Fe, through the mountains and scorching desert: all that they had lost and suffered; everything they would enjoy once they reached Mesilla; and the "want of feeling, poor generalship, and cowardice" of their commander, Henry Hopkins Sibley.[14] He had brought them into these desert wastelands with promises of personal glory and the creation of a Confederate empire, and then he had hidden in his wagon at Valverde and in his luxurious quarters in Albuquerque, and let his men fight the Yankees on their own. The only carriages they had not burned during their journey along the mountain route were Sibley's. They jolted along Coopwood's Trail in advance of the reeling troops, carrying Sibley, Rafaél and Manuel Armijo and their wives, and a handful of other New Mexican dignitaries with Confederate leanings.

"Mexican whores can find room to ride in his wagons," an embittered Texan wrote in his diary, "while the poor private soldier is thrown out to die on the way."[15]

Davidson and his friends had praise for their own officers, however, and for Bethel Coopwood, the spy company commander who had sworn that he could guide the Sibley Brigade safely through this mountain retreat.[16] Although it had taken a huge toll on the men, the detour had achieved its goal. They had avoided a battle with Richard Canby's soldiers and were safely below them, heading toward their strongholds in Arizona Territory.

On April 30, when they finally established their camps around Mesilla, the men of the Sibley Brigade let out a collective sigh. When they thought about all they had endured in the previous three weeks, they could hardly believe it.

"Surely a march over such a country and made by men mostly on foot, not accustomed to walking, was never surpassed," claimed one of Davidson's 5th Texas comrades. It was yet another long haul in a campaign characterized by them, necessitated by the nature of the high desert region in which they had chosen to fight. The Confederates saw these marches as epic achievements in the American Civil War, actions as noteworthy as their battle victories at Valverde and Glorieta, and their occupation of Albuquerque and Santa Fe. That these were journeys marked by suffering and death made them even more historic.

"It reminds one," a Texan noted, "of Bonaparte's celebrated march over the Alps."[17]

Throughout the month of May 1862, the men of the Sibley Brigade encamped in southern New Mexico Territory, nursing their cracked and
bleeding feet, and scrounging through the Brigade's remaining wagons
for scraps of clothing. There were funerals to attend every day. The Texans
mourned comrades they were putting in the ground as well as the untold
number of men they had left in Santa Fe, Albuquerque, Peralta, and on
Coopwood's Trail. They reckoned that all told, they had lost 30 percent
of the Brigade: more than eight hundred men killed, wounded, felled by
disease, or taken prisoner during the campaign. It was an egregiously high
casualty rate, among the highest in the Confederate Army during the Civil
War. Those Texas boys' names had been "dropped from the roll," Bill Davidson reflected, but all would be remembered.[18]

When they were not contemplating the disasters of the campaign, and
if they could find a nub of a pencil and some paper, the Texans wrote
letters home. They crowded around the mail wagons, passing around the
newspapers that had come into Mesilla from San Antonio since they had
left in February on their march up the Rio Grande.[19] The news seemed
to track with the Sibley Brigade's own campaign. General Earl Van
Dorn, transferred from his command in Texas to the battlefields of the
trans-Mississippi West, had lost to the Yankees at Pea Ridge in northwestern Arkansas in early March, forced to retreat on the second day of that
battle because he had left his wagon train far behind the field and could
not resupply his men.

The Battle of Shiloh, farther east in Tennessee, appeared to have gone
much the same way. The Confederates had had the upper hand on that
first day, April 6, as they pushed the federals back toward the docks at
Pittsburg Landing, on the Tennessee River. But the Yanks had come back
at them the next day with thousands of fresh troops, pouring off the riv-
erboats and onto the battlefield. It was the bloodiest battle the Texans had
ever heard of, with more than twenty-three thousand casualties. The Texans were also distressed to learn that Union gunboats had been able to
pass the massive and well-armed forts guarding the mouth of the Mississippi River and were threatening to lay siege to New Orleans.

None of these events boded well for the Confederacy or for the Texans
encamped around Mesilla. The Union Army was now in control of Missouri, northern Arkansas, and southern Louisiana. If they succeeded in
taking all three of those states, Texas would be cut off from the rest of the

Confederacy. Texans would have to rely on the boats steaming and sailing across the Gulf to bring food, supplies, and soldiers in and out of the state. Davidson and the other soldiers of the Sibley Brigade began to feel a sense of urgency about their situation. It was clear that their campaign to take the West had failed. Most of the men felt that they should leave Confederate Arizona as soon as possible, and return home to help defend their beloved Texas against a Yankee invasion.

Davidson and the others could not set out on their own, of course. They had to wait for orders. They had heard next to nothing from Henry Sibley since they arrived in Mesilla. Two weeks after their return he had sent out an address to the troops.

"It is with unfeigned pride and pleasure," Sibley wrote, "that I find myself . . . congratulating the Army of New Mexico upon the successes which have crowned their arms in the many encounters with the enemy during the short but brilliant campaign."

He praised their valor at Valverde, Glorieta, Albuquerque, and Peralta, and counted as one of their achievements their march along Coopwood's Trail, an "almost unprecedented evacuation, through mountain passes and over a trackless waste of a hundred miles through a famishing country." Like his men, Sibley was sure that the retreat in particular "will be duly chronicled, and form one of the brightest pages in the history of the Second American Revolution."

The Proclamation contained few hints about the future of the Brigade, however. Sibley acknowledged that the offensive campaign for New Mexico was at an end, but cautioned the men to "constantly bear in the mind that at any moment you may be called into activity."[20] Would Canby's troops descend upon their camps around Mesilla? Would Sibley suddenly decide that it was not over and make one last attempt to take Fort Craig and reestablish the Confederacy's foothold in New Mexico Territory? The Texans did not know.

Henry Sibley would have liked to consult with John Baylor regarding the Confederacy's hold on the Mesilla Valley and Tucson, but when he arrived he found Baylor gone and his letter of resignation on the desk at headquarters. Sibley was enraged when he read the letter, in which Baylor had attacked him personally, and when he heard about Baylor's raid across the border into Mexico, which had almost instigated an international incident. Sibley wrote to Governor Terrazas of Chihuahua and apologized on behalf of the Confederate government for the Corralitos Raid. If he had known about the transgression before Baylor left Arizona, Sibley assured the governor, he would have held the Texan accountable.

Sibley also forwarded Baylor's Apache Extermination Order, which had sanctioned the betrayal and murder of Apaches at a peace parlay, to the Confederate War Department. Jefferson Davis had been trying to secure the allegiance of Native groups in Indian Territory, and Baylor's order might imperil that project. Perhaps the raid and the order would lead to Baylor's dismissal from the Confederate service. In Sibley's view, he deserved it.[21]

The general turned from these matters to the tricky business of explaining to the Confederate War Department why he had failed to capture and occupy New Mexico Territory. His strategy was to lay the blame elsewhere. Neither the War Department nor the state of Texas had given him enough money to acquire arms, blankets, uniforms, or sufficient food for his men, he complained. This had delayed his campaign, and made his men feel devalued. Furthermore, the help he had anticipated from Hispano New Mexicans, Apaches, and Navajos had not materialized. It also turned out that the secessionists in New Mexico were vociferous but few in number. Most of the wealthy Hispano ranchers and merchants, whom Sibley had been so sure would flock to the Confederate side, were only interested in retaining their own power, and so their loyalties fluctuated accordingly.

Also unexpected was the constant siphoning off of their mules, horses, cattle, and sheep by Apache and Navajo raiders. The presence of the Confederate Army in New Mexico had provoked rather than discouraged these activities. Sibley did not advocate for extermination, as Baylor had, but did inform his superiors that he had decided, "as good policy, to encourage private enterprises against [Navajos] and the Apaches, and to legalize the enslaving of them."

The root of the problem for the Confederates, however, had been the high desert landscape itself. With its aridity, lack of water, and long distances between towns and forts, New Mexico was a disaster for large-scale military operations, only notable for "the multiplicity of its defensible positions," which favored the Union Army. A continuous supply of food, "the indispensable element" of any long-term military campaign, "cannot be relied upon." Further, Sibley noted, the desert was so aesthetically repellant that by the end of the campaign, his soldiers "manifested a dogged, irreconcilable detestation of the country and the people."

Sibley dipped his pen in ink once again and wrote his final assessment of the landscape he had spent the past year trying to conquer.

"It is proper that I should express the conviction," he wrote, "that, except for its political and geographical position, the Territory of New Mexico is not worth a quarter of the blood and treasure expended in its conquest."

In light of these considerations, Henry Sibley concluded, he intended to leave the Mesilla Valley and "move by slow marches down the country."[22] He would gather the Brigade at Fort Bliss in Texas and then send them by companies along the Rio Grande to Fort Quitman. From there they would take the military road back to San Antonio. Given their lack of horses, wagons, and supplies, and given that the spring was now turning to summer, it would be a difficult march. But there was really no other choice. He could not hold the country for much longer. Another battle with Richard Canby on the outskirts of Mesilla could only end in defeat and surrender.

What was more, there was a rumor that another Union army was on the move toward Mesilla, traveling rapidly from Los Angeles through Arizona on the Butterfield overland mail route. It was best to leave soon, before the Yankees could amass another large fighting force on the Texans' flank. The Sibley Brigade would disappear into the deserts of West Texas, where Sibley was sure Union troops would not follow him.

In early June 1862, Davidson and Company A moved to Fort Bliss, happy to be back in the state of Texas. They spent most of their days there trying to buy clothes, hats, and provisions for the march back to San Antonio. The Texans had finally been paid, but in Confederate scrip. The Anglo and Mexican merchants who gathered along the bridge crossing the city's *acequia madre*, and sold lettuce, onions, and mince pies, refused to take that currency, insisting on gold or silver coin. The Texans offered old clothes, shoes, and paper for trade, but they were rebuffed.[23]

Unable to purchase supplies, the Texans decided to steal them. In small groups, they rode across the Rio Grande into Mexico and took wagons, beef cattle, work oxen, and weapons from Mexican ranches.[24] The victims of these thefts launched their own retaliatory raids, attacking Confederate foraging patrols and camps. The Texans saw the logic in these strikes.

"Had we been successful and remained conquerors of the country," wrote one private, "all these things would have been forgotten, but now being fugitives, they felt secure in harassing us in every possible way."[25]

Bill Davidson fell victim to one of these raids on Company A's camp outside Fort Bliss.

"A Mexican stole my mule," he complained, "and took it over to [Mexico] and sold it. Although I found it over there and duly claimed it, . . . Mexico refused to give it up."[26]

———————

In mid-June 1862, Bill Davidson left Fort Bliss on foot and, with Company A, marched to Fort Quitman. The journey of one hundred miles took more than a week. The river was running high and fast, swollen by the spring melt, and it spread over the valley and forced the Texans to "follow a circuitous route around the hills, throw[ing] us out of the shade and into sand, and render[ing] our journey much more tedious and laborious than it would otherwise be." The gnats buzzed around their faces, "thick as grains of sand, almost."[27]

When they finally reached Quitman, Davidson and his comrades "were all foot sore and weary. The rest we had [in Mesilla] healed our sores, but the skin was tender and a few days' tramp made them as sore as ever."[28] The Confederates dreaded jumping off into the deserts of West Texas. They were without horses or mules, with the sun blazing down upon them. But they could not turn back. Their only option was to place one foot in front of the other on the road home.

In early July 1862, Bill Davidson and his comrades took one last look at the Rio Grande, and then turned their faces to the east. Only a few miles along, they began to pass "broken down wagons and carcasses of dead horses, and oxen that had starved for water." This was it: the end of the Confederate campaign for New Mexico. The Texans had mismanaged time, supplies, and natural resources in an unforgiving theater of war, and they had suffered for it. The West remained in the hands of the Union, and the Confederacy was surrounded on all sides by states and territories loyal to Abraham Lincoln. The Confederates lost access to the goldfields of the West, and the Pacific Coast's deepwater ports. The dream of creating a continental Confederacy built on the labor of slaves in the fields and the mines, and the possibility of extending that empire of slavery into Mexico, had evaporated like a desert mirage.

Leaving Fort Quitman on that hot summer day in 1862, Bill Davidson and the men of the Sibley Brigade looked at the ruins of Henry Sibley's failed campaign, and limped on.[29]

12

Carleton

The rumors that Henry Sibley had heard were true. At the same moment that the Texans began their retreat out of Confederate Arizona, Union colonel James Henry Carleton and more than 1,500 men of the 1st California Volunteers were encamped at Fort Yuma on the Colorado River, on the California-Arizona border. Several steamers and a ferry were tied up on the west bank of the river, waiting for soldiers to load and unload their contents. The high bluffs around the fort, which commanded an excellent view of the deserts extending to the horizon in all directions, were packed with wagons and soldiers.[1]

In the fall of 1861, when the Union Army's commanders in California had received word of John Baylor's successful invasion of New Mexico, they decided that their soldiers should go on the offensive. They considered and discarded several plans of attack before hitting upon a workable strategy in December.

"I propose to send Colonel Carleton . . . to reopen the southern mail route," George Wright, commander of the Department of the Pacific, suggested, to "recapture Forts Buchanan, Thorn, Fillmore, and Bliss."[2]

Carleton, a career military man who had spent the previous twenty years as an officer in 1st Dragoons (a cavalry unit), had begun training recruits outside Los Angeles in early December 1861. He instructed his officers to "drill, drill, drill" the volunteers, who had mustered into infantry, cavalry, and artillery companies, putting them through their paces with their knapsacks on to get them used to carrying their own supplies. Carleton was sure that by working hard every day, the 1st California Volunteers would "become perfect as soldiers, as skirmishers, as marksmen."[3]

The men grumbled at first, but Carleton, lean and straight-backed with a clipped beard and intense gray eyes, inspired them. They came to appreciate his dedication to their training, knowing that it would help them survive what was to come.[4]

Moving more than 1,500 men across a massive desert was a logistical challenge. The men could carry some supplies with them (strips of dried beef and hard bricks of pemmican made of meat, fruit, and fat), but the army would have to establish a network of supply depots along the route. Carleton sent companies of experienced soldiers with two of his officers, Edwin Rigg and Joseph Rodman West, to stock these depots, and clean out roadside wells and springs. Then he sent off orders to fill the wagon trains waiting in Los Angeles. Soon they were packed with sacks and barrels of flour, beans, coffee, sugar, and vinegar. Carleton also issued orders for the volunteers to gather nettles, mustard greens, and other plants growing around their camps, which they could eat to "freshen the blood," preventing scurvy.[5]

The 1st California, made up of miners from all over the state, was supposed to leave Los Angeles in early January 1862 and proceed on the Butterfield overland mail route to the Rio Grande. General Wright was confident that this army would succeed. It was made up of hardy volunteers used to life in the California gold mines, "ready and anxious for active service" and ably commanded by Carleton, "an officer of great experience, indefatigable and active."

"We have the power and will," Wright boasted, "to drive every Rebel beyond the Rio Grande."[6]

It soon became apparent, however, that the 1st California would not be leaving in January. Every day for almost six weeks, "torrents of water [had been] precipitated on the earth," the *Los Angeles Star* reported. "It seemed as if the clouds had been broken through, and the waters over the earth and the waters under the earth were coming into conjunction." Immense amounts of water came "fretting and boiling" through the city, sweeping thousands of orange trees and grapevines downstream. The San Gabriel River overflowed, seemed to pause, and then gathered itself and pushed on, carving a new channel through the plains toward the Pacific Ocean. The city's business district was flooded, the water seeping through the tiniest of cracks, causing adobe buildings to sag and then dissolve into the streets.[7]

Los Angelenos had never seen anything like it, this "Noachian deluge." Sixty-six inches of rain fell on the city in forty-five days. The roads in and out were impassable, suspending mail and telegraph communications and making it impossible to move vehicles of any kind.[8] As a result, the Union Army's campaign to retake Arizona was delayed for more than three months.

James Carleton knew that nature often made a mockery of the military's desires. While he waited for the rains to stop and the roads to dry, Carleton continued to train his men and look to every minute detail of the upcoming march. One day, he sent out orders to the cobblers supplying the 1st California, specifying that the soles of the men's boots be sewn to the uppers rather than attached with wooden pegs. In the hot desert air, Carleton knew, the pegs would shrink and the boots would fall apart.[9]

By mid-March 1862, the Californians were finally able to start moving eastward. Carleton sent small companies of men out every few days, using the same strategy of staggering troops as Henry Sibley had when he moved his men through West Texas. As the time for Carleton to depart Los Angeles drew nearer, he contemplated taking his family with him. His wife, Sophia, and two children, Eva and Henry, had traveled with him from fort to fort throughout the 1850s. Like the Canbys, the Carletons had built a family at frontier garrisons. But that spring, Sophia was pregnant. If she joined him, she would have to deliver the baby on the road to Fort Yuma. The Carletons decided it was best for her to remain with the children in Los Angeles, and he would send for them when he could.[10]

In early April 1862, Carleton bid his family goodbye, mounted his horse, and rode off with his staff and a company of soldiers on a road that soon entered the San Bernardino Mountains. When they began to descend the eastern slopes of that range, the Sonoran desert opened up before Carleton's contingent in a series of sand flats, drifts, and small hills dotted with mesquite.

"The whole distance [is] one unbroken waste of blinding white sand, which reflects the rays of the sun with terrible lustre and withering effect," one of Carleton's officers wrote. "Men, mules, and horses sink under its power, as if suddenly blighted, losing all energy."[11]

Given that the sun was already scorching, Carleton sent out orders that his army was to march only at night, setting out at 4 p.m. every day and halting at dawn.[12] Using the light of the moon and hundreds of torches to illuminate the road, the 1st California Volunteers marched steadily eastward along the Butterfield route. They arrived at Fort Yuma in early May, having lost no men during a march of over three hundred miles.

The 1st California spent two weeks at Fort Yuma, recuperating from their long march. Carleton established his headquarters and then sat down with Major Rigg, who had been organizing supplies and receiving soldiers at Fort Yuma for months. Rigg confirmed an unfortunate piece of news. One of Carleton's favorite officers, an Irishman named William McCleave, had been captured by the enemy. McCleave had been with one of the first companies Carleton had sent forward. When McCleave arrived at Fort Yuma, Rigg had ordered him to ride east and make contact with Ammi White, a Unionist who ran a flour mill at Pima Villages, a small trading center outside of Tucson. When McCleave knocked on White's door, he met with a man he thought was the mill owner. He was actually Sherod Hunter, whom John Baylor had sent with the Arizona Rangers to occupy Tucson. Hunter had done so, and then pushed west to Pima Villages, where he took both Ammi White and McCleave prisoner.[13]

Carleton was aggrieved, and Rigg commiserated.

"A whole staff could not compensate us for the loss of McCleave," Rigg believed.

Worse, the Confederates now knew that Carleton's army was in Arizona, and that they planned to march on Tucson. The loss of Ammi White and his flour stores was also a blow. Perhaps something good would come out of this, though, a lesson for the men.

"It may turn out to be a good thing that these men have been taken," he wrote to General Wright, "it will make all others more vigilant."[14]

The bad news did not end there, however. Rigg had sent two companies of soldiers to try to rescue McCleave. This command had passed through Pima Villages in mid-April and moved on, surprising several Confederates posted at the foot of a red, volcanic shard called Picacho, forty miles west of Tucson.[15] In the firefight that followed, the Union soldiers managed to take three prisoners but it cost them. One of the Californians was shot in the heart, another in the back. An officer who dismounted in order to secure the Confederate prisoners was shot in the neck and died instantly.[16]

When Union reinforcements arrived, they rolled the bodies of their three comrades in blankets and buried them in the desert sands below Picacho Peak. Then they brought the horses and the Confederate prisoners back to Fort Yuma. Carleton went to the guardhouse to interview them, and learned that McCleave had been sent on to Mesilla, where John Baylor was deciding what to do with him.[17]

The three Californians who fell at Picacho were the first battle casualties that the 1st California had suffered in the fight for control of Confederate Arizona. Carleton thought it was likely that the battles to come would be fought in a similar manner: small groups of soldiers in close combat, fighting it out in thickets of scrub brush and cactus.

———————

In mid-May 1862, the 1st California—now also known as the "California Column"—boarded ferries, crossed the Colorado River, and stepped into Confederate Arizona. They moved forward as they had on the first part of the march, staggered in small companies and marching from dusk until dawn on the Butterfield route, which followed the Gila River. Even at night, the late-spring heat was unrelenting, "decidedly Plutonian," according to one soldier.[18] Men and animals pulled into camp each morning, their bodies encrusted with dust and their parched tongues hanging out of their mouths. Cutting willow and cottonwood limbs from the trees that fringed the river, the soldiers constructed bowers to give them some relief from the glaring sun. These leafy structures ran in regular rows by company, resembling "booths of a fair, alive with military life."[19]

If they could have seen the camps of their fellow Union soldiers in Virginia that spring, the Californians would have been astonished at the similarities. Over the previous winter, the Army of the Potomac had built themselves row upon row of log cabins, decorating them with tree limbs and planting flowers along sidewalks out front. Whenever and wherever men went to war, they used what they could to protect themselves from the elements.[20]

The men of the Column who had first traveled to California overland had seen vast deserts before. Those who had arrived by ship had not, and were amazed. One morning, a soldier climbed from camp up the slopes of nearby Antelope Peak. From its summit, where a Union flag was already flying, he had a splendid view of the surrounding country.

"I could trace the bright sheen of the Gila, in its winding course, for many miles above and below, coming, as it were, from the same source as the rising sun," he wrote to a newspaper in California. Out from its banks "stretches the bleak desert, and in the distance, broken ranges of mountains and solitary peaks, looking like immense pyramids."[21]

On May 23, 1862, after another four days of hard marching and a shortcut across a waterless stretch where the Gila arced northward, Carleton's contingent arrived at Pima Villages. They were exhausted and thirsty but cheered by the greetings of hundreds of their comrades, who had been building a fort adjacent to White's mill. From these men, Carleton learned that the Confederate ranger Sherod Hunter had abandoned Tucson and was heading back to Mesilla. Carleton's officer Joseph Rodman West was on the move toward that town already, with several companies of cavalry under his command. Carleton was pleased. Tucson would be a major supply depot for the remainder of the Union campaign to retake Arizona.[22] He waited to hear from West. After he did, the rest of the California Column would move toward the Queen City of the Desert.

The next day, a rider came into Pima Villages from Tucson, carrying a note.

"I have the honor to report the occupation of this place, by the forces under my command," West wrote. "The colonel commanding can rely upon this place being held against the enemy."[23]

There had been no battle. West had been cautious in his approach, moving quietly through the fields, gardens, and corrals west of Tucson and then sending three detachments into town from different directions. There was a brief moment of panic when some cavalrymen spied what they thought were sharpshooters up on the roofs of the town buildings. The men laughed with embarrassment when these turned out to be canales: wooden spouts that extended two feet from the roofs, protecting the adobes from the cascades of rain that came during monsoon season. The Californians confirmed that Sherod Hunter and his Arizona Rangers had left a few days before, and Tucson was nearly empty.[24]

Soon after reading West's report, Carleton welcomed several Pima and Maricopa chiefs to his headquarters. They rode into Pima Villages followed by one hundred mounted warriors, their skin painted and feathers in their hair. These two Native communities had cultivated the land along the Gila for hundreds of years, building a large network of acequias to water their fields. Their foodstuffs had kept American miners and Butterfield mail route workers alive during precarious times in the 1840s and '50s. By the summer of 1862 they had several thousand acres under cultivation near Pima Villages, lush fields filled with corn, wheat, pumpkins, and melons.

The men of the California Column stopped their work and gathered around to gawk at the warriors. "It was quite a novel and curious spectacle," one of them commented.[25]

"They are the finest Indians I have ever seen," Carleton wrote after the council. The Pima and Maricopa chiefs were shrewd traders and had been careful not to officially ally themselves with Sherod Hunter during the Confederates' brief occupation of Pima Villages. In their talk with Carleton, they agreed to sell the Union Army wheat and produce in exchange for manta, a red cloth that was a common currency of exchange in the Southwest, and muskets to help them defend their communities against Apache raids.[26] As part of the deal, Carleton ordered his soldiers not to disturb any of their fields or attack any of the women in Pima and Maricopa villages.[27] He was pleased that this first meeting with the region's Indians had gone so smoothly. Surely even the Apaches, with their reputation for resistance to American armies along this route, would see that peace and trade with the California Column were in their best interest.

This diplomatic success achieved, Carleton turned eastward once again. After spending a week in Pima Villages, he ordered small detachments forward along with one battery of artillerists, with orders to have their cannons ready to fire a salute the moment he rode into Tucson.[28] On June 1, 1862, once he had seen the battery on its way, Carleton and his staff left Pima Villages.

The road they followed took them through heavy sand canyons and past "old foundations, mounds, and pieces of broken pottery, scattered for miles over the plain," all evidence of the former villages of the Hohokam peoples, who had farmed maize in the deserts of the Southwest before any European had even thought about setting foot on the continent.[29] A high, broken range of mountains came into view, and soon Carleton's contingent pulled into camp at Cañada del Oro.

"In a bed of the cañon is a beautiful, bold, mountain stream," one of Carleton's officers reported, "and the scenery is quite romantic—the mountains, forming the background, running up to curiously shaped summits, suggesting the idea of old castles."[30] The area had been mined in the late 1850s but only along the streambeds and not for long. Western Apaches, a band of Chiricahuas who often joined Mangas Coloradas and Cochise for raids into Mexico, had chased the Anglo miners from their claims.

Some of the soldiers were curious and prospected a bit along the mountain stream, dipping their tin baking pans into the water and swirling them around.

"All got 'color,'" one of them reported, "and all come to the conclusion that rich diggings could be found."[31]

The men of the California Column believed that their five-hundred-mile march from Los Angeles to Tucson would have two results: the liberation of Arizona Territory from the Confederacy and the development of its mineral resources. Their experiments at Cañada del Oro confirmed that the Territory was rich in gold, and copper and silver, too, perhaps.[32] Casting a longing look back at the mineral-laden stream, the California Column made one more long push through the desert. On June 7, 1862, they rode into Tucson.

The Union flag was already waving above the town. On cue and according to orders, a four-gun battery fired salutes to James Carleton, to the California Column, and to the Union. Carleton dismounted and made a speech to his soldiers, praising them for their fortitude on the long march across the desert from Los Angeles. Then he made his way to his headquarters, a handsome house on the plaza. It had been abandoned by a notorious secessionist, and Joseph West had confiscated it on behalf of the Union Army.[33]

Tucson, like other frontier towns in the Southwest, was inhabited by a diverse mix of people in the early 1860s: Hispanos born in Mexico who found themselves living north of the border after the American victory in 1848 and the Gadsden Purchase in 1854; Apache, Maricopa, Pima, and Papago (Tohono O'odham) women and men working as guides, servants, teamsters, or farmers; and Anglo-Americans, predominantly men, who had migrated from the southern states to make their fortunes as miners, merchants, or gamblers. Most of these Anglos were secessionists and had welcomed Sherod Hunter and his men when they had ridden into town bearing John Baylor's Arizona Territory proclamation in February 1862.[34]

Several of these Confederate sympathizers had left with Hunter, but Carleton suspected that many remained in town, or were hiding out in the surrounding mountain ranges. He was determined to root them out and restore order to Tucson, which in his view had too long been controlled by "cutthroats, gamblers, and loafers who have infested this town to the great bodily fear of all good citizens." The day after his arrival, Carleton established martial law in the city and informed the residents that any adult man choosing to remain would have to swear an oath of allegiance to the United States, or be expelled from the Territory. Secessionist talk or symbols would not be tolerated. If there was proof that any person said anything "to impair that veneration which all good patriots should feel for our country and Government," they would be punished accordingly.[35]

After issuing these initial proclamations and orders, Carleton left his headquarters and walked to the bustling business district, where he turned off onto a smaller side street. There, a local blacksmith named Ramón Pacheco had his shop. Almost immediately upon entering Pacheco's smithy, Carleton found what he had come for. Turned on its long edge and partly buried in the ground for stability, an elongated slab of iron resembling a kidney bean sat in the middle of the shop. Two holes were bored in one end and a flat surface gleamed along the top, where Pacheco pounded hot metal into sheets to form horseshoes, wagon tires, and handcuffs for prisoners at the town guardhouse.[36]

Carleton had read about this anvil in John Bartlett's *Explorations*, an account of his journey marking the boundary line between the United States and Mexico in the early 1850s. Carleton had brought a copy of the book with him on the march, thinking it would be a useful guide to landmarks along the road. In addition to describing his meeting with Mangas Coloradas among the ruins of Santa Rita del Cobre, Bartlett had given an account of this blacksmith's anvil in Tucson. Pacheco had found the four-foot-long iron hunk in the mountains south of town and had managed to load it into his cart and haul it back to Tucson. A considerable feat, given that it weighed more than six hundred pounds. All of the explorers and scientists who had seen it since then had agreed. It was a "remarkable meteorite," hurled from the heavens into the Southwestern desert an untold number of years before.[37]

Carleton had always been interested in collecting evidence of the nation's natural histories. In 1843, as a young officer in the U.S. Army, he met John James Audubon, who was hunting birds and animals along the Missouri River for his naturalist studies. Carleton and his dragoons accompanied Audubon's party for several days, and the two men became friends. Carleton gave Audubon a bearskin and a set of elk antlers, and in exchange Audubon presented him with four colored plates from his *Quadruped* series.[38] Since then, Carleton had collected the bones and hides of deer, antelope, and bighorn sheep across the West, and sent these specimens to the Smithsonian Institution, which had been founded in Washington, D.C., in 1846.[39]

Initially Carleton had been merely curious about Pacheco's meteorite, but once he saw it, he knew he wanted it. He had no definitive proof that Pacheco had made horseshoes or other items for Sherod Hunter, but the blacksmith's presence in Tucson during the Confederate occupation was evidence enough for Carleton. The Confiscation Act, passed by Congress and signed by President Lincoln in 1861, gave him the power to seize any property used to support the Confederate cause. The Union armies in the East had been using this measure to confiscate crops, animals, and enslaved men and women from rebels in the southeastern states. Carleton invoked it and took the meteorite from Pacheco, promising that he would replace it with another, more quotidian anvil. As his men heaved the meteorite onto the bed of a wagon, Carleton ordered them to send it with a wagon train heading west to Fort Yuma. From there, it would be loaded onto a boat sailing down the Colorado River to the Gulf of California, and then to San Francisco. He wrote to General Wright and notified him that the meteorite was en route.

"I desire you to present this [meteorite] to the City of San Francisco," Carleton wrote, "to be placed upon the PLAZA, there to remain for the inspection of the people and for examination of the youth of the city forever."

On permanent and public display, the meteorite from Tucson would be an object of instruction for city residents. Additionally, Carleton boasted, "It will be a durable memento of the march of the *Column of California*."[40]

––––––––

This massive wartime souvenir rolled westward in mid-June 1862, along with Confederate prisoners. Carleton's sweeps of the town had rounded up "eight or ten suspicious characters who had been prowling about the place ever since Hunter's departure," observed one California volunteer. "They are a portion of a set of bad men who have had things all their own way, scorning all law; but affairs have taken a turn, and I think their jig is up."[41]

Carleton did not think there were any Confederates holed up at Fort Buchanan (south of Tucson) or Fort Breckinridge (north), but he sent companies of soldiers there to make sure, and to reoccupy these installations for the Union. Turning his attention from the traitors in his midst to allies in New Mexico, Carleton wrote to Richard Canby, informing him that Tucson was now in Union hands. He explained the actions he had taken, including the fact that he had declared himself the military governor of the Union Territory of Arizona, which now extended from the California border to Tucson. It was a move worthy of John Baylor, and one that Carleton did not hesitate to make as the commander of an invading army in a massive theater of war. There was not time to ask for permission from General Wright or Richard Canby, and Carleton saw it as within his rights to make such a decision.

The California Column, Carleton added, would remain in Tucson until the monsoon rains filled the water holes and springs along the 275-mile road to Mesilla. Carleton thought they might be able to set out in early July 1862, and arrive in time to "cooperate with you in driving the Rebels from New Mexico." News traveled slowly across the vast reaches of the desert, and so Carleton had not received word of the status of the war in New Mexico before he left Los Angeles, and no dispatches had arrived from Santa Fe since then. So Carleton also asked for information as to the location and strength of Canby's forces and the condition of the Sibley Brigade. After signing the letter, he handed it to a courier and ordered him to find Richard Canby, wherever he might be, and deliver it to him.[42]

Over the next several weeks, Tucson residents who had fled from the Confederates began to return, and Mexican traders poured in, setting up stands from which they sold beef and pepper pies, cakes, watermelons, pomegranates, and peaches.[43] The owners of gambling dens and saloons reopened their establishments, after paying the Union Army the first of their $100 monthly taxes to keep their businesses running.[44] The 1st California continued to drill, as the quartermaster gathered huge mountains of supplies and the Column's wainwrights repaired most of the wagons. The journey from Fort Yuma to Tucson had been instructive regarding the effects of the intense heat and the dry desert air: the wood shrank and cracked and spit out nails.

"The tires have to be cut and reset," Carleton noted, "and a large amount of other repairs have to be made to keep them from going to pieces."[45]

The men were in good shape, considering how far they had marched through a parched desert in the summertime. The California Column had faced many of the same obstacles as the Sibley Brigade, but Carleton managed his own supplies and the natural resources of the mineral landscape of Arizona much better than Sibley had done in Texas. This kind of leadership was essential to any military campaign in this region. It boded well for the California Column's engagements to come.

A few days after Carleton sent him off, the courier with the note for Richard Canby came riding back into Tucson. He had been spooked by the prospect of potential encounters with the Chiricahuas, who were said to be attacking travelers throughout Apachería. Disgusted, Carleton dismissed the courier and sent for the California Column's most experienced scout. John W. Jones had worked on and off for the U.S. Army while ranching his land near Fort Yuma, and had been running messages and spying for Carleton in Arizona since January 1862. Carleton trusted

Jones's ability to navigate the Butterfield mail route and avoid run-ins with Mangas Coloradas and Cochise.

Carleton gave him two letters: one written on military stationery and sealed, and one written on tissue paper and rolled up tightly to look like a *cigarito*. The stationery was a decoy, giving false information about the California Column's numbers and position. Carleton ordered Jones to proceed to the Rio Grande and find the Union commander. If he was captured, Jones was to eat the tissue paper, which contained Carleton's real message to Canby, and turn over the decoy letter to the Confederates. On June 16, 1862, Jones rode out of Tucson, accompanied by an officer named Lieutenant Wheeling and a Mexican guide named Chávez.[46]

A few days after Jones left, "huge masses of snow-white clouds piled themselves upon each other" and darkened the desert skies. "Not a breath stirred the leaves of the mesquite," wrote one of Carleton's officers, "and the air stood collected, as if awaiting the shock of an assailing host." There was a roar of thunder and "down came the rain in perfect Niagras: flash flash flash hissed the electric fluid as it lighted up the scene: boom, boom, boom: bang, bang, bang: roar, roar: crash, crash thundered the columbiads of the skies, while the frightened wind fled shrieking along the reverberating plain and through the mountain gorges."[47]

It was the first of the summer monsoons in Arizona, and in its wake, Carleton called in one of his officers, Edward Eyre, and told him that the army needed to know the location of roadside water supplies and whether or not the Confederates had left anyone to guard them. He was to take 140 men with him and "make a reconnaissance of the country; discover the [Confederate] army's position, force, and general condition, and report accordingly."[48] As they moved eastward, Eyre's men would carry the flag of the United States with them, reclaiming more of Arizona Territory with every step.[49]

On June 21, 1862, the men of the California Column watched Eyre's company depart with envy. In their opinion, they were in the best fighting condition of any Union army in the Civil War, and they wanted to give the Texans a go. They were worried that they would never have the chance, that John Baylor and Henry Sibley were "phantoms that will disappear at our approach." That the Civil War would end while they were in the middle of the desert, "a long ways from anywhere."

"*Nos veremos*," one of them sighed. We will see.[50]

13

Mangas Coloradas

Three riders had emerged out of the Dragoon Mountains and onto the plain to the east, moving fast across the flats. One was dressed in a Union Army uniform and the other two in the plain clothes of the frontier. They were riding mules and leading several additional mounts by the reins. It was John Jones and his two escorts, Lieutenant Wheeling and Chávez, bearing dispatches from James Carleton for Richard Canby. It was June 18, 1862.

Chiricahuas who had been posted on the lower slopes of Apache Pass raised a smoke as the riders began to climb up out of the plain into the mountains. When they neared the summit, a group of Chiricahuas rode down on the Americans. A running fight ensued. Chávez was shot in the hip and fell off of his horse. Jones and Wheeling kicked their mules into a gallop, leaving the wounded man behind. The Apaches caught up with Wheeling not far from the top of the pass and dragged him from his mount. They continued to chase Jones down the east side of the mountains and onto the desert floor.

"Now let's have a race!" one of Cochise's warriors taunted Jones as they thundered after him.

"*Mucha buena mula!*" yelled another. "*Mucho bravo Americano!*"

The Chiricahuas pursued Jones until sundown, but he was able to outride them. As he disappeared over a rise in the road, they turned back toward the pass. By then the rest of the Chiricahuas had already stripped Chávez and Wheeling and tied them each to a set of four poles, hoisting them up off the ground. They built fires underneath their captives and then stood over them as their bodies burned, filling their torsos with arrows and slashing their arms and legs with lances.[1] After this death ritual for their enemies was over, Cochise left Chávez's and Wheeling's bodies where they were, as warnings to all Americans who might try to follow them through the pass.

One week later, a much larger contingent of riders appeared on the road, 140 men led by Edward Eyre, sent from Tucson to reconnoiter the Butterfield route.[2] Cochise was wary. He preferred to fight when he had the advantage of numbers as well as position. Eyre's group was large, and well armed. On the cool, dark morning of June 25, Cochise let the Americans climb all the way up the road into the pass and watched as they camped at the abandoned Butterfield stage station. A small group of California soldiers, including Eyre, took the animals to Apache Spring, unaware that the Chiricahuas were tracking their every move. In a deep gulch behind a ridge on the north side of the spring, a small group of warriors waited for the signal to strike, hidden from the soldiers' view.

Soon, three Californians walked into the gulch with their horses. They had disobeyed Eyre's strict orders not to wander from camp. Four shots rang out. The three men fell to the ground. Cochise watched as Eyre and his men scrambled to mount their horses and take shelter at the stage station. After a moment, Eyre and an interpreter emerged from the ruins, waving a white flag. When they came within speaking distance of one of Cochise's warriors, the interpreter told him in Spanish that Eyre wanted to speak to their chief. Cochise's men—about one hundred of them, all armed with rifles and pistols, and a few with single-barreled shotguns in addition to bows and arrows—gathered around, and Cochise came forward. Eyre began to speak.

"We are Americans," he said, "our great Captain lives in Washington, and we wish to be friends of the Apaches."

Cochise responded to this statement with amusement, thinking back on his experience talking peace and friendship with Lieutenant Bascom before Cut the Tent.

"I am only traveling through your country," Eyre said, "and all that I ask is that you not interfere with my men or animals. Our great Captain is at Tucson with a large number of soldiers."

This was a valuable piece of information. Cochise now knew that there was a considerable American force in western Apachería, and that this "great Captain" was likely coming his way soon. Eyre assured him, however, that James Carleton wanted only "to have a talk with all the Apache chiefs and to make peace with them and make them presents."

Cochise considered all of this and then answered, in Spanish.

"I have a great desire to be friendly with the Americans," he said. "Neither your men nor your animals will be molested." He then asked for tobacco and food, and Eyre gave him all that he could spare.[3]

Cochise watched Eyre return to the stage station. After the American returned, a party of thirty soldiers pounded out of it, riding toward the gulch near the spring. The bodies of the three soldiers had been found. While he and Eyre had been talking, Cochise's warriors had stripped them and lanced their limbs, and left their bodies lying where they fell. The Americans' search party came back with the three dead men slung over their horses. Eyre ordered several soldiers to bury their comrades near the station, marking their graves with pieces of board.

After this, some of the soldiers rode out into the hillsides but could find no sign of Cochise or his men. The Chiricahuas knew how to make themselves invisible in the high desert landscape. Eyre and his men gave up and returned to their camp, packed, and left at dusk, marching down onto the plains east of the mountains. They did not send a messenger back toward Tucson, to warn Carleton about the Chiricahuas in force at Apache Pass. A man alone would never make it.

After the Americans had gone, Cochise sent his messengers out to his father-in-law, Mangas Coloradas, and the war chiefs of the other Chiricahua bands. He suspected that there would be a big battle at the pass very soon. He needed Mangas and his other allies to come and join him in the fight.[4]

———

In late June, Mangas Coloradas's scouts signaled to him from their positions above his camp in the Mogollon Mountains west of Mesilla. Two riders were approaching. Chiricahuas. When they arrived in camp, Cochise's messengers told Mangas about the recent fights at Apache Pass. Would the war chief come with his Chihennes and Bedonkohes, and help Cochise defeat these new enemies? Mangas Coloradas did not hesitate. As the couriers galloped away with his message for Cochise, he began to assemble his warriors for a journey to the Chiricahua Mountains.

It had been almost a year since his last real fight: the attack on Pinos Altos in September 1861. They had planned that attack perfectly, descending on the mining camp from multiple positions and burning several buildings. Their success had not been without costs, however. The Chiricahuas had lost three war chiefs and several other warriors in the effort, more than in any other battle with the Americans. After that, Cochise had turned his horses southward into Mexico, and Mangas took his people back to the Mogollons. Mangas's band set to work harvesting acorns and piñon nuts, planting small fields with corn and melons, and hunting the deer whose meat would sustain them through the winter.[5]

Mangas Coloradas's seventy years were weighing heavily on him, and he had wanted some time to rest after so many months of hard fighting. The cycle of vengeance for the U.S. Army's betrayal of the Chiricahuas at Cut the Tent, which had begun in January 1861, had been completed. Most of the Americans and Mexicans who had tried to mine copper or silver in Apachería had fled to Mesilla or Santa Fe. Only a handful remained in Pinos Altos, protected by a small detachment of Arizona Guards. Mangas was convinced that the Chiricahuas had retaken control of Apachería.

He was pleased by this, and by the number of horses that his men had been able to steal from the American military camps.[6] Mangas was aware of the white man's fight. Their conflict provided the perfect opportunity to launch a series of raids against both armies, with their long wagon trains and their huge beef and horse herds moving along the roads of New Mexico and Arizona. Mangas did not want to attract too much of either army's attention. Targeted strikes, launched quietly at night, brought in a few hundred animals from the camps without many casualties.

In the spring of 1862, as the weather grew warmer, Mangas had thought he might make peaceful overtures to the Arizona Guards at Pinos Altos. This had always been his strategy with the towns of northern Mexico. His warriors raided, the Mexicans retaliated, one side asked for peace, and the negotiations began, with enslaved women and men used as leverage. The communities remained peaceful for a time, until the next raid was warranted. In this way, Mexican towns and Chiricahuas created and sustained a violent but constructive coexistence.[7] These American armies and the towns they protected might remain along the eastern border of Apachería, so perhaps it was best to talk peace with them.

In March 1862, he had moved his camp southward toward Pinos Altos, and sent emissaries to approach the captain of the Guards. Soon, Mangas received word that the captain wanted to meet. But some of his men found out that the Guards were planning to set a trap for him. The Confederate John Baylor had ordered the Guards to lure the Chiricahuas into a peace parlay, then kill the adults and enslave the children.[8] Mangas had withdrawn his people from Pinos Altos immediately and gone to the

Mogollons. Although he was amenable to signing treaties with his enemies when it suited him, Mangas Coloradas began to wonder if peace was
possible with any Americans, Union or Confederate. The only alternative
now seemed to be war.[9]

<hr />

When Mangas Coloradas arrived at Apache Pass in July 1862, he found
three other Chiricahua bands who had also answered Cochise's call. Now
there were more than two hundred warriors encamped along the ridges
and gullies around the pass, tucked in among the junipers, oaks, and piñon
pines. Here, they would have the advantage of surprise, and they would
hold the high ground. They would also control access to Apache Spring,
which was the only water source in a sixty-mile radius. Cochise's people
were already working on breastworks that would protect the spring, gathering rocks and dragging them to hillsides above it. From their perches
behind the breastworks, Chiricahuas could shoot down on anyone who
sought to approach the spring, from any direction.[10]

While Mangas Coloradas, Cochise, and the other war chiefs planned
their ambush, their warriors gathered their arrows, sharpened the points
on their lances, stockpiled ammunition for their guns, and waited.[11] As
the sun rose on July 15, ninety uniformed men with several wagons in
tow sloshed their way through the alkali playa in the flats below Apache
Pass. The summer monsoons had come, and the mud in the plains was
"half-knee-deep." After slogging through the gray-white sludge, the Californians, under the command of Captain Thomas L. Roberts, marched
along twenty miles of dusty road at a pace "fast enough to test the mus-
cles of men who had become hardened by their march from the Pacific
coast" in the rising heat. James Carleton had sent Roberts and his men
to cache supplies along the Butterfield route for the rest of the California
Column, who would follow over the next week. Carleton had not received
dispatches from Eyre regarding the condition of the road or the presence
of Chiricahuas, so he sent Roberts to make his way as far as Apache Pass,
and then send a report back to Tucson.[12]

The Chiricahuas moved into position. Mangas Coloradas and his warriors hunkered behind rocks and boulders along the trail leading to the
stage station. Cochise gathered his men in the breastworks around the
spring, and higher up in the hills surrounding the pass. He placed one of
his men who was an especially adept sharpshooter in the notch of an oak
tree above the spring. Mangas and Cochise watched the soldiers straggle

into the pass. They were a smaller force than Eyre's company, and their wagons were lagging behind. The Chiricahuas felt confident that an easy victory was at hand.[13]

Mangas Coloradas waited until Roberts's horsemen dismounted at the stage station and heaved the saddles from their horses. At his signal, the Chiricahuas leapt out from behind the rocks and unleashed a "murderous volley" at the Californians at the rear of the column.[14] One of the soldiers collapsed, blood soaking the dust from a bullet wound to his brain. The other Californians scattered as Mangas's men charged. Roberts, who was up near the spring with the cavalry, heard the gunfire and rushed back down the trail to join the fight, shouting at his artillerymen to get there as fast as they could. The Californians rapidly set up their cannons—"new and terrible weapons, huge guns mounted on wheels," as the Chiricahuas later described them—and threw a few shells into the hills.[15] They crashed into the dirt where the Apaches lay concealed. At this, Mangas and his men scattered and took shelter in the surrounding ravines. Aiming their rifles at the slopes, Roberts's soldiers took shots and then moved forward, making their way slowly up toward the stage station.[16]

The Californians gathered in and around the station as the captain discussed a battle plan with one of his officers. If they hoped to win this fight with the Chiricahuas, the Californians needed to take Apache Spring. Roberts divided his men into two groups. One would make a dash for the spring and the other would cover them with gun and cannon fire.

"Boys, there is water," the captain said, "we must have it or die. I ask no man to do more than I shall try to do. I expect no man to do less. This is no place for cowards or skulkers; if I fail to do my duty men shoot me down for by God I will shoot down the first man who shows the white feather here today!"[17]

The Californians cheered, and Cochise's men readied themselves behind their breastworks. They waited until the soldiers came within fifty yards of the spring and then Cochise gave the signal. The Chiricahuas fired and the Californians fell back. The artillerists lobbed shells into the hills, but given the sharp angles, they missed their marks. The Chiricahuas taunted the Californians, and the soldiers responded with "fierce and brutal curses from cracked lips and swollen tongues." They turned to Roberts and implored him to get them back into the fight.[18]

Roberts came up with another plan. Instead of charging the spring, his men would run up the ridge above it, in an attempt to take the breastworks. If they could hold those, they could "whip the Indians and get out of this scrape."[19] The Californians re-formed and dashed forward, ten men at a time, before lying down and firing their rifles up the slope to cover the charge of another ten men. In the meantime, the artillerists fixed their trajectories and began to hit their targets. One shot blew apart the tree in which the sharpshooter had been sitting, leaving nothing but a slivered stump where the oak had been. Cochise's men in the breastwork north of the spring continued to fire down on the charging Californians, but the soldiers kept coming. They ultimately gained the top of the rocks and clambered over them, dispersing the Chiricahuas, who ran back down the other side of the ridge and disappeared into a gully.[20]

Once the Californians controlled the breastwork, Roberts sent a contingent of men to the spring to fill as many canteens and camp kettles as they could before Cochise could regroup and charge their position. He also called over six cavalrymen and gave them orders to ride hard down the trail west of the pass and onto the flat, where Roberts had left most of his train. They were to tell the wagon master that under no circumstances was he to come up the road. Roberts could not risk a moonlight attack on the wagons when the Chiricahuas would again have the advantage.[21]

Through field glasses, one of Roberts's officers watched as the six horsemen pounded down the trail to the west. Following them was a group of thirty mounted Chiricahuas, led by Mangas Coloradas. As the Americans dashed down the mountain, Mangas and his men rode after them, and into a gully on the west side of the trail. When the Californians made it to the flats, they slowed their pace, and one of them, a private named John Teal, dismounted in order to rest his horse. His compatriots pulled away from him, and within moments, Mangas Coloradas and his men emerged from the gully and fired on them. The soldiers looked back at Teal "but self-preservation, the first instinct of nature getting the better of their valor, they galloped off," leaving the private to take care of himself.[22]

The Chiricahuas closed in around Teal, who remounted his horse. Mangas Coloradas threw himself on the ground in order to brace his rifle for a better shot at the Californian, who was frantically turning his mount in circles and firing his gun in every direction. Mangas took his shot, but Teal saw it coming and leapt out of the saddle. The bullet hit the horse in the chest and it wheeled off, trailing blood on the road. Teal crawled through the desert grass, trading gunfire with the Chiricahuas. As the sun began to sink, one of Teal's bullets found its mark. Mangas Coloradas fell back in the arms of his warriors and they dragged him into the darkness.[23]

Later that night, Thomas Roberts abandoned his position in the breast-works and retreated back the way he had come, down the Butterfield road to where the wagon train was waiting, more than twenty miles away. Co-chise directed his men to reoccupy the works around Apache Spring and sent scouts to the other Chiricahua camps to get their battle reports. They had lost nine men in the fight that day, and many others were injured. Mangas Coloradas's wound was serious, and several of his warriors sent word to Cochise that they were going to take him to the northern Mexi-can town of Janos to get help.[24]

Cochise turned his attention to the Americans, who were already marching back to the pass, now with twice as many men and the wagon train. He readied his warriors, but this time, the Californians' assault on Apache Spring was organized and unrelenting. The artillerists pounded Cochise's positions with shot and shell. He knew a losing fight when he saw it and pulled his men out of the breastworks and farther up into the hills. Then he ordered a retreat, following Mangas Coloradas into Mexico. On July 16, 1862, the Chiricahuas lost control of Apache Spring, the most valuable resource in western Apachería.[25]

This did not mean that the war with the Americans was over, however. Throughout the Chiricahuas' history, they had engaged in battle with Mexicans and Americans, winning and losing and always returning to the fight. The Chiricahuas did not see one loss as the end of the war. They still had experienced war chiefs and a knowledge of the desert and all of its resources. If more soldiers came, they would fight them. If the U.S. Army built a fort at Apache Spring, they would attack it. They would do what they could to defend Apachería and assert their power as a people. In their view, the Chiricahuas' struggle with the U.S. Army had just begun.

14

##

Canby

O n July 4, 1862, having survived their clash with the Chiricahuas at Apache Pass, Edward Eyre and his men arrived on the Rio Grande and encamped at Fort Thorn, raising the Union flag above its walls.

"This was the first time the stars and stripes floated on the Rio Grande below Fort Craig since the occupation of the country by the Confederate troops," Eyre wrote in a dispatch to Richard Canby, "and it being the anniversary of our National Independence was not calculated to dampen the ardor of the command."[1]

That same day, the citizens of Santa Fe gathered in the plaza to celebrate the nation's founding. Louisa Canby walked the short distance from her home with Richard, and they mingled with Union officers and their wives, a small group of men wearing the medals and sashes of the Masons and Oddfellows (fraternal organizations whose membership included the most prominent citizens of the city), and Hispano and Anglo parents with their children. The Palace of the Governors had been prepared for the occasion. Bright green cedar and pine boughs encircled each of the thirty wood pillars that held up the portico, giving "a cool and refreshing appearance to the whole street."[2]

Governor Henry Connelly stepped up onto the platform that had been built in front of the Palace, and began to speak.

"*Cuando en el curso de los acontecimientos humanos,*" Connelly said, "*se hace necesario para un pueblo disolver los lazos políticos que le han unido con otro y asumir entre los poderes de la tierra . . .*"

The crowd applauded throughout Connelly's reading of the Declaration of Independence, their cheers growing louder as the governor spoke

144

the document's final line: *"Nos comprometemos mutuamente nuestras vidas, nuestras fortunas, y nuestro sagrado honor."*[3] Connelly acknowledged the applause and then turned to welcome Richard Canby onto the stage.

Louisa listened as her husband read the entire Declaration again, this time in English. Then Connelly and Richard read George Washington's Farewell Address in both languages. Once again, the crowd shouted their approval. A procession followed: a brass band playing patriotic tunes, followed by Connelly, Richard and his staff, the civil officers, and members of the territorial legislature. Louisa, the other officers' wives, and the rest of the revelers came after them, moving toward the parade ground north of the Palace. There, Louisa watched the soldiers run the Union flag up a beautiful new pole, which had been erected after the Union Army had retaken the city. As the banner ascended and then unfurled in the breeze, "enthusiastic cheers broke forth from the surrounding throng" and echoed through the streets of the city.[4]

"The good people of Santa Fe," the editors of the *Santa Fe Gazette* declared, "showed that the patriotic fire blazes in their bosoms with undiminished ardor." The citizens' love for America's political institutions "has not waned with [the] passing of time, nor decreased by the melancholy events of the past twelve-month."[5]

It seemed impossible that Santa Fe and its residents had undergone so many changes in the previous year. The invasion of the Texans. The mustering in of volunteers from towns all over New Mexico and Colorado. The flight of the Territory's political leaders. The bloody and terrifying battles at Valverde, Apache Canyon, and Glorieta Pass. The surrender of Santa Fe and its conversion into a hospital for the Confederate wounded. The retreat of most of the Texans. And the restoration of Santa Fe to the Union. So much had happened, and so many lives had been lost.

After Henry Sibley had abandoned Santa Fe in April, Louisa and her friends had continued to visit the Confederate wounded, doing "all they could to lighten the sadness of hospital life," bringing the men flowers, food, books, and newspapers. When some of the Texans had convalesced sufficiently to organize a vaudeville club, Louisa attended their entertainments and applauded their efforts.[6] Two weeks after Sibley departed, Richard's second in command, Benjamin Roberts, arrived in Santa Fe and declared the wounded men prisoners of war. Roberts and his staff took responsibility for the Texans, issuing them rations from the quartermaster's stores. This had eased Louisa's burden considerably.[7]

Louisa's obvious concern and care for the Texans, and the fact that she had met with Henry Sibley, had caused some consternation among the city's leaders. Some of them suspected her of leading the Texans to the Navajo stores cached at the Indian Agency. In May 1862, when Richard returned from Fort Craig, however, the talk of her potentially treasonous actions had quieted to a murmur. The *Gazette* lauded her care of the Confederates and praised the other ladies in town who had helped her. Her actions reflected well on her and on the work that civilian women did in occupied towns, and in the wake of Civil War battles. It also suggested that acts of kindness were not totally unknown in the context of warfare.

By the end of May, about half of the Texan wounded had recovered enough to travel. Richard paroled them and ordered them out of the Territory. The day before they left for Texas, the Confederates held a meeting at the hospital and voted to approve a resolution. On their way out of town, they stopped by the *Gazette* office and asked that the paper publish it.

"*Resolved*," it read, "that we should be doing violence to our feelings were we to leave this place without expressing to the ladies of Santa Fé and, through them, to those who have aided them in their mission, our profound gratitude for the deliberate kindness which has been shown to many of us in suffering and sickness, and the attention and courtesy which has been extended to all."[8] While the Texans applauded Louisa's acts of mercy, the citizens of Santa Fe recognized Richard's victory. Even the *Gazette*, which had sometimes been critical of his military leadership, had nothing but good things to say after he returned.

"Never, perhaps, was an army brought into the field, organized, and disciplined in the midst of as many unfavorable and discouraging circumstances," the editor wrote, "as those encountered by the Commander of this department."[9]

Richard assured everyone in Santa Fe and the Union War Department that the Texans were soundly beaten. Their Confederate army was broken and their resources depleted. He could have forced them to fight another battle in Mesilla and then surrender, but he did not have the resources to feed and house another army as large as his own. So he had followed them until they turned westward on their detour through the San Mateo Mountains, and then he had let them go. Richard kept soldiers at Fort Craig under the command of Kit Carson, and sent others to forts in the

Territory, in order to defend those locations in the event of another Texas invasion.[10] But Richard doubted that they would see Sibley or his men again. Union scouts were reporting that most of them were on the road to San Antonio.

"All apprehension that may be entertained in reference to the return of the Texans to New Mexico may be confidently dismissed," the papers declared. "[There is] not the least probability of their coming back."[11]

After the celebrations of July 4, several of the Canbys' old friends began to return to Santa Fe. In early August, Surveyor General John Clark came to see Louisa. His trip to Washington, D.C., had been productive. He met with Commissioner Edmunds, as well as Secretary of War Stanton and President Lincoln himself.

He "was well received by all," Clark reported, although it really was "fatiguing this running after great men."[12]

In mid-April he had returned to Illinois to spend time with his family. Once he was sure that the Texans were on the run, he had made plans for his return to New Mexico. The trip from Fort Leavenworth along the Santa Fe Trail had taken little more than a month and there had been no trouble along the way.

Clark was eager to talk to Richard about the battles in New Mexico. While he had heard some accounts of Valverde during his short stay at Fort Union back in March, he had only read in the eastern papers about subsequent events. Richard indulged him but talked in detail only about Valverde, as this was the one battle he had commanded himself. An adequate defense of McRae's battery would not have changed the fortunes of the Union that day, Richard thought.

"The column of Texans charging was full 1000 strong," he told Clark, "and they were desperate, it being their last chance. They [had to] take the battery or be destroyed."[13]

The Canbys and Clark talked of national developments as well. Once the news had reached Washington that Richard had forced the Texans to retreat from New Mexico, the U.S. Congress passed the bills that would encourage the colonization of the West by free Anglo farmers. The Homestead Act provided any adult citizen loyal to the Union with 160 acres of surveyed government land. They were required to "improve" the land by cultivating it and building structures on it within five years. Congress also passed the Pacific Railway Act a few months later, authorizing two companies, the Central Pacific and the Union Pacific, to begin construction on a transcontinental railroad. Much to the disappointment of the citizens of Santa Fe, the line would not be built along the southern route through New Mexico and Arizona. It would be constructed farther north, on the 42nd parallel through Nebraska, Wyoming, Utah, and Nevada and into northern California. Both of these measures would bring hundreds of thousands of Anglo settlers to the western territories and states, to make the Republican Party's dream of an empire of free labor manifest. Both legislative acts also required that military and civilian officials like Richard Canby and John Clark wrest control of the West's lands from Native peoples and from Hispanos who could not prove their ownership.[14]

Clark and the Canbys chatted, and made plans for future gatherings. Clark's arrival in town coincided with a return to normalcy in Santa Fe. There were dinner parties and weddings and walks around town.[15] The streets buzzed with activity. Wagons were rolling in from every direction, and all of the merchants' stores had reopened, their shelves full of goods.

Richard Canby's troops controlled all of New Mexico Territory, and by August 1862 James Carleton had marched his California Column through Confederate Arizona, effectively returning it to the Union. After the Battle of Apache Pass, the Californians occupied that vital way station on the Butterfield route. Several weeks later Carleton arrived on the Rio Grande and then moved south, crossing into Texas to retake Fort Bliss and Fort Quitman. He found these deserted and raised the Union flag above them, then sent 1st California soldiers to do the same at Fort Davis, in West Texas.

Carleton wrote to Richard, asking for permission to pursue the Sibley Brigade.

"We have not crossed the continent thus far to split hairs," he wrote, "but with an earnest resolution to do our duty whatever be our geographical position. . . . It would be a sad disappointment to those from California if they should be obliged to retrace their steps without feeling the enemy."[16]

Richard was unmoved, denying Carleton's request to engage with the last of Sibley's retreating troops. He believed that an invasion of Texas was impracticable, given "the length of the march, the desert character of the country to be traversed, [and] the scarcity of supplies on the route." The Union did not have resources to subsist Confederate prisoners of war, or enough troops to garrison all of the forts in West Texas. These soldiers, in Richard's opinion, would be more usefully employed elsewhere in New Mexico and Arizona.[17] Richard ordered Carleton to parole any Texans he found, and to make sure that the federal installations in southern New Mexico Territory were well provisioned and guarded.[18]

While Carleton was at Fort Quitman, the Canbys began to hear rumors about their own future. The papers reported that Richard had been relieved of duty in New Mexico and ordered to report to Washington, D.C. Their friends hastened to their house to confirm this news, and Richard told them the truth, which was that he had received no official orders.[19] A few days later, however, the word did come. Richard was promoted to brigadier general of the Union Army and was instructed to turn over command of the Department of New Mexico to James Carleton. He would then travel to Washington, D.C., to serve as a military advisor to Secretary of War Edwin Stanton.

It was hard to know what the Canbys would find when they arrived at the Union capital city. In the spring of 1862, the Union Army's fortunes in the eastern theater had seemed bright. Ulysses S. Grant's troops had won at Shiloh, and New Orleans had fallen. The latter, Santa Fe residents were certain, "will prove the most severe blow upon the cause of secession that it has felt since the commencement of the war."[20] They also had high hopes for the Union's march up the Virginia Peninsula and felt sure the federals would take Richmond in that assault. The campaign, which had taken place in late June and early July 1862, had been "sanguinary in the extreme," the eastern papers reported, but had achieved nothing for the Union Army. Union general George McClellan had withdrawn his troops down the Peninsula, and it was said that the cheers of the secessionists in Virginia could be heard as far north as the U.S. capitol building.[21]

In September 1862, during her final weeks in New Mexico Territory, Louisa Canby maintained her social schedule in the midst of her travel preparations, finding the time to attend the final examination exercises at the female school run by the Sisters of Laredo. She listened as the girls recited dialogues in English and Spanish and played the piano, and she distributed books and medals as prizes. There was fine needlework and crochet to admire, and Louisa and the other ladies of Santa Fe found much to applaud in the girls' achievements.[22] She made one final visit to the Santa Fe hospital in late August, to say goodbye to the few Confederate sick and wounded who still remained in the city. They, too, were leaving New Mexico soon and traveling south to Fort Bliss. She talked with them about their health, and about what they would do after making their way home. Many of them expressed their disgust for Henry Sibley, for deceiving them into the expedition, and then exacerbating the disasters they had faced along the way.[23]

The departure of the last of the Texan invalids was both an end and a beginning for Louisa Canby. Her work as a Civil War nurse, for the moment, was done. It was possible that she might take on such responsibilities in the future, as they would be posted among the massive army camps and many hospitals of Washington, D.C. They always needed volunteers and would welcome her as an experienced caregiver of men with war wounds. In mid-September, Santa Fe residents read the first reports from the battlefields of Bull Run (Manassas), where the Union and Confederate armies had met for the second time in two years of warfare. It was another devastating Union loss.

In the aftermath of Second Bull Run, there were numerous reports about the movement of rebel troops. Robert E. Lee, in command of the Confederate Army in Virginia after Joseph Johnston was wounded during the fights on the Peninsula, was taking his troops northward into Maryland. Perhaps the Canbys would arrive in time for Richard to be sent to that battlefield, to help protect the North from invasion just as he had defended New Mexico Territory. If so, Louisa would accompany him. It was what she had always done, and would continue to do.

———

Richard Canby had chosen September 22 for their departure from Santa Fe. The afternoon before, John Clark came and sat with Louisa for half an hour. When he left, he promised to bring her a bouquet of flowers in the morning, to take with her in the coach. Clark was melancholy, as the Canbys had constituted the best part of his society in Santa Fe, and he believed it "very likely I shall never see either of them again."[24] That night Richard went to a dinner party that James Carleton threw for him. The new commander of the department had arrived in Santa Fe a few days before. All of the Territory's important military and civil officials were there, and they toasted Richard all evening long, commending him on everything that he had achieved during his command in the Territory. Their toasts echoed the judgment of the citizens of New Mexico.

"He has won for himself golden opinions from those who have impartially scrutinized his course," the *Gazette* judged, "either during the time of the Texan invasion or when there was no enemy to encounter but the wild Indian." He did his duty to the Territory and to the country, and no one could find fault with his conduct.[25]

Richard lauded the efforts of his own officers and soldiers, and those of the California Column. He asked Carleton to relay to the 1st California the gratification he and the Union Army of New Mexico felt "at the fact that troops from the Atlantic and the Pacific slope—from the mountains of California and Colorado, acting in the same cause, impelled by the same duties, and animated by the same hopes—have met and shaken hands in the center of this great continent."[26]

The next morning, Louisa climbed into a coach that would take her to Denver. The road from there to Council Bluffs, Iowa, was considered to be a safe route, although reports were coming in of a Sioux uprising in southwestern Minnesota. Richard would travel separately, taking the Santa Fe Trail stage to Fort Leavenworth in Kansas. On the seat next to Louisa was the bouquet that John Clark had given her. That morning he had visited the famed garden of Bishop Jean-Baptiste Lamy, a four-acre oasis behind the Cathedral of St. Francis of Assisi. It was planted with fruit trees, flowering shrubs, and flowers. Louisa took the bouquet that he picked for her there with great pleasure.[27]

At nine o'clock Louisa's carriage and Richard's stage left Santa Fe, accompanied by twenty citizens on horseback, including John Clark and James Carleton. The procession made its way out of the city on the Santa Fe Trail, climbing toward Apache Canyon. At the mouth of the canyon, the group halted. One of the army officers opened bottles of champagne and another produced glasses. They all toasted to the Canbys' good health and said their final goodbyes. After a half hour of conviviality, Louisa climbed back into her coach and it rolled on.[28] During her time in New Mexico, she had seen the Territory imperiled and then saved for the Union, the path cleared for the future Anglo conquest of the region. Perhaps she would return to Santa Fe with Richard after the war was over. Or perhaps, as John Clark believed, she would never see him or New Mexico Territory again.

15

===

Ickis

The day the Canbys left Santa Fe was unremarkable for Alonzo Ickis and Dodd's Independents. They had arrived in the city in mid-August 1862 after spending four months at Fort Craig, drilling and standing guard and occasionally riding out after Navajos who had stolen horses and mules from the army's herd. Mostly the soldiers had reclined on blankets under shady bowers they built with willow branches, bent into arcs and staked into the sandy ground. Ickis had been bored, hungry, and reluctantly reconciled to the fact that their active campaign against the Confederates had come to end for the present.[1]

Ickis was delighted to be in Santa Fe. They were not staying at Fort Marcy on the hill above the city. The Texans had converted that installation into a cemetery during their occupation, so the Union officers decided to abandon it. Instead, Dodd's men were housed in a long, low adobe building just off the plaza that had once belonged to the wealthy Armijo brothers. It had been confiscated by the Union Army after the Armijos fled with Henry Sibley. Each day, after gathering for roll call, Ickis and the others had breakfast and then reported for duty. If they were lucky, they would ride out into the mountains north of the city to procure wood, or accompany a wagon train to cut hay in the rolling tablelands near the Rio Grande. These opportunities to leave the garrison and see the country, especially as the weather cooled and the leaves began to change color, did the men some good. There was always the possibility that a raiding party of Navajos would descend upon them, and Dodd's men could make a dash into the mountains. These pursuits rarely resulted in a fight or the retrieval of stolen animals, but they made for good stories later, around a warm fire.

Much of the time, though, Dodd's Independents were assigned to fatigue duty: unloading bags of wheat and barrels of vinegar from wagon trains; sweeping the parade ground; or collecting adobe bricks from corrals and warehouses that had been destroyed during the retreat of Union forces back in March. Or, they could be selected for guard duty. James Carleton had made it known that the martial law that Richard Canby had instituted in the city would continue on for the foreseeable future. The army needed soldiers to roam the streets of Santa Fe with pistols and clubs, keeping order as civilians began to return in large numbers. This kind of duty was replete with opportunities. The men could linger at the scene of the town's many cockfights. Or they could look in on a game of three-card Mexican monte in progress, cheering on the players trying to guess which card would turn up in the center of the table. If they were on guard duty the night of a fandango (which, these days, was pretty much every night in Santa Fe), Ickis and the boys could station themselves outside the entrances, searching men and women for concealed weapons before letting them in the doors. If Dodd's men secured passes, they could attend the fandangos themselves, drinking and dancing and buying treats for the Anglo and Hispano ladies. It was little wonder that most soldiers in the Union Army thought Santa Fe was the best military posting in the West.[2]

In the month since their arrival Ickis had watched other companies of Union soldiers march in and out of the city.[3] Dodd's men said goodbye to the men of the 1st Colorado, who headed to Fort Union.[4] Another company of Coloradans went east as well, ordered to pursue Kiowas responsible for robbing a wagon train on the Santa Fe Trail.[5] Dodd's men did get one good assignment. In early September they escorted the paymaster's wagon train down to Peralta and back. Other than that, they stayed put in Santa Fe.

Their officer, Theodore Dodd, had always argued for using his "Rocky Mountain Bearded Saints" wherever stout hearts and strong arms were wanted.[6] The boys had enlisted for three years, and most of them, as much as they loved the entertainments of Santa Fe, wanted to get back into active service. By late September 1862 it had become clear that some sort of campaign was afoot. The newly re-formed 1st New Mexico—all of the best men recruited from the Hispano regiments that had fought against the Texans—was gathering supplies in Santa Fe and preparing to head out.

Half of them would march south to Albuquerque and then turn west toward Navajo country. Carleton had ordered them to build a fort in the lava fields south of the mountain that the Navajos called Tsoodzil, and the Americans called Mount Taylor. This site was flanked by thousands of acres of excellent pasturage. It was also the crossroads of two major road-ways: the U.S. Army's military road from Albuquerque to Navajo country, and a Native trail that moved southwest toward Zuñi Pueblo. From their new fort, Union soldiers could control routes in and out of the Navajo homeland. The post would be called Fort Wingate, after a career army officer who died from the wounds he sustained at Valverde.[7]

The rest of the soldiers of the 1st New Mexico were heading in the other direction, to Fort Stanton, a Union installation nestled in the foot-hills of the Sierra Blanca Mountains, one hundred miles due east of Fort Craig. Union troops had abandoned Stanton in the wake of Isaac Lynde's humiliating surrender to John Baylor in July 1861. The Texans had oc-cupied it for only a few weeks that summer, until Mescalero Apaches at-tacked and killed a contingent of their troops and Baylor recalled them to Mesilla. On their way out, the Texans had set fire to the fort, burning out the interiors of all the buildings but leaving their thick stone walls intact. In the year since, the Mescaleros had reoccupied their homelands in the Sierra Blancas, living on the game they hunted in the piñon and juniper forests, and the cattle they raided from Hispano ranches and army wagon trains.[8]

The soldiers marching to Fort Stanton were to build shelters for them-selves and then prepare for an extended campaign against the Mescale-ros. James Carleton had identified this band of Apaches as a threat to the Union Army's control of New Mexico. Like the Chiricahuas and the Na-vajos, they had exploited the Sibley Brigade's invasion of the Territory and "commenced robbing the inhabitants of their stock and killed in various places a great number of people." In order to control the Mescaleros, the army needed to reoccupy Stanton with five companies of soldiers, four of which "would operate against the Indians until they have been punished for their recent aggressions."[9] To lead them in this campaign, Carleton had chosen Kit Carson.

"The worldwide reputation of Colonel Carson, as a partisan," the gen-eral wrote in his orders, "gives a good guarantee that anything that may be required of him which brings into practical operation the peculiar skill and high courage for which he is justly celebrated, will be well done."[10]

Carleton based this command decision on more than just Carson's rep-utation, however. The two men had once been acquainted, and Carleton was a great admirer of the frontiersman. Eight years before, when Carleton had been stationed in Albuquerque, he had used Carson as a guide on a chase after Jicarilla Apaches who had killed several of his soldiers. After a few days of following a cold trail through the Sangre de Cristo Mountains, Carson checked signs and declared "they would overtake the fleeing foe by two o'clock that same afternoon." Carleton had scoffed and offered a wager. If they did find the Jicarillas by then, he would give Carson a beaver hat. From a summit in the Raton Mountains, Carleton and Carson looked down upon a camp of Jicarillas. Carleton took out his timepiece: 2:07 p.m. Carson was disgusted that he had been wrong by seven minutes, but Carleton considered that this was close enough, and that Carson had won the wager. Six months later, he ordered a black beaver hat from a haberdashery in Boston and asked that an inscription be printed inside the liner: "*Kit Carson* from his friend *James Henry Carleton*, U.S.A. Fischer's Peak Raton Mountains Sunday June 4th, 1854, 2 o'clock p.m."[11]

In early October 1862, Kit Carson and his 1st New Mexico Volunteers left Fort Union for Fort Stanton, with orders to take the fight directly to the Mescaleros. It was the first campaign against New Mexico's Native peoples, and an expression of a new Union Indian Policy in the West. The army would make no treaties. Instead, Carleton would go to war in order to force the Apaches and Navajos from their lands. In his view, if the army did not take the initiative, there might be a Native uprising in New Mexico as there had been in Minnesota just a few months before. There, the Dakota Sioux had already been placed on reservations, but the chaos of the Civil War had resulted in the cessation of annuities. Starving Dakotas first attacked the Lower Sioux Agency and then Anglo settlements along the Minnesota River Valley. The Union Army pursued them, and the armed conflict lasted for more than a month, leaving hundreds of Dakota men and women, Union Army soldiers, and Anglo civilians dead.[12]

Carleton wanted to avoid this kind of situation by making a powerful first strike against the Mescaleros.

"All Indian men of that tribe are to be killed whenever and wherever you can find them," Carleton instructed Carson. The soldiers were not to be so harsh with the women and children. They would be taken prisoner and fed at Fort Stanton until Carleton sent Carson further instructions about them. He was not to engage in any peace talks, only violence.

"We believe if we kill some of their men in fair open war," Carleton informed Carson, "they will be apt to remember that it will be better for them to remain in peace." The army would send the survivors to live on reservations, guarded by Union Army soldiers and forced to change their ways. War first. Then relocation. And then, ultimately, civilization.[13]

———

While the 1st New Mexico Volunteers marched out against the Mescaleros, Alonzo Ickis continued to do fatigue duty and get up to trouble in and around Santa Fe. In a scuffle in late October 1862, Ickis was "wounded by a pistol shot, the ball passing through the fleshy part of the thigh." He shrugged off the injury. It was "only a flesh wound" and he would be all right in a couple of days.[14] While his injury healed and the boys waited for news of Kit Carson's fights against the Mescaleros, Ickis spent his time reading the city papers, and the others that had come in on the mail trains. After so many months without any information about how the war was progressing, he was eager to know how the Union Army was doing in other theaters.

The *Santa Fe Weekly Gazette* published the first dispatches from the battlefield of Antietam in mid-October, more than a month after the battle had occurred. The one-day struggle was "fought with great violence on both sides," the newspaper reported, and "the carnage has been awful." In the end, both sides declared victory: the Confederates because their defenses above Antietam Creek had held, and the Union because in the days after the battle, Robert E. Lee had withdrawn his Confederate troops back to Virginia. The articles were unclear regarding the extent of the casualties. One reported that the dead "are thickly strewn all over the field; in many places lying in heaps."[15]

Dodd's Independents knew what it was to face the enemy across a river, and to charge his position. They could not imagine, however, the scale of these battles in the East, the tens of thousands of troops, the astonishing number and condition of the dead. It was unlikely that they would ever participate in such a fight. Unless the Texans returned, they would never see another battle like Valverde. Instead, they would be fighting small bands of Apaches or Navajos, creeping through tablelands and over mountain passes for months at a time, "proceeding with great caution, without noise or trumpets or drums."[16]

While Ickis and the others contemplated their future Indian fights, couriers arrived from Fort Stanton with the rather astonishing news that the war with the Mescaleros was already over. An advance unit of the 1st New Mexico had attacked and killed several Mescaleros outside Fort

Stanton before Carson had arrived. This show of force in addition to the destitute condition of many Mescalero bands resulted in the surrender of more than one hundred men, women, and children by the end of October. Carson wrote Carleton to tell him the news, and to inform him that he was sending three Mescalero chiefs to Santa Fe, to negotiate their removal to a reservation Carleton had picked out, a stretch of land along the Pecos River in central New Mexico, called Bosque Redondo.[17]

Ickis and the boys would have liked to see the Mescaleros enter Santa Fe and walk to the Union Army headquarters on the plaza. They had seen Indians only from very far away, receding into the distance on horseback after stealing their horses. Before the Mescaleros arrived, however, Dodd's Independents did something that so enraged James Carleton that he banished them from the city forever.

The trouble began on a Saturday afternoon, November 8. There were the usual arrivals and departures of wagon trains, and burros loaded with corn, flour, wood, and hay barreling their way through the city streets. Dodd's men had been ordered to clean their quarters, as they usually did on Saturdays. It had been the custom of the company officers (Theodore Dodd, especially) to distribute whiskey to Ickis and the boys afterward. It was a small reward for the tedious work. That day, however, the post was under the command of Henry Wallen, an officer who had been sent to Santa Fe to inspect the garrison and its soldiers. He had observed Dodd's men several days before and found that they "evidenced but slight acquaintance with the company drill" and were not practiced at firing their weapons. In addition, their uniforms were mismatched and their kits were haphazard. The company's request for whiskey would not help them to improve their soldiering, and so Wallen refused.

At first, Ickis and the others were befuddled. They returned to their quarters, where they discussed the matter and decided that they would confront Wallen and demand their customary reward. Again, the major said no. Dodd's Independents were outraged. This behavior clearly deserved a reprimand.

"Booooo! Boooooo! Booooo!" the Coloradans shouted at Wallen. The opposite of "three cheers," this was the ultimate "token of their esteem" for the major.

Wallen ordered the men back to their quarters and reported the matter to James Carleton. Dodd's Independents had not been under Carleton's command for very long, but they already understood that he was an uncompromising disciplinarian. It did not seem likely that he would let this act of insubordination go unpunished. At sundown, the orders came. Dodd's men were to gather up their kits and march more than eighty miles to Fort Union. There they would report to the guardhouse and await their fates.

Ickis packed up his belongings, including his well-worn diary, and joined his comrades as they marched on the double-quick out of the city. That night they bivouacked on the Santa Fe Trail, and discussed what might happen to them. Perhaps they would stay at Fort Union awhile, or be sent out of the department entirely. Rumors had been circulating around town that the Confederates were on the move again, marching up the Pecos River in central Texas to attempt another invasion of New Mexico Territory. If that were true, Ickis and the boys would be perfectly positioned to give the Texans another go.[18]

When they arrived at Fort Union, Dodd's Independents reported to the guardhouse as ordered. The soldiers there did not see that they had any business jailing their compatriots, and so Dodd's men camped "in the bottom," between the fort and the foothills. This suited them perfectly. The sutlers had also set up out there, and so they had easy access to extra grub and, of course, whatever whiskey was on offer. The boys of the 1st Colorado came to see them, and agreed with Dodd's men that Wallen had clearly been in the wrong.

"Not till a squad of officers arrived from the States who knew not the stuff of which the Colorados are made, did they ever have any difficulty with their officers," one 1st Colorado private reckoned. Anyone who had been in the region long enough or knew of the trials Dodd's Independents were subjected to in the previous year could not help but admire them.

"They are men of superior physique," their fellow Coloradan judged, "hardy, iron bound fellows, neither to be scared at being snowed in and reduced to every extremity while crossing the mountains on their way south from Garland, marching on foot through the blinding sands of the Rio Grande from Santa Fe to Fort Craig at the rate of thirty miles per day, or at withstanding, alone and unsupported, the furious charge of the Texas Rangers."

Dodd's Independents were men of the first water, and they did not deserve to be treated so unfairly.[19]

Ickis and the others were the talk of Fort Union until a company of soldiers, their fellow Coloradans who had left Santa Fe in early October to chase Kiowa raiders on the Texas border, came riding in. Ickis had thought they would never see these boys again, but there they were, with prisoners in tow. They were not Kiowas, however. And no one could have been more shocked than Dodd's men when they discovered who the captives were: a ragged group of miners, led by the legendary Green Russell, the first man to find gold in the streams of Colorado. The man whose discoveries had brought them all to the Rockies in the spring of '59.

Russell, his brothers, and most of their friends were Georgians. When they heard that the war had begun out in South Carolina, they had not declared for one side or the other but had remained in their gulches in the Rockies, quietly working their claims. They had monitored the Sibley Brigade's progress in the newspapers and decided that if New Mexico and then Colorado came under Confederate control, they would make their southern sympathies known and support Sibley in whatever way they could.

When Russell heard that the Texans had been turned back at Glorieta, he knew his party had to leave Colorado and return home to the Confederacy. Having gathered forty pounds of gold nuggets and dust in saddlebags and packed several wagons with their gear, the Russell party came down from the mines. They made their way southward, skirting Fort Garland and heading toward Taos, and then cut through the mountains eastward to Las Vegas, the hardscrabble frontier town south of Fort Union. From there they had hoped to follow the Pecos River into Texas. They discovered too late that Union soldiers were already in the area, scouting for Kiowas. The soldiers ambushed the miners in early November. After determining that they were Confederates, the Coloradans took the Green Russell party prisoner and started with them toward Fort Union.[20]

For the next few months, the captive miners, the Coloradans, and three hundred army regulars hunkered down at Fort Union together, as snow squalls blanketed the area with deep drifts. Once again the rumor circulated. John Baylor was amassing six thousand men in western Texas for another invasion of New Mexico. Once again the rumor died. None of the Union Army's scouts had found any Texans along the waterways and routes into Texas, and none of the wagon train drivers heading into Fort Union on the Santa Fe Trail had seen anything suspicious along those lines.[21]

By the end of December 1862, James Carleton had decided that keeping so many soldiers garrisoned at Fort Union and feeding them through an inactive winter was not the best course of action. He had been looking for another reason to send Dodd's Independents out of New Mexico, and so he ordered them to report to Fort Lyon in southern Colorado Territory. There, the troublemakers would fall under the command of the Department of Missouri. Perhaps its commander could find a way to control them.[22]

———

Around Christmas 1862, one year after he had begun his march to war in New Mexico, Alonzo Ickis packed up his belongings and began to make his way to Colorado. He did not know what 1863 would bring. Maybe Dodd's Independents would fight the Plains Indians that had been attacking trains along the Santa Fe Trail. Maybe they would be sent even farther east over the rolling prairies toward the Mississippi River. Ickis had been in the mountains and the high deserts of Colorado and New Mexico for so long, it would feel strange to be back in the green, rolling hills and the swampy sloughs of the Midwest. What the war would look like there, he could not tell. At least he would be there with his fellow Colorado miners. Dodd's Independents had helped to defend New Mexico Territory and keep the West in Union hands. They would stick together until the end.

PART THREE

Land of Suffering

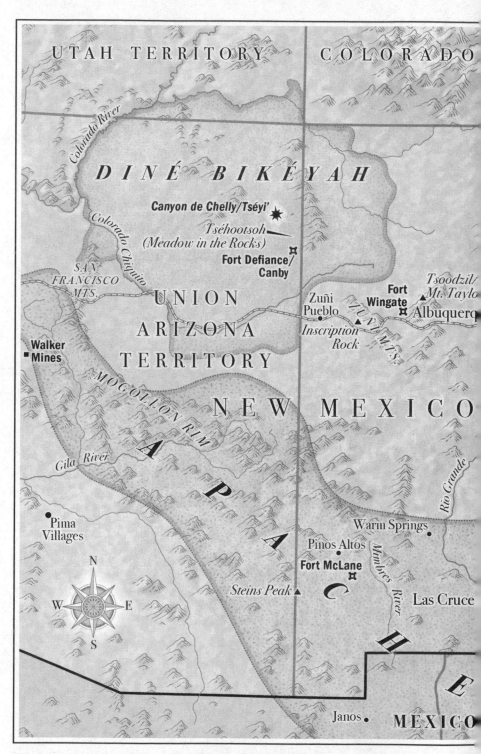

The Southwestern Theater, Summer 1862–Summer 1868

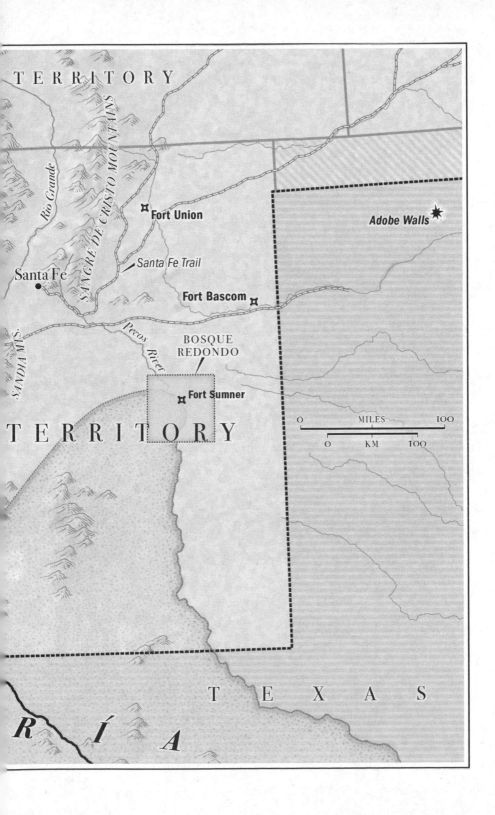

TERRITORY

Rio Grande

SANGRE DE CRISTO MOUNTAINS

¤ **Fort Union**

Santa Fe Trail

Santa Fe •

SANDIA MTS.

Pecos River

Fort Bascom ¤

BOSQUE
REDONDO

¤ **Fort Sumner**

Adobe Walls ✸

TERRITORY

O	MILES	100
O	KM	100

T E X A S

R Í A

16

Mangas Coloradas

After Mangas Coloradas was injured during the Battle of Apache Pass, his men took him to the Mexican town of Janos.[1] Founded as a mission by Franciscan priests, Janos was one of Mexico's northernmost presidios, a walled garrison of soldiers surrounded by farms and ranches. Thriving fields of grain and vegetables lined the *acequia madre* pulling water from the Rio de Janos, and cattle and horses grazed in the lands beyond. Janos was a center of trade in northern Mexico. Several roads spiraled out of town, westward toward Sonora, northeast toward El Paso, and southward to the larger cities of central Mexico. Janeros called the road moving due north the Chiricahua Trail, for Apaches had been using it to raid and trade and make war on Janos since the seventeenth century.[2]

When the Chiricahuas appeared in mid-July 1862 with their injured war chief barely keeping his seat on his horse, the Janeros were not surprised to see him. They knew Mangas Coloradas well. Sometimes he swept into Janos just as the sun was rising, gathering up horses from the corral and galloping off before the townspeople could muster a militia to follow. Other times he descended upon Janos in a fury, not raiding but killing in revenge for an act of violence perpetrated by the townspeople or other northern Mexicans. Often Mangas came with plunder to trade: cloth, cattle, horses, and Mexican slaves. For these he almost always wanted ammunition in exchange, a vital resource in the borderlands. Sometimes, after extended periods of warfare and raiding, Mangas and his Chiricahuas made peace treaties with the Janeros, and received rations from the Mexican Army garrison posted there. This was the first time, however, that Mangas Coloradas had come seeking medical attention.[3]

Mangas's men spoke to several townspeople before finding the doctor, a "white Medicine Man skilled in healing wounds." They were not sure if they could trust him, but they had no choice.

"If you kill Mangas Coloradas," they warned the doctor, "we will kill every person in the village." With shaky hands, the physician was able to extract the bullet. He did what he could to prevent infection around the wound, and bandaged Mangas up.[4]

The Chiricahuas stayed in Janos for several weeks as Mangas recovered. Then they heard about northern Mexican militias gathering in the mountains and desert grasslands around Janos. The raids of several Apache bands in the area had provoked their ire, and even though Mangas's Chiricahuas were not directly responsible for these recent attacks, the militias would fight any Apaches they found in their path. Mangas Coloradas was healing and could lead his men into another battle, but their small band would be outnumbered. The war chief had stayed alive as long as he had by avoiding such situations. In mid-August 1862, Mangas and his men made their way back north of the border.[5]

———

By the fall, Mangas Coloradas had returned to his stronghold in the Mogollon Mountains. In his absence, the Americans had established a significant presence in Apachería. There was a company of soldiers camped around Apache Spring, making preparations to build a fort. James Carleton had sent soldiers to reoccupy forts near Tucson, and to mining towns across the region to offer military protection to their residents. The Chiricahuas had been wrong to think that the white man's war might weaken the American Army. Instead, after a brief withdrawal from Apachería, Union soldiers had returned in force, and now they were considerably stronger foes.

Mangas Coloradas had always been a pragmatist when it came to warfare and diplomacy. He attacked his enemies when he had advantages of position and number. When the odds were not in the Chiricahuas' favor, he brokered peace. Back in the Mogollons and still recovering from his wound, Mangas decided that for the moment, his people could not mount a successful campaign against the Americans. Winter was coming on, and he wanted to plant some fields in the mountain valleys of his stronghold before the snows came.

In September 1862, Mangas Coloradas sent a message to James Carleton. He wanted the new commander of the American Army in New Mexico to know that he was back in Apachería. The Chiricahuas' attacks on civilians, armies, and wagon trains along the Butterfield road over the past two years, Mangas argued, had been provoked. The Americans had come to Apachería and "attacked & killed many of his people." The Chiricahuas had fought back in self-defense, trying to retain control of their land. Now he wished to return to his former pursuits, Mangas assured Carleton, and was "anxious for peace."[6]

James Carleton read Mangas Coloradas's message, and refused his request to talk. When Carleton had come through Apache Pass over the summer, he had seen the graves of Lieutenant Wheeling and Chávez and several 1st California soldiers and was incensed. He did not trust Mangas's word, and did not believe that the Chiricahuas would cease their raiding or their attacks on the U.S. Army even after a peace treaty. Carleton was in the midst of planning his campaign against the Mescaleros and would soon turn west toward Apachería. There, his strategy would be the same: make war first, force a surrender, and then remove the survivors to a reservation. He would make no treaties with the Chiricahuas.[7]

When Mangas Coloradas received word of Carleton's refusal to make peace, he was disappointed but not discouraged. Perhaps he did not need to negotiate with the Union Army but could come to an agreement with Americans living within his stronghold. And so he turned to the miners of Pinos Altos, a town that was thriving again now that the California Column had arrived and its soldiers had reoccupied nearby Fort McLane. Mangas viewed Pinos Altos as he did Janos. Sometimes the Chiricahuas warred with the town's inhabitants. Other times they raided their stock or wagon trains. Sometimes they made peace with them. It was a complicated, symbiotic relationship, one that was always subject to change.

In November 1862, Mangas appeared on the outskirts of Pinos Altos and sent a messenger with his request to negotiate a peace. The memory of the Chiricahuas' attack on the town the previous year was still vivid for some residents, and they were nervous. Many of the recent arrivals in Pinos Altos, however, had no experience with Mangas Coloradas, and they wanted to keep it that way. If the Chiricahuas would let them mine their claims without fear of attack, perhaps it was worth talking about. A group of miners, along with a handful of 1st California soldiers who had just arrived in town, gathered and set out on the path up the hillside, to see what terms Mangas Coloradas wanted to offer. That they took matters into their own hands was not unusual in 1860s New Mexico. Towns and forts were so far apart in the southwestern desert that civilians and military personnel often acted on their own authority, without consulting government officials or superior officers.

One member of the group was a man named Jack Swilling, a former Confederate who had switched sides after Henry Sibley's retreat and had been working as a Union express rider until a few weeks before. Swilling had drifted into Pinos Altos then, convinced that there was still enough gold in the hills above the town to make mining worthwhile.[8] Like his fellow miners, Swilling was prepared to make an agreement with Mangas Coloradas, if it meant the Chiricahuas would let them return to their prospecting.[9]

When the Pinos Altos group approached Mangas's camp, the chief came forward and made signs of peace. Then he told them, in Spanish, that he wanted to return to the Mogollons and live out the rest of his days looking after his grandchildren. He would agree to trade at Pinos Altos but not raid the mines if they would agree not to attack Chiricahua camps. The miners conferred with the soldiers. They told Mangas that if all of the war chiefs of the Chihenne and Bedonkohe bands came to Pinos Altos to sign a peace agreement, then they would agree. What was more, the California soldiers suggested, "we will issue to you, from the Government, blankets, flour, provisions, beef, and all manner of supplies."[10]

Mangas agreed, and promised to return to Pinos Altos in a few months with as many of his war leaders as he could convince to make peace. He and his men galloped out of the town and down to the Butterfield road, and then turned west. A few days later, as they neared the jutting form of Steins Peak, they saw the winter camp of Geronimo, who had fought with Cochise and Mangas Coloradas at Cut the Tent in 1861 and at Apache Pass in 1862. Mangas, as the chief of both the Chihennes and the Bedonkohes, had often sent Geronimo to other bands of Chiricahuas as an emissary, to convince them to join in war parties. After Mangas had been injured at Apache Pass, Geronimo became the recognized war leader of the Bedonkohes. Mangas needed to convince him that peace, not war, was in their future.[11]

Mangas Coloradas called Geronimo's people into council and told them what he wanted to do. The miners and soldiers at Pinos Altos had promised rations, he said, and if the Bedonkohes came with him, they could claim blankets and food, and then return to their hunting grounds, able to feed their families throughout the winter. It was always a hard season for the Chiricahuas, and the sudden presence of so many American soldiers along the Butterfield road and at Apache Pass suggested that they might not be able to move as freely in pursuit of game and plunder as they had in previous winters. Some of the Bedonkohes were amenable, but Geronimo was astonished.

"I do not believe that the people at [Pinos Altos] will do as they say," he told Mangas. "Therefore I oppose the plan."[12]

Geronimo had good reason to distrust the Americans. The treachery of the soldiers at Cut the Tent had "angered the Indians and revived memories of other wrongs." He also viewed peace treaties as opportunities for the Chiricahuas' enemies—Mexicans and Americans—to lure his people into a sense of security, and then attack. This had happened to Geronimo in 1851, when the people of Janos had proposed peace, the Bedonkohes had accepted, and the two communities had celebrated together in town. When Geronimo returned to his band's camp in the fields that surrounded Janos, he had found the bodies of his mother, his wife, and his three young children scattered across the ground. That moment had given Geronimo his impetus for war. Every battle he had fought in since then was an act of revenge for that betrayal.[13]

Mangas Coloradas recognized Geronimo's objections, and the long history of both Mexican and American duplicity. He knew the dangers, but he also believed that the Americans, now that their battles against the Texans had ended, would want peace along the Butterfield road. After the Battle of Apache Pass, Mangas had understood that the American Army was intent on invading Apachería from all directions. The Chiricahuas might soon be surrounded and would lose any advantage they might have in negotiations. He explained to Geronimo that this might be the best time to secure a permanent peace.[14] His arguments were persuasive.

"It was ultimately decided," Geronimo remembered, "that with part of the tribe Mangus-Colorado [sic] should return to [Pinos Altos] and receive an issue of rations and supplies." Geronimo would not go, however. He would wait with the other half of his band at Steins Peak, and Mangas would send him word.

"If the white men would keep the treaty faithfully," Geronimo promised, "the remainder of the tribe would join him and we would make our permanent home at [Pinos Altos]."

Geronimo gave Mangas's men guns and ammunition, "so that in case of treachery they would be prepared for any surprise."

As Mangas Coloradas disappeared into the eastern horizon, Geronimo was struck by how contented he and his people seemed. They believed "they had found white men who would be kind to them, and with whom they could live in peace and plenty."[15]

From Geronimo's camp, Mangas's party rode to the Mimbres River and turned north to Ojos Calientes ("Warm Springs"). Here, Chihennes led by Victorio, an experienced war leader, had settled into their winter villages. Victorio was short and muscular, soft-spoken in councils, and fierce on the battlefield.[16] Like Geronimo, he was skeptical of the Americans' intentions. And like Geronimo, he ultimately relented. But Victorio insisted that if Mangas Coloradas was determined to return to Pinos Altos, he and several of his warriors would accompany him as bodyguards. Mangas agreed.

By early January 1863, more than one hundred Chiricahuas gathered in the mountains around Pinos Altos: Mangas's band of men, women, and children; half of Geronimo's Bedonkohes; and Victorio and his Warm Springs warriors. In his talk with the miners back in November, Mangas had agreed that he would stay in this camp above the town and wait for a signal from Jack Swilling. Then he and Victorio, along with a few others, would come into Pinos Altos to negotiate for peace.[17]

––––––––––

At sunrise on January 17, 1863, a white flag appeared above Pinos Altos. It was Jack Swilling's signal. Mangas Coloradas sent out scouts to survey the town and look for any suspicious activity. They returned to the Chiricahua camp and reported that nothing seemed amiss. The next day, shortly before noon, Mangas Coloradas began walking to Pinos Altos on an old mountain trail. He had over a dozen warriors with him, including one of his sons, Sethmooda, and Victorio. As they approached the outskirts of town, Jack Swilling emerged from the chaparral, with several other miners.

Then, abruptly, Swilling let out a yell.

Mangas paused. What did Swilling mean by this shout? Was he sending another signal, to the American soldiers this time? Nothing stirred in Pinos Altos, however, and so Mangas Coloradas continued along the trail toward Swilling. The two men came close enough to one another to shake hands, and as they did, Swilling reached up and laid his hand on the chief's shoulder. At this, thirty men rose up from behind scrub brush and leveled their guns at Mangas Coloradas.

The chief flinched. As a sign of good faith his party had not brought their bows or guns.

"*Resistencia significa la destrucción de toda su grupo,*" Swilling told Mangas. Resistance means the destruction of your entire party.

It had not taken much convincing for Swilling to betray the Chirica-hua chief. In the months since his parlay with Mangas Coloradas, he had joined up with a group of prospectors under the leadership of a western adventurer named Joseph Reddeford Walker. Swilling told them about his upcoming peace treaty with Mangas, and Walker suggested an alternative plan: they would capture the Chiricahua chief and use him as ransom to ensure that they would not be harmed as they prospected in Apachería over the winter of 1863. Swilling agreed, and the adventurers invited the 1st California Volunteers to take part in the scheme. Their captain, Ed-mund Shirland, accepted.[18] These were the men who were now pointing their weapons at the Chiricahua chief.

When Mangas Coloradas saw what the situation was, he turned and waved off Victorio, Sethmooda, and the rest of his men, urging them to return to the Chiricahua camp.

"Beware," he said to them, "we are not fooling with Mexicans now."

They objected, but Mangas Coloradas instructed them to gather the women and children, and ride as quickly as possible to Victorio's encamp-ment at Warm Springs.

"Tell my people," he said, "to look for me when they see me."

Then he turned and followed Jack Swilling into Pinos Altos.[19]

———

The miners and soldiers gave Mangas Coloradas a wild sorrel pony, and the party rode for Fort McLane, the reoccupied fort that sat between Pinos Altos and the Butterfield route. Mangas rode in stony silence, his mouth a grim line across his face. The men in Swilling's party snuck looks at the legendary Chiricahua along the way.

"Altogether he presented quite a model of physical manhood," one of them noted. "If Mangas ever had any or many peers amongst his own people in personal appearance, I never saw them."[20]

They rested briefly overnight and then continued on. On January 18, 1863, they arrived at Fort McLane. The camp was full of Union soldiers. Joseph Rodman West and several companies of California troops had just arrived, marching in from Mesilla. James Carleton had sent orders to West to begin a widespread campaign against the Chiricahuas in southern New Mexico and Arizona, giving him the same instructions he had relayed to Kit Carson before his war against the Mescaleros.

"The campaign to be made by this expedition must be a vigorous one," Carleton wrote, "and the punishment of that band of murderers must be thorough and sharp." Like the Mescaleros, "the men are to be slain wherever and whenever they can be found, and the women and children may be taken as prisoners."[21]

Fort McLane would be the headquarters of West's campaign. From there, small patrols would head out into the strongholds of Mangas Coloradas, Cochise, Victorio, and Geronimo. Joseph West was confident of the campaign's success.

"With guides and a good force," he wrote to Carleton, "a severe castigation could most likely be inflicted upon the Indians."[22]

———

Jack Swilling knew nothing about James Carleton's and Joseph West's larger plans. He was acting strictly out of self-interest. He rode at the head of the party, looking forward to presenting Mangas Coloradas to Walker, the leader of the adventurers, and setting out for the gold country. Captain Shirland, however, had other ideas. When they arrived at Fort McLane, he went directly to Joseph West's headquarters and reported that he, not Swilling, had captured the legendary Chiricahua chief.[23] A disappointed Swilling was forced to turn his captive over to the Union Army. As the party dismounted, General West came out to meet them.

Mangas Coloradas towered over West, a short man with a voluminous beard and dark, abundant curls on either side of his head. The general summoned a translator, and then began to pepper Mangas with questions. He wanted to know if the Chiricahuas were responsible for an attack on a Union wagon train the previous October, in which one of West's men was killed. Mangas Coloradas protested his innocence, but West did not believe him. He wanted to know what the chief really wanted with these overtures of peace he was making to the miners at Pinos Altos.

Mangas Coloradas, seeing that West was enraged and thus unlikely to be persuaded by anything he said, refused to answer. His silence made West apoplectic. The general continued to harangue Mangas Coloradas, ultimately informing him that there would be no peace treaty under any circumstances. West decided, however, to incarcerate Mangas Coloradas rather than kill him on the spot.

"The remainder of your days," West said, "will be spent as a prisoner in the hands of the U.S. authorities. Your family will be permitted to join you, and you will be well treated." This would ensure that Mangas Coloradas "never should have it again in his power to perpetrate such atrocities."

ALONZO FERDINAND ICKIS, C. 1864

From Ickis, Alonzo Ferdinand. *Bloody Trails along the Rio Grande: The Diary of Alonzo Ferdinand Ickis*. Edited by Nolie Mumey. Denver, Colo.: Old West Publishing Company, 1958. Permission courtesy of Linda Lebsack Books, Denver, Colorado. Image courtesy of Harvard University Libraries.

BRIGADIER GENERAL JOHN ROBERT BAYLOR
PC1000, Tucson Main Photo Collection, Portraits: Baylor, John Robert,
Negative #25679. Courtesy of Arizona Historical Society Library and Archives.

LOUISA HAWKINS CANBY, C. 1864
Mary Louise Speed Photograph Collection, 990PC49x.13.
Courtesy of Filson Historical Society.

JAMES CARLETON, 1866
Courtesy of Palace of the Governors Photo Archives (NMHM/DCA),
Negative No. 22938.

COLONEL KIT CARSON, 1864
Courtesy of Palace of the Governors Photo Archives (NMHM/DCA),
Negative No. 007151.

JOHN A. CLARK, NEW MEXICO SURVEYOR GENERAL, C. 1860S
Courtesy of Palace of the Governors Photo Archives (NMHM/DCA),
Negative No. 047652.

WILLIAM LOTT DAVIDSON, C. 1880s
From Daniell, Lewis E. *Personnel of the Texas State Government,*
with Sketches of Distinguished Texans. Austin, Tex.: Smith, Hicks & Jones, State Printers,
1889, p. 422–23, di_11328. Courtesy of Dolph Briscoe Center for
American History at the University of Texas at Austin.

"Juanita, a Navaho Woman," by Charles Milton Bell, 1874

Courtesy of National Anthropological Archives, Smithsonian Institution,
Photo Lot 90-1, number 211.

However, any attempt to escape from Union Army custody, West warned the Chiricahua chief, meant that "his life would be immediately forfeit."[24]

West ordered his soldiers to give Mangas a blanket and to put him under guard in one of the ruined fort buildings. The soldiers pushed the chief into a small room with no roof and set up a guard post outside the open doorway. The weather had been pleasant that day, but darkness fell early and the temperatures plummeted. The Chiricahua chief untied the strings around his knee-length deerskin moccasins, wrapped the blanket around his long body, and tried to sleep.

The camp eventually grew quiet as the soldiers bedded down in their tents. Mangas could hear some intermittent sounds. The muffled footsteps of a sentry on duty. The crackling of a fire that soldiers had built out of logs from one of the fort's abandoned buildings. Low laughter from Mangas's guards.

Suddenly, several rocks hit the packed dirt where Mangas lay. They were small chunks of adobe, lobbed by the guards in an attempt to hit him. He did not move. There was a pause. Then a stinging sensation and searing pain, along his legs and feet. The soldiers had fixed bayonets on the ends of their guns and heated them in the fire. They then extended them through the doorway and touched the hot metal to his skin. Mangas drew his legs up, pulling the blanket to cover his feet so that they could not get at him. Again, the sting and the pain. Mangas was outraged. He raised himself on his elbow and shouted out into the dark.

"No soy un niño con quien jugar!" I am no child to be playing with.

There were flashes of light and the deafening sound of two guns discharging. Mangas Coloradas fell onto his side, several bullets lodged in his chest, others passing through, "marking the frozen ground beyond . . . for a distance of five or six feet with an unbroken line of blood." Someone stepped into the room, pressed a pistol against the back of his head, and fired.[25]

The gunshots awakened most of the soldiers, who stirred from their bedrolls. An officer went to Mangas Coloradas's cell and then made his way through the camp to Joseph West's tent.

When granted admission, the officer informed West that Mangas Coloradas had been shot while attempting to escape.

"Is he dead?" West asked.

"He is, sir," he replied.

"Very well, Sergeant, then let his guard go to sleep."[26]

The next morning, the weather was extremely cold and a thin layer of frost covered Mangas Coloradas's body. Walker's adventurers and the California soldiers came to gawk, and to search the body for souvenirs.[27] They left him where he lay until noon. General West sent five soldiers in to shift the chief's body onto a blanket and carry it out beyond the boundary of the camp to a gully. They tipped the blanket and watched the body tumble into the declivity, and then heaved a few shovelfuls of dirt on top of it.

For the next few days the camp buzzed with the rebuilding of Fort McLane's structures and the departure of soldiers in pursuit of Mangas Coloradas's and Victorio's bands. One company returned to report that they had attacked a small group of Chiricahuas who had lingered outside Pinos Altos, waiting to hear what had happened to their chief. Among the Apaches killed was Sethmooda, Mangas Coloradas's son. One of the chief's wives was also wounded. Captain Shirland came back to report his success in a fight against Victorio and his warriors near Warm Springs. He had killed nine Chiricahuas and brought back thirty-four mules and horses. He and his men rode into Fort McLane with scalps dangling from their saddles.[28]

Fort McLane's physician, D. B. Sturgeon, was busy with other matters in the days after Mangas Coloradas's death. When he was able to secure some time and several soldiers to help him, he followed the path out to the chief's grave beyond the fort. They exhumed Mangas's body and brought it back to camp. In his tent, Sturgeon severed Mangas's head and placed it in a large black kettle filled with boiling water. When nothing but the skull was left, Sturgeon carefully removed it and placed it in a trunk in his tent. Over the next few months Union soldiers came in to see the skull. It was so large and well formed, one of them proclaimed, that "it was the wonder of all who saw it."[29]

Geronimo waited at Steins Peak until February 1863, looking every day for Mangas's runners, carrying word that his peace treaty had been agreed to and that the Bedonkohes should come to Pinos Altos for rations. No one came. Eventually Geronimo heard that Mangas Coloradas "had been treacherously captured and slain." He packed up his camp and moved southward toward Mexico.[30]

It was not until later that he and his people found out about the beheading. To the Chiricahuas, this was worse than death, for Apaches believed that they passed through eternity with their physical bodies. The betrayal of Mangas Coloradas, and the murder and subsequent mutilation of his body, was to Geronimo "perhaps the greatest wrong ever done" to the Chiricahuas in their history with the Americans. The Union Army may have thought that by killing Mangas, they had won the war against his people, and that the Chiricahuas would finally submit. They also probably assumed that the large number of soldiers that the Civil War had brought to New Mexico and Arizona would intimidate the Chiricahuas into surrendering to the Union Army. Instead, during the spring and summer of 1863, the Chiricahuas began a long-term campaign of their own, a war of revenge for the death of Mangas Coloradas.[31]

17

==

Clark

Four months after Mangas Coloradas's death, New Mexico surveyor general John Clark stumbled out of the foothills of the Mogollon Mountains and into a lush valley filled with grama grass. This land had been part of Mangas's stronghold for more than forty years. Now white tents were scattered on the top of a bluff at a big bend in the Gila River. Union soldiers had established this U.S. military post, called Fort West after Joseph Rodman West, as a depot for the Union Army's campaign against the Chiricahuas.

Clark had left Fort Craig two weeks before with a small group of Union soldiers. He was reconnoitering the area as part of his survey of New Mexico Territory, trying to find land that the federal government could sell, mine, or distribute under the Homestead Act. The trip had been both harrowing and unproductive. The trail they had followed seemed to double back on itself every mile, and the team had gotten lost more than once.[1] Along the way they had found only narrow valleys in what appeared to be a series of endless canyons.

"The result of my expedition may be summed up in a few words," he wrote later to James Edmunds, the commissioner of the General Land Office. "I found no arable land West of the Rio Grande."[2]

After returning to New Mexico from his furlough, Clark had proposed a series of expeditions like this one, "for the purpose of ascertaining what proportion of land there may be, suitable for settlement and cultivation in those districts."[3] Edmunds had agreed, eager to know more about New Mexico's and Arizona's agricultural and mineral prospects. In March 1863, Clark had set out on his first official expedition, joining James Carleton on a trip down the Pecos River to the new Indian reservation at Bosque Redondo in central New Mexico. He had left for the trip through the Mogollons soon after he returned from the Bosque. After each journey, Edmunds expected Clark to make as complete a report of the exploration as possible, which would be distributed for the benefit of the Union Congress and the Lincoln administration.

Although the federal government was focused on waging war against the Confederates in the East during the spring of 1863, they were still invested in retaining control over the West. Now that the Union Army had turned back the Texan invasion, the conquest and Anglo settlement of the region was once again possible.

In December 1862, in his Second Annual Address to Congress, Abraham Lincoln had reaffirmed the Republican administration's belief in the prospects of the western states and territories, and their importance to the Union. Before they could develop this region, however, the government had to know more about its lands and resources. Therefore the President had advocated "a scientific exploration of the mineral regions in those Territories with a view to the publication of its results at home and in foreign countries—results which cannot fail to be auspicious."

Once the findings of these explorations had been disseminated, the government could act.

"The immense mineral resources of some of those Territories," Lincoln had written, "ought to be developed as rapidly as possible. Every step in that direction would have a tendency to improve the revenues of the Government and diminish the burdens of the people."

By now it was clear that the Civil War was not going to end anytime soon, and the federal debt was skyrocketing. The Union Congress had already passed two Revenue Acts, levying income taxes on northern citizens and increasing excise taxes on a variety of items including playing cards, telegrams, leather, and iron. If the lands of New Mexico and Arizona were arable, and its mountains threaded with rich veins of gold, silver, or copper, land sales and mineral extraction could help pay for the war and ease the tax burden on northerners. This kind of development would not be cheap but Lincoln believed it was worth the investment.

"It is worthy of your serious consideration," the President urged Congress, "whether some extraordinary measures to promote that end cannot be adopted."[4]

John Clark was more than happy to take up the mantle of explorer and to work toward the government's and the Republican Party's aims in this regard. From the moment he had arrived in New Mexico Territory, he had taken to its climate and geography. Although he was almost fifty years old, he was a robust man, taking daily walks up into the mountains around Santa Fe. On these rambles, he took pleasure in observing New Mexico's landscapes and assessing their potential. This new role, as surveyor ex-plorer, was one to which Clark was uniquely suited.

While the trip to the Mogollons was disappointing from a land sur-vey perspective, Clark did make some intriguing discoveries regarding the Southwest's mineral prospects. He spent several days at Fort West, meeting many of the officers and enlisted men. Most were California miners. Some had prospected along the route of their long march from Los Angeles. They told Clark that "the whole District from the mountains near Fort Stanton to the Rio Colorado [to] the West"—most of southern New Mexico and the new Union Territory of Arizona, organized in Feb-ruary 1863 with the borders we know today—"is exceedingly rich in the precious metals, & in copper, lead & iron. In some parts of it, there is an abundance greater."[5]

The soldiers also said that after the death of Mangas Coloradas, Jo-seph Reddeford Walker's group of gold-seeking adventurers had left Fort McLane to explore the mountains north of Tucson and Pima Villages. If Walker's group found veins worth working, Clark knew, the government would need to make the mines accessible to Anglo migrants, building roads wide enough for wagons, establishing hay camps and way stations to keep the wagon trains supplied, and constructing forts garrisoned with soldiers to protect emigrants and miners. Before that work could be done, however, the Union Army needed to seize control of New Mexico and Arizona from Apaches and Navajos. They had to exterminate or remove these peoples, Clark believed, if the region was to be peaceful and pro-ductive. The death of Mangas Coloradas and Joseph West's subsequent pursuit of the Chiricahuas were the first steps in this fight.

"As soon as the Indians are [dispossessed] of those sections upon & near the water courses," Clark wrote to Edmunds, "I look for magnificent results."[6]

━━━━━━

Clark had been back from the Mogollon expedition for two months when a letter arrived in Santa Fe, detailing the discoveries that Joseph Redde-ford Walker's adventurers had made in Arizona Territory. The letter gave a "full account of flattering prospects for the future of our New Eldorado," arguing that the mountains north of Pima Villages were much richer in minerals than the state of California.[7] As proof, the author of the letter enclosed specimens of gold from the new mines. Clark was delighted.

"I have no doubt of the wealth of that country in minerals," he wrote in his diary, "and I trust it is now in a fair way to be developed."[8]

It did not take long for gold fever to take possession of Santa Fe's residents. A few days after the letter arrived, Clark visited James Carleton at his headquarters and the two men spent "a half hour discussing the question of protection to mines, &c." Clark was invited to attend a meeting of prominent men in Santa Fe "who have an interest in the new discoveries of gold & silver." They were military men (including Carleton), government officials, and businessmen. Each man would contribute money and whatever other support he could toward the exploration and development of the mines in Arizona. They had the power of arms, laws, and money behind them, an ideal consortium for backing exploratory ventures into Arizona's goldfields. They called themselves the Santa Fe Mining Company.

The group discussed the reports from the Walker mines and agreed that the details were tantalizing, but probably untrustworthy. As even most miners acknowledged, "since gold was first discovered in the Rocky Mountains, men will lie about their exploits upon second-hand information." Several of the men proposed to send an agent to Arizona, "to make an examination & report." They all agreed that the man to go was John Clark. He would act as an agent for the company in Arizona, while still reporting to the government as surveyor general. If possible, he would appoint a man already working at the mines to stake claims and provide status reports.[9] Once this plan had been decided upon, it came together in a matter of days. James Carleton provided Clark with an army escort of twenty 1st California soldiers with mining expertise, to accompany him on the journey.

"When you arrive at the new diggings," Carleton instructed the captain of the escort, "I want each of your men to prospect and wash, and I want you to report the exact time they severally work, and the amount of gold each one obtains in return for his labor during that time."

The soldiers' statistics, combined with Clark's assessments, would accurately represent the Arizona goldfields. If they found that the mines were rich, "there will, on your return, be a revolution in matters here which no man now can ever dream of."[10]

By June 18, 1863, all of the arrangements for the expedition had been made. Before they left, Clark wrote to Commissioner Edmunds, making the case for this latest foray into Arizona mining country. The intelligence received from the Walker party, he wrote, "is deemed of such importance by the Governor of this Territory, and other Federal officers, that, in order that the people abroad may not be deceived and that the Government may have the earliest and most authentic information concerning these discoveries, I have been advised and strongly urged to visit the scene of the reported discoveries [and] ascertain the facts concerning them."

Clark would be gone for two months, he told Edmunds, during which time he would make a thorough examination of the country and report his findings "at the earliest day practicable." Such a journey was an important one, for the Southwest and for the Union.

"The development of the mineral resources of our country and an increased production at this time of the precious metals," Clark wrote, "is a matter of national interest."[11]

In mid-August 1863, Clark's party encamped on a grassy prairie in the San Francisco Mountains of northern Arizona. There had been delays of all kinds at the outset of the expedition, and the party had been forced to change their route. Clark had initially planned to travel to Arizona along the Butterfield road from Mesilla to Tucson, then on to Pima Villages and northwest to the mountains. But since the death of Mangas Coloradas, the Chiricahuas had been attacking civilian and wagon trains, towns, and forts in southern New Mexico and Arizona. Joseph West's campaign had made no headway against them. Clark's group had to pivot and head out over a more northerly road that took them from Albuquerque westward through Navajo country.[12]

The expedition had traveled quickly. Most of the men in the party rode horses or mules, and they had only three wagons with them. They stopped briefly to gather supplies at Fort Wingate and at Zuñi Pueblo.[13] The soldiers in Clark's escort heard from the Zuñis that the Navajos were in the area and so had been alert, scanning the landscape for signs of Navajo raiders out en masse, and posting a close watch on their horses and mules at night. There had been no attacks, however.

In the second week of August, they had arrived in the San Francisco Mountains, north of where the Walker mines were reported to be. Clark noticed granite outcroppings in large quantities, definitive signs that they had entered the mineral region. Soldiers fanned out from the prairie camp into the mountains to find Joseph Reddeford Walker and his party of miners. On August 15, one of the soldiers returned to report that he had found them, digging holes in the creekbeds just over the next ridge.[14]

Clark and the captain of the army escort started for the Walker mines. After climbing up and down an exceedingly rough trail over the ridge and through a valley, they found A. C. Benedict, the miner who had written the letter that caused such a sensation in Santa Fe. Benedict told them that Walker's men had moved to the east, and that he would take them there. Along the way, the miner described all the discoveries that had been made along several creeks in the region since June. There were already more than one thousand miners in the area, establishing claims and panning in every ravine. Clark arrived at Walker's camp and despite his fatigue, he was jubilant.[15]

"Your letters . . . found their way to New Mexico," Clark told the miners. He informed them that his group had been sent by General James Carleton to search for them.

"[We have] been out some months," he added, "and found [you] by accident at last."[16]

Clark spent the next few days with Walker's men. There was not enough running water in the creeks and rivers to use a sluice to separate the gold from the dirt, so most of the miners were using rockers. He watched them shovel loads of soil into these high-sided wooden boxes and then move them back and forth on their curved legs. The dirt fell through a series of sieves, trapping pebbles on top and the dust below. Some of the pebbles "had color": flecks or veins of gold. The miners pocketed these and tossed the rest back on the ground. Clark tried his hand at the rocking and with the miners' permission, dug around in the gravel near the creekbeds, looking for gold nuggets. He found several, and some of the miners gave him other small specimens.[17] A few of the claims were "of course paying better than others & some paying very largely."[18]

On August 22, Clark left on a short trip into the mountains with Walker himself and eleven Union soldiers. Over the next few days they panned in every stream they came upon, and found color in each one. Many of the ridges were "full of quartz ledges, some of them probably silver bearing & some of them with gold," and others had granite ledges "traceable upon the surface for great distances . . . giving good indication of gold & silver & some of copper." Clark examined one of A. C. Benedict's silver lodes and took several specimens to carry home.[19]

The next week, Clark's group headed to the Antelope diggings, a series of ravines at the base of a high mountain nearby. Here Clark found a pack train from Pima Villages, carrying newspapers from California. War news dominated their pages. After months of lobbing cannonballs into the city of Vicksburg, Mississippi, the Union Army there under Ulysses S. Grant had finally forced it to surrender. Port Hudson had also fallen, which meant that now the entire length of the Mississippi River was in Union hands. The Confederates, after their win at Chancellorsville, Virginia, in May, had marched north under Robert E. Lee, crossing into Pennsylvania. A new Union Army general, George Meade, had stopped this invasion of the North at Gettysburg, and pushed the Confederates back into Virginia.

All of this news was "very gratifying to me and all lovers of our country," Clark crowed.[20]

He tucked the newspapers away in his saddlebags and turned toward a steep trail that led to the summit of Antelope Mountain. At the top Clark found a large depression in the smooth rock and a group of men crouched down in the dirt, working over the ground with butcher knives. Even with these rudimentary tools, they had uncovered gold nuggets of all shapes and sizes. How the gold had come to be there on the mountaintop was unknown. The miners' best guess was that the quartz vein had been pushed up near the surface, which had then been eroded through exposure to the weather.

Clark walked around and was ultimately introduced to the leader of the mining company on Antelope Mountain, who turned out to be none other than Jack Swilling, the betrayer of Mangas Coloradas. The two men talked not of Chiricahuas but of lodes. Swilling told Clark that the Antelope placer had already yielded "20,000 dollars & not half the ground has yet been worked over." He gave Clark a fine specimen of gold for himself and two for General Carleton. Clark observed the miners for a few more hours and then descended the mountain on a steep trail that he thought even a goat would hesitate to use, to the camps below.[21]

Clark returned to Walker's mines with A. C. Benedict, and along the way they discussed the Santa Fe Mining Company's interests. Benedict agreed to act as an agent for the company, locating quartz lodes for its investors over the next several months. By September 1, Clark had seen enough of the country to be convinced of its potential as the next El Dorado. He mounted his mule and, along with the Union Army escort, left the Arizona gold country to make his way back to Santa Fe.[22]

Clark's party made the trip from the mines back to Zuñi Pueblo in less than half the time it had taken them to come out.[23] On September 10, as they reached a creek west of the pueblo, fifty Zuñi warriors emerged out of the piñon-juniper woodland. They were armed and ready for a fight, assuming that John Clark's party were Navajos. The two peoples often fought one another, and had been engaged in a series of raids and reprisals in recent months. After a tense few moments, all parties lowered their weapons.

"We have indeed been most fortunate," Clark sighed with relief, "or rather God has most signally protected & prospered us thus far on our journey & to Him I return most hearty thanks."[24]

The next day Clark's expedition moved on and met an advance guard of Union troops, mounted and on their way west. They were with Kit Carson's army, starting out on their campaign against the Navajos.[25] Carson would be arriving at Zuñi Pueblo in an hour, the soldiers said, if Clark wanted to speak with him.

Clark rode to the pueblo, dismounted, and waited. In a short time, Kit Carson and around four hundred men came into sight. Carson rode up the narrow trail into the pueblo, and he and Clark sat down for a talk. Over the summer, with the Mescaleros subdued and the Chiricahuas elusive, James Carleton had turned his prodigious energy toward organizing another Indian campaign. The Navajos had a long history of raiding Hispano towns and ranches as well as fighting the U.S. Army. These were reasons enough, Carleton believed, to make war upon them. Now that gold had been discovered in Arizona, Carleton had another justification for this new campaign: the road to the Walker mines lay through Navajo country. He needed to remove them from their lands, to make the development of the region (and his own investment in the Santa Fe Mining Company) viable.

Carleton had therefore sent word to Manuelito and the other Navajo headmen that they had until late July 1863 to surrender to Union troops at Fort Wingate. If they did not, "every Navajo that is seen will be considered hostile and treated accordingly ... the door now open will be closed." The Navajos had not surrendered, and so Carleton sent Kit Carson to "prosecute a vigorous war upon the men of this tribe until it is considered at these headquarters that they have been effectually punished for their long-continued atrocities."[26]

Carson had arrived at the site of old Fort Defiance while Clark had been exploring the Walker mines, and used it as a base to launch the Navajo campaign. He had had a few skirmishes with Navajo fighters since then and now he was out on an extended scout, to determine the location of Navajo bands and assess their strength. Clark informed Carson about the favorable conditions along the road to the Arizona mines and Carson was happy to hear it. He had been trying to decide which trail would have the most resources for his men and their animals as they pushed farther west into Navajo country.

The men chatted a bit more about the state of the war in the East. Then John Clark bid Kit Carson farewell, mounted his mule, and rode out of Zuñi Pueblo toward the Rio Grande. When he returned to Santa Fe, the residents of that city would certainly want to know what he had found in his expedition to the Arizona mines. Clark's information would also inform the next step of the Union Army's war for the West: the extermination or removal of the Navajos and the Anglo occupation of their lands.

18

Tséyi'

I t was the middle of July 1863 when the spies Manuelito had positioned on the high mesas around Tséhootsoh informed him that a large group of soldiers were heading for the ruins of old Fort Defiance. The Americans were back, in the heart of Diné Bikéyah.

The Navajos had hoped that the Americans' Civil War had brought an end to *Nahondzod* ("the Fearing Time"), but over the past year there had been signs that their conflict had merely been a lull in this period of intense violence for the Diné. In the summer of 1862, the Navajos' enemies had begun to reappear in the homeland. The Hopis and Utes came from the north and the Zuñis from the south. Hispano raiders reappeared, bent on stealing sheep from Navajo herds and capturing children to sell into slavery. And in October 1862, the Union Army had started building Fort Wingate on the black lava south of Tsoodzil ("Blue Bead"), the sacred mountain to the southeast.[1]

Then soldiers arrived at Fort Defiance and began to rebuild it. Manuelito weighed his options, and decided that it was not the right time to attack. Juanita packed up the family's belongings, and with more than five hundred men, women, and children of their band, they moved up and over the Defiance Plateau to the tablelands beyond. They brought as many sheep as they could herd easily and as much cached grain as they could carry, but they had to abandon their cornfields. Perhaps they would be able to find some piñon trees in this new place and pick the nuts from their sticky-sweet green cones. Otherwise, they would have to rely on small sacks of seeds and dried cactus fruit that Juanita and the other women had already gathered, and the hunting skills of the men, to keep them fed.[2]

A few weeks later, as summer was turning to fall, large dust clouds rose with regularity along the road south of old Fort Defiance: the American Army, led by Kit Carson, was moving through Diné Bikéyah, looking for Navajos to fight. Juanita packed up again, and the family journeyed out to the western edge of the homeland. Here was the Colorado Chiquito, a river large enough for fishing and washing, and abundant caves in the San Francisco Mountains for shelter and concealment. Family groups dispersed across this landscape, maintaining enough distance from one another to provide wood and edible plants for everyone, while remaining close enough to spread the word quickly if any of the enemies should come upon them by surprise.[3]

After John Clark left Zuñi Pueblo, Kit Carson walked through the town's streets and past its large adobe church. The Zuñis were using the sanctuary as a stable, giving their horses some protection from the weather, and from raiders. Following a narrow passage, Carson entered a small plaza. At its center was a pole lodged in the dirt, with fourteen Navajo scalps tied to it.[4]

Carson went to see the governor of the pueblo, who confirmed the Zuñis' enmity toward the Navajos, and their desire to help the Union Army in their campaign. Carson was happy to hear it. The Zuñis had been allies of the Navajos in the past, trade partners with kin ties, and he had not been sure if they would help him. The governor supplied Carson with three men as guides and offered to sell him a considerable quantity of corn to feed his soldiers and their mounts.[5]

The next day, Carson set out with four hundred 1st New Mexico Volunteers and twenty Zuñi warriors. Over the next two weeks, Carson's army marched west, searching for encampments of Navajos to bring to battle. Each day Carson rode out in front with some of his soldiers and the Zuñis, on the alert for tracks of horse or sheep herds, abandoned campsites, and fires whose smoke signaled to other Navajos the presence of the Americans. They found nothing, and continued marching west until they arrived on the banks of the Colorado Chiquito. The Zuñis told Carson that Manuelito's band had come out this way in the previous weeks, but there was no sign of them. After marching eighty-five miles up the waterway, toward the enormous rift in the ground that the Americans would later name the Grand Canyon, Carson decided that "no Indians have been on the River within this distance since last Spring."[6]

Frustrated, Carson ordered most of the 1st New Mexico to march the two hundred miles back to old Fort Defiance (which had been renamed Fort Canby, in honor of the former commander of the department), on the road they had come in on. He took 150 soldiers with him on a more circuitous, northerly route through the Painted Desert, its ridges decorated with red, pink, yellow, and brown ribbons of rock. They passed by the jutting black cones and spires of Hopi country, and then rode toward the Defiance Plateau. Reports said that several Navajo bands regularly planted and hunted in this area. In search of them, Carson urged his men onward. Soon they found a small cluster of hogans, which looked to have been recently abandoned. Carson's men searched the village and piled everything they found in the center: saddles and bridles, a rifle, blankets, baskets, and hides.

"[All of] this I destroyed," Carson reported later to Carleton.[7] The soldiers set fire to the pile and then to the hogans, the smoke billowing up into the air. They were back at Fort Canby two days later.

The Navajo campaign so far, Kit Carson believed, had produced mixed results. His men had not had the opportunity to fight the Navajos, but they had become familiar with the western reaches of the Navajo homeland, and they had destroyed one village. Ruination was part of James Carleton's campaign plan, which he had organized over the summer. Carleton had never faced the Navajos before, but he understood that Navajo culture was decentralized, with multiple bands led by headmen like Manuelito living in *rancherías* spread out all over their territory. They had fast horses, and at the first sign of trouble, they disappeared into the mountains and canyons with their families and their giant herds of sheep.

Carleton concluded that Union troops could never bring enough Navajos to a battlefield to have a definitive fight like Valverde, Apache Canyon, or Glorieta Pass. Instead, Carleton decided, the Union Army of New Mexico would embark on a campaign of "constant hard scouting with now and then a skirmish; the idea being to wear the Indians out by capture of their herds of sheep and ponies . . . the destruction of their fields of corn, beans, pumpkins, etc."[8] Soldiers would be posted around springs and wells, controlling access to water, the most precious resource in the Navajo homeland. This kind of "vigorous warfare," which an increasing number of Union generals were advocating as an effective tactic against the Confederates in the South, would destroy the Navajos' means of subsistence in the West. It would weaken them to the extent that they could no longer survive in their own territory. They would be forced to surrender and give over their lands to the United States to save themselves. Then the Union Army would move all of the Navajos to Bosque Redondo, the reservation that James Carleton had established in central New Mexico. There they would be contained and surveilled, and converted into full-time farmers and Christians. They would no longer raid Anglo and Hispano ranches or towns, and they would not prevent emigrants from making their way to the Arizona mining camps.

Carleton did not invent vigorous warfare as a military strategy. Americans had adapted this form of fighting from indigenous people themselves, and had used it effectively against many other Native communities in the United States since the eighteenth century. In 1830, Andrew Jackson had initiated large-scale removals of Native Americans from their homelands to reservations far from white communities. And the idea that if Native Americans could not be exterminated physically, they should be annihilated culturally and converted into "true Americans," had informed federal Indian policy for years. This three-step method for dealing with the "Indian Problem"—destruction of homelands, removal from them, and incarceration on reservations—was already well established by the time James Carleton began to apply it as part of the Union war effort in New Mexico in 1863.[9]

Kit Carson had no fixed opinion on the matter. On the one hand, he believed that whites had often been the instigators of violence with Native communities in the West. On the other hand, he knew that Chiricahuas and Navajos would continue to resist the Union Army's removal and reservation policies until they were forced, somehow, to capitulate.[10] Carson preferred fighting Indians to burning fields, but he understood the utility of vigorous warfare and he implemented it without mercy as part of his service to the Union.

Carson hoped that the Navajos would see the smoking ruins his soldiers left across their homeland, and that they would understand what this track of devastation meant: that the Americans would come after them whenever and wherever they pleased, and that they would keep coming.[11]

One morning in the fall of 1863, as the leaves began to turn to yellow and orange, Juanita walked with the children through the forests, looking for wild fruit and for seeds to grind into flour for winter cakes.[12] Meanwhile, Manuelito went out to hunt along one of the Colorado Chiquito's creeks. When he returned, he was without his rifle and had a harrowing story to tell.

While he and two of his warriors had been concealed in the brush along the creek, lying in wait for deer or antelope, American soldiers had suddenly appeared on the riverbank. There were too many of them. The three Diné could not hope to fight them successfully, so Manuelito opted for another approach. He gestured to his men to give him their guns, and rose slowly out of the brush, holding the rifles in the air, making signs of peace. One of the soldiers dismounted and came forward, and Manuelito indicated he wanted to talk. The Americans had no interpreter, however, and so were not prepared to enter into any negotiations. The soldiers conferred, and then took the rifles from Manuelito and rode away. They clearly had not recognized him. If they had, they would have taken him prisoner, or shot him where he stood.[13]

The loss of the rifles was a grievous turn in their fortunes. With the winter coming on, deer were especially crucial to their survival. They could eat the meat fresh or jerk it to save for later, and Juanita and the other women could use the hides for making moccasins and leggings to keep themselves and the children warm. Two years of drought had thinned the deer herds, however, and with the American soldiers roaming the country, the men could not afford to go far afield on hunting trips. Out here in the San Francisco Mountains, they were encroaching on Tonto Apache lands, and would fall prey to their attacks if they wandered too close to their villages. The Hopis and Zuñis, too, continued to be a threat.

It got so that many of the Diné could not sleep for worrying. They were constantly on the move, gathering up their belongings and their children and encamping for a few days before doing it all again. The sheep that did not die of exposure or starvation, they killed for meat and wool. Because they could not send men out to raid New Mexican settlements (they were too far away now, and the American army stood between them and the Rio Grande) Juanita and Manuelito's herd shrank considerably. This was another cause for anxiety.[14]

Sometimes runners would come bearing messages from other Diné headmen, telling of corn and wheat fields in ashes, hogans reduced to piles of charred wood. They also told of Diné raiders who had struck back at the Union soldiers, in the heart of their army camps. As the winter snows began to fall, Navajos attacked the wood and hay camps north of Fort Canby and managed to take forty-eight mules from right under the white men's noses. The soldiers gave chase, but even in their diminished state the Diné's horses were too much for them and the raiders escaped.[15] Perhaps this would convince the Americans not to ride out again before spring. They would be too tired from chasing the Diné and have too few animals to ride or to pull their wagons.

In early January 1864, however, a messenger came bearing troubling news. Spies had seen several groups of soldiers setting out from the fort, trudging through a foot of fresh snow. They were not heading toward Juanita and Manuelito's camp on the Colorado Chiquito. Instead, the soldiers had turned north toward one of the Diné's most important places of refuge, a breathtaking canyon whose bottomlands were planted with corn and more than three thousand peach trees. The Navajos called it Tséyi' ("Deep in the Rock"). The Americans called it Canyon de Chelly.

Carson had not wanted to march into Canyon de Chelly in the middle of winter. In November, after he returned from his fourth scouting mission against the Navajos, he decided that there was no reason to remain at Fort Canby for the next few months. The weather conditions would prevent his troops from making extended marches in the high desert, and the men (and their horses and mules) needed a few months to recuperate from the strenuous campaigns of the fall.[16]

Carson asked James Carleton for a two-month leave. He would come to Santa Fe to discuss Navajo campaign strategies and then go to Taos to see Josefa and the children. He had not seen his family since the previous spring. He missed them, and he was not feeling well. Carson had turned fifty-three on Christmas Eve, having spent most of his life on horseback and sleeping in the dirt. His throat hurt him almost daily. He thought it was a legacy of an incident a few years before, when his horse had thrown him and dragged him by the neck down a steep embankment.[17] He wanted to go home to rest before he began chasing Navajos again.

Carleton denied his request.

"Now, while the snow is deep," Carleton wrote to Carson, "is the true time to make an impression on the tribe."

Although winter campaigns were uncommon in other theaters of the American Civil War, they were prevalent in the longer history of U.S. Army conflicts with Native peoples in the West. The harsh conditions meant that most communities were vulnerable. Attacks launched in winter were often successful. And given that Carson's men had destroyed about two million pounds of grain during their summer and fall scouts, the Navajos could not depend upon their fields for sustenance. Their suffering would drive them out of the mountains, Carleton believed, and into the Union Army's arms.[18] This plan made perfect sense to Carleton, but he knew that Carson needed extra motivation. So he promised that if Carson captured at least one hundred Navajos in the winter campaign, he could bring them to Santa Fe himself, and then go to Taos to see his family.[19]

Heartened by this, Carson began to prepare for a winter assault on the heart of Navajo country. As he dictated orders to his adjutant, the soldiers of Fort Canby got their tents and kits in order and sang a song that one of them had penned when a storm had covered the fort's grounds with a foot of white powder.

> *"Come dress your ranks, my gallant souls, a-standing in a row,*
> *Kit Carson he is waiting to march against the foe;*
> *At night we march to Moqui o'er lofty hills of snow,*
> *To meet and crush the savage foe, bold Johnny Navajo.*
> *Johnny Navajo! O Johnny Navajo!*
> *We'll first chastise, then civilize, bold Johnny Navajo!"*[20]

On January 7, 1864, at the head of a column of almost four hundred Union soldiers, Carson approached the western entrance of Canyon de Chelly. When they neared the rim, Carson halted and sent out orders to circle the wagons, pitch the tents, and establish a base of operations. They would reconnoiter the canyon from this end and wait for one of Carson's officers, Albert Pfeiffer, to arrive. At the outset of the march from Fort Canby, Carson had sent Pfeiffer with a smaller detachment of soldiers to approach the canyon from the east. The plan was for both forces to operate along the rim of the canyon and in its interior, trapping the Navajos concentrated in the bottomlands between them, and forcing their surrender.[21]

Carson rode to the canyon's edge and looked down. Its smooth red walls plunged into a wide valley covered with bright white snow. Carson knew almost nothing about the canyon's dimensions, its extent or how deep it was. U.S. Army troops had marched into it on three different occasions before now. Once in 1849, after Stephen Watts Kearny had swept through the region on the way to California, and then again in 1858 and 1859, as preludes to Richard Canby's Navajo campaign. None of these expeditions had produced maps, however, and the reports lacked any useful geographic detail. The officers who wrote them had merely noted their relief at having managed to find their way out. The commander of the 1858 expedition concluded his report of Canyon de Chelly with an ominous recommendation: "No command should ever again enter it."[22]

Carson sent some scouts off around the northern rim of the canyon and then took some men and rode along the undulating southern edge for five miles. He did not find any kind of trail to the bottom. Discouraged, he returned to camp, where he found the scouts he had sent to the northern rim. They reported a skirmish with a small band of Navajos, killing eleven and wounding five. They had brought in several prisoners and 130 sheep and goats. The Canyon de Chelly fight had begun.[23]

The next day, January 14, Carson rode once again along the meandering edges of the canyon.[24] He had unobstructed views of large sections of bottomlands, and the icy wash that meandered through them. There was no sign of Pfeiffer coming from the east. Carson pulled on his reins, turning his horse around to go back the way they had come. On the ride to camp, three Navajos materialized out of the scrub brush, waving a flag of truce. Carson halted, dismounted, and called over his interpreter.

"They want to come in with their people," the interpreter told Carson, "and submit."

Carson told them what General Carleton had instructed him to say, a message that the general wanted all Navajos to hear and understand.

"You must come in and go to the Bosque Redondo," Carson said, "or we will pursue and destroy you. We will not make peace with you on any other terms. You have deceived us too often and robbed and murdered our people too long—to trust you again at large in your own country. This war shall be pursued against you if it takes years, now that we have begun, until you cease to exist or move. There can be no other talk on the subject."

The three Navajos seemed to understand, and so Carson continued.

"Your people might come unmolested to my camp up to ten o'clock A.M. tomorrow," he promised, "but after that time if you do not come, my Soldiers will hunt you up and the work of destruction [will] recommence."[25]

The three Navajos left, and Carson continued back to camp, drawing near just as night was falling. As his party rode in, to Carson's surprise and gratification, Albert Pfeiffer stepped out to greet him. Over the previous week his friend had "accomplished an undertaking never before successful in wartime—that of passing through the Cañon de Chelly from East to West, and this without having had a single casualty of his command."[26] They went back to Carson's tent, and Pfeiffer told him the whole story.

Pfeiffer's detachment had been marching for five days from Fort Canby before they reached the eastern end of Canyon de Chelly. The snow had been so deep that they lost the trail several times, and the cold was so severe that two of his men removed their boots to find their toes black with frostbite. As they marched, smoke wafted up into the air ahead of them, signals notifying the Navajos of the enemy's arrival. The next day, before they entered the canyon, Pfeiffer divided his men into three parties. One group walked ahead, with picks and shovels at the ready, to remove any obstructions they found in their way. Next came the main body of soldiers, all of them on foot. The rear guard followed on horseback, leading the rest of the detachment's animals. Pfeiffer would ride back and forth among all three groups, so that he could respond immediately to any threat.

On January 11, Pfeiffer's command moved forward into Canyon de Chelly. The walls rose up around them, covered with scrub oak. They picked their way slowly along the wash. The ice was thin and cracked under the hooves of the mules, who were carrying the command's supplies. Some of the animals broke through and sank breast-deep into the wash, thrashing and kicking while the soldiers grabbed their reins and pulled them out of the freezing water. One mule's legs went out from under him and he landed with such force that his belly skin burst open, spilling his entrails all over the ice. The soldiers took the bags from his back and left him there, a brown mound in a growing patch of bright red blood.

The next morning, after Pfeiffer's men came through a big bend in the canyon and began moving southwest, bullets began to hit the snow and ice all around them. Then the rocks came, aimed at the heads of both men and horses. The soldiers looked up and could barely make out the Navajos leaning over ledges high above them. Almost sixty years before, the Navajos had made a stand against Spanish soldiers from these strongholds high up in the canyon walls. They had succeeded in defending the canyon against those foes, but the effort had cost many lives.

On this day, Pfeiffer's men took cover and drew beads on the forms they saw moving above them. First one Navajo warrior and then another fell from the ledge and landed on the bottomlands beside them. The bullets continued to zing and the rocks to plummet into their midst. In the late afternoon, one of the soldiers shot a Navajo woman who had been cursing at them and hurling shards of wood. The Union Army marched on.

At some points the canyon widened out, looking to Pfeiffer like a beautiful savannah. Here there were large cornfields, irrigated by acequias dug into the bottomlands. At other places, the walls almost seemed to converge, forcing the soldiers to march in single file along a meandering course. Along the way Pfeiffer spied villages tucked up among the rocks, "solidly built, and remarkable for [their] substantial and beautiful masonry." Puebloans had built these structures hundreds of years before, then abandoned them in search of better croplands. Rock spires towered above the canyon floor, and on some ridges "Navajos jumped about . . . like Mountain Cats, hallooing at me, swearing and cursing, and threatening vengeance on my command, in every variety of Spanish."

That night, the soldiers halted at the convergence of their canyon with another, which headed off to the southeast. Here they had plenty of wood, and a secure position at the base of a gigantic rock that lunged out of the canyon wall like the prow of a ship. From here, the soldiers kept watch for Navajos approaching from the east, south, and west. None came. The soldiers made camp, pitching their tents and building fires at the base of the rock. The smoke rose slowly into the cold air, and as some soldiers looked up to follow its trail into the night sky, they saw a large group of Navajos perched on ledges above them. They were so high up, they looked like crows.

Pfeiffer calculated the distance and decided it was a waste of ammunition to try and shoot them out of their mountain fastness. Through the night, they could hear faint echoes from above. The Navajos were cursing at them again, but their words were carried away by the wind. Pfeiffer and his men slept on their guns that night. As their fires burned down to ashes, the Navajos lowered buckets from the ledges, to dip into the wash for water.

The next morning, Pfeiffer and his men continued their march to the west. The canyon walls sloped more gently down and the bottomlands widened. That evening, they saw the fires at Carson's camp and rode into it in triumph, having come safely through what Pfeiffer called the "Gibraltar of Navajodom." It was one of the canyon's two major arteries, which the Hispanos had named Cañon del Muerto ("Canyon of Death").[27]

The Union soldiers under Pfeiffer's command had not fought any major battles with the Navajos, but they had marched an army through the heart of their homeland. The kind of message this would send to the Navajos was articulated almost a year later by William Tecumseh Sherman regarding his march through Georgia. "If the North can march an army right through the South, it is proof positive that the North can prevail in this contest," Sherman wrote to Ulysses S. Grant in November 1864, "leaving only open the question of its willingness to use that power."[28]

———

The Navajos understood what this demonstration meant. The next morning a contingent of sixty men, women, and children arrived in Kit Carson's camp, having abided by his deadline.[29] A few hours later, more Navajos came in, and Carson talked with them. They told him that their people wanted to surrender but feared that if they came in, Union troops would murder them. Carson selected one of the Navajos, furnished him with rations, and told him to find as many of his people as he could and tell them that the American troops were there to feed them, keep them warm, and take them to Fort Canby.

"Tell them," he instructed the Navajo man, "that they will have the protection of the troops, providing they came in with the bona fide intention of immigrating" to the reservation at Bosque Redondo.

The man took his rations and left, promising to bring a great many Navajos back to Carson's camp.[30]

As he surveyed the scene at Canyon de Chelly, Carson decided that his campaign had now accomplished all that was possible. The army had shown the Navajos there was no canyon, no mountaintop, no desert expanse, in which they were safe from pursuit. They had demonstrated that the Union Army would destroy the Navajos if they did not submit, and that once they had surrendered, the soldiers would treat them humanely. Carson felt sure that once all of the Navajos understood these vital points, they would capitulate.[31]

The next day Kit Carson left his camp at Canyon de Chelly and started back to Fort Canby. He wanted to make sure that the soldiers there were ready to receive Navajo prisoners, and he needed to send out additional expeditions in other directions.

"Now is the time to prosecute the campaign with vigor," he informed General Carleton, "and effect the speedy removal of all the Indians."[32]

By January 21, 1864, Carson was back at Fort Canby. Three days later, there were two hundred Navajos encamped outside the fort's walls. More were turning up every hour.[33] Carson was satisfied. He had captured enough Navajos to ensure that he would see Josefa and the children again. On January 26, Kit Carson left his second in command, Captain Asa B. Carey, to oversee the surrenders at Fort Canby and rode out of the gates with 270 Navajos, bound for the Rio Grande. He would send the prisoners on to Bosque Redondo from there, and then return home to Taos.[34]

This was the first in a series of forced removals that the Navajos remembered collectively as the Long Walk. Over the next several months, groups ranging in size from 150 to 2,000 would leave Fort Canby or Fort Wingate and make their way along a number of routes to Bosque Redondo. Some went to Santa Fe and Fort Union before heading south along the Pecos, while others went through Albuquerque, up over the Sandia Mountains, and east toward the reservation. Most of the Navajos were on foot and drove their small sheep and goat herds in front of them. They had few blankets or tents to keep them warm for the journey of more than four hundred miles. When Navajos became tired or ill, armed Union soldiers forced them to resume their march on the road moving east. Hundreds died of starvation or froze to death. Some tried to escape and others were stolen away by Hispano raiders, who assessed the Navajos' vulnerability on the Long Walk and exploited it. The Navajos lost count of the days they were on the road. To many of them, it seemed like years.[35]

―――――――

As their people's Long Walk began more than 150 miles away, Juanita, Manuelito Segundo, and Shizie huddled in their shelter in the San Francisco Mountains, seeking protection from the winter wind. Juanita made moccasins and leggings from the deerskins that Manuelito managed to bring in, and ventured out to hunt for Apache plume, a shrub that grew on the rocky hillsides. In the spring it would produce soft pink tendrils, but now its branches were brown and green. After Juanita cut a bunch and dried them in the warm air of the shelter, Manuelito would scrape off their bark with a knife, sand them into shafts, straighten them in the heat of the fire, and then attach feathers to one end, plucked from turkeys or eagles.[36] Although their band still had a good number of guns, they relied on these arrows and their bows for hunting, and for battle. Kit Carson's army might come for them soon, and they needed to be ready.

Messengers appeared on the horizon, bearing news of a Union Army attack on Tséyi' and the surrender of thousands of Diné. It was said that many of the other headmen had brought their bands into Fort Canby, and that the army was giving them blankets and food.[37] The soldiers had promised not to attack any Navajo who wished to capitulate and had told them that at the new Indian reservation at Bosque Redondo, the army would protect them from the Utes, the Zuñis, and the Hispanos.

There were other reports, however, that the Diné gathered at Fort
Canby had no shelters and were freezing to death, and that the food the
soldiers were giving them was poisoned.[38] Manuelito consulted with Juanita. He trusted her instincts and often asked for her counsel.[39] They decided not to go into Fort Canby just yet. They would wait out the winter
with as many of their band who wanted to stay with them in the mountains near the Colorado Chiquito. They would decide what to do when the
spring came, and the leaves pushed their way out of the dirt.[40]

In March 1864, Manuelito's scouts saw shapes moving against the sky.
They were soldiers sent out by Kit Carson, whom the Diné now called
Rope Thrower. He wanted Manuelito and his people to come into Fort
Canby and surrender. They could keep their sheep, goats, and horses.[41]

Manuelito called the band's men, women, and children together to
discuss their options. Some of them wanted to go to Fort Canby. The winter had been brutal, and they saw no way they could continue to survive
along the Colorado Chiquito without corn crops or a steady supply of
sheep. It was clear that if they did not go, Rope Thrower would continue to
burn their crops and hogans, to chase them from place to place until they
died of exhaustion. Manuelito relented. Before he and Juanita surrendered, however, Manuelito wanted to consult with the headmen of other
bands who were already encamped around Fort Canby, waiting for their
removal to Bosque Redondo. They would go in a few months.[42]

In early May 1864, Juanita and Manuelito and several other families
rode into Tséhootsoh. Juanita had not been home for more than a year. The
grasses had greened in the warm spring sun, and there were fires dotting
the hills around Fort Canby. Since Kit Carson had taken the first group of
Navajo prisoners to the Rio Grande in January, thousands of Diné had come
and gone from the fort, and endured the suffering of the Long Walk.[43] The
two hundred men, women, and children still encamped around the fort
were trying to make the best of things. They were not used to the strange
foods that the soldiers had given them: flour that they had at first stirred into
water and eaten raw, and coffee beans that they had thought they should eat
like piñons. The bacon tasted odd and they did not know how to prepare it.
Many Navajos had sickened and died from eating the rations. Others were
so far gone from starvation that they died despite the food in their bellies.[44]

On May 9, 1864, Manuelito gathered his warriors and went to Fort
Canby to talk to Rope Thrower. But Carson was not there. He had left for
Santa Fe a few weeks before, and Asa Carey was once again in command
of the post.

"We do not wish to go to the Bosque," Manuelito announced to Carey, "but desire to stay in this country near this post and plant this year." His band would live peacefully at Tséhootsoh and make no trouble for the soldiers at Fort Canby.

Carey was skeptical. He repeated James Carleton's message to all the Navajos.

"There is but one place for you," he said, "and that is to go to the Bosque."

Manuelito wanted assurances that it was not a trap. He wanted to speak to another headman, a friend whom he trusted, who had already made the four-hundred-mile Long Walk to the Navajo reservation.

"Send for Herrera Grande," he said. "He has been at the Bosque, and I want to see him."

Manuelito still suspected that as soon as the Americans got all of the Navajos corralled in one place, far from their homeland, they would massacre them. He believed that Herrera Grande would tell him the truth about the reservation, and then he would know whether or not to give himself and his family up to the Union Army.[45]

Carey agreed, and sent a messenger east to Bosque Redondo. While they waited for Herrera Grande to arrive, Juanita and Manuelito settled into their camp north of Fort Canby. They did as they had always done at Tséhootsoh, hunting and gathering seeds and plants to lay aside for the winter.

On June 20, a group of Navajos arrived from the Bosque, but Herrera Grande was not with them. He had refused to leave the reservation, and so the Union Army had sent four other headmen in his place. Manuelito rode to Fort Canby and sat with them. They told him that the Bosque was a flatland with a meandering river whose salty water had made many of the Diné sick. They had spent the spring digging acequias and planting corn and wheat in large fields next to the riverbanks. Hopefully the seeds would take and they would be able to eat corn again in the fall.[46]

Manuelito was unconvinced. Flatlands with bad water would not keep his family or his sheep alive. And he did not believe that the Americans had the manpower or the knowledge of the landscape of Diné Bikéyah to keep him from his territory. After saying goodbye to the Bosque Navajos, Manuelito consulted with a few of his warriors and they formulated a plan. He went to the fort and told the officers there that his band needed just a few more weeks to prepare for the march to Bosque Redondo. Juanita continued to gather supplies, and they corralled their sheep and horses.

One morning in mid-July 1864, soldiers rode out to Manuelito's camp and found it deserted. The small group, with more than five thousand sheep and hundreds of horses, had disappeared into the forests of the Defiance Plateau.[47]

The Union Army's winter campaign against Tséyi' had been definitive, resulting in the removal of thousands of Diné to Bosque Redondo. Even some of Manuelito and Juanita's people had broken with them and surrendered. But the rest of the band (100 to 150 of them now), along with another 2,000 Navajos, remained in Diné Bikéyah, determined to resist the Union Army's attempts to force their capitulation. It would be a difficult path, but one of their own choosing.[48]

19

Carleton

Although he had not been able to force Manuelito to surrender in the summer of 1864, General James Carleton had reason to be pleased with his latest campaign. Thousands of Navajos had been removed to Bosque Redondo, and the soldiers stationed at Fort Sumner, the Union installation on the reservation, had immediately put them to work. They dug irrigation ditches with their bare hands and readied three thousand acres of land along the Pecos River for planting corn. The fall harvest from these fields should produce enough to feed all six thousand Navajo captives, and the four hundred Mescalero Apaches who had removed there the previous year.

There had been some problems, of course. No large-scale operation was without them, in Carleton's experience. He had been sure his destructive campaign against the Navajos would succeed, but he had not anticipated such a large number of men, women, and children would surrender, and he was unprepared. Carleton had already been forced to purchase more than $500,000 worth of wheat, corn, and meat as well as cloth and blankets. Local merchants, aware of Carleton's desperation, raised their prices. In addition, Bosque Redondo was over 150 miles southeast of Santa Fe. Although this was ideal in terms of the reservation's isolation from Hispano settlements, the distance made transportation of goods egregiously expensive.

Since early spring, Carleton had been writing frantic letters to the commander at Fort Sumner, Henry Bristol, to urge him to work the Navajos and Mescaleros harder in the fields. They needed a large harvest of corn, and smaller yields of grain, melons, onions, and tobacco, if the prisoners were to survive. This was a key element of the federal government's reservation plan: the army would provide support for the Navajos and Mescaleros, but only until they could subsist themselves at Bosque Redondo.[1]

Carleton had hoped that he would have the help of New Mexico Territory's Office of Indian Affairs to support the Navajos and Mescaleros at the Bosque. But Superintendent Michael Steck had refused. Steck had been an Indian agent in New Mexico since the early 1850s, and President Lincoln appointed him superintendent in 1863. While he was a proponent of the reservation system in theory, Steck had opposed Bosque Redondo since its inception, arguing that the Mescaleros and Navajos were traditional enemies and should not be forced to live together in the same space. In addition, Steck believed that there was not enough arable land at the Bosque to support such large numbers of people living in close proximity. In his view, the Mescaleros could stay at Bosque Redondo, but the Navajos should be sent back to their homelands and placed in settlements there. In any case, he told Carleton, because the Bosque Indians had surrendered to the Union Army and were prisoners of war, they were not the responsibility of the federal Bureau of Indian Affairs, or New Mexico's Indian agency.[2]

Carleton, who did not tolerate criticism or resistance of any sort, dug in.

"The Navajos should never leave the Bosque," he wrote to the War Department, "and never shall if I can prevent it."[3]

If the Navajos could bring in all of their crops, they could feed themselves, and Carleton could declare yet another victory for the Union in the West.

━━━━

In August 1864, while he was battling Steck for resources, Carleton received a letter from Henry Bristol. The Navajos had gone through the fields to check the corn, Bristol wrote, and when they peeled the husks away from several cobs, they found them pulverized into mush.[4] This meant that earlier in the summer, swarms of tiny moths, light brown with one small white spot on each forewing, had deposited their eggs in the warm, moist soil of the bottomlands along the Pecos. When these eggs hatched, hundreds of thousands of cutworms crept out of the grass and up the cornstalks, boring into the husks, gorging themselves on the tender kernels, and leaving behind furrows of slime.[5]

"This will do some damage," Bristol concluded.[6]

Carleton was stunned. He ordered Bristol to examine all of the Navajos' fields to see if any of the plants were salvageable, and tried to convince himself that the situation was better than Bristol feared. A few days later, however, the soldiers confirmed that the cutworms had devastated almost all of the Bosque's three thousand acres of corn.[7]

"This was a visitation from God!" Carleton lamented. "No human forecast could have prevented it."[8]

Every letter Carleton received after that bore similarly terrible news.

A wagon train heading for New Mexico on the Santa Fe Trail was attacked by Comanches and Kiowas riding up from their territories in the Texas Panhandle. The large sacks of flour the wagons had carried, bound for Bosque Redondo, had ended up strewn across the prairies.[9] An unexpected cold snap in northern New Mexico wiped out the corn and wheat fields there.[10] Violent thunderstorms rolled across the plains, one after the other, pounding the wheat crop at Bosque Redondo into the mud and flooding many of the Navajos out of their rudimentary shelters. The Mescaleros managed to save some of their wheat by harvesting it with butcher knives while the hail pelted them in the fields. But they only had enough to feed their small band.[11]

In October, Carleton ordered Bristol to hold a council with the Navajo headmen and inform them that they must bear the awful loss with fortitude.

"Tell them to be too proud to murmur at what cannot be helped," the general urged. "We could not foresee the total destruction of their corn crop, nor could we foresee that the frost and hail would come and destroy the crop in the country."

Carleton could not believe that this was what the Almighty had in store for him, or for the Navajos.

"Do not be discouraged," he admonished his prisoners. "Work hard, every man and woman, to put in large fields next year, when, if God smiles upon our efforts, [you] will, at one bound, be forever placed beyond want, and independent."[12]

It was not supposed to have turned out this way. From the first moment Carleton had seen Bosque Redondo, he had believed in its potential. It was the winter of 1852, and he and a company of dragoons were scouting the lands south of Fort Union. They had come up over a ridge and seen the valley of the Pecos laid out before them, impossibly green in an endless landscape of brown plains. Large groves of cottonwood trees, their branches silver with frost, clustered along the banks of the river. Mexican herders had named the valley for these cottonwoods: Bosque Redondo ("Round Forest"). This vision of the Bosque had remained vivid for Carleton even after he left New Mexico for service in California. When he returned ten years later and began to plan for the Union Army's campaign against the region's Native peoples, he thought immediately of the Bosque as the location for a reservation.[13]

"I had seen that the . . . rich bottomlands there were capable of growing crops sufficient to support a large population," he believed. In addition, the valley was surrounded by a large expanse of high desert prairie, which would act as both pasturage and a buffer between the Indians and Hispano and Anglo settlements in the area. They would also act as a topographical fence line. Any Indian who tried to escape the reservation would be easily spotted, and would be unable to elude pursuit and capture.

"I feel justified in saying," Carleton wrote, "that there is not another spot of vacant land, between the Pecos River and the Colorado of the West, which possesses any two of these essential elements for a Reservation, *much less, all of these elements*."[14]

The Union War Department had supported his vision. President Lincoln approved an order creating Bosque Redondo as a reservation in January 1864, and Congress appropriated $100,000 for its maintenance.[15] Contained along the Pecos, the Navajos and Mescaleros would become productive members of American society. This was their only possible future. If the Union Army did not save the Indians from themselves, Carleton and the War Department believed, the Navajos and Apaches, like "the races of mammoths and mastodons, and the great sloths," would disappear from the face of the earth.[16]

In the fall of 1864, Carleton was managing the disaster he had created at Bosque Redondo when he received a series of beseeching letters from Colorado's governor, John Evans. Kiowas and Comanches were riding into southern Colorado to raid towns and wagon trains, and the soldiers stationed at forts in the area needed reinforcements. Carleton thought back on the good work that Colorado soldiers had done in the fight against the Texans.

"When we were menaced and in trouble you came to help us," he replied to Evans, "and you may be sure that . . . we will respond to your call, as far as possible, to the last man that can be spared."[17]

Carleton ultimately sent Evans what he believed to be New Mexico's greatest resource in the fight against Indians: Kit Carson. The frontiersman had resigned from the army in September and gone back to Taos to be with his family, but Carleton knew that Carson would answer another call to serve his country. In early November 1864, with a large contingent of Utes, Mescaleros recruited from the Bosque, and 350 soldiers of the 1st New Mexico Volunteers—another of the Union's multiracial fighting forces in the West—Carson set out for a newly constructed Fort Bascom, near the Texas border. Carleton was sure that this new Indian campaign would be triumphant.

"Your knowledge of the haunts of the Indians of the plains," Carleton wrote to Carson, "and the great confidence the Ute Indians have in you as a friend and as a leader, point to yourself as the most fitting person to organize, direct, and bring this enterprise to a successful issue."[18]

In mid-December, while he was in southern New Mexico on a tour of the forts there, Carleton received a battle report from Kit Carson. A few weeks earlier, on November 25, 1864, Carson and his men had marched into the Texas Panhandle and found more than one thousand Kiowas and Comanches encamped outside of the ruins of a former trading fort called Adobe Walls. When the Indians discovered the soldiers' presence, wave after wave of warriors attacked the Union contingent, firing rifles from horseback and wheeling away just in time to avoid the soldiers' artillery fire. The ruins of Adobe Walls provided effective cover for Carson's men, but it seemed the wiser course to fall back, burn and loot the Kiowa lodges they had overrun, and save their own wagon train. In his report to Carleton, Carson explained that once the full strength of the Comanches had become apparent, "it became impossible for [me] to chastise them further."[19]

The Battle of Adobe Walls was not a conclusive victory, but perhaps the Kiowas and Comanches would think twice before attacking another American wagon train or outpost on the Santa Fe Trail. Carleton congratulated himself for choosing Carson to lead this campaign, and Carson for leading it so ably.

"This brilliant affair adds another green leaf to the laurel wreath," he wrote to his favorite officer, "which you have so nobly won in the service of your country."[20]

The war news from the East was also gratifying. Union cavalry commander Phil Sheridan had pushed the Confederates from the Shenandoah Valley in Virginia, while William Tecumseh Sherman had occupied

Atlanta and then begun to march eastward through Georgia. In the election in November, Abraham Lincoln had been reelected as President of the United States. Carleton was disappointed in this bit of news. He supported the Union, but he was a military man and had voted for one of his own, Democrat and former Union Army general George McClellan.[21]

Some of the local papers had reported these events. They had also printed anti–Bosque Redondo editorials, grumbling about how feeding the more than eight thousand Navajos now at the reservation was driving up grain prices for all New Mexicans. There were also personal attacks on Carleton himself.

"Major Pomposo," they called him, with "his military cap worn precisely six inches from the extreme tip of his nose . . . his eyes like Mars, that threaten and command as with slow and measured tread, each step exactly twenty-eight inches." The general might pretend that Bosque Redondo was a humanitarian effort, the editorials jeered, but it was really an "unscrupulous design for his personal aggrandizement." The authors recommended that readers refer to the reservation not as Bosque Redondo but as "Fair Carletonia."[22]

Carleton was enraged. He pulled out several sheets of paper and began to write a declaration, addressed to the people of New Mexico.

"Finding myself in command of the troops within your borders," he wrote, he had determined that to "cure this great evil from which your territory had been so long a prey, some new remedy must be adopted."[23]

He had been victorious in what he was sure was the last Navajo War in New Mexico, and he had sent his prisoners of war to Bosque Redondo. In the end, Carleton argued, the reservation would create wealth for all New Mexicans. The removal of the Navajos would open huge tracts of valuable land to cultivation and ranching, and clear the path to the mining districts of Arizona. Soon, Carleton imagined, the tracks of a transcontinental railroad would be laid across those lands, and all of the Territory would prosper. Carleton, aided by soldiers from New Mexican communities and fully backed by the Department of War and the Lincoln administration, had done all of this not to promote *his* interests, but the interests of the people of New Mexico.

"This matter has commanded my attention, my study, and my anxiety, for nearly two years," he noted, "All I can ask is that you will raise no unreasonable clamors against the important measures which have been inaugurated for your own good."[24]

Carleton signed the declaration, folded the sheets into an envelope, and sent it by the next mail coach to the *Santa Fe Weekly Gazette*. The editor was a friend of his and a supporter of Bosque Redondo, and would print it in its entirety. Then, perhaps, the critics would be quieted, and the people of New Mexico would understand and appreciate what he had done for them.

———

Carleton spent the winter back in Santa Fe, seeing to every detail at Bosque Redondo. He thought of little else, even his family back in California. He had not seen Sophia and the children for almost three years, and had never met his youngest daughter. The roads through the desert were too long and dangerous for them to travel upon, and Carleton would never request a furlough to visit them while there was so much work to do in New Mexico.

Primary among his objectives was bringing the Navajo War to a close. This meant forcing the last of the Navajo headmen to surrender with their bands. Carleton was particularly interested in capturing Manuelito, whom he saw as the most powerful of the remaining resisters.[25] Because Manuelito seemed to value Herrera Grande's opinion, Carleton wrote and asked the commander at Bosque Redondo to send him and several other headmen, along with the interpreter Jesus Arviso, to see him in Santa Fe.[26]

On February 15, 1865, the Bosque Navajos arrived at Carleton's headquarters in Santa Fe. After greeting them, Carleton asked them to go back to their homeland and find Manuelito and his band.

"Tell them that this is the last warning they will have," Carleton said, "that if they come in now, their stock shall remain as their own."

Manuelito would have five weeks to comply with this order. If he and his people were not at Fort Wingate, on the southeastern border of the Navajo homeland, by April 1865, "the door will be shut" and what happened next would be their own fault and nobody else's.

"We will fight them," Carleton promised, "the people will fight them, and the Utes will fight them, and they will be destroyed."[27] Their children would be enslaved, and ultimately, they would be exterminated.

Herrera Grande and the other headmen agreed to go to their homeland and relay this message to Manuelito and the other fugitive Navajos. A few days later, they left, accompanied by a Union Army escort. While Carleton awaited their return, he continued to send multiple orders to the Bosque every day, monitor the Territory for any secessionist activities or rumors of invasion, and read the papers. William Tecumseh Sherman had arrived in Savannah and presented that city as a Christmas gift to President Lincoln before turning northward into South Carolina. And there was reason to hope that the recent meeting of Union and Confederate diplomats at Hampton Roads in Virginia would be successful and that peace would be the result.

Many soldiers serving in New Mexico had expressed regret that they had not experienced the great battles in the war's bloodiest theaters in the East. Carleton himself would have liked the chance to fight Henry Sibley's forces along the Rio Grande. But the work that the California Column had done since they arrived was, in his view, vital to the future of the country. He and his men would clear New Mexico of the Indian threat and pave the way to the gold buried in the mountains of Arizona. This, he believed, was his service to the Union cause.

"If I can develop the mineral wealth in this country—although I get none of it myself," he wrote to his sister, "I shall have fulfilled my mission."[28]

On March 20, 1865, Carleton received word that Herrera Grande and his party were on the outskirts of Santa Fe. They came to army headquarters, and the Navajo chief began to tell the story of their meeting with Manuelito.

It had taken them two weeks to travel to the lands south of Zuñi Pueblo, where the Bosque Navajos sat down with Manuelito and his brother Cayetanito. Herrera Grande conveyed Carleton's message, and urged his fellow headman to surrender to the Union Army. Manuelito considered his friend's words, and then spoke.

"My stock is so poor," he said, "I cannot travel to the Bosque now."

Herrera Grande told him that Carleton had not authorized him to extend the deadline for surrender.

"It is no use to discuss the matter," another Bosque headman interrupted. "If you do not go the Bosque [now], worse will come to you."

"If you stay," warned another, "you could lose not only your stock but your lives."

"The dead cannot be called back," Herrera Grande said, "and you better think of this."

Still Manuelito resisted. Several women and children in his band began to cry out in protest. They were starving, and they saw the consequences of remaining in Diné Bikéyah, constantly on the run.

Cayetanito joined the conversation.

"My animals are also poor, and I want to remain."

At this, Herrera Grande stood up.

"I have delivered my message," he told the brothers, "and now we will go back to the Bosque."

Manuelito turned to address his people.

"My god and my mother live in the West," he announced, "and I shall not leave them. There is a tradition that my people shall never cross the Rio Grande, the Rio San Juan, or the Rio Colorado. We also cannot pass three mountains, and we cannot leave the Chuska mountains, my native hills." The Navajo country was theirs by birth and by right, and even in these direst of circumstances, Manuelito would not leave.

"I will remain, and will suffer the consequences of either war or famine," Manuelito concluded. "Now I have nothing to lose but my life, and this they can take whenever they please. But I will not move." Carleton and his Union Army were welcome to come and attack him, Manuelito insisted, but if they killed him, "innocent blood would be shed."

Herrera Grande had heard enough.

"I have done all I can for your benefit," he told Manuelito. "I have given you the best advice. I now leave you as if your grave were already made."[29]

Three days after hearing Herrera Grande's account of the meeting, James Carleton sent a letter to the commander at Fort Wingate with instructions to ambush Manuelito at Zuñi Pueblo the next time the headman came to trade. It would save his people from extermination.

"Try hard to get Manuelito," he admonished the captain. "It will be a mercy to those whom he controls to capture or kill him at once."[30]

In mid-April 1865, glorious news began to arrive from the East. The Union flag flew once again over Fort Sumter and Charleston. Both that city and Columbia, the capital of South Carolina, had fallen to Sherman's troops. There were also reports from Virginia that the Confederates had abandoned Richmond and Petersburg, and the armies were fighting in the farmlands west of those cities.

A few days later, the papers reported the Confederate Army's surrender at Appomattox. James Carleton issued a general order expressing the "gladness and thankfulness which fill all our hearts" when "our brethren, both North and South, will forget the rancor engendered by this unhappy quarrel which has so long estranged them from one another, and will soon, as of old, clasp hands again under the flag of our fathers, and alike feel proud that they are citizens of THE GREAT REPUBLIC."[31]

The cannons at Fort Marcy boomed, firing the national salute. In Albuquerque there were "bonfires, illuminations, fireworks . . . together with speechmaking and general jollification."[32] The thought that the Civil War in the East might actually be over filled all of the city's residents with relief and elation.

"It diffuses a community of feeling," the Santa Fe Weekly Gazette observed, "and makes all feel that they have an interest in the success acquired by any portion of the army, no matter where it may be located."[33]

The next week, the mood in Santa Fe changed. The Palace of the Governors, the merchants' stores, La Fonda, and private homes were all draped in black fabric. President Abraham Lincoln had been assassinated.

There was a public meeting on April 29, during which local politicians gave speeches lauding Lincoln's presidency. The New Mexico legislature passed a series of resolutions sending sympathy to the other states and territories of the Union, to Congress and the president's cabinet, and to Lincoln's family.

"We the people of New Mexico," they declared, "proud of our position as an integral portion of this great republic and holding ourselves faithful citizens of our Government and observers of the public peace . . . do lament the melancholy occurrence that has deprived us of [this] great man and citizen."[34]

—————

The end of the conflict in the East did not mean an end to the struggle for the West. James Carleton continued to focus on pursuing Chiricahuas, rounding up Manuelito and the remaining resistant Navajos, and keeping the Bosque Indians alive and contained.

In mid-June 1865, disturbing news reached him from the reservation. In the middle of the night, two headmen left with more than five hundred of their people.[35] Carleton immediately fired off a series of letters, ordering companies of soldiers from Fort Sumner and Fort Union into the field, and authorizing New Mexican militias to chase down the runaways, before they could cross the Rio Grande.

This breakout had occurred at the worst possible time for James Carleton. As armed and mounted Anglos and Hispanos fanned out across the high desert plains of central New Mexico in search of the fugitives, a delegation of politicians arrived at Fort Union. They were there to examine the Union Army's actions against Native peoples during the Civil War.

During the war, a series of violent events—the Dakota War in Minnesota in 1862 and the massacre of Cheyennes and Arapahos at Sand Creek (led by John Chivington, who had destroyed the Confederate wagon trains at Glorieta) in 1864—had prompted the creation of a congressional committee to study "the condition of the Indian tribes and their treatment by the civil and military authorities of the United States." James Doolittle, a Republican senator from Wisconsin, was appointed as its chair, and its other members were two congressmen and a representative from the U.S. Army.[36]

The Doolittle Commission was going to Colorado to investigate Sand Creek, and so Congress asked them to make the trip south to Bosque Redondo as well. The extraordinary cost of maintaining the reservation (more than $1,000,000 a year) and the high mortality rate (between 10 and 20 percent) were concerning. The Doolittle Commission was to observe conditions there, and report their findings.[37] For his part, James Doolittle felt sure that the commission would "return home more than ever impressed that the Republic, over which the flag of the Union now floats so triumphantly, is indeed continental."[38]

James Carleton and most of his staff met the commission at Fort Union and hosted them there overnight. The next day they left for Bosque Redondo. On June 25, 1865, the party arrived and took a tour of Fort Sumner and the reservation.

"Their crops [are] looking well," a member of the commission observed, "and the Indians [are] willing to work."[39]

The next day, the commission sat down with the Mescalero chiefs and the Navajo headmen. They wanted to know about their families, how much stock they had, if their rations were large enough, and if they had enough fuel for their fires. They were particularly interested in the quality of the water. Doolittle had heard reports about the alkaline nature of the Pecos River, and that it made both the captive Indians and the soldiers sick.

"There is plenty of good land and water," Herrera Grande began in a generous tone, "plenty to raise crops for the whole tribe." There was a pause. "The men are working like mules," he added.

"Work is civilization," Doolittle interjected. "Work makes the white man great."

Herrera Grande shrugged this comment off, and then became much less conciliatory. He began to explain that there were no trees left at the reservation. The Diné had to walk long distances for wood. It took an immense amount of labor to till three thousand acres and maintain the acequias that watered them, and the overwork was making them sick. The Navajos had helped to build an Indian hospital, but the patients who went there died, and so no one had gone back. Their own medicine men had tried to cure the Diné but could not. At the Bosque, they did not have access to the herbs and plants they usually used to heal the sick.

"Every day some of [the people] have died. So many of them are dying," the chief said, "[it's] as though they were shooting them with a rifle."[40]

All of the chiefs agreed that they were not getting enough to eat. The ration of meat was often spoiled, and there was too little flour to make bread to fill the bellies of their children. They needed corn and they needed more sheep, and wagons to help them transport wood from groves far north of the Bosque.

These were things they needed, right now. What they *wanted* was to go home.

"If we were sent back," the chiefs promised, "we would never commit an act of hostility [again]."

They were even willing to abide more forts in Diné Bikéyah, if that is what it took.

"You could send troops," they urged, "to see that we kept our promise."

"Do you want us," Doolittle asked, "to tell the Great Father and the great council that you would like to be sent back to your old country?"

"Yes, we would all like to go," they said without hesitation. "We would go straight back the way we came."[41]

Two days later, Carleton and Doolittle rode out of Fort Sumner onto a long straight road heading north. The Avenue, as the soldiers called it, was lined with young cottonwood trees planted by the Navajos. It skirted a slough on the east bank of the Pecos before passing through thousands of acres of lush corn. The crop would be ready for harvest in another month or two. The commission had heard abundant testimony regarding the cutworms' devastation the summer before, but both the Navajos and the soldiers were optimistic that their fields would survive this year. Carleton hoped so. Many of his plans depended on it.

James Carleton had not learned anything new from the testimonies of the Navajos or the soldiers posted at Fort Sumner. The problems they identified—poor water, lack of fuel, widespread illness—had been issues at the Bosque from the beginning. Despite this, Carleton continued to believe that the reservation could be a success. And he was encouraged that the majority of the soldiers and other personnel at Fort Sumner spoke of their support for the reservation policy, and favored the Bosque site over other locations in Navajo country. The commission members seemed to agree.

"No improvement can be suggested by me, in regard to Indian Affairs in New Mexico," the military representative observed in a letter to the War Department. Carleton's supervision seemed to him to have created ideal conditions on this particular reservation, which he saw as a model system for civilizing the Southwest's Indians. "Life and property are enjoyed in security there," he concluded.[42]

As Carleton and Doolittle rode into Santa Fe Plaza, cannons boomed in honor of the commission. City officials made speeches from a platform placed in front of the Palace of the Governors, and the military band played national airs. Carleton was pleased to discover that Doolittle and his son, who had accompanied the commission, would be boarding in the same house as John Clark. The surveyor general would make sure that Doolittle heard all about the rich quartz veins of Arizona, and how the removal of the Navajos to Bosque Redondo would make their extraction possible.[43]

For the next four days, the city of Santa Fe hummed with excitement. When the commission members were not taking testimonies they were touring the town, visiting the convent school, and calling on territorial officials. There were musical soirées and parties every night. July 4 was particularly festive. The fighting in the East had ended, Jefferson Davis had been captured, and everyone was hopeful about the future of the country. In the evening, there was a grand ball, planned and paid for by the city's most prominent citizens, including James Carleton and John Clark.[44]

When Carleton sat down with the commission to record his testimony, he repeated many of the same arguments he had made in his declaration to the citizens of New Mexico in December 1864. Bosque Redondo was the ideal site for a reservation, he argued. They had just been unlucky with the cutworms and the storms. It was cheaper to feed the Navajos at the reservation than fight them in their homeland. In passing, he mentioned the hostility that many wealthy Hispanos and Anglos had for the Bosque. He thought he knew the reason for their resistance.

"When this system goes into successful operation," Carleton said, "there will be no more tribes from which they can capture servants."[45]

Doolittle's interest was piqued. He had advocated for the 13th Amendment abolishing slavery, which the Union Congress had passed in January 1865, and which everyone was sure would be ratified by the end of the year. And when President Lincoln had signed the legislation creating Arizona Territory back in February 1863, slavery had been outlawed there, and in all the western territories. The United States could not allow slavery to exist in any form in the West, given the immense price that had been paid over the past four years to abolish it.

Doolittle questioned Carleton further about the New Mexico slave trade, and Carleton told him that there were still about three thousand enslaved Indians living in households across the Territory. The Union's war against the Navajos, Carleton argued, had kept those numbers from growing.

"The Indians upon the reservation, if properly cared for by the military commander," Carleton told the commissioners, "run no risk of being stolen or attacked."[46]

In Carleton's view, Bosque Redondo was a prison created to emancipate Native peoples from slavery. It was part of the civilizing process, and a vital element in the Union's larger plan for the region. This concept of the reservation system in New Mexico, with all of its seeming ironies, seemed to satisfy Doolittle.

By July 6, 1865, the commission members had collected all of the testimony they needed from Santa Fe's residents, and they prepared to leave for Taos. Carleton rode with them to a ridge north of the city, and then bid them adieu. He returned to his headquarters, confident that the commission would recommend to Congress that the government continue to support Bosque Redondo. He was a stubborn man, and he believed in his reservation project. He would see it through to the end.[47]

———

As Santa Fe settled back into its normal rhythm of trading activity and city gossip, the Navajos at Bosque Redondo turned from the fields along the Pecos River to walk back to their dirt-covered huts. Behind them, just above the waving tassels of the corn plants, a mass of light-colored moths rose up and took flight.

20

Juanita

It was the summer of 1866. More than a year had passed since Herrera Grande had come to Diné Bikéyah from the Bosque to try to persuade Manuelito to surrender to the Americans.

"It is no use killing up horses in coming for me," Manuelito had told his fellow headman. "I will never go voluntarily."[1]

At that moment, Juanita had cried out in protest. The lands along the Colorado Chiquito had plenty of wood for fires and deer to hunt, but Juanita could never gather enough plants and seeds to feed little Shizie and Manuelito Segundo. They were hungry all the time. Although her husband usually considered her counsel, he had not listened to her that winter. He vowed to fight the Americans to the death, if he had to.

"I will shed my blood on my own land," he told her, "and my people will have the land even if I die." The Great Spirit had given Diné Bikéyah to the Navajos, he had insisted, the valleys and the high mesas and the four sacred mountains. The people were supposed to be there, and they would not leave.[2]

Others in the band had not been persuaded by Manuelito's words. Over the past year, Juanita would wake up in the morning and find another family gone, having taken what few sheep and goats they still owned and headed east to surrender.[3]

Juanita and Manuelito had been careful. They moved their small band regularly to elude pursuers, and to avoid exhausting their food and fuel supplies. But the enemies always seemed to find them. In the summer of 1865 they had been surprised by a group of Hispano raiders. The Navajos fled into the trees, dragging their children and whatever household goods

they could carry. They found out later that Hispanos were riding throughout Diné Bikéyah, hunting for the Navajos who broke out from Bosque
Redondo just as the Doolittle Commission arrived. The relentlessness of
their raids left Manuelito's band with no time for rest, or for hunting and
gathering.[4]

When the winter snows covered the tablelands in 1865–66, they had
moved to the northeastern edge of Diné Bikéyah. There, the Utes had attacked, dispersing them once again. Some Navajos did not come back.
They were either captured by the Utes or they found their way to the
Americans, finally overcome by the exhaustion of constant resistance.[5]
And then in the spring of 1866, as they prepared to move back west
toward the Colorado Chiquito, the Hopis had struck their camp. Several
Navajos were killed and the Hopis withdrew with a significant portion
of the band's small sheep herd. Manuelito stumbled back from the fight,
blood seeping from his left arm and side.[6]

Now it was the end of summer, and Juanita and Manuelito were on the
move once again. This time they were headed east, through the southern
part of the homeland. Huge brown spires of rock appeared on the right,
rising up from the scrub brush. The Zuñis called it A'ts'ina ("Place of Writing on the Rock"), for the words that the outsiders had carved in its soft
surface, marking their passage. Juanita and Manuelito, their children, and
the twenty remaining members of their band did not stop there. They kept
moving, grimly, toward their destination. They urged along a small herd
of sheep and goats, skinny and parched after a summer of drought.

When they passed through the Zuni Mountains and turned north,
their horses' hooves clattered on great sheets of glossy black lava. The old
stories said that these flows were the dried blood of a giant, killed by the
Changing Woman's twin boys in a war against the Navajos' enemies.[7] In
the distance, they could see the high blue slopes of Tsoodzil, the sacred
mountain that marked the southeastern border of Diné Bikéyah. In the
valley below, smoke from campfires wafted up into the air among a handful of adobe buildings and white shelter tents.

On September 1, 1866, a group of soldiers rode out of Fort Wingate
and approached them. Their captain greeted the party, and Manuelito
told them that after more than two years of resistance, he and his small
band were finally surrendering to the U.S. Army.[8] Juanita and her children
joined him, and they all moved northward toward the fort. Soon they
would leave Diné Bikéyah. It would be Juanita's first time east of Tsoodzil.
She did not know how far they were going, or if they would ever return.

For the next few days, Manuelito's band encamped at Fort Wingate. Because of the time they had spent near Fort Canby two years before, Juanita was at least somewhat familiar with the rations they now received (soft brown flour, salty hunks of bacon fat, and hard coffee beans) and how to prepare them. Juanita could only hope that her children's bodies would adjust to this new diet quickly and that they would feel full, for the first time in a long time.[9]

When they left Fort Wingate, only a small detachment of soldiers accompanied them. They were a small group compared to the massive trains that had left for Bosque Redondo during the Long Walk of 1864. The road had dried after the summer's monsoon rains and they made good time. It did not take long to pass beyond the boundaries of Diné Bikéyah and enter the territory of the Hispanos and Anglos. Each night, after they stopped to make camp, Manuelito stood up and talked to his people. They had suffered over the past few years, he said, chased through the tablelands by their enemies. They had lost children to raiders or to death. He was not sure what awaited them at Bosque Redondo. He was still their headman, and he wanted them to trust him.

"You should listen to me and follow me," Manuelito said, "and maybe one day we will get to go back."[10]

As they traveled eastward, Juanita and Manuelito passed small mounds of dirt on the side of the road, the graves of Navajos who had died of starvation, exposure, or exhaustion on their Long Walk to Bosque Redondo. Over the past few years, stories had filtered back to Diné Bikéyah about the dead who had been left behind during these forced marches. It was said that a pregnant woman, about to give birth and too weak to walk on any longer, stopped to rest by the side of the road.

"Go ahead," she had told her parents, "things might come out all right with me." And so they had left her, and kept walking. A few minutes later, they heard a gunshot. The soldiers did not allow them to go to their daughter and cover her body.[11]

These remnants of past Long Walks seemed portentous. Signs of terrible things to come.

As they neared the Rio Grande, Juanita and the other Navajos who had never been this far east looked around in wonder. There were large fields of corn, ripe and ready for harvest, crisscrossed by narrow channels of water. Fruit trees in long rows, reminders of the peach orchards at Tséyi', chopped down and burned by Kit Carson's men. And the towns, hundreds of flat-roofed adobe buildings with glass windows and wooden doors, clustered together along the banks of the river. The Rio Grande seemed enormous to the Navajos, after living so long amongst creeks, mountain streams, and shallow washes.[12] Its waters rushed and eddied and clawed at the banks as they flowed south.[13]

"There was a tradition among my people," Manuelito had been insisting for the past several years, "that we should never cross the Rio Grande."[14] In mid-September 1866 he and Juanita were forced through its waters. Their meager herd went first. The animals were already weak and they struggled. Several of them were swept away in the current. Then the Navajos stepped into the water, the wet sands sucking at their feet, and grabbed several ropes tied to a raft made of logs. A group of soldiers on the eastern bank began to pull another set of ropes, and the raft began to move across the river. The current pulled at their clothes and tried to drag them away. Juanita and her children hung on tightly until they reached the other side, and clambered up the bank.[15] After their clothes had dried, they were moved to a corral outside Albuquerque and penned in with their animals.

Walking uphill from there, they soon crossed through the Sandia Mountains, and descending through forests of dark green piñon and juniper, they came into a broad, open plain. It was a strange country, a flatland with almost no trees, painted various shades of brown. The Navajos knew they were moving through this country, but they could not tell how fast or for how long. The land, every day, looked the same. They saw dark shapes on the horizon that could have been mountains, but they could also have been mirages. It was unsettling, not having anything to rest their eyes against.[16]

They turned north and came to the Santa Fe Trail, following the route that Confederate troops had taken toward Glorieta Pass and their last disastrous fight with the Union Army in 1862. Instead of going all the way to Fort Union, Manuelito's band turned and followed the road along the Pecos River to the south. They could not see the river itself. Its winding, shallow depths were hidden behind large scrub bushes and scraggly cottonwood trees. The road undulated, and then smoothed out. They were back in the seemingly featureless plain again, the home of coyotes and rattlesnakes.[17]

In early October 1866, Juanita, Manuelito, and their children walked through a gate and moved down the avenue and fields lying fallow on both sides. They had arrived at Bosque Redondo.

———————

The avenue led directly to Fort Sumner, where Juanita and the rest of their small band were corralled and counted. The soldiers gave them more rations and then sent them back north, on a road that crossed a wide acequia and then followed it, arcing through rolling prairies. Here they found the Diné, thousands of them. The soldiers had insisted that the Navajos cluster together in bands, and so Juanita and Manuelito found their way to their people, who had come to the reservation before them. They shed tears of joy at meeting their family members again. Then they wept in sorrow after hearing the stories they had to tell.[18]

Juanita and Manuelito learned that for more than two years, the Navajos had been worked almost to death, called out of their dirt huts in the morning by the ringing of a giant bell, delivered to the Bosque from St. Louis the previous summer. They were sent to plow the land, plant seeds, and dig out acequias. After November 1865, the Navajos had labored alone. The 350 Mescalero Apaches at the Bosque left en masse one night and did not return.[19] The first two years, the cutworms had eaten up the corn before the Diné could take it from the fields.

This year's harvest had looked promising until just a few weeks before Juanita and Manuelito arrived, when black clouds had rolled across the plains toward the Bosque. The rain fell in sheets and then the hail came, pounding the corn into the mud. The storms had caused the waters of the Pecos to rise, its currents running so hard and fast that they tore up the dam that the Navajos had built to funnel water into the acequias, and to catch logs that were floated downstream from woodcutting camps to the north. Loose rocks, chains, and bags all broke loose from the dam with the rush of water.

The Navajos could not explain why so many disasters had befallen them at the Bosque. They could only say that the ground was never intended for them.[20]

Juanita and Manuelito looked out into the prairie and saw just a few sheep and goats. What had happened to the large herds that so many of the people had brought with them to the Bosque? Some had been stolen away by Comanches and Kiowas, who rode up from the red dirt plains of western Texas to make quick strikes against the Bosque herds. Others had died of starvation. The lands around the reservation, which the soldiers had told them were a storied rangeland, did not grow enough of the nutritious grasses and shrubs that their animals had gotten fat upon in Diné Bikéyah. Still others, rooting around for anything that looked edible, had eaten plants that poisoned them. There were fewer than one thousand sheep at the Bosque now. This was a shock to Manuelito's band, whose members themselves had owned tens of thousands of churros before the Fearing Time.[21]

Juanita had brought a small herd with her, and she would have to tend to them carefully to ensure that they continued to provide for her family: the wool that she would use to weave the blankets that would keep them warm this winter; the goat milk that would help Shizie and Manuelito Segundo remain healthy; and meat in the event that the army's rations proved too meager to sustain them all.

This seemed likely, for Juanita and Manuelito's people reported that the rations were, in fact, paltry. To receive their share, Navajos gathered every other day at the Issue House, a long and low adobe building in the southernmost part of the Bosque. Some of the Navajo men worked inside, slaughtering twenty-eight cattle each ration day to feed the people. In their first year at the Bosque, the cattle had come up from southern New Mexico Territory along *El Camino Real*, or from the ranches on the Santa Fe Trail. Soon, however, a new kind of cow appeared on the reservation: light brown animals with massive horns extending horizontally from their heads. They were longhorns from Texas, driven up the Pecos River from the huge ranchlands of the Confederacy. After Union troops took Vicksburg in 1863, Texas ranchers could no longer send their cattle eastward across the Mississippi River. Instead, they had found a ready market for their cattle at Bosque Redondo.[22]

After killing the longhorns at the Issue House, Navajo butchers removed the entrails and drained the blood into pails, carefully setting them aside to distribute later. The Navajos lucky enough to secure the blood would stir it into cornmeal to make a thick, nutritious porridge. The butchers then cut the meat into three-quarter-pound portions, to be handed to the Diné waiting outside with their ration tickets and food baskets. After procuring their meat, they exchanged their tickets for a pound of flour per person.[23] They often pleaded for more, but the soldiers were strict and almost never made exceptions. This meant, the Diné told Juanita and Manuelito, that they had to try to obtain food in other ways.

During the first year they were at the Bosque, the Navajos had realized how easy it would be to forge ration tickets, which initially were made of metal. The talented silversmiths among them produced more than three thousand counterfeits before the army was able to shut down this practice by converting to handwritten paper tickets.[24]

Navajos could take advantage of the army's systems in other ways, however. Manuelito could apply to the soldiers for a pass to go hunting. There were deer, antelope, and rabbits to be had on the plains east of the Bosque. Although the army was worried about sending men off the reservation with bows and arrows, they knew that this was essential to diversifying the Navajos' diets, so they allowed it. Hunting without a pass was easy, too. The soldiers guarding the reservation boundaries were posted so far apart it was a simple thing to sneak by them.[25]

On the reservation, Juanita could send Shizie and Manuelito Segundo to the Indian School that the army had built, and the children would come home with extra ration tickets as a reward for attendance. And if Manuelito proved himself valuable to the soldiers as a worker, he might be able to earn extra food. The army had started to pay the men in rations when they made adobes for Fort Sumner's buildings or repaired corral fences.[26]

Once the crops matured enough to be edible, the Navajos could also take corn and melons from the fields planted near the Pecos. They did not believe this was theft. The Diné had plowed and planted these lands, and the bounty, when harvested, would come back to them in the form of rations anyway. Sometimes outright thievery was necessary, though, if their families were hungry enough. While the Mescaleros had still been living in lean-tos south of Fort Sumner, the Navajos had raided their fields. The soldiers, who had their own garden that they tended to at the fort, built a wall around their crops to try and deter the Navajos from taking their vegetables, but the Navajos found the wall easy to scale.[27]

Sometimes, the people said, it was the soldiers who came sneaking into Diné camps, hunting for women. They offered rations in exchange for sex. Some women agreed, others were raped. The officers at Fort Sumner turned their eyes away, and the soldiers were never punished for their crimes. The Navajos at the Bosque put their own heads down, and did whatever they had to in order to feed themselves and survive.[28]

———

Juanita and Manuelito would figure out how to obtain enough food. But first they had to build themselves a shelter. By the time they arrived in the fall of 1866, the days were getting shorter and colder. They heard tell of the harsh winters on the New Mexico plains, with the howling winds and driving blizzards that half-buried the huts that the Navajos had built for themselves. These shelters bore almost no resemblance to the hogans that Juanita had lived in for most of her life, which were carefully constructed and oriented to reflect the Navajos' relationship with the gods and the cosmos. These reservation huts were mere holes in the ground with a dirt roof covered in animal skins.

The Diné had to construct their houses this way. Their people told Juanita and Manuelito how quickly the trees had disappeared from the riverbanks after the first large groups of Navajos arrived in 1864. They had hoped that the woodcutters working north of the Bosque would send poles down the river, but then the dam had washed out.[29] They had become desperate for building material and for firewood. They cut limbs off of the trees that they had planted along the avenue and the acequias, and stole stakes that enclosed the corrals. They felled mesquite trees and dug out their roots, but soon these disappeared from the Bosque as well, and they had to go farther and farther to find them. Some of the people set out into the plains with sheepskins, hooking as many cockleburs as they could before returning to toss the spiky seeds into their fires.[30]

Juanita and Manuelito had no choice but to build their hut like the others, digging down into the dirt to create the floor and packing mud, grasses, and sticks together to make a roof. Manuelito went out hunting with his men, sometimes with a pass but more often without, and brought back skins to cover the roof. Juanita turned her attention to her flock of sheep. She also managed to find enough wood to build herself a loom.

Like many other women at the Bosque, Juanita went to work making blankets and clothing for her family. Every now and again the army brought in more sheep, but increasingly they sent in wagons of raw wool or, sometimes, yarn already spun at factories in the East. Juanita and the other weavers at Bosque Redondo made use of all of these materials. They also used bayeta cloth, a cheap red textile that the government provided, and army uniforms that they secured by trading with the soldiers. Carefully unraveling the threads, the women wove them into their blankets, creating lines and triangles in red and blue.[31]

Together, Juanita and Manuelito worked to protect their family and their people, and they survived their first winter at Bosque Redondo. In the spring of 1867, the soldiers called the Navajos back out into the fields to plow and plant their crops. The Diné did so without enthusiasm. They continued to sing songs and say prayers while they dropped the seeds into the dirt, in order to ensure a good crop. But most of them had lost faith in what the fields along the Pecos could provide for them. To the Navajos, Bosque Redondo was a cursed place. They called it Hwéeldi. The Land of Suffering.[32]

Over the previous three years, some of the Navajos on the reservation had responded to its terrible conditions by attempting to escape, as the Mescaleros had in November 1865. Every few months, the soldiers who counted the Navajos each morning would find some people missing, in small family groups or larger bands. The soldiers would sound the alarm and ride them down. Some would return on their own.

In the summer of 1867, after having been there for less than a year, Manuelito began to think about breaking out of Bosque Redondo. In July, there was a fracas with drunk soldiers, who said that the Navajos were stealing horses from the army's herd. Manuelito acted as a negotiator, helping to ease the tension and avoid a shootout. But the incident had left the Diné in a constant state of anxiety and suspicion. The new superintendent of Indian affairs in New Mexico, A. B. Norton, came to speak to them after the debacle.

Herrera Grande spoke for the people and once again described the hardships that the Navajos faced at Hwéeldi.

"What does the government want us to do—more than we have done?" he asked Norton. "Or more than we are doing?"[33]

Norton promised to take action, but the Navajos did not expect much. He was just another of a long list of American officials who arrived at the Bosque, asked some questions, and left. Nothing ever changed.

Soon after, the monsoons of August destroyed the dam that Navajos had rebuilt along the Pecos. When the river's waters fell a few weeks later, the acequias ran dry. Several weeks of no rains lowered the Pecos to a trickle, and the ground cracked in the dry heat. The corn harvest failed once again.[34] Manuelito had several talks with another headman named Barboncito, and they began to make plans to leave the reservation with their people.

One night in late September 1867, Juanita wrapped blankets around herself and the children and ushered them quietly out of their hut and into the darkness. They had to rely on the light of the moon and stars to find their way along the paths that wound through the reservation camps. The group of Navajos grew to more than three hundred, heading north first and then west. Four headmen, including Barboncito and Manuelito, were leading the way. They had picked an opportune time. Most of the soldiers were away chasing after Comanches, and Fort Sumner's commander would not be able to send men after them for several days.[35]

Once they left the boundaries of the reservation, the Diné split into smaller groups, creating a confusing track for the soldiers to follow. They headed for the Sandia Mountains. If they made it to the Rio Grande and then through its waters, they thought the army might not chase them down. Before they reached the Sandias, however, the journey had taken its toll. Their horses and mules were suffering, for the grasses in the plain were withered and the arroyos were dry. Hispano militias, whom the U.S. Army had authorized to pursue them, were drawing closer every day. Then came the soldiers themselves, sent to persuade Manuelito to return with his people. If he would not, they had been ordered to make them return by force.[36]

Three weeks after their breakout, Juanita and Manuelito turned their horses back toward Hwéeldi. Their flight had been an act of resistance, a protest against the horrific conditions at the reservation, and it had brought them a small taste of freedom. But once again, in order to ensure that they and their children would survive, they had to surrender to the U.S. Army.

21

Clark

The week after Juanita's and Manuelito's return to Bosque Redondo, John Clark left his office and walked to the Santa Fe Plaza. What had been an open square filled by wagons and animals in 1861 was now a fenced-off grassy space with walkways that converged at the center. Union soldiers had built these walks and set out trees along them in 1862–63, as part of a city improvement project. On October 24, 1867, New Mexico's civil and military administrators arranged themselves around a patch of dirt in the middle of the plaza and waited for a ceremony to begin.[1]

Clark was one of the few officials there who had been at his post since the beginning of the Civil War. In April 1866, the War Department had relieved James Carleton of duty, much to the delight of his enemies in New Mexico. Although his superiors had lauded his efficiency in the march from Los Angeles and his tenacity in the Union Army's campaigns against the Apaches and Navajos, his Bosque Redondo project had cost the federal government millions of dollars and caused a political uproar in New Mexico. It was time for him to leave, and turn his talents toward the Indian Wars in Texas. General George Getty, who replaced Carleton, was presiding over the day's events in the plaza.[2] Henry Connelly was no longer governor, and the citizens of New Mexico had elected a new territorial delegate, Charles Clever, to represent the Territory's interests in Congress. Clark recognized John Evans, the former governor of Colorado Territory, standing with A. B. Norton, New Mexico's new superintendent of Indian affairs. A small contingent of the city's Masonic brotherhood marched up to the center of the plaza, and the ceremony began.

Getty introduced everyone, and the new governor delivered an oration (which was then, as in the Santa Fe tradition, translated into Spanish). Then the McGee brothers—Irish architects who advertised themselves in the *Gazette* as builders of public and private buildings, mills, smelters, stone cellars, and foundations—brought a large square stone up one of the walkways and laid it carefully in the dirt. The Masons crossed their arms at their breasts in unison, then raised them above their heads and dropped them to their sides, conferring their honors upon the site. The audience applauded and then dispersed.[3]

Over the next six months the McGees were planning to add several more stones to the foundation and four columns at the corners, which would support an obelisk whose tip would tower thirty-three feet above the plaza. On each side of the base, the brothers would place a marble slab, and chisel into them memorials to the heroes of the Union Army who had fallen in battles against the Confederates at Valverde, Apache Canyon, Glorieta Pass, and Peralta. One of the panels would also laud the men who died in Union Army campaigns against the "Savage Indians" of New Mexico.[4]

One evening later that week, Clark searched through his papers for the account he had written about the Battle of Valverde. Finding it tucked between the pages of one of his leather-bound diaries, he read the description with interest. Back in March 1862, Clark had been shocked at the outcome of the battle, dismayed at Richard Canby's inaction and what he perceived to be the cowardice of most of the Union Army's volunteers during the Confederates' final charge. At the time the only Union officer he praised was Alexander McRae, the artillery commander who stood by his guns until the very end. McRae "fired his pistol until his charges were exhausted & finally was killed by the side of his guns," Clark had written with admiration. "Such heroism is sublime—He could not have died a more glorious death, or in a better cause."[5]

The previous spring, the body of Captain McRae had arrived in Santa Fe. His family had paid to exhume the body from the grave at Fort Craig in order to rebury it in the States.[6] While his name would not be listed individually on the Union Soldiers' Monument in the plaza, surely all Santa Fe residents would remember McRae's brave deeds when they read the name "Valverde" cut into the marble.

Clark had been in Santa Fe since July 1866, after taking a yearlong leave of absence to be with Jane and the children in Illinois. He had spent his time since his return on additional expeditions to the Arizona gold country, hearing and deciding disputes over land claims, writing reports, and drawing maps of New Mexico Territory. In the fall of 1867, when his workdays were done, Clark often found himself immersed in the past, reading accounts of the Civil War or leafing through *Bancroft's History of the United States*.[7] It seemed more comforting to read about what had come before than to contemplate his present in Santa Fe, or the future of the nation. When Clark had returned to New Mexico, he found most of his friends and their wives gone, or about to leave the Territory. Recently he had been having "blue days," during which he keenly felt his isolation from his family and the lack of congenial society in Santa Fe. When Clark sat down with his diary at the end of such days, he found he had nothing to say.

"A day without incident," he sighed. "A blank in my life."[8]

This did not mean that nothing was happening in Santa Fe. Within a few months of his return there had been four murders in the city and numerous robberies. Clark had worried that this crime spree would lead to vigilantism, but things had calmed down since then and such a "terrible remedy for the violation of law" was not necessary.[9]

The political scene in New Mexico, however, was tumultuous. Anglo and Hispano New Mexicans continued to be bitterly divided on the future of Bosque Redondo, even after James Carleton's departure from the Territory. There were rumors that the reservation would soon be taken from the War Department and turned over to the Bureau of Indian Affairs, which was part of the Department of the Interior. Clark believed this would be a serious mistake. He had always agreed with Carleton that without constant military surveillance and force of arms, all Indians would revert to their former ways. The Bosque Navajos were still not self-sufficient, and breakouts were becoming more common. If a meticulous man like James Carleton and the soldiers under his command could not force the Navajos to become civilized, what could Indian agents do? Clark was sure that this new oversight arrangement would fail.

While the army struggled to subdue the reservation Navajos, the other Native peoples of the Southwest—the Chiricahua Apaches to the west, still angry about the murder of Mangas Coloradas, and the Plains Indians to the east, engaged in an all-out war against whites in revenge for the Sand Creek Massacre—continued to wreak havoc along the region's roads, killing American travelers and attacking ranches. It seemed to Clark that a general Indian War was about to erupt across the West in the fall of 1867.[10]

The continued vulnerability of the Anglo and Hispano citizens of New Mexico had been a theme in the recent election for New Mexico's territorial delegate. That contest had resulted in a number of clashes between the supporters of Charles Clever and those of his opponent, José Francisco Chaves. Clark had watched as armed gangs marched through Santa Fe and to the quarters of their candidates, urging them into conflagratory speeches before building bonfires and shooting off rockets and roman candles, illuminating the plaza.[11] As soon as the votes had been counted, the election was disputed. In the end, Clever was declared the winner. Clark was not pleased. The two men had never been on good terms, and word had reached Clark that Clever planned to lobby for his removal as surveyor general of New Mexico once he reached Washington, D.C.

"I trust that it will be in my power to repay with interest some of the individuals who I know desire & will work underhandedly for my removal," Clark noted grimly. "Time brings all things even."[12]

Such shenanigans angered and depressed him. He had hoped to serve out his term in peace, to "attend strictly to the duties of my office and to keep aloof of the political quarrels of the politicians."[13]

———

It was becoming harder and harder to remain distant of local or national politics, however. Clark was still a committed Republican, one of the only government officers in New Mexico who was loyal to that party. But the growing antagonism between the Republican-controlled U.S. Congress and President Andrew Johnson worried him. Clark had been out on a surveying trip to Arizona when Johnson became president in the wake of Lincoln's assassination. The Tennessee War Democrat, an avowed advocate of free labor and enemy of secession, had been recruited to the ticket in 1864 in order to woo moderates to a national "Union" party of Republicans.

Clark was in Santa Fe in the summer of 1865, testifying before the Doolittle Commission about conditions at Bosque Redondo, when Johnson began pardoning one hundred Confederates a day and returning their confiscated lands to them. When Johnson announced that the states of the former Confederacy need only recognize the 13th Amendment abolishing slavery, nullify secession, and repudiate the Confederate war debt in order to rejoin the Union, Republicans like Clark were enraged. The former rebel states should be forced to do more to provide for and protect the rights of millions of freed people within their borders, as a requirement of readmission. And under no circumstances should former Confederates be allowed to hold public office.[14]

Clark had been back home in Illinois in 1866, a state dominated by the more moderate wing of the Republican Party, when the Radical Republicans in Congress formed their Joint Committee on Reconstruction. They had passed a series of bills to ensure the rights of newly freed African Americans, and to provide for their education and employment. While he was on his way back to New Mexico that summer, Clark read newspaper accounts of the passage of the 14th amendment, which granted citizenship to "all persons born or naturalized in the United States, and subject to the jurisdiction thereof" and denied former Confederates the right to run for any office, civil or military.[15]

In mid-March 1867, Clark and his fellow New Mexico residents heard about the flurry of legislation that Congress had passed at the beginning of the month: the Military Reconstruction Act, which divided the South into military districts and empowered the army to protect African-American rights; and the Tenure of Office and Command of Army Acts, which was passed to prevent President Johnson from removing cabinet members Lincoln had appointed, who were in charge of implementing the Radical Reconstruction plan. Johnson had immediately vetoed these measures, of course, but Congress had passed them over his veto on the very same day. Although Clark hoped that the Radicals and Johnson might come to some sort of compromise regarding Reconstruction policies, he supported Republican measures and believed that they would benefit the nation as a whole as well as the former states of the Confederacy.[16]

"[Virginia and her kindred States in the South] will make greater advance during the next twenty-five year[s] in material & intellectual development and in true ideas of liberty and of the proper relation of man to man," Clark believed, "than in all their previous existence."[17]

Reconstruction would be accomplished, if only under military rule.

"We shall have peace and unity again," Clark declared.[18]

Congress had also passed measures in which Clark was particularly interested, funding two geological explorations of the western territories. One would survey the 40th parallel through northern California, Nevada, and eastern Wyoming. The other would map out all of the western territories adjacent to the Rocky Mountains. Clark was envious. His own plans for exploration had been curtailed by the attachment of the Territory of Arizona to the surveying district of California. He would no longer be sent to map out that mineral-rich region for the General Land Office, and the Department of the Interior.[19]

Clark also read with satisfaction that in March 1867 Congress had passed an act abolishing peonage and Indian slavery in New Mexico. The governor issued a proclamation declaring that this new federal law would be enforced, and that enslaved Apaches and Navajos working in New Mexican households and enslaved Hispanos living in Native communities would henceforth be free. Since then, however, Clark had seen no real change in the labor systems of the Territory. When asked, New Mexican slaveholders insisted that they told their slaves that they were free, but they had chosen to remain in the homes in which they had been domesticated.

"They prefer a life among our people," one editorial in the *Santa Fe New Mexican* insisted, "to one among their own."[20]

It was unclear what it would take to abolish Indian slavery in New Mexico once and for all. Given the U.S. Army's treatment of the Navajos at Bosque Redondo, it did not appear that Congress could send military forces to the Territory with the same instructions as those they sent to the former states of the Confederacy. The Republicans clearly did not see Indian slavery as the same sort of immoral system as African-American enslavement. They took the same stance they had since 1863, fighting simultaneously for black emancipation and indigenous incarceration. Both practices served their ultimate goal, to take possession of the lands of the entire continent, and give them over to free laborers. Perhaps Congress thought that Indian slavery in the Southwest would just fade away, as the region's tribes were forced onto reservations and converted to civilization.

———

Through the fall and winter of 1867 Clark continued to work on whatever land claims came to his attention and drafted an updated map of New Mexico for the General Land Office.[21] On New Year's Day he mused about what the year 1868 would bring for him and his family.

"It is one of the wisest provisions of a good Providence that we do not have the power of reading the future," Clark decided. "We can only wait & hope."[22]

Although Charles Clever had not yet acted against him, it was still possible that Clark would be removed from his post, and sent home to Illinois. Some of his friends had suggested that the surveyor general position in Utah might be an option, and he had promised to consider it. Jane had urged him to think about running for Congress from his home district. Clark thought this an absurd possibility, given that the field was already so crowded. What intrigued him more was the prospect of working for a railroad company.

Since the passage of the Pacific Railway Act in 1862, engineers had been laying the transcontinental track at a rapid pace, moving the iron line westward from Council Bluffs, Iowa, toward a union with the Central Pacific somewhere in the Rockies. Clark had met the treasurer and chief engineer of the Union Pacific when they came through Santa Fe to survey possible spur routes. Clark had "proffered all assistance in my power & any information in my possession" and they seemed to appreciate it. Surely this or another railroad company would need a man like him, who had a knowledge of the West, and who could make credible maps to help sell its lands to the public. Railroads would change everything in the West, and Clark wanted to be a part of that important process.[23]

Despite these connections and a host of possibilities, Clark still felt unsettled. He often found himself staring off in the distance during the workday, "constantly building castles which I fear have little foundation to support them."[24]

Soon he received word that gave him focus. The furlough he'd requested had come through, and he would leave for Illinois to see Jane and the children. Jane had been managing an enormous household in his absence. At any given moment fourteen people were living there, giving her not a moment's rest. They had been married for twenty-nine years, and in the past six years he had left her alone for months at a time. Clark went out to the stores in Santa Fe looking for a gift for her, one that would commemorate their time together and their time apart. He found what he was looking for: a beautiful breast pin. To purchase it, he exchanged an old chain, a pocket pistol, and a half ounce of gold from the Arizona mines.[25]

———

In February 1868, as John Clark traveled eastward toward home, the news broke that after months of conflict over the military enforcement of the Reconstruction Acts, President Johnson had removed Secretary of War Edwin Stanton from his post. Stanton refused to recognize the order or vacate his office.[26] Clark had followed all of these developments from Santa Fe, and felt anxious about the turmoil this was creating in Washington. It had been clear since the summer that Johnson was "pursuing a course that may finally result in his impeachment."[27]

Clark decided that he would stop for a few weeks to see his family but then travel on to Washington, D.C. If Congress was going to remove President Johnson from power, he wanted to be seated in the galleries to watch the proceedings. Then he would return home through Chicago, where the Republicans would be meeting in May to nominate a presidential candidate. It was almost certain that Ulysses S. Grant would be their man, a fact that pleased Clark. Grant was the northern hero of the Civil War and the current general of the armies. He had broken with Johnson over the president's stance on Reconstruction, arguing that reconciliationist measures repudiated all that Union soldiers had fought and died for during the Civil War. Grant was also a proponent of the reservation system, and believed that Indian removal and "civilization" programs were necessary to bring peace to the western states and territories. This policy position endeared him to the Anglo and Hispano residents of New Mexico. Furthermore, Grant had expressed no interest in the presidency, which made him even more popular. There was little doubt of his election if nominated.[28]

"With Grant for our candidate next year all will be well again," Clark believed, "so I do not despair of the Republic."[29]

22

Juanita

John Clark's route out of New Mexico in 1868 took him north of Bosque Redondo, where the grasses had begun to green up in the spring sunshine. When army officers called the Navajos into the fields to furrow the soil and prepare for planting corn, they refused. The crops had failed four years in a row. To the Diné, it was obvious that the land would never give them anything, no matter how hard they worked. The officers did not try to force them. The reservation was now under the authority of the Bureau of Indian Affairs, and the number of soldiers garrisoned at Fort Sumner had been reduced. It would be impossible to round up thousands of resistant Navajos and attempt to oversee their labor.[1]

In March 1868, the Diné's Indian agent sent word that he wanted to see Manuelito and a few of the other headmen. The agent, Theodore Dodd—the same man who had commanded Alonzo Ickis's company of Colorado miners in 1861–62—told them about a letter he received. Congress had been debating about the future of Bosque Redondo, which was still costing the federal government many times its annual appropriation of $100,000. James Carleton's misjudgments regarding the reservation's location and the large number of Navajos who ended up there, along with the constant environmental disasters and acts of Navajo resistance, had led them to consider abandoning the reservation altogether. If this occurred, an official in Washington wanted to know what the Navajos preferred to do.

"If they left Bosque Redondo," he queried, "would the Navajos be willing to go to their former home, or to lands in the Indian territory west of Arkansas?"[2]

Manuelito and the others expressed the desire they had been repeat-
ing over and over to Dodd since he had arrived: they wanted to return to
Diné Bikéyah. The soil in the homeland was more productive, they argued. There would be an abundance of timber to build their hogans, and
they could gather beans, wild potatoes, and fruits to subsist themselves
while their crops ripened. The headmen left the meeting sure that Dodd
would report their wishes, but not optimistic that the government would
listen. They had answered such questions in councils and meetings and
interviews since 1865, and these conversations had come to nothing.[3]

In April, Dodd called for Manuelito once again. He wanted Manuelito
and Barboncito to ride with him to Santa Fe and talk with the military
commander of the Department of New Mexico. Juanita and the children—
Manuelito Segundo (almost a teenager now), along with nine-year-old
Shizie, and the new baby, Alk'iníbaa—watched him head off on horseback
on the road north. In Santa Fe, Manuelito and Barboncito met with General George Getty, who told them that another government delegation
was on the way, members of a Peace Commission. They were tasked with
negotiating peace treaties with the Plains Indians, and with making a final
decision about Bosque Redondo. The headmen returned to the reservation to await this new delegation.[4]

As the days turned into weeks, the Navajos grew restless. Some talked
of leaving again, en masse, as they had tried to do the previous fall. Manuelito climbed to the top of his hut and talked to his people about 'Iiná
("life").

"'Iiná does not end," he said, "it goes on. [We] must hold on to the
future with all of our strength."[5]

In mid-May, a large group of Navajos gathered at the eastern boundary of Bosque Redondo, where the grasses of the Pecos Valley turned into
the red dirt of western Texas. They scattered across the land and began to
search for a coyote, an intelligent and adaptive animal that the Diné believed had knowledge beyond that of the people. Whenever they did not
know what might happen, they asked Coyote.[6]

Someone found the animal, a female sleeping in the short brush after
a long night of hunting. The Diné formed a large circle and began walking
toward her, until there was no space between them. Coyote was skittish,
her long, bushy tail sweeping the ground. When Barboncito stepped into
the circle and faced her, she calmed. He came close and grabbed her long
snout, and pulled a white shell bead out of his pouch. The shell was from
Sisnaajini (the whites called it Blanca Peak), one of the four sacred moun-

tains of the homeland.[7] Barboncito put the bead in Coyote's mouth, and then let her go. The Diné took a step back, and then another, to give the animal some room. She turned clockwise and then walked off, to the west.

The Navajos began to smile. Coyote had given her answer. They would be going back to Diné Bikéyah.[8]

––––––––––

A few days after the Coyote ceremony, on May 27, 1868, the members of the Peace Commission arrived at Bosque Redondo. A small wagon train processed through the gates at the north end of the reservation, escorted by an army band playing lively tunes. When the wagons arrived at Fort Sumner, several men stepped out. One was General Getty, and with him was a man immediately recognizable to all of the soldiers assembled there: William Tecumseh Sherman, famed Civil War commander and current lieutenant general of the Army of the United States. With a few flecks of white in his red beard, Sherman had the same stern and disapproving look he sported in his wartime photographs.

The other, a shorter man with an abundance of dark brown hair and a voluminous mustache and goatee, was less familiar. Samuel F. Tappan had been in New Mexico Territory before. He had come to the Rockies to mine for gold in 1860, and in March 1862 he had come with the 1st Colorado and fought the Texans at Glorieta Pass. After garrisoning Fort Craig for a few months with Alonzo Ickis's company of "Brave Mountaineers," Tappan had marched back to Colorado with his regiment and mustered out of the Union Army. He knew Theodore Dodd from those days, and it was a strange coincidence that both men found themselves at Bosque Redondo in May 1868, to help determine the fate of the Navajos. It was Tappan who had written to Dodd a few months before, asking about the Navajos' preference for a new reservation location.[9]

The report of the Doolittle Commission, which had visited the Bosque in 1865, had finally been published in January 1867. The testimony recorded within it had spurred Congress to create the Peace Commission, and empower its members to call together the Native peoples of the Plains and hammer out treaties with them. It was a precarious time in the history of the nation, with the impeachment trials of President Johnson and the violent opposition of southern whites to Reconstruction. In order to reintegrate the nation, the federal government was exerting most of its military power in the South. At the same time, it needed to take full command of the West and create some order out of the violent chaos of the Civil War.[10]

The peace commissioners had been doing this nationalizing work since the summer of 1867, and had already signed two important treaties with Native peoples in Kansas and Wyoming. From Laramie, Samuel Tappan had headed south toward New Mexico, following a portion of the route he had taken with the 1st Colorado six years before. Sherman had joined him at Fort Union. He was coming west on the Santa Fe Trail after testifying in Andrew Johnson's impeachment trial.

As Tappan and Sherman settled into their quarters at Fort Sumner and made plans to speak to the army's officers about conditions at Bosque Redondo, General Getty sent messengers to the Navajo camps. One of them informed Manuelito that the commissioners wanted to meet with the headmen the next day.

━━━━━

It was already warm by the time Juanita and Manuelito arrived at the fort at 11 a.m. on May 28. The soldiers had erected a large tent over part of the grounds for shade. Underneath its canvas roof, Tappan and Sherman sat, flanked by Getty and General Benjamin Roberts, who had fought at the Battle of Valverde and was now the commander of Fort Sumner. Juanita stayed behind as Manuelito entered the tent and sat with Barboncito and five other headmen. There was a buzzing in the air: the murmured conversations of a growing crowd of Navajos settling in beside Juanita to listen to the proceedings; the calls of birds and the hum of early-summer insects; and the clicking and scraping of a photographer, fixing images and moving glass plates, attempting to capture the scene.[11]

Sherman stood.

"The Commissioners are here now for the purpose of learning and knowing all about your condition," he began, "and we wish to hear from you the truth and nothing but the truth."

He paused while his words were translated from English into Spanish, and then from Spanish into Navajo.

"We find you have done a good deal of work here in making acequias," Sherman continued. On their ride down the avenue and subsequent tours of the fields along the Pecos, the commissioners had noticed that the Navajos had done no plowing or planting that spring, and that their herds of sheep and goats were minuscule. The Navajos had clearly "sunk into a condition of absolute poverty and despair." Sherman was curious about how this had come to be.

"Before we discuss what we are to do with you," he concluded, "we want to know what you have done in the past and what you think about your reservation here."[12]

There was another pause as the translators did their work. Then Barboncito stood and began to speak. To him and all the other headmen, it was obvious that it was Bosque Redondo that was to blame for the destruction of their crops, and the deaths of the people and their animals.

"Our Grand-fathers had no idea of living in any other country except our own," he said, "and I do not think it right for us to do so."[13]

Barboncito told Tappan and Sherman what the headmen had been telling government officials for years now. The Navajos had worked hard, building acequias and making adobes, and trying to coax corn and wheat out of the ground. They had brought many sheep, goats, horses, and mules with them to the reservation, but the animals had died, or had been stolen by Comanches and Kiowas.

"I thought at one time the whole world was the same as my own country," that the land would produce for Navajos wherever they were. "But I got fooled," Barboncito said. "This ground was not intended for us."[14]

Evidence of this was suggested by the number of deaths on the Long Walk and at Bosque Redondo, almost 20 percent of the population. So many of the people had perished, Barboncito said, it was hard to know the number.

"Some work at the acequias [and] take sick and die," he said. "Others die with the hoe in their hands. They go to the river to their waists and suddenly disappear. Others have been struck and torn to pieces by lightning."

It did not seem to matter what precautions they took or herbs they gathered or ceremonies their medicine men performed.

"Whatever we do here causes death."[15]

The Diné had been waiting, Barboncito said, and hoping. Waiting for the commissioners to arrive, hoping that General Sherman would do all he could for the Navajo. It was a hope that "goes in at my feet and out at my mouth." Barboncito looked directly at Sherman.

"I am speaking to you now as if I was speaking to a spirit," he said, "and I wish you to tell me when you are going to take us to our own country."[16]

———

Barboncito's words confirmed for Sherman all he had seen and read about Bosque Redondo, and about the Navajos' desperate situation. He was also aware that Navajos had been in a constant state of warfare with the United States since the 1840s. He wanted to make sure they understood how vulnerable they were, and would continue to be.

"You are right, the world is big enough for all the people it contains and all should live at peace with their neighbors," Sherman said. "[But] the Navajos are very few indeed compared with all the people in the world. They are not more than seven leaves to all the leaves you have ever seen." It was the American government's intention to do what was right, however. "Right to *you*," Sherman emphasized, "and right to *us* as a people."[17]

The general went on to present the Navajos with two options.

"For many years we have been collecting Indians on the Indian Territory south of the Arkansas," he noted, "and they are now doing well." Some of these Native peoples, who had aligned themselves with the Confederacy, had given up a large tract of their lands as part of a peace treaty negotiated in 1865. Sherman thought there was enough rich bottomland on this tract to support the more than seven thousand Navajos currently at the Bosque. He also believed that concentrating all of America's Indians in one place would help the U.S. Army control them.[18]

"Send some of your wisest men to see for themselves," Sherman urged, "if they like it we will give you a reservation there."

The other option was to send the Navajos back to their own country. Sherman pulled out a map and gestured to Barboncito to come over and see it. The map showed the four sacred mountains of Diné Bikéyah, Fort Canby, and the territories of the Utes and the Pueblos.

"If we agree [to send you back], we will make a boundary line outside of which you must not go except for the purpose of trading," Sherman said. "We must have a clearly defined boundary line and know exactly where you belong to." The Navajos could defend their own lands from any Ute or Apache incursions, but they must not pursue them beyond the border.

"The Army will do the fighting," Sherman said, "You must live at peace."[19]

———

After all of Sherman's words had been translated, Barboncito considered the two options only briefly. The Navajos would not send any of their people to Indian Territory.

"I hope to God you will not ask me to go to any other country except my own," he said. "It might turn out to be another Bosque Redondo."[20]

Sherman asked him to choose ten headmen as representatives of all the Navajos. They would meet the next day to conclude the terms of the treaty. The first day of the council came to a close.

Tappan and Sherman went to Fort Sumner with Getty and Roberts, and the Navajos made their way back to their huts. Juanita and Manuelito had much to discuss: the powerful words of Barboncito; the general's equally forceful statements; the seriousness with which the commissioners and the soldiers treated the idea of the people returning to their homeland; and the hope that finally, they would be able to leave this place.

———

The next morning, Juanita and Manuelito were back at Fort Sumner, in the abandoned fields between the soldier's hospital and the Indian Issue House. The crowd was much larger that day. All of the Diné had heard about the first day's discussions, and Sherman had asked for the entire tribe to be present. Once again, Manuelito left Juanita and went to join nine other headmen in the tent.

First, there were some procedural matters to attend to. It was vital that the Navajos understood that Tappan and Sherman represented the U.S. government in good faith. And it was important that the Navajos agreed to have the headmen represent them.[21]

"We have come from our Capital, Washington, where our Government consists of a President and a great Council," Sherman began. "We are empowered to do now what is necessary for your good, but what we do must be submitted to our Great Father in Washington."

Sherman asked if ten headmen had been chosen to speak and sign for the Navajo people. Manuelito, Barboncito, and eight other men stood up. This was not an unfamiliar process to them. Many times in the past, the headmen of the various bands had represented their kin at gatherings of the Diné, where they made decisions about war and peace, and conducted ceremonies to ensure their well-being. They had also sent headmen to treaty negotiations with Spanish, Mexican, and American officials.

Sherman turned to the assembled crowd.

"Are you satisfied with these ten men?" he asked.

"*Aoo'!*" the crowd yelled out. Yes.

"We will now consider these ten men your principal men," Sherman acknowledged, "and we want them to select a chief . . . for we cannot talk to all the Navajos."

The Americans were always insisting that the Navajos choose a single leader. It was another way they tried to civilize them, to force them to adopt American forms of political leadership. But it was clear that if the people wanted to leave Bosque Redondo, they had to know what to protest and what to accept. Manuelito and the others conferred, and chose Barboncito to speak for them during the rest of the negotiations.

"From this time on," Sherman told the Navajos, "you must do as Barboncito tells you. With him we will deal and do all for your good."

All of the Navajos were unlikely to do anything that only one headman dictated, but the people were so close to going home that Manuelito and the others agreed to recognize Barboncito's actions as representative of the will of the Diné. Sherman went on to explain that everything would be put down in ink on paper, "so that hereafter there may be no misunderstanding between us."

Again, the general insisted, "we want to know if the whole Navajo nation is represented by those present and if they will be bound by the acts of these ten men."

The response rang out across the abandoned fields. "*Aoo'!*"[22]

Barboncito stood up, and once again made the feelings of the Diné known.

"It is true I never liked this place, and feel sorry for being here," he said, "from here I would like to go back [on] the same road we came by."

He began to imagine the return journey of the people, crossing the Rio Grande and visiting the Pueblo villages where so many Navajo kin resided. They would then go to Tséyi', the great canyon at the heart of the Navajo country, where so many had made their last stand against Rope Thrower. From there, Barboncito said, the people would disperse across the homeland, building their hogans and planting their fields between the boundaries of the four sacred mountains. They would live as they had before, with long distances between them, in order to manage their resources successfully.

"It would not do to put them all together as they are here," Barboncito said, "if separated they would be more industrious."

Barboncito had some concerns. The people wanted to farm and herd their animals in peace. But they also wanted to hunt in mountains in the western reaches of the homeland, and to trade in the Pueblo and Hispano towns to the east.

"I do not think it right to confine us to a certain part," Barboncito said. "We want to have the privilege of going outside the line to hunt and trade."

Sherman agreed.

"You can go outside the line to hunt: you can go to Mexican towns to trade," he said, "but your farms and homes must be inside the boundary line beyond which you have no claim to the land."

Barboncito was pleased.

"That is the way I like to be, and return the Commissioners my best thanks," he told Sherman. Once again, he began to envision the future.

"After we get back to our country it will brighten up again and the Navajos will be as happy as the land," he mused, "black clouds will rise and there will be plenty of rain. Corn will grow in abundance and everything look happy." At Bosque Redondo—Hwéeldi, the Land of Suffering—everything was black and red. That was not how it should be, it did not look right. Back in Diné Bikéyah, "everything should be white or yellow, representing the flower and the corn."[23]

———

Barboncito pulled himself from his vision and turned back to Sherman. His tone sharpened.

"I want to drop this conversation now and talk about Navajo children held as prisoners by Mexicans."

If the general was surprised, he did not show it.

"About four years ago we had slaves," Sherman replied, "and there was a great war about it, and now there are none. . . . [And] about [your] children being held as Peons by Mexicans, you ought to know that there is an Act of Congress against it."

If any Hispanos were still holding Navajo children as slaves, Sherman reassured them, the army officers in New Mexico would put the slaveholders in jail. Barboncito could apply to the judges and the land commissioners to locate their lost children. At the moment, however, the peace commissioners could not help the Navajos with this problem.

"That is a matter with which we have nothing to do," he said dismissively.

Sherman changed the topic and asked Barboncito about building schools and blacksmith and carpenter shops on the reservation, to teach Navajo children English and new skills. The headman assented, and the council appeared to be drawing to an end.[24]

Then, suddenly, Samuel Tappan spoke for the first time.

"How many Navajos are among the Mexicans now?" he asked Barboncito. Slavery was a topic of interest to Tappan. He had been an abolitionist before the war, moving from Massachusetts to Kansas in 1854 to help found the town of Lawrence, a Free State stronghold during the violent struggle over the future of slavery in the United States.[25]

"Over half the tribe," the headman replied.

"How many have returned within the five years?"

"Cannot tell."

Sherman interrupted.

"We will do all we can to have your children returned to you," the general promised. "Our government is determined that the enslavement of the Navajos shall cease and those who are guilty of holding them as peons shall be punished. All are free now in this country to go and come as they please."

After making this sweeping, optimistic statement, Sherman brought the council to an end, telling the Navajos that they would meet again the next day, to read out the treaty.[26]

On May 30, when the Navajo headmen arrived at the negotiation grounds, they had two additional headmen with them. Barboncito asked Sherman if they could be admitted as members of the Navajo council, and the general agreed. Then they were ready to commence business.

Sherman held up a sheaf of papers.

"We have it all written down on paper," he announced to the headmen and the thousands of Navajos who had once again gathered in the abandoned fields. "We do not consider it complete until we have all signed our names to it."

Sherman began to read the treaty, and its multiple provisions were translated for the Navajos.

"From this day forward," Article 1 of the treaty began, "all war between the parties to this agreement shall forever cease." The Navajos would deliver up any "bad men" who committed a wrong or depredation on "any one, white, black, or Indian, subject to the authority of the United States and at peace therewith," to be duly punished by the American courts. The government pledged, likewise, to bring to justice any whites who committed crimes against the Navajos.

The headmen indicated their assent.

Sherman read on, describing the boundary markers of the reservation in Diné Bikéyah, and the buildings the U.S. government agreed to construct there: a warehouse, carpenter and blacksmith shops, a school and chapel, and a building where the Navajo agent would reside and distribute annuities on the first of September every year, for ten years. The government would also provide equipment for the Navajos if any of them wished to farm.

"[Such an] individual," Sherman continued, "shall have the privilege to select . . . a tract of land within said reservation, not exceeding one hundred and sixty acres in extent." That individual would be the exclusive owner of the tract. Only he and his family could cultivate it, and the government would give them seeds and agricultural implements for the first several years of cultivation.[27]

Since the Navajos had arrived at Bosque Redondo in 1864, Union soldiers had been trying to persuade them to claim and farm their own plots on the reservation in this manner. The Diné had always been farmers. But for one man to hold bounded lands for himself and his family for the foreseeable future seemed nonsensical to them. The treaty stipulation did not seem to force individuals into land ownership, however, and it appeared that they could farm whatever lands they chose.

The headmen therefore assented, and Sherman read on.[28]

The Navajos, he said, would be required to send their children to English-speaking schools.

On the reservation, many of the Diné had resisted the soldiers' attempts to compel their children into the schoolhouse. They saw it as a form of theft, an attempt to take their culture from them. If this was a price they had to pay in order to return them to the homeland, however, they would pay it. The children could learn English and enough of the Americans' ways to trade with them. They would continue to speak Navajo and practice the ceremonies at all other times.[29]

The headmen assented.

The Navajos would also give up raiding, Sherman informed them. The government would give them fifteen thousand sheep and five hundred beef cattle in order to build their herds, along with articles they could not manufacture themselves. These should subsist the Navajos until they could bring in crops. They would not have to ride out and raid Hispano towns and ranches ever again.

The Navajos would also agree not to attack, capture, or kill Americans. Nor would they make any opposition to military posts or roads that the U.S. Army might build in the future, or protest the construction of railroads near their reservation at Diné Bikéyah.

At that moment, the iron rails of the first transcontinental railroad were approaching one another far north of Bosque Redondo, in Utah. It would not be long, however, before the railroad companies would build lines along the 35th parallel, connecting Santa Fe and Los Angeles. The government would compensate the Navajos for any damage that such construction might cause within their reservation lands, but the Navajos could not impede it.[30]

The Diné were unaware that according to the Peace Commission, this was the most important provision of the treaty. Congress had specifically instructed Sherman, Tappan, and the others to negotiate agreements with Native peoples that would "establish security for person and property along the lines of the railroad now being constructed to the Pacific and other thoroughfares of travel to the western Territories."[31]

The headmen assented.

The reservation at Diné Bikéyah was to be the Navajos' permanent home, Sherman said. Its lands could not be ceded without the agreement of three-quarters of the entire male population of the tribe. By signing the treaty, he reminded them, they would "relinquish all right to occupy any territory outside their reservation, as herein defined." They could hunt on contiguous lands if the amount of game justified the chase, but otherwise they were to remain on the homeland reservation and respect its borders.

The headmen were also expected, Sherman concluded, to induce the more than one thousand Navajos who had never come to Bosque Redondo to give up their nomadic ways and settle permanently on the reservation.[32]

The headmen assented. Then Barboncito spoke.

"We are very well pleased with what you have said and well satisfied with that reservation," he said. "It is the very heart of our country and is more than we ever expected to get."

Ganado Mucho, the newest member of the council, stood.

"We have been waiting for a long time to hear the good words you have now told us, about going back to our own country," he said. "I will not stop talking until I have told all the tribe the good news."[33]

When the council dispersed, the good news traveled swiftly from the abandoned fields, past the *acequia madre*, and into the Navajo camps to the east. Some of the treaty requirements, particularly the reservation border enforcement and the English education of their children, did not sit well with many Navajos. But the people were willing to do what they had to do to escape Hwéeldi. The headmen would sign the treaty, and the Diné would go home.

Early in the morning on June 1, 1868, a photographer set up his camera outside the Fort Sumner hospital. As the headmen assembled, William Tecumseh Sherman arranged the group underneath the shade of two large cottonwood trees. He placed the signers of the treaty in the first row, sitting side by side. Manuelito and Barboncito sat together on the photographer's right. A few other Navajos stood behind them and were flanked by Sherman, Tappan, and General Roberts and a few members of his staff. The photographer told the group to stay as still as possible while he exposed the plate.[34] As he rushed off to process the photographs, the Navajo headmen and the commissioners came together, for the final time, at the negotiation site.

The commissioners had laid out three copies of the treaty on a table. Each one was written out on the lined paper of a U.S. Army ledger book, with a thin blue stripe down the left side. The copies were of different lengths, given the handwriting styles of the various clerks, but Tappan and Sherman affirmed that the articles were as Sherman had read them to the Navajos two days before.

Sherman signed first, and then Tappan. They called up the headmen, pointing out to each his name, then the blank space between "his" and "mark." Each headman pressed the pen into each copy of the treaty, making an "X" in the space, affirming his own identity, the tribal sovereignty of the Diné, and their recognition of the authority of the United States of America. With the signing, the Navajos traded one reservation for another. They lost some of their power over their own lives, but won the right to shape their people's future in their homeland. It was a bittersweet moment.[35]

After all of the witnesses had signed each copy of the treaty, the clerks bound up the pages along the top, tying them with red ribbons. The commissioners gave one copy to Barboncito to take with him back to Diné Bikéyah. Sherman took one and gave it to a courier, who would ride with it to Fort Union and then send it eastward to the U.S. Congress in Washington, D.C. Samuel Tappan would take one copy back with him to the East Coast and file it among his papers.

Juanita and Manuelito and the Navajos left Fort Sumner en masse, returning to their camps to celebrate with ceremonies and dances, and to cook their meager rations into a feast. Sherman went back to his quarters and wrote an order to General Getty to prepare to remove the Navajos as quickly as possible. Congress had appropriated $150,000 for treaty expenses at Bosque Redondo, and Getty was to devote all of this money to procuring rations and wagons for the Navajos' journey back across the Rio Grande.

When he was done, William Tecumseh Sherman left Fort Sumner for Santa Fe. In one of his trunks was a large blanket with thin red and cream stripes interspersed with undulating lines of red and brown, some shot through with thin blue lines. The stripes were a traditional Navajo design, but the waving lines were a new pattern. If considered from above, they evoked the serpentine banks of the Pecos River. But if turned to the side, they suggested the peaks and valleys of Diné Bikéyah.[36]

A little more than two weeks later, on June 18, 1868, a wagon train ten miles long rolled down the avenue, through the rows of cottonwood trees that the Navajos had planted along it four years before. As more than seven thousand Navajos passed through the gate—some walking, some riding their horses, some of the older and more frail grandmothers and grandfathers packed in the wagons among sacks of corn—they did not look back. Medicine men stayed behind to perform a song that would protect the Navajos from suffering as much as they had in Hwéeldi. It was said that after the song was sung, the people should never talk about or return to that place again.[37]

Juanita and Manuelito and the three children traveled in the midst of the train as a family, herding along their horses and sheep.[38] The column moved slowly, only ten miles a day, and there was plenty of time for Juanita to talk with their friends and family. They discussed what fruits and seeds and piñon nuts they would gather up from the mountainsides and valleys, and how they would provide for their children and grandchildren. Some of them jumped and skipped and danced. Even the youngest among them seemed to have boundless energy, walking without ever tiring. The column created a cloud of dust that could be seen for miles around.[39]

Every evening, when the marching was done for the day, Juanita gathered wood to make fires and to construct a temporary shelter for her family. Over this structure she draped several of their blankets, which would protect them from the pounding rain and hail of summer storms. As she cooked dinner, some of the men went hunting for rabbits or antelopes. Others went to nearby towns to inquire about their sons and daughters who had been stolen from them and sold into New Mexican houses. Some gathered around a monte dealer, shouting and cheering as they gambled for arrows, rings, and money. In the mornings after breakfast, Juanita dismantled their shelter, repacked their belongings, and the family moved back out on the road. Every third day, they stood in line with baskets and blankets, turning in their ration tickets for a cut of fresh-butchered meat.[40]

By July 4 the Diné were making their way up into the Sandia Mountains. When they crested the pass, they could see the adobe buildings of Albuquerque laid out before them in the valley, and the silver ribbon of the Rio Grande winding through it. They passed through the city, and over the next few days the people, their animals, and the fifty wagons with them forded the Rio Grande. From there, it was a slow march up to the lip of the basin, where the grasses of the valley merged into pale brown sand scrub and waving fronds of light green sage.[41]

In mid-July 1868, the Navajos reached the tablelands. In the distance, they could see the hazy form of Tsoodzil, the Blue Bead.

"We wondered if it was our mountain," Manuelito said later, "and we felt like talking to the ground, we loved it so."[42]

As Juanita and her family crossed back into Diné Bikéyah, the summer monsoons came. The desert exploded with life: yellow and pink flowers opened on the tips of the cholla's spiny fingers; purple wildflowers sprang up in the meadows; and sunflowers lifted their heads. The Treaty of 1868 had been a victory, but not without cost. In order to secure a measure of freedom from the U.S. government, the Navajos had to accede to new methods of federal control. By signing the treaty, however, the government had acknowledged the Navajos' sovereignty as a people, and that was a significant achievement. Now they had come home. Returning to Diné Bikéyah after four years of imprisonment and exile, the Navajos were trees blooming after a cold, dark winter.[43]

Epilogue

The railroad tie was made of hard, durable California laurel and polished to a high sheen. In the center was a plaque: "The last tie laid on completion of the Pacific Railroad, May 1869." Two track workers lifted the tie out of Leland Stanford's train car, carried it over to the grade, and laid it down in its place. After setting the last rail sections over it, the workers dispersed and the dignitaries moved in. There were prayers and speeches and the presentation of four gold and silver spikes. One of them was offered by the governor of Arizona Territory.

"Ribbed with iron clad in silver and crowned with gold," Governor Anson Safford proclaimed, "Arizona presents her offering to the enterprise that has banded a continent and dictated a pathway to commerce."[1]

Stanford, the president of the Central Pacific Railroad Company, and Thomas Durant, the vice president of the Union Pacific, took turns tapping the ceremonial spikes into the tie. The track workers returned, removing the laurel tie and replacing it with one made of pine and four ordinary iron spikes. One of these had been wired to a telegraph line. Stanford and Durant swung away but failed to hit it. One of the workers stepped up, took the maul, and drove the spike home.

"D-O-N-E," was the message that flashed through the line to telegraph stations all over the United States. The first transcontinental railroad line had been completed.[2]

The Golden Spike Ceremony at Promontory Point, Utah, was a momentous event in American history. The transcontinental railroad now bound together with "an iron clasp" a nation that extended from the Atlantic to the Pacific. It fulfilled the destiny that so many Anglo-Americans had imagined for themselves, as journalist John O'Sullivan put it in 1845, "to overspread the continent allotted by Providence for the free development of our yearly multiplying millions."[3]

The speakers at the event lauded Stanford and Durant and the other businessmen and engineers who had built the track over the previous six years. They also acknowledged the Republicans in the Union Congress, who had passed the legislation in 1862 that enabled the construction of the road. No one at the ceremony made mention, however, of the series of events that made this "work so magnificent in conception, so marvelous in execution," possible: the Civil War in the West.[4]

In 1862, a multiracial army of Union soldiers repulsed a Confederate invasion of New Mexico Territory, and then campaigned against Apaches and Navajos to secure the Union's hold on the region. Some of these Union volunteers, like Alonzo Ickis, would go on to serve in other theaters of the war. After James Carleton sent Dodd's Independents out of New Mexico, they chased Confederate guerrillas across the trans-Mississippi West before mustering out of the Union Army in December 1864. After all of the violence and drunkenness of his war service, Ickis went back home to Iowa and lived a relatively quiet life on his family farm. He never returned to New Mexico, although he did move to Colorado with his wife, Ella, late in his life. He died in Denver in 1917.[5]

Kit Carson, whom Ickis and his fellow soldiers had so admired, did not go east after leading the 1st New Mexico against Kiowas and Comanches at Adobe Walls in 1864. He agreed to command the garrisons stationed at Fort Union and then Fort Garland, but in November 1867, he left the U.S. Army in the hopes of securing an appointment as an Indian agent in Colorado Territory. In January 1868, Carson and Josefa and their children moved to a ranch on the Arkansas River near Fort Lyon. Four months later, Josefa died after giving birth to their last child, and Carson's own throat condition worsened in the weeks afterward. On May 23, 1868— just as the peace commissioners were traveling to Bosque Redondo—he died at Fort Lyon. Seventeen years later, a sandstone obelisk was erected in front of the courthouse in Santa Fe, a monument to Carson's efforts on behalf of the Anglo and Hispano residents of New Mexico Territory, and his fights against its Native inhabitants. It bears the simple inscription: "He Led the Way."[6]

During the battles in New Mexico, even the Confederate Texans were in awe of Kit Carson. But they did not face him again. By the summer of 1862 the Confederacy had put their dream of a continental empire of slavery on hold and focused all of their attention on winning the war in the East. Bill Davidson joined in those fights, mustering into a reorganized contingent of the Sibley Brigade and fighting in the Battle of Galveston, Texas, and in the Red River campaign. After the war he went home, nursed his many war wounds (six in all), and set up a law practice in Richmond, a small town east of Houston. He got married, ran for local offices, and in the late 1880s wrote a series of articles on his wartime experiences under various pseudonyms, including "Dave Brown" and "U Bet."[7]

John Baylor claimed to have fought with Davidson at Galveston, but as a private. In the fall of 1862 he had been discharged from the Confederate Army as punishment for his Apache Extermination Order. After Galveston, Baylor recovered from his disgrace. He turned back to politics and was elected as a representative to the Confederate Congress in 1863. In Richmond, he lobbied for a second invasion of New Mexico Territory and served on the Indian Affairs Committee. After Appomattox, Baylor returned to Emy and to cattle ranching. He was fractious to the end. In the 1880s, while engaged in a dispute with a neighboring family, he stabbed the patriarch to death in front of the Uvalde County Courthouse, a crime for which he was never punished. Both Bill Davidson and John Baylor lived to be old men, and died surrounded by their families.[8]

Unlike many of the other soldiers who fought in the Civil War West, James Carleton never left the U.S. Army. After his removal from command in New Mexico, he spent several months exploring the mining region of Arizona, before returning to his hometown of Bangor, Maine, for the first time in many years. He never saw Sophia or his children after he left them in 1862. They remained in California while he continued his career as an army officer. By December 1868, he was back in the West, serving as lieutenant colonel in the 4th U.S. Cavalry in San Antonio. Carleton stayed there, organizing the Indian Wars in Texas until January 1873, when he contracted a severe case of pneumonia that killed him.[9]

By that time, little of James Carleton's reservation experiment at Bosque Redondo remained. Fort Sumner had been abandoned and its buildings auctioned off, and the cornfields had long since gone to fallow. Four hundred miles to the west, however, the Navajo reservation in Diné Bikéyah endured and grew larger.[10] After their journey back to the homeland in the summer of 1868, the Diné did not often speak of the Long Walk or their time at Hwéeldi. Juanita and Manuelito focused on rebuilding their herds and farmed on their lands near Tséhootsoh. In the winter of 1874–75, they both traveled to Washington, D.C., to meet with President Ulysses S. Grant to discuss the future of the reservation. Juanita was the only woman in the delegation. Grant did not provide them with many assurances, and so the Diné took matters into their own hands, purchasing additional lands and resisting the federal government's attempts to force them into individual land ownership.[11] Juanita helped to promote this work until her death in 1910. Her descendants, along with many other Navajos, preserved the stories of the Long Walk and Bosque Redondo and see them as pivotal moments in Diné history.[12]

Juanita lived to see many changes in Diné Bikéyah, including the laying of railroad tracks just south of the reservation boundary in the 1880s. John Clark, who had become increasingly enamored of railroads during his time in Santa Fe, left New Mexico for a surveyor general post in Utah in the summer of 1868 and was in Salt Lake City when the golden spike was driven into the transcontinental track. Soon after, he took a job as land commissioner for the Kansas, Fort Scott, & Gulf Railroad in Kansas City, where Jane and the children were finally able to join him. They lived in Kansas City for the next twelve years, until Clark died of cancer at the age of 67.[13]

Clark and Louisa Canby never did see one another again. In 1864 she and Richard left Washington, D.C., and went to New Orleans, where Richard took command of troops in the field. They remained in Louisiana until 1866 and went on to posts in Charleston, Austin, and Richmond. In all of these places, it was reported, "Mrs. Canby made her enemies love her."[14] In 1870, the Canbys took the transcontinental railroad to California and then went on to Portland, Oregon, where Richard directed campaigns against the Pacific Northwest's Native peoples. In the spring of 1873, during a negotiation with the Modocs, Richard was killed. Louisa took his body back to Indiana on a Central Pacific railroad car, and buried him in their hometown. She outlived him by fifteen years, staying with her family in Kentucky and with friends in Washington, D.C., working as a seamstress. When she died in 1888, veterans of the Sibley Brigade praised her for her work on their behalf in the spring of 1862. They called her the "Angel of Santa Fe."[15]

———

On a cold March day in 1881, another group of men gathered around another railroad tie in a windswept expanse of desert. An engineer for the

Atchison, Topeka, and Santa Fe Railroad bent down and tapped a ceremonial silver spike into the tie and the group broke out in applause.

"'Tis Done!" the *Santa Fe Daily Gazette* announced the next morning. "After all the surmises and rumors, the A.T. & S.F. R.R. and the Southern Pacific have at last been linked together."

The second transcontinental railroad, with rails that stretched from Kansas City to Los Angeles, had been completed.[16]

The newspaper accounts of the Silver Spike ceremony at Deming, New Mexico, all noted that the mood was surprisingly subdued. One journalist attributed this to the fact that "the officials of the lines are up to their ears in business, carrying out other railway projects." Another suggested that "a few years ago such an event would have been regarded as of national importance, but nowadays the country is so accustomed to gigantic enterprises that even the projectors of them do not think it worthwhile to make any parade over their completion."[17]

These immense enterprises, the railroads and the many other capitalist ventures they spawned, brought hundreds of thousands of Anglo emigrants to the West between 1869 and 1881. Populations in the western territories tripled and a network of railroads connected their capital cities. Corporations moved into the mining camps where Alonzo Ickis used to swing his pickaxe, buying up claims and digging deep shafts in the mountainsides. Many Americans believed that these developments would bring the West into a fully reunified nation.

This process had begun much earlier, however. It was a development made possible by Free Soilers and Republicans who had imagined a landscape of free labor in the West since the 1840s, and fought to defend it from Confederate invasion in the 1860s. It resulted from the conviction of Anglo Americans that if the region's indigenous peoples did not voluntarily give way before them, then the federal government and the U.S. military would force them to do so. The Union Army turned to this work of conquest and colonization during the 1860s, but their efforts were always contested. Apaches and Navajos fought to defend their territories. It was for this reason that the Civil War in the West continued beyond the end of the battlefield war in the East.

In early October 1881, just six months after the trains began running along the second transcontinental route through southern Arizona, the Chiricahua Apache chief Geronimo and more than three hundred of his people made their way toward the tracks from the mountains to the north. They had been encamped near a reservation that the U.S. government had created, where they had been imprisoned in 1877 after being lured into a peace parlay. In 1881, growing tensions with the U.S. Army provoked Geronimo to escape, and he and his people ultimately reached the railroad tracks on the flats below Apache Pass. When a westbound train approached, they climbed onto its freight cars and rode along until it slowed to climb up into the Dragoon Mountains. Here Geronimo's party disembarked, and then picked up the Chiricahua Trail south into Mexico. For the next five years, Geronimo and his fellow Chiricahuas continued to ride through Apachería, claiming it for themselves and in memory of Mangas Coloradas.[18]

Of those people who fought for control of New Mexico and Arizona in the 1860s, it was the Apaches and the Navajos who remained, building their homes and feeding their families in the lands their ancestors had given them. They, too, were almost constantly in motion, for the South-west has always been a landscape that requires mobility for survival. The exigencies of the Civil War pushed and pulled people along the roads and trails of Colorado, Texas, California, Arizona, and New Mexico as they tried to exert some measure of control over the high desert landscape, and one another. These struggles for power in the West exposed a hard and complicated truth about the Union government's war aims: that they simultaneously embraced slave emancipation and Native extermination in order to secure an American empire of liberty.

It was the American Civil War that brought all of the people in this book together: Mangas Coloradas, the Apache chief; Clark, the surveyor general; Canby, the army wife; Carson, the famous frontiersman; Juanita, the Navajo weaver; Ickis, the gold miner; Carleton, the Union colonel; Baylor, the ambitious rancher; and Davidson, the young lawyer. Their dreams, fears, flaws, and ambitions were all laid bare as they moved across the brown and scrubby deserts, the tree-covered mountains, and the red rock tablelands of the Southwest. Together, their stories reveal how the imagined future of the West shaped the Civil War, and how the Civil War became a defining moment in the West.

Acknowledgments

In 2014, I took a big leap away from academia and toward the writing life. I did so with the unwavering support of many friends and colleagues. My agent, Heather Schroder, immediately understood the kind of book I was trying to write about the Civil War West. Her guidance has been invaluable. From my very first conversation with her, Kathy Belden encouraged my approach to writing history differently. Her comments and suggestions along the way helped me to find my narrative voice. I hope that what has resulted is better than she imagined.

Many thanks to the design and production team at Scribner, particularly Rick Willett, Jason Chappell, and Sally Howe, for wrangling all of the details.

A National Endowment for the Humanities Public Scholar Award enabled me to focus on finishing the first draft of the manuscript in 2018. The ideas and arguments expressed in the book, however, do not represent those of the NEH. A timely grant from the Filson Historical Society brought me to Louisville, Kentucky, to dig into their collections related to Louisa and Richard Canby.

Fellow scholars have written fellowship and job letters on my behalf, and advocated for this project in other ways: Ari Kelman, Steve Berry, Steven Hahn, Clay Risen, and T. J. Stiles. Carole Emberton read the entire manuscript and offered incisive comments, especially regarding my unreasonable attachment to semicolons. Way back in 2013, Andy Graybill and Adam Arenson invited me to take part in the Civil War West Symposium at Southern Methodist University and the Autry Center, which gave me important feedback and introduced me to a host of wonderful western history scholars just as I began thinking about the book.

In the fall of 2014 I got in my car and set out on a research trip that took me to libraries, archives, museums, and historic sites around the Southwest. I am grateful to so many friends who offered me guest rooms and couches, and met me for dinner and drinks during my travels: Joe Beilein, Jr., Carole Emberton, Sara Sukalich and Matt Mingione, Amy Wood, Brian Craig Miller and Nick Messing, Ken and Elise Davis, Randy Egan, Anne and Jerry Moore, Sam Truett, Gingy Scharff and Chris Wilson, Rebecca Cohen, Ben Irvin, Lonn and Dedi Taylor, Catherine Clinton, Greg Chico, Natalie Ring and Jon Daniel, Jeanne Lopiparo, Juliet Wagner, Nancy and Trey Grayson, and Dave and Emma Kieran.

Historians could not do their work without the help of archivists and librarians. I am thankful for the wisdom and patience of the experts at the Western History Collection, Denver Public Library; Stephen H. Hart Research Library, History Colorado; Fray Angélico Chávez History Library and Photo Archives, New Mexico History Museum; Arizona Historical Society; Briscoe Center for American History, University of Texas, Austin; University of Colorado, Boulder Archives; New Mexico State Records Center and Archives; Archives and Special Collections, Branson Library, New Mexico State University; University of Arizona Special Collections; Center for Southwest Research and Special Collections, University of New Mexico; C. L. Sonnichsen Special Collections, University of Texas, El Paso; National Archives and Records Administration, Washington, D.C.

When I wasn't sitting in reading rooms peering at Civil War–era documents, photos, and maps, I was out and about visiting historic sites. The park rangers and staff members at Navajo Nation Museum, Bosque Redondo Memorial and Fort Sumner Historic Site, Fort Craig National Historic Site, Glorieta Battlefield at Pecos National Historical Park, Fort Union National Monument, Fort Garland Museum, Bent's Old Fort National Historic Site, Fort Selden Historic Site, Fort Bowie National Historic Site, Picacho Peak State Park, and Fort Davis National Historic Site welcomed me to these important places and shared their knowledge with me. I am especially grateful to Paul Tohtsonie, facility manager at New Mexico Navajo South Facility Management, who took me around Second Fort Wingate's grounds and then out on a spontaneous excursion to try to find Shash Bitoh in the hills above the site. We did not find it, but we had a great conversation along the way about the importance of family and community histories.

As I began to write, a number of colleagues invited me to talk to their students and communities about the Civil War West. These talks, and the challenging questions the audiences posed, helped me to refine my ideas. Thank you to Amy Kohout and the History Department at Colorado College; Ann Little and the History Department and Public Lands History Center at Colorado State University; Gingy Scharff and the History Department at University of New Mexico; Pete Carmichael and the Civil War Institute at Gettysburg College; David Spanagel and the Humanities and Arts Department at Worcester Polytechnic University; Julie Mujic and the History Department at Sacred Heart University; Natalie Ring and the School of Arts and Humanities at University of Texas, Dallas; Bob Lytle at the New Bedford Civil War Roundtable; Steve Berry, Brian Allen Drake, and the History Department at the University of Georgia; Chandra Manning and the History Department at Georgetown University; and Conrad Wright and the Boston Environmental History Seminar at the Massachusetts Historical Society.

I could not have written this book without the important work of those historians of this time and place who have come before me, particularly Jennifer Nez Denetdale, Gerald E. Thompson, Jerry D. Thompson, John P. Wilson, and Andrew E. Masich. No one has done more than these historians to unearth primary documents that give voice to the complicated histories of the Civil War West.

I have also benefited from encouragement and excellent feedback from my fellow writers in Boston: BookSquad's Liz Covart, Sara Georgini, Kevin Levin, Heather Cox Richardson, Nina Silber, Caitlin Hopkins, Conevery Valencius, Chris Parsons, Laurel Daen, Tom Thurston, and Seth Jacobs; Freelance Writers Meetup friends Jack Cheng, Kaila Kuban, Lauren Paul, and Suzanne Greenwald; and Kevin Birmingham, Gabi Gage, Mo Moulton, and Tobey Pearl of Writers Anonymous. I must also thank the wonderful folks at Haute Coffee in Concord, Mass., and Saltbox Kitchen in West Concord, Mass. I wrote many of these pages sitting at the tables in their cafés, fueled by delicious coffee and snacks.

A number of good friends have been relentless in their support of this project, including Tita Chico (who was also a marvelous host during my research time at the National Archives) and the OWGs: Carole Emberton, Amy Wood, and Natalie Ring. Thank you to Nancy Serrano-Wu for Friday lunches and Spanish translation help.

Dan Nelson never wavered in his belief that this book would come to fruition. He is and will always be my favorite person in the world.

    Researching and writing about the Civil War West meant that I was able to go home to Colorado quite often during the past four years. My parents, John and Lynn Fritschel, fed and housed me, and were always interested to know what I was finding in the archives. I only wish that Genevieve Miles Riddle and Mathilde Bodensieck Fritschel could have been there to talk about this project with me. My grandmothers were two very different women, but they shared a fierce love for their families, the deep sorrow of loss, and an abiding strength and sense of self.

    This book is dedicated to them, and to all of the grandmothers.

Abbreviations

AHS Arizona Historical Society, Tucson

DBC Dolph Briscoe Center for American History, University of Texas at Austin.

DPL Denver Public Library

FAC Fray Angélico Chávez History Library, New Mexico History Museum, Santa Fe, New Mexico

FHS Filson Historical Society, Louisville, Kentucky

NARA RG 49, Box 92–93 National Archives and Records Administration Record Group 49: Records of the Bureau of Land Management [General Land Office], Letters Received from the Surveyors General of Public Land States, 1826–1883 [New Mexico, 1862–1870]

NARA RG 92, Box 1093, Entry 225 National Archives and Records Administration Record Group 92: Records of the Office of the Quartermaster General 1774–1985, Consolidated Correspondence File 1794-1915 [Packet; Fort Sumner, NM, 1864]

NARA RG 393 Part IV, Vol. 106, Entry 1218 National Archives and Records Administration Record Group 393, Part IV: Records of the U.S. Army Continental Commands, 1817–1947, Supplemental Letters Sent [from Fort Sumner, NM], 1864–1865

NARA RG 393 Part IV, Vol. 107, 108, and 109, Entry 1217 National Archives and Records Administration Record Group 393, Part IV: Records of U.S. Army Continental Commands, 1817–1869, Letters Sent [from Fort Sumner, NM]

NARA RG 393 Part IV, Vol. 114, Entry 1234 National Archives and Records Administration Record Group 393, Part IV: Records of the U.S. Army Continental Commands, 1817–1947, Morning Reports of Indians, 1866–1867 [Fort Sumner, NM]

NMSRCA New Mexico State Records Center and Archives, Santa Fe

OR United States War Department, *The War of Rebellion: A Compilation of the Official Records of the Union and Confederate Armies* (Washington, D.C.: Government Printing Office, 1880–1901)

SHL Stephen H. Hart Library, History Colorado, Denver

UA University of Arizona Special Collections, Tucson

UNMD University of New Mexico Digital Collections

Notes

Prologue

1 Jefferson Davis, Speech before the Democratic State Convention, July 6, 1859, as in *Jefferson Davis, Constitutionalist: His Letters, Papers, and Speeches*, ed. Dunbar Rowland, vol. 4 (Jackson: Mississippi Department of Archives and History, 1923), 70.

2 Republican Party Platforms of 1856 and 1860, *The American Presidency Project*. https://www.presidency.ucsb.edu/documents/republican-party-platform-1856 and https://www.presidency.ucsb.edu/documents/republican-party-platform-1860.

3 "The Comet," *Harper's Weekly* 5, no. 238 (July 20, 1861): 450; *Santa Fe Gazette*, July 6, 1861, p. 2, and July 27, 1861, p. 4.

Part One

Chapter 1: Baylor

1 Jerry D. Thompson, *Colonel John Robert Baylor: Texas Indian Fighter and Confederate Soldier* (Hillsboro, Tex.: Hill Junior College, 1971), 4, 24; Randolph B. Campbell, *Gone to Texas: A History of the Lone Star State*, 2nd edition (New York: Oxford University Press, 2012), 205.

2 Thompson, *Colonel John Robert Baylor*, 5; Federal Census, Fayette County, Texas, 1850.

3 Baylor to Emy, February 6, 1854, and November 7/9, 1855, John R. Baylor Family Letters, Baylor (John Robert) Family Papers, DBC; Thompson, *Colonel John Robert Baylor*, 1, 5.

4 Thompson, *Colonel John Robert Baylor*, 6–7.

5 Baylor to Fan, April 5, 1857, Baylor Family Papers, DBC.

6 Earl Van Dorn, General Orders No. 8 (May 24, 1861), *OR* I:1, p. 574; Thompson, *Colonel John Robert Baylor*, 25.

7 Campbell, *Gone to Texas*, 244.

8 Thompson, *Colonel John Robert Baylor*, 26.

9 H. E. McCulloch to John R. Baylor, July 21, 1861, in John P. Wilson, ed., *When the Texans Came: Missing Records from the Civil War in the Southwest* (Albuquerque: University of New Mexico Press, 2001), 148.

10   Baylor Report to Captain T. A. Washington, September 21, 1861, in *OR* I:4, p. 17; Thompson, *Colonel John Robert Baylor*, 29.

11   Martin Hardwick Hall, "The Skirmish at Mesilla," *Arizona and the West* 1, no. 4 (Winter 1959): 346.

12   Hall, "The Skirmish at Mesilla," 346; William S. Kiser, *Turmoil on the Rio Grande: The Territorial History of the Mesilla Valley, 1846–1865* (College Station: Texas A&M Press, 2011), 149, 161.

13   Kiser, *Turmoil on the Rio Grande.*

14   W.W. Mills letter, as in Kiser, *Turmoil on the Rio Grande*, 149.

15   Hall, "The Skirmish at Mesilla," 346–47; Ray C. Colton, *The Civil War in the Western Territories: Arizona, Colorado, New Mexico, and Utah* (Norman: University of Oklahoma Press, 1959), 13–14; George Henry Pettis, "The Confederate Invasion of New Mexico and Arizona," in *Battles and Leaders of the Civil War*, vol. 2 (New York: The Century Co., 1887), 103; Isaac Lynde to E. R. S. Canby, from Fort McLane, N.M., June 24, 1861, in Wilson, ed., *When the Texans Came*, 29; Thompson, *Colonel John Robert Baylor*, 32; John Baylor Report to Captain T. A. Washington, September 21, 1861, in *OR* I:4, p. 17.

16   Hall, "The Skirmish at Mesilla," 348–49; Kiser, *Turmoil on the Rio Grande*, 247 n. 43.

17   Hall, "The Skirmish at Mesilla," 349.

18   John Robert Baylor Report to Captain T. A. Washington, September 21, 1861, in *OR* I:4, p. 18.

19   Baylor Report to Captain T.A. Washington, September 21, 1861, in *OR* I:4, p. 18.

20   Norman R. Malm, "Climate Guide, Las Cruces, 1892–2000" (Las Cruces: New Mexico State University, 2003), 1; G. E. Griffith, J. M. Omernik, M. M. McGraw, G. Z. Jacobi, C. M. Canavan, T. S. Schrader, D. Mercer, R. Hill, and B. C. Moran, *Ecoregions of New Mexico* (Reston, Virginia, U.S. Geological Survey, 2006).

21   Baylor Report to Captain T. A. Washington, September 21, 1861, in *OR* I:4, p. 18.

22   Baylor Report to Captain T. A. Washington, September 21, 1861, in *OR* I:4, p. 18.

23   Isaac Lynde Report, August 7, 1861, *OR* I:4, p. 5.

24   Baylor Report to Captain T. A. Washington, September 21, 1861, in *OR* I:4, p. 18; "Terms of Surrender of U.S. Troops to C.S. Troops, July 27, 1861, San Augustine Springs, N. Mex.," *OR* I:4, p. 7; Lorenzo Thomas, General Orders no. 102, November 25, 1861, *OR* I:4, p. 16.

25   Lewis Roe, "With Canby at Valverde, NM, February 21, 1862," *National Tribune*, November 3, 1910, 7, in *From Western Deserts to Carolina Swamps: A Civil War Soldier's Journals and Letters Home*, ed. John Wilson (Albuquerque: University of New Mexico Press, 2012), 63–64.

26   Baylor Report to Captain T. A. Washington, September 21, 1861, in *OR* I:4, p. 19; Thompson, *Colonel John Robert Baylor*, 42; Roe, "With Canby at Valverde," 63–64.

27   Statement of Captain [Alfred] Gibbs, [n.d.], *OR* I:4, 40, p. 11.

28   Thompson, *Colonel John Robert Baylor*, 43; Colton, *The Civil War in the Western Territories*, 17.

29   John R. Baylor, "Proclamation to the People of the Territory of Arizona," August 1, 1861, *OR* I:4, pp. 19–20; John R. Baylor to Robert Baylor, June 4, 1861, the Portal to Texas History, http://texashistory.unt.edu/ark:/67531/metapth30594/; Thompson, *Colonel John Robert Baylor*, 45; Jerry D. Thompson, *A Civil War History of the New Mexico Volunteers and Militia* (Albuquerque: University of New Mexico Press, 2015), 4.

30   John Baylor to Earl Van Dorn, August 3, 1861, *OR* I:4, p. 23; Thompson, *Colonel John Robert Baylor*, 72.

31 Earl Van Dorn to L. P. Walker, August 10, 1861, in *OR* I:4, p. 97.

32 Judah Benjamin to Jefferson Davis, Report of the Confederate Secretary of War, December 14, 1861, *OR* 4:1, p. 791.

33 Fan to Baylor, September 18, 1861, and Baylor's mother to Baylor, October 28, 1861, Baylor Family Papers, DBC.

34 *Mesilla Times*, July 27, 1861, as in Thompson, *Colonel John Robert Baylor*, 31.

35 John Baylor to Earl Van Dorn, August 3, 1861, *OR* I:4, p. 23; Thompson, *Colonel John Robert Baylor*, 72.

36 Thompson, *Colonel John Robert Baylor*, 71–72.

37 John Baylor to P. O. Hébert, September 24, 1861, *OR* I:4, p. 109.

Chapter 2: Mangas Coloradas

1 John Cremony, *Life Among the Apaches* (San Francisco: A. Roman and Co., 1868), 47–48; Edwin R. Sweeney, *Mangas Coloradas: Chief of the Chiricahua Apaches* (Norman: University of Oklahoma Press, 1998), 28; Dan L. Thrapp, *The Conquest of Apacheria* (Norman: University of Oklahoma Press, 1967), 14; Paul Andrew Hutton, *The Apache Wars* (New York: Crown, 2016), 40–41.

2 Sweeney, *Mangas Coloradas*, 146–47.

3 Lance R. Blyth, *Chiricahua and Janos: Communities of Violence in the Southwestern Borderlands* (Lincoln: University of Nebraska Press, 2012), 143.

4 Sweeney, *Mangas Coloradas*, 20, 21–22.

5 Juliana Barr, "Geographies of Power: Mapping Indian Borders in the 'Borderlands' of the Early Southwest," *William and Mary Quarterly* 6, no. 1 (January 2011): 8, 9, 12.

6 Waterman Ormsby, *The Butterfield Overland Mail*, ed. Josephine M. Bynum and Lyle H. Wright (San Marino, Calif.: Huntington Library, 1942), 143, 149, 157, 162; Sweeney, *Mangas Coloradas*, 145; Amy S. Greenberg, *A Wicked War: Polk, Clay, Lincoln, and the 1846 U.S. Invasion of Mexico* (New York: Alfred A. Knopf, 2012), 121.

7 Journal of Captain A. R. Johnston, October 20, 1847, in Lt. Col. William H. Emory, *Notes of a Military Reconnoissance [sic] from Fort Leavenworth, in Missouri, to San Diego, in California* . . . (Washington, D.C.: Wendell and Van Benthuysen, 1848), 578–79; Hutton, *The Apache Wars*, 22–23.

8 Sweeney, *Mangas Coloradas*, 144.

9 Brian DeLay, *War of a Thousand Deserts: Indian Raids and the U.S.-Mexican War* (New Haven, Conn.: Yale University Press, 2009); Laverne Harrell Clarke, "Early Horse Trappings of the Navajo and Apache Indians," *Arizona and the West* 5, no. 3 (Autumn 1963): 236.

10 Sweeney, *Mangas Coloradas*, 31–32, 45, 142–44.

11 Johnston Journal, October 20, 1847, in Emory, *Notes of a Military Reconnoissance*, 579.

12 William H. Emory Diary, October 20, 1847, in Emory, *Notes of a Military Reconnoissance*, 60.

13 Sweeney, *Mangas Coloradas*, 168–69.

14 Sweeney, *Mangas Coloradas*, 229–31.

15 Sweeney, *Mangas Coloradas*, 236.

16 Sweeney, *Mangas Coloradas*, 259, 243–44.

17 Sweeney, *Mangas Coloradas*, 259–61.

18 Kevin Waite, "Jefferson Davis and Proslavery Visions of Empire in the Far West," *Journal of the Civil War Era* 6, no. 4 (December 2016): 548–52.

19 Sweeney, *Mangas Coloradas*, 390–91.

20 Sweeney, *Mangas Coloradas*, 397.
21 Edwin R. Sweeney, *Cochise: Chiricahua Apache Chief* (Norman: University of Oklahoma Press, 1991), 148–58.
22 Sweeney, *Cochise*, 160–63; Daniel Robinson, "Eyewitness to the Bascom Affair: An Account by Sergeant Daniel Robinson, Seventh Infantry," ed. Douglas C. McChristian and Larry L. Ludwig, *Journal of Arizona History* 42, no. 3 (Autumn 2001): 287–89.
23 Sweeney, *Cochise*, 160–63; Robinson, "Eyewitness to the Bascom Affair," 292, 293.
24 Sweeney, *Mangas Coloradas*, 417.
25 Sweeney, *Mangas Coloradas*, 418–19.
26 Sweeney, *Mangas Coloradas*, 421.

Chapter 3: Canby

 1 *Mesilla Times*, October 3, 1861, in Wilson, ed., *When the Texans Came*, 150.
 2 *Mesilla Times*, October 3, 1861, in Wilson, ed., *When the Texans Came*, 151; Sweeney, *Mangas Coloradas*, 424; L. Boyd Finch, *Confederate Pathway to the Pacific: Major Sherod Hunter and Arizona Territory, C.S.A.* (Tucson: Arizona Historical Society, 1996), 93.
 3 *Santa Fe Gazette*, October 19, 1861, 2.
 4 John Clark Diary, October 10–29, 1861, FAC.
 5 Max L. Heyman, Jr., *Prudent Soldier: Biography of Major General E. R. S. Canby, 1817–1873* (Glendale, Calif.: Arthur H. Clark Co., 1959), 34–35.
 6 Heyman, Jr., *Prudent Soldier*, 41–42.
 7 Jefferson Davis, *Report of the Secretary of War*, December 4, 1854, in *Message from the President of the United States to the Two Houses of Congress . . .* , Part II (Washington, D.C.: A. O. P. Nicholson, Printer, 1854), 4, 5–6.
 8 Verity G. McGinnis, "Agents of Empire: Officers' Wives in British India and the American West, 1830–1875," *Pacific Historical Review* 83, no. 3 (August 2014): 378, 382, 392–93.
 9 Mary Craig to Lou Canby, from Georgetown, Kentucky, November 28, 1858, Folder 5, Edward Richard Sprigg Canby Papers, FHS.
10 Heyman, Jr., *Prudent Soldier*, 44–50.
11 Heyman, Jr., *Prudent Soldier*, 61–70.
12 James Buchanan, "A Proclamation," May 18, 1858, in *The Utah Expedition: Letters of Capt. Jesse A. Gove, 10th Inf., U.S.A. of Concord, N.H., to Mrs. Gove, and special correspondent of the New York Herald* (Concord: New Hampshire Historical Society, 1928), 229–30; Donna G. Ramos, "Utah War," *HistoryNet.* http://www.historynet.com/utah-war-us-government-versus-mormon-settlers.htm.
13 Jesse Gove to Maria Gove, June 28, 1857, in *The Utah Expedition*, 5, 6.
14 Gove to Maria, July 20, 1857, in *The Utah Expedition*, 17.
15 Gove to Maria, August 14, 1857, in *The Utah Expedition*, 37.
16 William Seville, *Narrative of the March of Co. A, Engineers from Fort Leavenworth, Kansas to Fort Bridger, Utah, and Return (May 6 to October 3, 1858)* (Washington Barracks, D.C.: Press of the Engineer School, 1912), 22.
17 Seville, *Narrative of the March of Co. A*, 5; Gove to Maria, September 17, 1857, in *The Utah Expedition*, 57–58.
18 Gove to the *New York Herald*, June 4, 1858, in *The Utah Expedition*, 268.
19 Gove to Maria, October 3, 12–20, 1857, in *The Utah Expedition*, 69, 75–81.
20 Heyman, Jr., *Prudent Soldier*, 105; Miss E. R. Snow, "The Ladies of Utah, to the La-

dies of the United States Camp in a Crusade against the 'Mormons,'" *Deseret News*, October 14, 1857, p. 252.

21 Snow, "The Ladies of Utah," p. 252.

22 Gove to Maria, June 18–July 8, 1858, in *The Utah Expedition*, 174–81; Journal of Albert Tracy, March–April 1858, *Utah Historical Quarterly* 13 (1945): 1–2.

23 John Hawkins to Lou Canby, August 26, 1859, and Aunt McDougal to Louisa, November 12, 1859, Folder 6, Canby Papers, FHS.

24 Fannie Hawkins to Lou, from Cottage Grove, November 18, 1858, and [Mathilde] Gardner to Mrs. Canby, December 18, 1859, Folders 5 and 6, Canby Papers, FHS; Gove to Maria, June 26, 1858, in *The Utah Expedition*, 177; Heyman, Jr., *Prudent Soldier*, 108–10.

25 William A. Carter to his wife, November 12, 1858, in Heyman, *Prudent Soldier*, 110.

26 Heyman, Jr., *Prudent Soldier*, 113–32; Robert M. Utley, *Frontiersmen in Blue: The United States Army and the Indian, 1848–1865* (Lincoln: University of Nebraska Press, 1967), 171–73.

27 Durwood Ball, *Army Regulars on the Western Frontier, 1848–1861* (Norman: University of Oklahoma Press, 2001), 197; Heyman, Jr., *Prudent Soldier*, 137–40; Utley, *Frontiersmen in Blue*, 173.

28 *Santa Fe Gazette*, June 22, 1861, p. 2, July 6, 1861, p. 2, and August 17, 1861, p. 1.

29 *Santa Fe Gazette*, June 15, 1861, p. 2, and June 29, 1861, p. 2.

30 *Santa Fe Gazette*, June 22, 1861, p. 2.

31 Lydia Spencer Lane, *I Married a Soldier; or, Old Days in the Old Army* (Philadelphia: J. B. Lippincott Co., 1893), 123–26.

32 Lane, *I Married a Soldier*, 127, 179.

33 Clark Diary, November 29, 1861, FAC.

34 Clark Diary, February 1, 1862, FAC; "Military Preparations," *Santa Fe Gazette*, February 1, 1862, p. 2; LeeAnn Whites and Alecia P. Long, introduction to *Occupied Women: Gender, Military Occupation, and the American Civil War*, ed. Whites and Long (Baton Rouge: Louisiana State University Press, 2009), 3–6.

Chapter 4: Davidson

1 Jerry D. Thompson, "Introduction," *Civil War in the Southwest: Recollections of the Sibley Brigade*, ed. Jerry Thompson (College Station: Texas A&M University Press, 2001), xii; Bill Davidson account, in *Civil War in the Southwest*, ed. Thompson, 9.

2 "The Alamo," *Texas Almanac Online*, http://texasalmanac.com/topics/history/alamo.

3 Davidson, in *Civil War in the Southwest*, ed. Thompson, 10; Donald Frazier, *Blood and Treasure: Confederate Empire in the Southwest* (Reprint, College Station: Texas A&M Press, 1995), 91; Anne Sarah Rubin, "'Seventy-Six and Sixty-One': Confederates Remember the American Revolution," in *Where These Memories Grow: History, Memory, and Southern Identity*, ed. W. Fitzhugh Brundage (Chapel Hill: The University of North Carolina Press, 2000).

4 Theophilus Noel, *A Campaign from Santa Fe to the Mississippi: Being a History of the Old Sibley Brigade* (Shreveport, La.: Shreveport News Printing Establishment, 1865), 8.

5 Jerry D. Thompson, *Henry Hopkins Sibley: Confederate General of the West* (College Station: Texas A&M University Press, 1996), 56–57, 58, 224–25; Martin Hardwick Hall, *Sibley's New Mexico Campaign* (1960; reprint, Albuquerque: University of New Mexico Press, 2000), 27, 28.

6 Samuel Cooper [on behalf of President Jefferson Davis], Orders to Henry Sibley, July 8, 1861, *OR*, I:4, p. 93; Samuel Cooper, Orders to Earl Van Dorn, July 9, 1861, in Wilson, ed., *When the Texans Came*, 144.

7   Davidson, in *Civil War in the Southwest*, ed. Thompson, 5.
8   Davidson, in *Civil War in the Southwest*, ed. Thompson, 5; Frazier, *Blood and Treasure*, 96.
9   Baylor to Sibley, October 24, 1861, *OR* I:4, chap. 40, p. 127.
10 Davidson, in *Civil War in the Southwest*, ed. Thompson, 10.
11 Thompson, "Introduction," *Civil War in the Southwest*, ed. Thompson, xv; Frazier, *Blood and Treasure*, 118.
12 Davidson, in *Civil War in the Southwest*, ed. Thompson, 5, 9, 10; William Randolph Howell Diary, November 7, 1861, in *Westward the Texans: The Civil War Journal of Private William Randolph Howell*, ed. Jerry D. Thompson (El Paso: Texas Western Press, 1990), 68.
13 Noel, *A Campaign from Santa Fe*, 9.
14 Thompson, *Henry Hopkins Sibley*, 228.
15 Campbell, *Gone to Texas*, 192–93.
16 Noel, *A Campaign from Santa Fe*, 10; Thompson, *Henry Hopkins Sibley*, 227, 228; Howell Diary, November 10, 1861, in *Westward the Texans*, ed. Thompson, 69.
17 Davidson, in *Civil War in the Southwest*, ed. Thompson, 11–12; Thompson, *Henry Hopkins Sibley*, 231; Howell Diary, November 11–17, 1861, in *Westward the Texans*, ed. Thompson , 69.
18 Howell Diary, November 18, 1861, in *Westward the Texans*, ed. Thompson, 70.
19 Howell Diary, November 20–22, 1861, in *Westward the Texans*, ed. Thompson, 70; Thompson, *Henry Hopkins Sibley*, 232, 237.
20 Howell Diary, November 24–27, 1861, in *Westward the Texans*, ed. Thompson, 70–71; *Civil War in the Southwest*, ed. Thompson, 12; Frazier, *Blood and Treasure*, 121; Hall, *Sibley's New Mexico Campaign*, 33–34.
21 Davidson, in *Civil War in the Southwest*, ed. Thompson, 12.
22 Howell Diary, November 24–27, 1861, in *Westward the Texans*, ed. Thompson, 71; Hall, *Sibley's New Mexico Campaign*, 34.
23 Howell Diary, November 30–December 3, 1861, in *Westward the Texans*, ed. Thompson, 71–73.
24 John E. Hart, in Frazier, *Blood and Treasure*, 122.
25 Hall, *Sibley's New Mexico Campaign*, 34; Davidson, in *Civil War in the Southwest*, ed. Thompson, 12–13.
26 Howell Diary, December 12–15, 1861, in *Westward the Texans*, ed. Thompson, 74.
27 Davidson, in *Civil War in the Southwest*, ed. Thompson, 13–14.
28 Davidson, in *Civil War in the Southwest*, ed. Thompson, 14–15.
29 A.M. Jackson [for Henry Hopkins Sibley], General Orders No. 10, December 14, 1861, *OR* I:4, pp. 157–58.
30 Davidson, in *Civil War in the Southwest*, ed. Thompson, 15.
31 Henry H. Sibley, "Proclamation to the People of New Mexico," December 20, 1861, *OR* I:4, pp. 89–90.
32 Frazier, *Blood and Treasure*, 125; Kevin M. Levin, *Searching for Black Confederates: The Civil War's Most Persistent Myth* (Chapel Hill: University of North Carolina Press, 2019).
33 Henry H. Sibley, General Order No. 2, January 9, 1862, as quoted in Hall, *Sibley's New Mexico Campaign*, 36.

Chapter 5: Juanita

1 Ruth Roessel, *Women in Navajo Society* (Rough Rock, Ariz.: Navajo Resource Center, 1981), 15, 72, 107, 109.

2 Peter Iverson and Monty Roessel, *Diné: A History of the Navajos* (Albuquerque: University of New Mexico Press, 2002), 14, 19, 20, 23.

3 Iverson and Roessel, *Diné: A History of the Navajos*, 3, 23.

4 Iverson and Roessel, *Diné: A History of the Navajos*, 21–24; Lance R. Blyth, "The Navajo–New Mexico War, 1800–1880: Struggle for a Pastoral Borderland," unpublished manuscript (courtesy of the author), 7–9.

5 Blyth, "The Navajo–New Mexico War"; James F. Brooks, *Captives and Cousins: Slavery, Kinship, and Community in the Southwest Borderlands* (Chapel Hill: University of North Carolina Press, 2002).

6 Frank McNitt, *Navajo Wars: Military Campaigns, Slave Raids, and Reprisals* (Albuquerque: University of New Mexico Press, 1972), 117; John K. Hillers, "Cliff Ruins near Fort Wingate, New Mexico" [photograph], c. 1873–1879, Library of Congress Prints and Photographs Division, Washington, D.C.

7 McNitt, *Navajo Wars*, 117–118.

8 J. Lee Correll, *Through White Men's Eyes: A Contribution to Navajo History*, Vol. 1 (Window Rock, Ariz.: Navajo Heritage Center, 1976), 180; McNitt, *Navajo Wars*, 119.

9 David E. Wilkins, *The Navajo Political Experience* (rev. ed., New York: Rowman and Littlefield, 2003), 73; McNitt, *Navajo Wars*, 118; Iverson and Roessel, *Diné: A History of the Navajos*, 39.

10 Jennifer Nez Denetdale, *Reclaiming Diné History: The Legacies of Navajo Chief Manuelito and Juanita* (Tucson: University of Arizona Press, 2007), 8, 57–58, 60–61; Andrés Reséndez, *The Other Slavery: The Uncovered Story of Indian Enslavement in America* (Boston: Houghton Mifflin, 2016), 233; Virginia Hoffman, "Manuelito," *Navajo Biographies*, vol. I (Phoenix, Ariz.: Navajo Curriculum Center Press, 1974).

11 Iverson and Roessel, *Diné: A History of the Navajos*, 41; McNitt, *Navajo Wars*, 195, 198, 199.

12 McNitt, *Navajo Wars*, 277–79; Blyth, "The Navajo–New Mexico War," 190–91; Hoffman, "Manuelito," 84.

13 Hoffman, "Manuelito," 91; Blyth, "The Navajo–New Mexico War," 210–11.

14 McNitt, *Navajo Wars*, 382; Iverson and Roessel, *Diné: A History of the Navajos*, 47; Denetdale, *Reclaiming Diné History*, 69–70.

15 Iverson and Roessel, *Diné: A History of the Navajos*, 2, 48; McNitt, *Navajo Wars*, 403.

16 McNitt, *Navajo Wars*, 390–91, 397–98; Blyth, "The Navajo–New Mexico War," 218–20.

17 McNitt, *Navajo Wars*, 403, 405.

18 *U.S. Treaty with the Navajos, 1861*, http://www.lapahie.com/Dine_Treaty_1861.cfm; Iverson and Roessel, *Diné: A History of the Navajos*, 48; McNitt, *Navajo Wars*, 413–15.

19 Roessel, *Women in Navajo Society*, 106.

20 Hoffman, "Manuelito," 94.

21 Denetdale, *Reclaiming Diné History*, 5, 142; Blyth, "The Navajo–New Mexico War," iii; Roessel, *Women in Navajo Society*, 101–2.

22 Susan Kent, "The Differentiation of Navajo Culture, Behavior, and Material Culture: A Comparative Study in Culture Change," *Ethnology* 22, no. 1 (January 1983): 83–84; Maureen Trudelle Schwarz, *Molded in the Image of Changing Woman: Navajo Views on the Human Body and Personhood* (Tucson: University of Arizona Press, 1997), 48, 110.

23 Denetdale, *Reclaiming Diné History*, 142, 150–51.

24 Brooks, *Captives and Cousins*, 28, 40, 82, 85–88, 241; Reséndez, *The Other Slavery*, 6–7; Denetdale, *Reclaiming Diné History*, 141.
25 Denetdale, *Reclaiming Diné History*, 140–41; Brooks, *Captives and Cousins*, 246.
26 Schwarz, *Molded in the Image of Changing Woman*, 18, 20–21, 39; Iverson and Roessel, *Diné: A History of the Navajos*, 8–11; Denetdale, *Reclaiming Diné History*, 144; Roessel, *Women in Navajo Society*, 74.
27 Denetdale, *Reclaiming Diné History*, 8; Roessel, *Women in Navajo Society*, 109–10.
28 Iverson and Roessel, *Diné: A History of the Navajos*, 2, 11.

Chapter 6: Ickis

1   Alonzo Ickis Diary, December 25, 1861, DPL.
2   Ickis Diary, January 1, 1862, DPL.
3   Ickis to his sister Cass, July 7, 1861, in Alonzo Ferdinand Ickis, *Bloody Trails Along the Rio Grande: The Diary of Alonzo Ferdinand Ickis*, ed. Nolie Mumey (Denver, Colo: Old West Publishing Company, 1958), 25–26.
4   *Cañon City Times*, October 7, 1861, in Ickis, *Bloody Trails*, ed. Mumey, 27; E.R.S. Canby to William Gilpin, September 8, 1861, *OR* I:4, pp. 68–69.
5   "Volunteers Wanted!" and "Capt. C.D. Hendren and Lieut. J.C.W. Hall of the Colorado Volunteers, arrived from Fort Garland last week," *Cañon City Times*, October 7, 1861, and Ickis to Johnathan F. Ickis, October 25, 1861, in Ickis, *Bloody Trails*, ed. Mumey, 27, 28.
6   Ickis Diary, October 27, 1861, DPL.
7   Ickis Diary, December 11, 1861, DPL.
8   Ickis Diary, December 12, 13, and 21, 1861, DPL.
9   Hampton Sides, *Blood and Thunder: The Epic Story of Kit Carson and the Conquest of the American West* (New York: Anchor Books, 2007), 3.
10 Duane A. Smith, *The Trail of Gold and Silver: Mining in Colorado, 1859–2009* (Boulder: University Press of Colorado, 2011), 50, 53; Ovando J. Hollister, *The Mines of Colorado* (Springfield, Mass.: Samuel Bowles & Co., 1867), 130.
11 Ickis Diary, January 3, 1862, DPL.
12 Ickis to Cass, July 7, 1861, in Ickis, *Bloody Trails*, ed. Mumey, 25–26; E. H. N. Patterson, "My Impressions of the New El Dorado and Its Surroundings" (August 18, 1859), in Leroy R. Hafen, ed., *Overland Routes to the Gold Fields, 1859, from Contemporary Diaries* (Glendale, Calif.: Arthur H. Clark, Co., 1942), 192.
13 Ickis Diary, January 8, 1862, DPL.
14 Emily E. Kieta, "The New Mexico Fandango," *Wagon Tracks* 19, no. 3 (2004–2005): 11–15.
15 Ickis Diary, January 6, 1862, DPL.
16 Ickis Diary, January 8, 1862, DPL.
17 Ickis Diary, January 10, 1862, DPL.
18 Ickis Diary, January 16, 1862, DPL.
19 Clark Diary, January 18, 1862, FAC; Ickis Diary, January 15, 1862, DPL.
20 Ickis Diary, January 17, 1862, DPL.
21 Ickis Diary, January 13 and 17, 1862, DPL.
22 Ickis Diary, January 16, 1862, DPL; Ickis to Thomas, May 14, 1862, in Ickis, *Bloody Trails*, ed. Mumey, 30.
23 Ickis Diary, January 23, 1862, DPL; Ickis to his brother Thomas, May 14, 1862, in Ickis, *Bloody Trails*, ed. Mumey, 30; Clark Diary, January 22, 1862, FAC.

24 Ickis Diary, December 22–23, 1861, DPL; Ickis to Thomas Ickis, May 14, 1862, in Ickis, *Bloody Trails*, ed. Mumey, 29–30.

Chapter 7: Valverde

1 Thompson, *A Civil War History of the New Mexico Volunteers and Militia*, 111, 115.
2 Clark Diary, October 16, 1861, FAC.
3 Thompson, *A Civil War History of the New Mexico Volunteers and Militia*, 67.
4 Ickis Diary, January 31, 1862, DPL.
5 Ickis Diary, December 8, 1861, and February 8, 1862, DPL.
6 Ickis Diary, February 1–2, 1862, DPL.
7 Ickis Diary, February 1, 1862, DPL; Porter, *Account of the Confederate Attempt to Seize Arizona and New Mexico*, 14, SHL.
8 John Taylor, *Bloody Valverde: A Civil War Battle on the Rio Grande, February 21, 1862* (Albuquerque: University of New Mexico Press, 1995), 23; Davidson, in *Civil War in the Southwest*, ed. Thompson, 19.
9 Davidson, in *Civil War in the Southwest*, ed. Thompson, 19.
10 Davidson, in *Civil War in the Southwest*, ed. Thompson, 23.
11 Davidson, in *Civil War in the Southwest*, ed. Thompson, 23; Ickis Diary, February 16, 1862, DPL; Taylor, *Bloody Valverde*, 25 26; Howell Diary, February 16, 1862, in *Westward the Texans*, ed. Thompson, 86–88.
12 Davidson, in *Civil War in the Southwest*, ed. Thompson, 24.
13 Canby to Adj. Gen of the US Army, March 1, 1862: *OR* I:9, p. 288.
14 Phil Fulcrod, "Battle of Valverde," in *Civil War in the Southwest*, ed. Thompson, 53.
15 Ickis Diary, February 16, 1862, DPL; *Civil War in the Southwest*, ed. Thompson, 23; Report of Henry Hopkins Sibley, May 4, 1860, *OR* I:9, p. 507.
16 Report of Henry Hopkins Sibley, May 4, 1860, *OR* I:9, p. 507.
17 E.R.S. Canby to Adj Gen of the US Army, March 1, 1862, *OR* I:9, p. 288.
18 Bell, "The Campaign of New Mexico," p. 57, as in Alfred B. Peticolas, *Rebels on the Rio Grande: The Civil War Journal of A. B. Peticolas*, ed. Don E. Alberts (Albuquerque: Bickerstaff's Historical Publications, 2013), 36–37; Taylor, *Bloody Valverde*, 32–33; Report of Henry Hopkins Sibley, May 4, 1860, *OR* I:9, p. 507.
19 Peticolas, *Rebels on the Rio Grande*, ed. Alberts, 37–38; "Valverde," www.newmexico history.org.
20 Howell Diary, February 19, 1862, in *Westward the Texans*, ed. Thompson, 88.
21 Taylor, *Bloody Valverde*, 35.
22 Ickis Diary, February 20, 1862, DPL.
23 Fulcrod, in *Civil War in the Southwest*, ed. Thompson, 52; Taylor, *Bloody Valverde*, 33; Canby to Adj. Gen of the US Army, March 1, 1862: *OR* I:9, pp. 288–89.
24 Davidson, in *Civil War in the Southwest*, ed. Thompson, 24.
25 Taylor, *Bloody Valverde*, 33–34.
26 Robert Scott to C.A. Dupree, April 10, 1925, as in Taylor, *Bloody Valverde*, 39.
27 Peticolas, *Rebels on the Rio Grande*, ed. Alberts, 38–39; Taylor, *Bloody Valverde*, 38; "Three Privates" and Fulcrod, in *Civil War in the Southwest*, ed. Thompson, 52, 65.
28 Davidson, in *Civil War in the Southwest*, ed. Thompson, 46, 52.
29 Report of Col. Benjamin Roberts, February 23, 1862, *OR* I:9, p. 494; Canby to Adj. Gen of the US Army, March 1, 1862: *OR* I:9, p. 489.
30 Canby to Adj. Gen of the US Army, March 1, 1862: *OR* I:9, p. 489; Taylor, *Bloody Valverde*, 43, 44.

31   Davidson, in *Civil War in the Southwest*, ed. Thompson, 25.
32   William Laughter, "Battle of Valverde," in *Civil War in the Southwest*, ed. Thompson, 61.
33   Davidson, in *Civil War in the Southwest*, ed. Thompson, 25; Taylor, *Bloody Valverde*, 41.
34   Davidson, in *Civil War in the Southwest*, ed. Thompson, 25.
35   Taylor, *Bloody Valverde*, 52.
36   Davidson and "Three Privates," in *Civil War in the Southwest*, ed. Thompson, 26, 28, 65–66.
37   Ickis to Thomas, May 14, 1862, in Ickis, *Bloody Trails*, ed. Mumey, 34.
38   Taylor, *Bloody Valverde*, 46; Canby to Adj Gen US Army, March 1, 1862, *OR* I:9, 489–90.
39   Laughter, in *Civil War in the Southwest*, ed. Thompson, 62.
40   Ickis Diary, February 21, 1862, DPL; Report of Col. Benjamin Roberts, February 23, 1862, *OR* I:9, p. 495.
41   Davidson, in *Civil War in the Southwest*, ed. Thompson, 29; Peticolas Diary, February 21, 1862, in *Rebels on the Rio Grande*, ed. Alberts, 43; Report of Major Henry Raguet, February 23, 1862, *OR* I:9, p. 516.
42   Peticolas Diary, February 21, 1862, in *Rebels on the Rio Grande*, ed. Alberts, 43–44.
43   Ickis Diary, February 21, 1862, DPL.
44   Ickis Diary, February 21, 1862, DPL; Ickis to Thomas, May 14, 1862, in Ickis, *Bloody Trails*, 30, 34; Taylor, *Bloody Valverde*, 67; Captain P.W.L. Plympton to Captain H.R. Selden, February 24, 1862, in *When the Texans Came*, ed. Wilson, 242.
45   Davidson, Phil Clough, "Battle of Valverde," and "Three Privates," in *Civil War in the Southwest*, ed. Thompson, 32, 47, 67; Report of William Scurry, February 22, 1862, *OR* I:9, p. 514.
46   Report of William Scurry, February 22, 1862, *OR* I:9, pp. 514–15.
47   Peticolas Diary, February 21, 1862, in *Rebels on the Rio Grande*, ed. Alberts, 44.
48   Captain P.W.L. Plympton to Captain H.R. Selden, February 24, 1862, in *When the Texans Came*, ed. Wilson, 242; Taylor, *Bloody Valverde*, 72; Ickis Diary, February 21, 1862, DPL.
49   Davidson, in *Civil War in the Southwest*, ed. Thompson, 33.
50   Davidson and Fulcrod, in *Civil War in the Southwest*, ed. Thompson, 33, 56; Taylor, *Bloody Valverde*, 35.
51   Davidson and "Three Privates," in *Civil War in the Southwest*, ed. Thompson, 33–34, 68; Taylor, *Bloody Valverde*, 79.
52   Report of William R. Scurry, February 22, 1862, *OR* I:9, p. 515; Davidson, in *Civil War in the Southwest*, ed. Thompson, 34–35.
53   Fulcrod, in *Civil War in the Southwest*, ed. Thompson, 56.
54   Davidson, in *Civil War in the Southwest*, ed. Thompson, 34.
55   Davidson, in *Civil War in the Southwest*, ed. Thompson, 37.
56   Ickis Diary, February 21, 1862, DPL; Ickis to Thomas, May 14, 1862, in Ickis, *Bloody Trails*, 30, 34.
57   Joseph Bell to Lt. Charles Newbold, February 26, 1862, in Wilson, ed., *When the Texans Came*, pp. 64–65; Ickis Diary, February 21, 1862, DPL; Taylor, *Bloody Valverde*, 87.
58   Davidson, in *Civil War in the Southwest*, ed. Thompson, 37; Ickis Diary, February 21, 1862, DPL; Ickis to his brother Thomas, May 14, 1862, in Ickis, *Bloody Trails*, 30, 34.
59   Ickis Diary, February 21, 1862, DPL.
60   Report of Colonel Christopher Carson, February 26, 1862, *OR* I:9, pp. 502–3; Davidson, in *Civil War in the Southwest*, ed. Thompson, 34–35; Thompson, *A Civil War History of the New Mexico Volunteers and Militia*, 123.

61 Canby to Adj Gen US Army, March 1, 1862, *OR* I:9, p. 491.
62 Fulcrod, in *Civil War in the Southwest*, ed. Thompson, 58.
63 Ickis to his brother Thomas, May 14, 1862, in Ickis, *Bloody Trails*, ed. Mumey, 30–34.
64 Davidson, in *Civil War in the Southwest*, ed. Thompson, 37; Report of Lt. Col. William R. Scurry, February 22, 1862, *OR* I:9, p. 515; Report of Major Henry W. Raguet, February 23, 1862, *OR* I:9, p. 518.
65 Davidson, in *Civil War in the Southwest*, ed. Thompson, 40.
66 Davidson, in *Civil War in the Southwest*, ed. Thompson, 71–73.
67 Ickis to his brother Thomas, May 14, 1862, in *Bloody Trails*, ed. Mumey, 30, 34.
68 Fulcrod and Davidson, in *Civil War in the Southwest*, ed. Thompson, 59, 73.
69 Ickis Diary, February 22, 1862, DPL.
70 Ickis Diary, February 23, 1862, DPL.

Part Two

Chapter 8: Baylor

1 "Battle of Valverde!!" *Mesilla Times*, February 1862, reprinted in *San Antonio Herald-Extra*, March 16, 1862, Beinecke Library, Yale University.
2 Finch, *Confederate Pathway to the Pacific*, 119.
3 Baylor to Emy, January 12/13, 1862, and Fan to Baylor, December 30, 1861, Baylor Family Papers, DBC.
4 Henry Hopkins Sibley, General Orders No. 10 (December 14, 1861) and No. 12 (December 20, 1861), *OR* I:4, pp. 157, 159.
5 Mark E. Nackman, "The Making of the Texan Citizen Soldier, 1835–1860," *Southwestern Historical Quarterly* 78, no. 3 (January 1975): 232.
6 "John Henry Moore," *Handbook of Texas Online*, https://tshaonline.org/handbook/online/articles/fmo30.
7 Campbell, *Gone to Texas*, 169–70; Anna Muckleroy, "The Indian Policy of the Republic of Texas, III," *Southwestern Historical Quarterly* 26, no. 2 (October 1922): 145.
8 George D. Harmon, "The United States Indian Policy in Texas, 1845–1860," *Mississippi Valley Historical Review* 17, no. 3 (December 1930): 394; Campbell, *Gone to Texas*, 201; Fan to Baylor, December 9, 1855, Baylor Family Papers, DBC.
9 Thompson, *Colonel John Robert Baylor*, 11.
10 Baylor to Fan, April 28, 1857, Baylor Family Papers, DBC.
11 Harmon, "The United States Indian Policy in Texas, 1845–1860," 401; Thompson, *Colonel John Robert Baylor*, 13–16.
12 George Wythe Baylor, *Into the Far, Wild Country: True Tales of the Southwest*, ed. Jerry D. Thompson (El Paso: Texas Western Press, 1996), 153.
13 Baylor, *Into the Far, Wild Country*, 159.
14 Baylor, *Into the Far, Wild Country*, 171.
15 Finch, *Confederate Pathway to the Pacific*, 39–40, 43, 45, 55, 78.
16 *Mesilla Times*, January 8, 1862; Finch, *Confederate Pathway to the Pacific*, 108.
17 John R. Baylor to [Henry McCulloch], September 24, 1861, *OR* I:4, p. 110.
18 Jefferson Davis, Proclamation [re: *An act to organize the Territory of Arizona*, passed January 18, 1862], February 14, 1862, in Thomas Edwin Farish, *History of Arizona*, vol. 2 (San Francisco: Filmer Brothers, 1915), 94–95.
19 Thomas W. Cutrer, "Reily, James," *Handbook of Texas Online*, http://www.tshaonline.org/handbook/online/articles/fre26.

20 Sibley to Cooper, January 3, 1862, *OR* I:4, p. 167; A.M. Jackson to Reily, December 31, 1861, *OR* I:4, p. 168.

21 Reily to John Reagan, January 1862, *OR* I:50, part I, pp. 825–26, as in J. Fred Rippy, "Mexican Projects of the Confederates," *Southwestern Historical Quarterly* 22, no. 4 (April 1919): 294.

22 Sibley to Cooper, January 3, 1862, *OR* I:4, p. 167; A.M. Jackson to Reily, December 31, 1861, *OR* I:4, p. 168; Luis Terrazas to Henry Sibley, January 11, 1862, *OR* I:4, p. 172.

23 Martin Hardwick Hall, "Colonel James Reily's Diplomatic Missions to Chihuahua and Sonora," *New Mexico Historical Review* (July 1956): 236.

24 Kelley to the *Austin State Gazette*, January 4, 1862, p. 2, as in Thompson, *Colonel John Robert Baylor*, 60.

25 *Mesilla Times*, December 19, 1861; Finch, *Confederate Pathway to the Pacific*, 103.

26 *Mesilla Times*, December 19, 1861; Finch, *Confederate Pathway to the Pacific*, 103; Thompson, *Colonel John Robert Baylor*, 61.

27 Baylor, *Into the Far, Wild Country*, 193; Fan to Baylor, December 30, 1861, and January 27, 1862, Baylor Family Papers, DBC.

28 Baylor to Emy, January 12/13, 1862, Baylor Family Papers, DBC.

29 Fan to Baylor, January 27, 1862, Baylor Family Papers, DBC.

30 Luis Terrazas to Henry Sibley, March 17, 1862, and Edward H. Jordan to Colonel J.A. Quintero, March 18, 1862, in *When the Texans Came*, ed. Wilson, 231, 233; Sweeney, *Cochise*, 194; Sweeney, *Mangas Coloradas*, 427; "The Raid of Rebels into Chihuahua," *New York Times*, May 29, 1862, p. 8.

31 James Reily to Henry Sibley, January 20, 1862, *OR* I:4, p. 174.

32 Luis Terrazas to Henry Sibley, March 17, 1862, in *When the Texans Came*, ed. Wilson, 232.

33 Juan Méndez to the Secretary of State of Chihuahua, March 26, 1862, in *When the Texans Came*, ed. Wilson, 234.

34 Baylor to Emy, January 12/13, 1862, Baylor Family Papers, DBC.

35 Thompson, *Colonel John Robert Baylor*, 77; Sweeney, *Mangas Coloradas*, 427.

36 Thompson, *Colonel John Robert Baylor*, 71.

37 Baylor to Thomas Helm, March 20, 1862, in Thompson, *Colonel John Robert Baylor*, 56–57, 77.

38 Baylor to Major A.M. Jackson, March 17, 1862, in Wilson, ed., *When the Texans Came*, 197.

39 Baylor to Emy, May 7, 1862, Baylor Family Papers, DBC.

Chapter 9: Clark

1 J.J. Bowden, "Jornada del Muerto Grant," *New Mexico History*, http://newmexicohistory.org/people/jornada-del-muerto-grant.

2 "An Act to Establish the offices of Surveyor-General of New Mexico," July 22, 1854, *United States Statutes at Large*, 33rd Congress, Session 1, Chapter 103, p. 309, https://www.loc.gov/law/help/statutes-at-large/33rd-congress/c33.pdf.

3 Clark Diary, October 9, 10, 1861, FAC.

4 Clark Diary, February 12, 1862, FAC.

5 Clark Diary, February 21, 1862, FAC.

6 John Monroe, "Making the Séance 'Serious': 'Tables Tournantes' and Second Empire Bourgeois Culture, 1853–1861," *History of Religions* 38, no. 3 (February 1999): 219–20.

7 Clark Diary, November 4, 1861, FAC.

8   Clark Diary, February 22 and 23, 1862, FAC.

9   Clark Diary, February 24, 1862, FAC.

10   Clark Diary, February 24 and 28, 1862, FAC.

11   1860 US Federal Census; Clark Papers Biographical Note, Clark Papers, FAC; John B. Ramsay, "John A. Clark," *New Mexico History*, http://newmexicohistory.org/people /john-a-clark; Fred Roeder, "The Journals of John A. Clark," *The American Surveyor* (April 5, 2009), http://www.amerisurv.com/content/view/6018/136/; Illinois Congressional Republicans to Abraham Lincoln, March 12, 1861, p. 2, Abraham Lincoln Papers, Manuscripts Division, Library of Congress; Appointment of John A. Clark as Surveyor-General of New Mexico Territory (1861), Clark Papers, FAC.

12   Richard W. Etulain, "Abraham Lincoln and the Trans-Mississippi American West: An Introductory Overview," in Etulain ed., *Lincoln Looks West: From the Mississippi to the Pacific* (Carbondale: Southern Illinois University, 2010), 33.

13   Daren Earl Kellogg, "Lincoln's New Mexico Patronage: Saving the Far Southwest for the Union," in Etulain ed., *Lincoln Looks West*, 140, 143.

14   Kellogg, "Lincoln's New Mexico Patronage," in Etulain ed., *Lincoln Looks West*, 137, 138, 139, 143.

15   *Santa Fe Weekly Gazette*, April 26, 1862, p. 1; John Clark Diary, February 28, 1862, and March 2–3, 1862, FAC.

16   Clark Diary, March 2, 1862, FAC.

17   Clark Diary, March 2–3, 1862, FAC.

18   Clark Diary, March 3, 1862, FAC.

19   Clark Diary, March 3, 1862, FAC.

20   "Second Fort Union," https://www.nps.gov/foun/learn/historyculture/the-star-fort.htm.

21   Clark Diary, March 4, 1862, FAC.

22   Clark Diary, March 5, 1862, FAC.

23   Clark Diary, March 6–7, 1862, FAC.

24   Clark Diary, March 7, 1862, FAC.

25   Clark Diary, December 31, 1861, FAC.

26   Clark Diary, March 7, 1862, FAC.

27   Ovando Hollister, *Boldly They Rode: A History of the 1st Colorado Regiment of Volunteers* (Lakewood, Colo.: The Golden Press, 1949), 47; Clark Diary, March 11, 1862, FAC.

28   Hollister, *Boldly They Rode*, 48.

29   Hollister, *Boldly They Rode*, 52; Clark Diary, March 11, 1862, FAC.

30   Clark Diary, March 11, 1862, FAC.

31   Homestead Act (May 20, 1862), *United States Statutes at Large*, 37th Congress, 2nd Session vol. 12, p. 392, https://memory.loc.gov/cgi-bin/ampage?collId=llsl&fileName =012/llsl012.db&recNum=423.

32   Abraham Lincoln to George McClellan, April 9, 1862, as in Doris Kearns Goodwin, *Team of Rivals: The Political Genius of Abraham Lincoln* (New York: Simon & Schuster, 2005), 432.

33   Clark Diary, March 12, 1862, FAC.

Chapter 10: Glorieta

1   Theophilus Noel, *Autobiography and Reminiscences of Theophilus Noel* (Chicago: Theo. Noel Co., 1904), 61.

2   Davidson and Fulcrod, in *Civil War in the Southwest*, ed. Thompson, 80, 90; Don E. Alberts, *The Battle of Glorieta: Union Victory in the West* (College Station: Texas

A&M Press, 1998), 16–17, 20; Sibley Report, May 4, 1862, *Southern History of the War: Official Reports of Battles, as Published by Order of the Confederate Congress at Richmond* (New York: Charles B. Richardson, 1864), 180.

3   Ellen Williams, *Three Years and a Half in the Army; or, a History of the Second Colorados* (New York: Fowler & Wells Co., 1885), 15–20.

4   James L. Donaldson, Quartermaster, Report, March 10, 1862, *OR* I:9, chap. 21, p. 527; Thompson, *Henry Hopkins Sibley*, 276.

5   *Santa Fe Weekly Gazette*, April 26, 1862, p. 1; Thompson, *Henry Hopkins Sibley*, 277.

6   Sibley's Proclamation to the People of Santa Fe (March 13, 1862), *Santa Fe Weekly Gazette*, April 26, 1862, p. 1; Alberts, *The Battle of Glorieta*, 15.

7   Alberts, *The Battle of Glorieta*, 15.

8   Peter Stark, *Last Breath: The Limits of Adventure* (New York: Penguin Books, 2002), 45–80, 135–50, *Ecoregions of New Mexico*.

9   Alberts, *The Battle of Glorieta*, 20–21; Peticolas Diary, March 22–25, 1862, in Peticolas, *Rebels on the Rio Grande*, ed. Alberts, 72–73; *Santa Fe Weekly Gazette*, April 26, 1862, p. 1.

10 Porter, *Account of the Confederate attempt to seize Arizona and New Mexico*, p. 17, SHL; John Miller to his father, April 3, 1862, *Pueblo Chieftain*, September 29, 1907, 10, in Wilson, ed., *When the Texans Came*, 260.

11 "Gen. Canby," *Daily Sentinel* (Raleigh, N.C.), September 11, 1867, 1, in William P. MacKinnon, "Epilogue to the Utah War: Impact and Legacy," *Journal of Mormon History* 29, no. 2 (2003): 228.

12 Jane E. Schultz, *Women at the Front: Hospital Workers in Civil War America* (Chapel Hill: University of North Carolina Press, 2004).

13 Williams, *Three Years and a Half in the Army*, 20.

14 Davidson, note attached to letter from J.H. Richardson (1888), in *Civil War in the Southwest*, ed. Thompson, 136.

15 Davidson, in *Civil War in the Southwest*, ed. Thompson, 82.

16 George Brown to his wife, April 30, 1862, in Hollister, *Boldly They Rode*, 167; Report of Major John Chivington, March 26, 1862, *OR* I:9, chap. 21, pp. 530–31; Davidson, in *Civil War in the Southwest*, ed. Thompson, 82; Hollister, *Boldly They Rode*, 63.

17 Davidson, note attached to letter from Love Tooke (1888), in *Civil War in the Southwest*, ed. Thompson, 137.

18 Davidson, in *Civil War in the Southwest*, ed. Thompson, 83.

19 Report of Col. William R. Scurry, March 31, 1862, *OR* I:9, 542.

20 Davidson, in *Civil War in the Southwest*, ed. Thompson, 84.

21 Davidson, in *Civil War in the Southwest*, ed. Thompson, 84; Report of Col. William R. Scurry, March 31, 1862, *OR* I:9, chap. 21, pp. 542–43; Peticolas Diary, March 27, 1862, in Peticolas, *Rebels on the Rio Grande*, ed. Alberts, 76.

22 Davidson and "Three Privates," in *Civil War in the Southwest*, ed. Thompson, 84, 93; Peticolas Diary, March 27, 1862, in Peticolas, *Rebels on the Rio Grande*, ed. Alberts, 76–77; Report of Col. William R. Scurry, March 31, 1862, *OR* I:9, chap. 21, pp. 542–43; Alberts, *The Battle of Glorieta*, 71, 78.

23 Davidson, in *Civil War in the Southwest*, ed. Thompson, 84; Alberts, *The Battle of Glorieta*, 67.

24 Report of Col. William R. Scurry, March 31, 1862, *OR* I:9, chap. 21, pp. 542–43; Davidson, in *Civil War in the Southwest*, ed. Thompson, 84.

25 Peticolas Diary, March 28, 1862, in Peticolas, *Rebels on the Rio Grande*, ed. Alberts, 77–78.

26 "Three Privates," in *Civil War in the Southwest*, ed. Thompson, 93; *Santa Fe Weekly Gazette*, April 26, 1862, 1.

27 Alberts, *The Battle of Glorieta*, 46; Report of Colonel John P. Slough, March 29, 1862, OR I:9, chap. 21, p. 533; Davidson, in *Civil War in the Southwest*, ed. Thompson, 84.

28 Davidson and "Three Privates," in *Civil War in the Southwest*, ed. Thompson, 85, 93; Alberts, *The Battle of Glorieta*, 87.

29 "Three Privates," in *Civil War in the Southwest*, ed. Thompson, 94.

30 Alberts, *The Battle of Glorieta*, 132.

31 Alberts, *The Battle of Glorieta*, 132–33; Reports of Col. William R. Scurry, March 30 and 31, 1862, OR I:9, chap. 21, pp. 542, 544; *Santa Fe Weekly Gazette*, April 26, 1862, p. 1; Davidson, in *Civil War in the Southwest*, ed. Thompson, 85.

32 Alberts, *The Battle of Glorieta*, 71–73, 128.

33 Alberts, *The Battle of Glorieta*, 132.

34 Alberts, *The Battle of Glorieta*, 133–35; Report of Major John M. Chivington, March 28, 1862, OR I:9, chap. 21, pp. 538–39; Chivington, "The Pet Lambs" (1890), Folder 65, Box 2, MSS 141, Colorado Volunteers: Civil War Collection, SHL.

35 As quoted in Alberts, *The Battle of Glorieta*, 135.

36 Davidson, in *Civil War in the Southwest*, ed. Thompson, 85.

37 Peticolas Diary, March 28, 1862, in Peticolas, *Rebels on the Rio Grande*, ed. Alberts, 85; Henry C. Wright Reminiscences, 1861–1862, reprinted in Michael L. Tate, ed., "A Johnny Reb in Sibley's New Mexico Campaign . . . Part II," *East Texas Historical Journal* 26, no. 1 (1988): 25.

38 Unidentified Texas soldier, in Alberts, *The Battle of Glorieta*, 143.

39 Davidson, in *Civil War in the Southwest*, ed. Thompson, 82.

40 Report of Brig. Gen. Henry Sibley, C.S. Army, March 31, 1862, OR I:9, chap. 21, p. 541; Reports of Col. William R. Scurry, March 30 and March 31, 1862, OR I:9, chap. 21, pp. 541–42.

41 Davidson, in *Civil War in the Southwest*, ed. Thompson, 86; Peticolas Diary, March 29, 1862, in Peticolas, *Rebels on the Rio Grande*, ed. Alberts, 87.

42 *Santa Fe Gazette*, April 26, 1862, p. 1.

43 Wayne R. Austerman, "'Sick, Dead and Discharged': Disease and the Defeat of the Confederate Campaign into New Mexico, 1862," *U.S. Army Medical Department Journal* (April–June 2007): 10.

44 Wright in Tate, ed., "A Johnny Reb in Sibley's New Mexico Campaign," 26.

45 Peticolas Diary, March 30, 1862, in Peticolas, *Rebels on the Rio Grande*, ed. Alberts, 87–88.

46 Peticolas Diary, March 30 and April 3, 1862, in Peticolas, *Rebels on the Rio Grande*, ed. Alberts, 87–88, 92–93.

47 *Santa Fe Gazette*, April 26, 1862, p. 1.

48 William R. Scurry, General Orders No. 4, March 28, 1862, in *Santa Fe Gazette*, April 26, 1862, p. 1.

49 Peticolas Diary, April 2, 1862, in Peticolas, *Rebels on the Rio Grande*, ed. Alberts, 92.

50 Fulcrod, in *Civil War in the Southwest*, ed. Thompson, 90; Alberts, *The Battle of Glorieta*, 157.

51 Peticolas Diary, April 5, 1862, in Peticolas, *Rebels on the Rio Grande*, ed. Alberts, 6.

52 Davidson, in *Civil War in the Southwest*, ed. Thompson, 99; Wright in Tate, ed., "A Johnny Reb in Sibley's New Mexico Campaign," 27.

53 *Santa Fe Gazette*, April 26, 1862, p. 1, and May 17, 1862, p. 2; Peticolas Diary, March 31, 1862, in Peticolas, *Rebels on the Rio Grande*, ed. Alberts, 91.

54 *Santa Fe Gazette*, April 26, 1862, p. 1, and May 17, 1862, p. 2; Davidson, in *Civil War in the Southwest*, ed. Thompson, 100; Alberts, *The Battle of Glorieta*, 152.
55 Report of Henry Sibley, May 4, 1862, in *Southern History of the War*, 181.
56 Thompson, *Henry Hopkins Sibley*, 292.
57 *Santa Fe Gazette*, April 26, 1862, p. 2; Tom Sharpe, "Confederate Army in Santa Fe," *New Mexico History*, newmexicohistory.org; Report of Henry Sibley, May 4, 1862, in *Southern History of the War*, 181.
58 Davidson, in *Civil War in the Southwest*, ed. Thompson, 100–101.
59 Wright in Tate, ed., "A Johnny Reb in Sibley's New Mexico Campaign," 27.

Chapter 11: Davidson

 1 Ickis Diary, March 1–April 8, 1862, DPL; E.R.S. Canby to Adjt. General of the Army, April 11, 1862, *OR* I:9, p. 550; Davidson, in *Civil War in the Southwest*, ed. Thompson, 102–3; Peticolas Diary, April 8–9, 1862, in Peticolas, *Rebels on the Rio Grande*, ed. Alberts, 97–98.
 2 Davidson, in *Civil War in the Southwest*, ed. Thompson, 119.
 3 Davidson, in *Civil War in the Southwest*, ed. Thompson, 119–20.
 4 Hollister, *Boldly They Rode*, 99–100.
 5 Davidson, in *Civil War in the Southwest*, ed. Thompson, 120.
 6 "Three Privates," in *Civil War in the Southwest*, ed. Thompson, 122–23; James Graydon to Col. Paul from Polvadera, N.M., May 14, 1862, *OR* I:9, pp. 671–72.
 7 Howell Diary, April 19, 1862, in *Westward the Texans*, ed. Thompson, 100; Hall, *Sibley's New Mexico Campaign*, 137; James Graydon to Col. Paul from Polvadera, N.M., May 14, 1862, *OR* I:9, pp. 671–72.
 8 Peticolas Diary, April 20, 1862, in Peticolas, *Rebels on the Rio Grande*, ed. Alberts, 113; Megan Kate Nelson, *Ruin Nation: Destruction and the American Civil War* (Athens: University of Georgia Press, 2012), 228–30; Joan E. Cashin, "Trophies of War: Material Culture in the Civil War Era," *Journal of the Civil War Era* 1, no. 3 (September 2011): 339–67.
 9 Peticolas Diary, April 21, 1862, in Peticolas, *Rebels on the Rio Grande*, ed. Alberts, 114; Hall, *Sibley's New Mexico Campaign*, 137–38.
10 "Three Privates," in *Civil War in the Southwest*, ed. Thompson, 124; Peticolas Diary, April 19, 1862, in Peticolas, *Rebels on the Rio Grande*, ed. Alberts, 111, 112; Frazier, *Blood and Treasure*, 254.
11 Peticolas Diary, April 22, 1862, in Peticolas, *Rebels on the Rio Grande*, ed. Alberts, 114, 115.
12 Peticolas Diary, April 24, 1862, in Peticolas, *Rebels on the Rio Grande*, ed. Alberts, 116–17; "Three Privates," in *Civil War in the Southwest*, ed. Thompson, 124; Howell Diary, April 24, 1862, in *Westward the Texans*, ed. Thompson, 101–2.
13 "Three Privates," in *Civil War in the Southwest*, ed. Thompson, 125.
14 Peticolas Diary, April 27, 1862, in Peticolas, *Rebels on the Rio Grande*, ed. Alberts, 118.
15 Peticolas Diary, April 27, 1862, in Peticolas, *Rebels on the Rio Grande*, ed. Alberts, 118.
16 Davidson, in *Civil War in the Southwest*, ed. Thompson, 120.
17 Howell Diary, April 21, 1862, in *Westward the Texans*, ed. Thompson, 101.
18 Davidson, in *Civil War in the Southwest*, ed. Thompson, 131.
19 Peticolas Diary, May 6–June 6, 1862, in Peticolas, *Rebels on the Rio Grande*, ed. Alberts, 127–36.
20 Henry Hopkins Sibley, Proclamation, May [14], 1862, in Peticolas, *Rebels on the Rio Grande*, ed. Alberts, 135.

21 Henry Sibley to Don Luis Terrazas, May 17, 1862, in Wilson, ed., *When the Texans Came*, 235; *Houston Tri-Weekly Telegraph*, October 17, 1862, as in Kiser, *Turmoil on the Rio Grande*, 183.

22 Sibley to Cooper, May 4, 1862, *OR* I:9, pp. 506–12.

23 Peticolas Diary, May [25], 1862, in Peticolas, *Rebels on the Rio Grande*, ed. Alberts, 140.

24 J.A.K. to the editor of the *Houston Tri-Weekly Telegraph*, July 8, 1862, in Wilson, ed., *When the Texans Came*, 311–12; Steele to Jose Urango and others in El Paso, July 11, 1862, in Wilson, ed., *When the Texans Came*, 312–13.

25 Wright in Tate, ed., "A Johnny Reb in Sibley's New Mexico Campaign," 31.

26 Davidson, in *Civil War in the Southwest*, ed. Thompson, 128.

27 Peticolas Diary, June 10, 1862, in Peticolas, *Rebels on the Rio Grande*, ed. Alberts, 146; Howell Diary, June 20–21, 1862, in *Westward the Texans*, ed. Thompson, 105.

28 Davidson, in *Civil War in the Southwest*, ed. Thompson, 127.

29 Peticolas Diary, May 23, 1862, in Peticolas, *Rebels on the Rio Grande*, ed. Alberts, 137; Davidson, in *Civil War in the Southwest*, ed. Thompson, 127.

Chapter 12: Carleton

1 Mansfield Report on Fort Yuma, 1854, as quoted in Justin Ruge, "Fort Yuma," militarymuseum.org; James Carleton, General Orders No. 1 and No. 9, May 15, 1862, *OR* I:50, pt. 1, p. 1075; George Wright to Lorenzo Thomas, May 13, 1862, *OR* I:50, pt. 1, p. 1069.

2 Wright to Thomas, December 8, 1861, *Records of California Men in the War of the Rebellion, 1861 to 1867*, ed. Richard H. Orton (Sacramento, Calif.: J. D. Young, 1890), 323.

3 Carleton, General Orders No. 3, in Constance Wynn Altshuler and Ben C. Cutler, "Military Administration in Arizona, 1854–1865," *Journal of Arizona History* 10, no. 4 (Winter 1969): 238; Andrew E. Masich, *The Civil War in Arizona: The Story of the California Volunteers, 1861–1865* (Norman: University of Oklahoma Press, 2006), 29.

4 John W. Robinson, *Los Angeles in Civil War Days, 1860–1865* (Norman: University of Oklahoma Press, 1977), 55–58; George Hand Diary, September 30, 1862, in "The California Column Occupies Tucson: George O. Hand's Diary, August 8–Dec. 12, 1862," ed. Neil P. Carmony *Journal of Arizona History* 26, no. 1 (spring 1985): 23; "Vidette," letter to the editors, *San Francisco Daily Alta California*, May 14, 1862, in Masich, *The Civil War in Arizona*, 163.

5 Carleton to Joseph West, March 29, 1862, *OR* I:50, pt. 1, p. 961.

6 George Wright to Lorenzo Thomas, December 8 and 9, 1861 [telegraph message], *Records of California Men in the War of the Rebellion*, 46, 323.

7 "The Rains—The Flood," *Los Angeles Star*, January 25, 1862.

8 Finch, *Confederate Pathway to the Pacific*, 120; Wright to Thomas, December 31, 1861, *Records of California Men in the War of the Rebellion*, 42; James M. McNulty Report, *OR* I:9, p. 596; Timothy Silver and Judkin Browning, *The Civil War: An Environmental History* (Chapel Hill: University of North Carolina Press, forthcoming 2020); Kenneth Noe, *The Howling Storm: Climate, Weather, and the American Civil War* (Baton Rouge: Louisiana State University Press, forthcoming 2021); Robinson, *Los Angeles in Civil War Days*, 87; J.M. Guinn, "Exceptional Years: A History of California Floods and Drought," *Historical Society of Southern California, Los Angeles* 1, no. 5 (1890): 36.

9 Masich, *The Civil War in Arizona*, 24.

10 Hunt, *Major James Henry Carleton*, 215–16.

11 "Vidette," letter to the editors, *San Francisco Daily Alta California*, May 14, 1862, in Masich, *The Civil War in Arizona*, 156.

12 Carleton, Special Orders No. 51, April 27, 1862, *OR* I:50, pt. 1, p. 1033.

13 Edwin Rigg to Carleton, March 20, 1862, *OR* I:50, pt. 1, pp. 939–40; Finch, *Confederate Pathway to the Pacific*,129; Sherod Hunter to John Baylor, April 5, 1862, *Records of California Men in the War of the Rebellion*, 45; David DeJong, "'The Granary of Arizona': The Civil War, Settlers, and Pima-Maricopa Agriculture, 1860–1869," *Journal of Arizona History* 48, no. 3 (autumn 2007): 231.

14 Rigg to Carleton, March 20, 1862, *OR* I:50, pt. 1, p. 940; Carleton to Wright, March 30, 1862, *OR* I:50, pt. 1, p. 962.

15 Masich, *The Civil War in Arizona*, 38; Aurora Hunt, *The Army of the Pacific, 1860–1866*, (Glendale, Calif.: The Arthur Clark Co.,1951), 85.

16 Masich, *The Civil War in Arizona*, 38; DeJong, "'The Granary of Arizona,'" 233; Akers Diary, April 23, 1862, Diary of Thomas Akers, 1861–1864, UA; *Sacramento Union*, May 23, 1862, in Hunt, *The Army of the Pacific*, 88–89.

17 Carleton to West, May 3, 1862, *OR* I:50, pt. 1, pp. 1048–49; "Vidette," letter to the editors, *San Francisco Daily Alta California*, May 14, 1862, in Masich, *The Civil War in Arizona*, 165; Masich, *The Civil War in Arizona*, 45.

18 "Vidette," letter to the editors, *San Francisco Daily Alta California*, June 8, 1862, in Masich, *The Civil War in Arizona*, 178.

19 "Dragoon," letter to the editors, *San Francisco Daily Alta California*, June 23, 1862, in Masich, *The Civil War in Arizona*, 192.

20 Akers Diary, April 21, 1862, UA; Nelson, *Ruin Nation*, 116–25.

21 Joseph West, "Journal of the March of Company C & Volunteers . . . from Camp Wright to Tucson," 1862, Joseph Rodman West Papers, DPL; "Dragoon," letter to the editors, *San Francisco Daily Alta California*, June 23, 1862, in Masich, *The Civil War in Arizona*, 192; Akers Diary, April 21, 1862, UA.

22 Carleton to Richard Drum, May 24, 1862, *OR* I:50, pt. 1, pp. 1094–95; Carleton to West, May 2, 1862, *OR* I:50, pt. 1, pp. 1045–46.

23 West to Benjamin Cutler, May 21, 1862, *OR* I:50, pt. 1, p. 1088.

24 Carleton to West, May 2, 1862, *OR* I:50, pt. 1, p. 1046; George H. Pettis, *The California Column: Its Campaigns and Services in New Mexico . . .* (Santa Fe: Historical Society of New Mexico Circular No. 11, 1908), 11; Masich, *The Civil War in Arizona*, 46.

25 "Vidette," letter to the editors, *San Francisco Daily Alta California*, June 29, 1862, in Masich, *The Civil War in Arizona*, 184–85; DeJong, "'The Granary of Arizona,'" 223–24.

26 Carleton to Richard Drum, May 24, 1862, *Records of California Men in the War of the Rebellion*, 50–51; West, "Journal of the March," 1862, DPL.

27 Carleton to Edward Eyre, May 25, 1862, *OR* I:50, pt. 1, p. 1098.

28 "N.," letter to the editors, *San Francisco Daily Alta California*, July 10, 1862, in Masich, *The Civil War in Arizona*, 203.

29 "N.," letter to the editors, *San Francisco Daily Alta California*, July 10, 1862, in Masich, *The Civil War in Arizona*, 203–4.

30 "N.," letter to the editors, *San Francisco Daily Alta California*, July 10, 1862, in Masich, *The Civil War in Arizona*, 204.

31 "N.," letter to the editors, *San Francisco Daily Alta California*, July 10, 1862, in Masich, *The Civil War in Arizona*, 204.

32 "N.," letter to the editors, *San Francisco Daily Alta California*, July 10, 1862, in Masich, *The Civil War in Arizona*, 204.

33 George Wright, Confiscation Circular, April 30, 1862, in "California Rebellion

War Claims," *Executive Documents of the Senate*, No. 11, 51st Congress, 1st Session (1889–90), 63; Constance Wynn Altshuler, "The Case of Sylvester Mowry: The Mowry Mine," *Arizona and the West* 15, no. 2 (Summer 1973): 149–50.

34 Masich, *The Civil War in Arizona*, 48–49; "N.," letter to the editors, *San Francisco Daily Alta California*, July 10, 1862, in Masich, *The Civil War in Arizona*, 205.

35 Carleton to Drum, June 10, 1862, *OR* I:50, pt. 1, pp. 1128–29; Carleton to Drum, June 10, 1862, and Carleton, "Proclamation," June 8, 1862, *Records of California Men in the War of the Rebellion*, 52–53, 55–56.

36 Aurora Hunt, *Major James Henry Carleton, 1814–1873: Western Frontier Dragoon* (Glendale, Calif.: Arthur H. Clark Co., 1958), 326, 329; Carleton Watkins, "The Carleton Aerolite," 1863 [photograph], in *Complete Mammoth Photographs*, ed. Weston Naef and Christine Hult-Lewis (Los Angeles: J. Paul Getty Museum, 2011), 32.

37 John Russell Bartlett, *Personal Narrative of Explorations and Incidents . . .* , vol. II (New York: D. Appleton & Co., 1854), 297–98; Carleton to Wright, June 30, 1862, in J. D. Whitney, *Notice of the Two Masses of Meteoric Iron Brought from Tucson to San Francisco, 1862 and 1863* (San Francisco: Town & Bacon, 1863), 6–7.

38 Carleton to John James Audubon, April 2, 1848, and *Audubon Journal*, October 1843, in John James Audubon, *The Missouri River Journals of John James Audubon*, ed. Daniel Patterson (Lincoln: University of Nebraska Press, 2016), 123–24.

39 Spencer F. Baird, *Report of the Assistant Secretary in Charge of the Natural History Department for the Year, 1850*, in *Publications of Spencer Fullerton Baird, in Bulletin of the US National Museum*, vol. 20 (Department of the Interior, Government Printing Office, 1883), 5.

40 Carleton to Wright, June 30, 1862, in Whitney, *Notice of the Two Masses of Meteoric Iron*, 6–7.

41 "N.," letter to the editors, *San Francisco Daily Alta California*, July 10, 1862, in Masich, *The Civil War in Arizona*, 205–6.

42 Carleton to Canby, June 11, 1862, *Records of California Men in the War of the Rebellion*, 48.

43 George Hand Diary, August 30, 1862, in "The California Column Occupies Tucson," 18.

44 Carleton Order, June 12, 1862, *Records of California Men in the War of the Rebellion*, 57.

45 McNulty Report, *OR* I:9, pp. 599, 600; Carleton to Drum, June 10, 1862, *Records of California Men in the War of the Rebellion*, 52–53.

46 Carleton to Canby, August 2, 1862, *OR* I:9, p. 557; Don M. Mahan, "John W. Jones: The Southwest's Unsung Civil War Hero," *Journal of Arizona History* 51, no. 3 (autumn 2010): 223, 224, 232, 233.

47 "Vidette," letter to the editors, *San Francisco Daily Alta California*, June 29, 1862, in Masich, *The Civil War in Arizona*, 188–89.

48 Carleton to Drum, July 22, 1862, *Records of California Men in the War of the Rebellion*, 57; "Vidette," letter to the editors, *San Francisco Daily Alta California*, July 23, 1862, in Masich, *The Civil War in Arizona*, 216.

49 Carleton, "Proclamation," June 8, 1862, *Records of California Men in the War of the Rebellion*, 55–56.

50 "N.," letter to the editors, *San Francisco Daily Alta California*, July 10, 1862, in Masich, *The Civil War in Arizona*, 208–09.

Chapter 13: Mangas Coloradas

1 Statement of John W. Jones, July 22, 1862, *OR* I:50, pt. 1, pp. 119–20; Mahan, "John W. Jones," 232–33; Carleton to Drum, July 22, 1862, *OR* I:9, p. 554.

2 Carleton to Edward Eyre, June 17, 1862, *OR* I:50, pt. 1, p. 98.
3 Eyre to Cutler, July 6, 1862, *Records of California Men in the War of the Rebellion*, 58–59.
4 Eyre to Cutler, July 6 and 14, 1862, *Records of California Men in the War of the Rebellion*, 58–59, 62; Sweeney, *Cochise*, 196–97; Sweeney, *Mangas Coloradas*, 429–30; Carleton to Drum, July 22, 1862, *Records of California Men in the War of the Rebellion*, 57; McNulty Report, *OR* I:9, p. 601; "Vidette," letter to the editors, *San Francisco Daily Alta California*, July 23, 1862, in Masich, *The Civil War in Arizona*, 216.
5 John G. Bourke, "Notes on Apache Mythology," *Journal of American Folklore* 3, no. 10 (July–September 1890): 211–12; Sweeney, *Mangas Coloradas*, 425, 426.
6 Sweeney, *Cochise*, 194.
7 Blyth, *Chiricahua and Janos*, x, 123.
8 Sweeney, *Mangas Coloradas*, 427; Baylor to Thomas Helm, March 20, 1862, in Thompson, *Colonel John Robert Baylor*, 56–57, 77.
9 John Greiner testimony in James R. Doolittle, *Condition of the Indian Tribes: Report of the Special Committee Appointed under Joint Resolution of March 3, 1865, with Appendix* (Washington, D.C.: Government Printing Office, 1867): 328.
10 "Horrible Massacre," *Santa Fe Gazette*, October 4, 1862, p. 2; Sweeney, *Cochise*, 201.
11 Sweeney, *Mangas Coloradas*, 430.
12 Thomas L. Roberts, "Journal of a March of a Detachment of the Column from California," *OR* I:50, pp. 129, 130–31; Sweeney, *Mangas Coloradas*, 430, 431.
13 Sweeney, *Mangas Coloradas*, 431–32.
14 Sweeney, *Mangas Coloradas*, 432.
15 Asa Daklugie account in Eve Ball, *Indeh: An Apache Odyssey* (Reprint ed., Norman: University of Oklahoma Press, 1988), 20.
16 Sweeney, *Mangas Coloradas*, 432.
17 Albert Fountain account, *Rio Grande Republican*, January 2, 1891, as in Sweeney, *Mangas Coloradas*, 433.
18 John Teal, "Soldier in the California Column: The Diary of John W. Teal," ed. Henry P. Walker, *Arizona and the West* 13, no. 1 (Spring 1971): 40–41; Sweeney, *Mangas Coloradas*, 433–34.
19 Fountain account, as in Sweeney, *Mangas Coloradas*, 434.
20 Sweeney, *Mangas Coloradas*, 433, 434–35.
21 Teal, "Soldier in the California Column," 40–41; Sweeney, *Mangas Coloradas*, 437; Report of John Cremony [to Roberts], July 16, 1862, *OR* I:50, pt. 1, p. 132.
22 Teal, "Soldier in the California Column," 41.
23 Teal, "Soldier in the California Column," 40–41; Sweeney, *Mangas Coloradas*, 437–38; Report of John Cremony [to Roberts], July 16, 1862, *OR* I:50, pt. 1, p. 132.
24 Sweeney, *Mangas Coloradas*, 439.
25 Sweeney, *Mangas Coloradas*, 439–40.

Chapter 14: Canby

1 Eyre to Cutler, July 6, 1862, *Records of California Men in the War of the Rebellion*, 60.
2 "The Fourth," *Santa Fe Gazette*, July 5, 1862, p. 2.
3 Spanish translation of the Declaration of Independence, *Semanario Político, Económico y Literario*, December 12, 1821.
4 "The Fourth," *Santa Fe Gazette*, July 5, 1862, p. 2.
5 "The Fourth," *Santa Fe Gazette*, July 5, 1862, p. 2.
6 Wright, in Tate, ed., "A Johnny Reb in Sibley's New Mexico Campaign," 27.

7 Wright, in Tate, ed., "A Johnny Reb in Sibley's New Mexico Campaign," 27; *Santa Fe Gazette*, April 26, 1862, p. 2; Alberts, *The Battle of Glorieta*, 160.

8 *Santa Fe Gazette*, May 31, 1862, p. 2; Wright, in Tate, ed., "A Johnny Reb in Sibley's New Mexico Campaign," 27.

9 "Col. Canby's Arrival," *Santa Fe Gazette*, May 10, 1862, p. 2.

10 E.R.S. Canby, General Orders No. 43, May 7, 1862, in *Santa Fe Gazette*, May 10, 1862, p. 2; Heyman, *A Prudent Soldier*, 182–83.

11 *Santa Fe Gazette*, May 31, 1862, p. 2.

12 Clark Diary, April 1 and 3, 1862, FAC.

13 Clark Diary, August 11, 1862, FAC.

14 Homestead Act, May 20, 1862, and Pacific Railway Act, July 1, 1862, *Statutes at Large*, 37th Congress, 2nd Session, 392–93, 489–98.

15 *Santa Fe Gazette*, August 9, 1862, p. 2; Clark Diary, August 20, 1862, FAC.

16 Carleton to Canby, August 2, 1862, as in Leo P. Kibby, "With Colonel Carleton and the California Column," *Historical Society of Southern California Quarterly* 41, no. 4 (December 1959): 342.

17 Canby to Carleton, August 11, 1862, OR I:50, p. 108.

18 Carleton to Drum, September 20, 1862, *Records of California Men in the War of the Rebellion*, 64–65.

19 Clark Diary, August 21, 1862, FAC.

20 *Santa Fe Gazette*, May 17, 1862, p. 2.

21 *Santa Fe Gazette*, May 17, July 12, July 19, July 26, 1862, August 2, August 9, 1862, all p. 2.

22 Clark Diary, August 28, 1862, FAC.

23 *Santa Fe Gazette*, August 30, 1862, p. 2.

24 Clark Diary, September 22, 1862, FAC.

25 Clark Diary, September 21, 1862, FAC; *Santa Fe Gazette*, August 30, 1862, p. 2.

26 Carleton, General Orders No. 85, September 21, 1862, OR I:15, p. 575.

27 Clark Diary, September 22, 1862, FAC; Marc Simmons, "Bishop Lamy's Garden," http://sfol.com/history/bishop.html.

28 Clark Diary, September 22, 1862, FAC.

Chapter 15: Ickis

1 Ickis Diary, April 24 and May 21, 1862, DPL; Hollister, *Boldly They Rode*, 121.

2 Charles A. Curtis, *Ordered West: The Civil War Exploits of Charles A. Curtis*, ed. Alan D. Gaff and Donald H. Gaff (Denton: University of North Texas Press, 2017), 82–83, 108; Ickis Diary, August 25, 1862, DPL.

3 *Navajo Roundup: Selected Correspondence of Kit Carson's Expedition Against the Navajo, 1863–1865*, ed. Lawrence Kelly, (Boulder, Colo.: The Pruett Publishing Company, 1970), 3, 8–9; Utley, *Frontiersmen in Blue*, 233.

4 Hollister, *Boldly They Rode*, 137.

5 James Carleton, General Orders No. 103, *Santa Fe Gazette*, December 27, 1862, p. 2.

6 J.H. Leavenworth to Thomas Moonlight from Fort Larned, August 13, 1862, OR I:13, p. 566.

7 E.R.S Canby, General Orders No. 81 (September 9, 1862) and Carleton, Special Orders No. 176 (September 27, 1862), in *Navajo Roundup*, ed. Kelly, 3, 8–9; Neil C. Mangum, "In the Land of Frozen Fires: A History of Occupation in El Malpais County" (1990), https://www.nps.gov/elma/learn/historyculture/upload/ELMA_hist .pdf; Ickis Diary, June 5, 1862, DPL.

8   Utley, *Frontiersmen in Blue*, 235; Dunlay, *Kit Carson and the Indians* (Lincoln: University of Nebraska Press, 2000), 242–43.

9   Carleton to Thomas, September 30, 1862, *OR* I:15, p. 576; Utley, *Frontiersmen in Blue*, 235; Dunlay, *Kit Carson and the Indians*, 242–43.

10 Carleton, Special Orders No. 176 (September 27, 1862), in *Navajo Roundup*, ed. Kelly, 8–9.

11 Hunt, *Major James Henry Carleton*, 139, 161.

12 Gary Clayton Anderson and Alan R. Woolworth, eds., *Through Dakota Eyes: Narrative Accounts of the Minnesota Indian War of 1862* (Minneapolis: Minnesota Historical Society, 1988); Micheal Clodfelter, *The Dakota War: The United States Army and the Sioux* (Jefferson, N.C.: McFarland & Co., 2006).

13 Carleton to Christopher Carson, October 12, 1862, *OR* I:15, p. 579.

14 Ickis Diary, October 22, 1862, DPL.

15 *Santa Fe Gazette*, October 11, 1862, p. 2.

16 James Carleton, endorsement on letter from William McCleave to West, July 15 [reprinted, August 6, 1863], in Doolittle, *Condition of the Indian Tribes*, Appendix, 124–25.

17 Kelly, *Navajo Roundup*, 12.

18 John Clark Diary, November 8–9, 1862, FAC; Hollister, *Boldly They Rode*, 152, 153–54; Henry Davies Wallen, Inspection Report: Fort Marcy, November 25, 1862, in *New Mexico Territory During the Civil War: Wallen and Evans Inspection Reports, 1862–1863*, ed. Jerry D. Thompson (Albuquerque: University of New Mexico Press, 2008), 52–53; "Vidette," letter to the editors, *San Francisco Daily Alta California*, May 14, 1862, in Masich, *The Civil War in Arizona*, 163.

19 Hollister, *Boldly They Rode*, 152, 153–54.

20 *OR* I:15, p. 153+; James Carleton, General Orders No. 103, *Santa Fe Gazette*, December 27, 1862, p. 2; Emma Dill Russell Spencer, *Green Russell and Gold* (Austin: University of Texas Press, 1966), 157–70; George Laird Shoup Diary, November 2–December 7, 1862, and Shoup to Captain W.H. Backus, n.d., George Laird Shoup Diary, SHL.

21 James Carleton to Joseph West, November 18, 1862, *OR* I:15, p. 599.

22 "Organization of the Troops in the Department of the Missouri, Major General Samuel R. Curtis, U.S. Army Commanding, December 31, 1862," *OR* I:22, part I, p. 891; "Organization of the Troops in the Department of the Missouri . . . February 28, 1863, [District of Colorado]," *OR* I:22, part II, p. 131.

Part Three

Chapter 16: Mangas Coloradas

1   Sweeney, *Mangas Coloradas*, 444; Hutton, *The Apache Wars*, 69; Kaywaykla account in *In the Days of Victorio: Recollections of a Warm Springs Apache*, ed. Eve Ball (Tucson: University of Arizona Press, 1970), 47.

2   Blyth, *Chiricahua and Janos*, 5, 7, 35.

3   Blyth, *Chiricahua and Janos*, 5, 123, 136, 151; Hutton, *The Apache Wars*, 15.

4   Asa Daklugie account in Ball, ed., *Indeh: An Apache Odyssey*, 20; Blyth, *Chiricahua and Janos*, 175; Cremony, *Life Among the Apaches*, 158–60.

5   Blyth, *Chiricahua and Janos*, 178.

6   Julius C. Shaw to AAG, September 20, 1862, in Sweeney, *Mangas Coloradas*, 444; Hutton, *The Apache Wars*, 95.

7 Carleton to West, October 3, 1862, *OR* I:50, part II, p. 148; Sweeney, *Mangas Colora-das*, 442, 445.

8 Andrew Wallace, "John W. Swilling," *Arizoniana* 2, no. 1 (Spring 1961): 16, 17; Hutton, *The Apache Wars*, 96–97.

9 J. William Fourr, *A Young Man's Life in the West*, n.d., Folder 4, J. William ("Billy") Fourr Papers, 1864–1983, AHS; Geronimo, *Geronimo's Story of His Life*, ed. S.M. Barrett (New York: Duffield and Co., 1906), 119–20; Hutton, *The Apache Wars*, 99.

10 Geronimo, *Geronimo's Story of His Life*, 119–20; Sweeney, *Mangas Coloradas*, 446.

11 Geronimo, *Geronimo's Story of His Life*, 46–47.

12 Geronimo, *Geronimo's Story of His Life*, 120.

13 Geronimo, *Geronimo's Story of His Life*, 44, 47–53, 118; Hutton, *The Apache Wars*, 15.

14 Asa Daklugie account in *Indeh: An Apache Odyssey*, ed. Ball, 19; Sweeney, *Mangas Coloradas*, 446; Hutton, *The Apache Wars*, 99.

15 Geronimo, *Geronimo's Story of His Life*, 121.

16 Robert Utley, "Victorio's War," historynet.com.

17 James Kaywaykla account in *In the Days of Victorio*, ed. Ball, 47, 48; Hutton, *The Apache Wars*, 99; Sweeney, *Mangas Coloradas*, 448.

18 Daniel Ellis Conner, *Joseph Reddeford Walker and the Arizona Adventure*, ed. Donald J. Berthrong and Odessa Davenport (Norman: University of Oklahoma Press, 1956), 35; Lee Myers, "The Enigma of Mangas Coloradas's Death," *New Mexico History*, http://newmexicohistory.org/people/the-enigma-of-mangas-coloradas.

19 Conner, *Joseph Reddeford Walker and the Arizona Adventure*, 36; Sweeney, *Mangas Coloradas*, 448–50; Hutton, *The Apache Wars*, 100.

20 Conner, *Joseph Reddeford Walker and the Arizona Adventure*, 37; Sweeney, *Mangas Coloradas*, 453.

21 Carleton to West, October 11, 1862, *OR* I:15, p. 580; Myers, "The Enigma of Mangas Coloradas's Death."

22 West to Cutler, November 2, 1862, *OR* I:50, part 2, p. 200.

23 West to Cutler, January 28, 1863, *OR* I:50, part 2, pp. 296–97; Records of First California Cavalry, [January 17, 1863], *Records of California Men in the War of the Rebellion*, 71; Myers, "The Enigma of Mangas Coloradas's Death."

24 West to Cutler, January 28, 1863, *OR* I:50, part 2, p. 296; Myers, "The Enigma of Mangas Coloradas's Death."

25 Conner, *Joseph Reddeford Walker and the Arizona Adventure*, 38–39; Sweeney, *Mangas Coloradas*, 457–58.

26 Sweeney, *Mangas Coloradas*, 457–58.

27 Conner, *Joseph Reddeford Walker and the Arizona Adventure*, 40; Hutton, *The Apache Wars*, 20–21, 102; Sweeney, *Mangas Coloradas*, 460.

28 1st Regiment of Cavalry Records, *Records of California Men in the War of the Rebellion*, 71; Sweeney, *Mangas Coloradas*, 460; Hutton, *The Apache Wars*, 102–3.

29 Conner, *Joseph Reddeford Walker and the Arizona Adventure*, 41; Sweeney, *Mangas Coloradas*, 460; Hutton, *The Apache Wars*, 102; Thrapp, *The Conquest of Apacheria*, 22; Ann Fabian, *The Skull Collectors: Race, Science, and America's Unburied Dead* (Chicago: University of Chicago Press, 2010), 2, 215; Orson Squire Fowler, "The Phrenology of Mangas Colorado, or Red Sleeve," in *Human Science or Phrenology: Its Principles, Proofs, Facts . . .* (Philadelphia: National Publishing Co., 1873), 1195–97.

30 Geronimo, *Geronimo's Story of His Life*, 121.

31 Geronimo, *Geronimo's Story of His Life*, 119; Conner, *Joseph Reddeford Walker and the Arizona Adventure*, 42.

Chapter 17: Clark

1 Clark Diary, April 8–24, 1863, FAC.
2 Clark to James Edmunds, May 25, 1863, NARA RG 49, Box 93; Clark Diary, April 8–24, 1863, FAC.
3 Clark to Edmunds, December 20, 1862, NARA RG 49, Box 93.
4 Abraham Lincoln, "Second Annual Message to Congress," December 1, 1862, https://www.americanantiquarian.org/Freedmen/Manuscripts/lincolnsecondannual.html.
5 Clark to Edmunds, May 25, 1863, NARA RG 49, Box 93.
6 Clark to Edmunds, May 25, 1863, NARA RG 49, Box 93; Sweeney, *Mangas Coloradas*, 462; Hutton, *The Apache Wars*, 103; Clark Diary, January 31, 1863, FAC.
7 Conner, *Joseph Reddeford Walker and the Arizona Adventure*, 104.
8 Clark Diary, June 12, 1863, FAC.
9 Clark Diary, June 13, 15, 16, 1863, FAC; Conner, *Joseph Reddeford Walker and the Arizona Adventure*, 97.
10 Carleton to Nathaniel Pishon, June 22, 1863, *Records of California Men in the War of the Rebellion*, 72.
11 Clark to Edmunds, June 18, 1863, NARA RG 49, Box 93.
12 Clark Diary, June 20–July 4, 1863, FAC.
13 Clark Diary, July 27–28, 1863, FAC.
14 Clark Diary, August 8–15, 1863, FAC.
15 Clark Diary, August 19, 1863, FAC.
16 Conner, *Joseph Reddeford Walker and the Arizona Adventure*, 130.
17 Clark Diary, August 20, 1863, FAC.
18 Clark Diary, August 21, 1863, FAC.
19 Clark Diary, August 22–25, 1863, FAC; Conner, *Joseph Reddeford Walker and the Arizona Adventure*, 131.
20 Clark Diary, August 28, 1863, FAC.
21 Clark Diary, August 18 and 29–30, 1863, FAC; Hiram C. Hodge, *Arizona As It Is; or, the Coming Country* (New York: Hurd and Houghton, 1877), 64–65.
22 Clark Diary, August 19, 23, 31–September 1, 1863, FAC.
23 Clark Diary, September 1–9, 1863, FAC.
24 Clark Diary, September 10, 1863, FAC.
25 Clark Diary, September 11, 1863, FAC.
26 Dunlay, *Kit Carson and the Indians*, 274; James Carleton, General Orders No. 15, June 15, 1863, in L. R. Bailey, *The Long Walk: A History of the Navajo Wars, 1846–1868* (Los Angeles: Westernlore Press, 1964), 153.

Chapter 18: Tséyi'

1 Curly Tso, John Smith, Howard Gorman, Sr., and Fred Descheene accounts, in *Navajo Stories of the Long Walk Period*, ed. Broderick H. Johnston (Tsaile, Navajo Nation: Dine College Bookstore/Press, 1973), 102, 137, 187, 210.
2 Roessel, *Women in Navajo Society*, 103–4, 110.
3 Kelly, *Navajo Roundup*, 41; Carson to Carleton, November 14, 1863, *Navajo Roundup*, ed. Kelly, 73.
4 Clark Diary, September 11, 1863, FAC.
5 Carson to Carleton, October 5 and November 10, 1863, in *Navajo Roundup*, ed. Kelly, 53–54, 73.
6 Carson to Carleton, October 5, 1863, in *Navajo Roundup*, ed. Kelly, 54.

7   Carson to Carleton, October 5, 1863, in *Navajo Roundup*, ed. Kelly, 55.

8   Asa B. Carey letter, 1909, in Edwin Legrand Sabin, *Kit Carson Days: Adventures in the Path of Empire* (New York: The Press of the Pioneers, 1935), 711; Dunlay, *Kit Carson and the Indians*, 271.

9   Mark Grimsley, *The Hard Hand of War: Union Military Policy Toward Southern Civilians, 1861–1865* (Cambridge: Cambridge University Press, 1995), 14–22; Mark E. Neely, Jr., *The Civil War and the Limits of Destruction* (Cambridge, Mass.: Harvard University Press, 2007), 5, 6–40.

10 Doolittle, *Condition of the Indian Tribes*, 5; Kit Carson testimony in Doolittle, *Condition of the Indian Tribes*, 96–97.

11 Carson to Carleton, October 5, 1863, and George W. Campbell report to Carleton, October 18, 1863, in *Navajo Roundup*, ed. Kelly, 53, 55; David Lavender, in David Remley, *Kit Carson: The Life of an American Border Man* (Norman: University of Oklahoma Press, 2011), 226; Dunlay, *Kit Carson and the Indians*, 277–78.

12 Roessel, *Women in Navajo Society*, 106, 108.

13 Carson to Cutler, December 6, 1863, in *Navajo Roundup*, ed. Kelly, 76.

14 Ason Attakai account, in *Navajo Stories of the Long Walk Period*, ed. Johnston, 125–26; Zonnie Ahtay account, in Dunlay, *Kit Carson and the Indians*, 268; Jennifer Nez Denetdale, *The Long Walk: The Forced Navajo Exile* (New York: Chelsea House, 2008), 55.

15 A.B. Carey to L.G. Murphy, October 13, 1863, Carey to Murphy, October 15, 1863, Carey to Murphy, October 29, 1863, Carey to Carleton, December 6, 1863, Jose Sena to L.G. Murphy, December 13, 1863, and Carson to Cutler, December 20, 1863, in Kelly, ed., *Navajo Roundup*, 65–67, 78, 82–83.

16 Carson to Carleton, October 5, 1863, in *Navajo Roundup*, ed. Kelly, 56; Kelly, *Navajo Roundup*, 68.

17 Kelly, *Navajo Roundup*, fn 35, p. 133.

18 Carleton to Thomas, September 6, 1863, Carleton to Carson, December 5, 1863, Carleton to Carson, December 31, 1863, in *Navajo Roundup*, ed. Kelly, 57, 69, 88.

19 Carleton to Carson, December 5, 1863, in *Navajo Roundup*, ed. Kelly, 69.

20 "Johnny Navajo," *Rio Abajo Press*, December 8, 1863, in William A. Keleher, *Turmoil in New Mexico, 1846–1868* (Santa Fe: Rydal Press, 1952), 314.

21 Carson to Cutler, December 26, 1863, in *Navajo Roundup*, ed. Kelly, 94; Dunlay, *Kit Carson and the Indians*, 294; Clifford E. Trafzer, *The Kit Carson Campaign: The Last Great Navajo War* (Norman: University of Oklahoma Press, 1982), 147.

22 Colonel D.S. Miles, in J. P. Dunn, *Massacres of the Mountains: A History of the Indian Wars of the Far West* (New York: Harper and Bros., 1886), 257–58, 265, 382, 485; L.G. Murphy to Abreu, December 11, 1863, in *Navajo Roundup*, ed. Kelly, 81.

23 Carson to Cutler, January 24, 1864, in *Navajo Roundup*, ed. Kelly, 98; Doolittle, *Condition of the Tribes*, 259.

24 Carson to Cutler, January 24, 1864, in *Navajo Roundup*, ed. Kelly, 98–99.

25 Carson to Cutler, January 24, 1864, and Carleton to Carson, September 19, 1863, Cutler/Carleton to Chacon [at Fort Wingate], October 21, 1863, in *Navajo Roundup*, ed. Kelly, 52, 99.

26 Carson to Cutler, January 24, 1864, in *Navajo Roundup*, ed. Kelly, 99.

27 Albert Pfeiffer to AAG Murphy, January 20, 1864, in Kelly, ed., *Navajo Roundup*, 102–5; Howard W. Gorman, Teddy Draper, Sr., Betty Shorthair, Akinabh Burbank, and Eli Gorman accounts in *Navajo Stories of the Long Walk Period*, ed. Johnston, 25, 44–49, 112, 128, 201; Oakee James, "Kit Carson Rounding Up the Navajo" (1969), UNMD.

28 William Tecumseh Sherman to Ulysses S. Grant, November 6, 1864, in *The Civil War and Reconstruction: A Documentary Collection* ed. William Gienapp, (New York: W.W. Norton, 2001), 256.

29 Carson to Cutler, January 24, 1864, in *Navajo Roundup*, ed. Kelly, 99.

30 Carson to Cutler, January 24, 1864, in *Navajo Roundup*, ed. Kelly, 100.

31 Carson to Cutler, January 24, 1864, in *Navajo Roundup*, ed. Kelly, 100–101.

32 Carson to Cutler, January 24, 1864, in *Navajo Roundup*, ed. Kelly, 100.

33 Carson to Cutler, January 24, 1864, in *Navajo Roundup*, ed. Kelly, 101.

34 Kelly, *Navajo Roundup*, 110.

35 Frank Apache, "Story of the Long Walk" (1969), UNM Digital; Herbert Zahne account, in *Navajo Stories of the Long Walk Period*, ed. Johnston, 233; Joseph Berney to Cutler, April 7, 1864, in *Navajo Roundup*, ed. Kelly, 115–16.

36 "Native Arrow Technology," Bosque Redondo Memorial Museum, Fort Sumner National Monument, Fort Sumner, New Mexico.

37 Kelly, *Navajo Roundup*, 111, 113, 119.

38 Carey to Cutler, February 14, 1864, in *Navajo Roundup*, ed. Kelly, 112; Eli Gorman, Yasdesbah Silversmith, and Hoske Yeba Doyah accounts, in *Navajo Stories of the Long Walk Period*, ed. Johnston, 202–3, 119, 224.

39 Jennifer Nez Denetdale, "Chairmen, Presidents, and Princesses: The Navajo Nation, Gender, and the Politics of Tradition," *Wicazo Sa Review* 21, no. 1 (spring 2006): 11.

40 Roessel, *Women in Navajo Society*, 109–10.

41 Oakee James, "Battles Around Civil War Time" (1969), UNMD; Kelly, *Navajo Roundup*, 129–30; Carson to Cutler, March 20, 1864, and Carson to Carleton, April 10, 1864, in *Navajo Roundup*, ed. Kelly, 140–41, 144–45.

42 Carey to Carleton, April 24, 1864, in *Navajo Roundup*, ed. Kelly, 152.

43 Carey to Cutler, February 21, 1864, Carleton to Thomas, February 27, 1864, Carey to Cutler, February 28, 1864, Carey to Cutler, March 6, 1864, Carey to Cutler, March 15, 1864, Carey to Cutler, March 27, 1864, Carson to Carleton, April 3, 1864, Carson to Carleton, April 10, 1864, in *Navajo Roundup*, ed. Kelly, 113, 119, 121, 122, 131–32, 138, 143, 144; *Santa Fe Gazette*, March 5, 1864.

44 Betty Shorthair, Yasdesbah Silversmith, Akinabh Burbank, Rita Wheeler, and Hoske Yeba Doyah accounts, in *Navajo Stories of the Long Walk Period*, ed. Johnston, 82, 113–14, 119, 131, 224; Denetdale, *The Long Walk*, 56.

45 Carey to Cutler, May 10, 1864, and Capt. P.W.S. Plympton to Carleton, June 20, 1864, in *Navajo Roundup*, ed. Kelly, 153–54, 160.

46 Carleton to Plympton, June 2, 1864, in *Navajo Roundup*, ed. Kelly, 154–55; Kelly, *Navajo Roundup*, 161.

47 P.W.S. Plympton to Carleton, July 11 and July 19, 1864, in *Navajo Roundup*, ed. Kelly, 161.

48 Kelly, *Navajo Roundup*, 161; Carleton to Thomas, August 29, 1864, as in "The Destruction of Navajo Orchards in 1864: Captain John Thompson's Report," ed. Stephen C. Jett, *Arizona and the West* 16, no. 4 (Winter 1974): 369.

Chapter 19: Carleton

1 Carleton to Thomas, February 7, 1864, and July 8, 1864, in Doolittle, *Condition of the Indian Tribes*, Appendix, 157, 187; Bristol to Cutler, May 13, 1864, NARA RG 393, Part IV, Vol. 107, Entry 1217; Kelly, *Navajo Roundup*, 160.

2 Edmund J. Danziger, Jr., "The Steck-Carleton Controversy in Civil War New Mexico," *Southwestern Historical Quarterly* 74, no. 2 (October 1970): 196–97; Gerald D. Thomp-

son, introduction to "James Carleton, *To the People of New Mexico*: Gen. Carleton Defends the Bosque Redondo," ed. Thompson, *Arizona and the West* 14, no. 4 (winter 1972): 350; Gerald Thompson, *The Army and the Navajo: The Bosque Redondo Reservation Experiment, 1863–1868* (Tucson: University of Arizona Press, 1976, 1982), 21, 24.

3 Carleton to Thomas, February 7, 1864, and March 19, 1864, in Doolittle, *Condition of the Indian Tribes*, Appendix, 157, 169.

4 Henry B. Bristol to Cutler, August 5, 1864, NARA RG 393, Part IV, Vol. 107, Entry 1217.

5 Ric Bessin, "Armyworms in Corn" (2004), https://entomology.ca.uky.edu/ef109.

6 Bristol to Cutler, August 5, 1864, NARA RG 393, Part IV, Vol. 107, Entry 1217.

7 Carleton to Bristol, August 22, 1864, in Doolittle, *Condition of the Indian Tribes*, Appendix, 191; Thompson, *The Army and the Navajo*, 49–50; Doolittle, *Condition of the Indian Tribes*, Appendix, 208.

8 Carleton, "*To the People of New Mexico*," 365.

9 *Santa Fe Gazette*, August 7, 1864, p. 2.

10 Carleton to Bristol, October 22, 1864, in Doolittle, *Condition of the Indian Tribes*, Appendix, 201.

11 Bristol to Cutler, August 19, 1864, NARA RG 393, Part IV, Vol. 107, Entry 1217; Lorenzo Labadie to Michael Steck, October 22, 1864, in Thompson, *The Army and the Navajo*, 50.

12 Carleton to Bristol, October 22, 1864, in Doolittle, *Condition of the Indian Tribes*, Appendix, 201; Dunn, *Massacres of the Mountains*, 469; Hunt, *Major General James Henry Carleton*, 285.

13 Hunt, *Major General James Henry Carleton*, 114, 274.

14 James Carleton Order, November 14, 1862, and Board of Surveys report, [December 1862], in Thompson, *The Army and the Navajo*, 14; Carleton, "*To the People of New Mexico*," 360–61.

15 William P. Dole to John Usher, January 14, 1864, and Abraham Lincoln, Bosque Redondo Approval, January 15, 1864, in *Indian Affairs: Laws and Treaties*, vol. 2 (Washington, D.C.: Government Printing Office, 1904, Part III, Executive Orders Relating to Reserves), 870.

16 James Carleton, Responses to the Questionnaire, July 25, 1862, in Doolittle, *Condition of the Indian Tribes*, 4, Appendix 422–23.

17 Carleton to Evans, June 26, 1864, in Doolittle, *Condition of the Indian Tribes*, Appendix, 185–86.

18 James H. Carleton, General Orders No. 32, October 22, 1864, and Carleton to Carson, September 18, 1864, in Doolittle, *Condition of the Indian Tribes*, Appendix 197–98, 268.

19 Carson Report of Adobe Walls, [December] 1864, in Sabin, *Kit Carson Days*, Appendix, 895; Sides, *Blood and Thunder*, 468.

20 Carleton to Carson, December 15, 1864, in Doolittle, *Condition of the Indian Tribes*, Appendix, 214.

21 Clark Diary, November 12 and December 14, 1864, FAC; Thompson, *The Army and the Navajo*, 58.

22 *Santa Fe New Mexican*, November 4, 1864, and December 16, 1864, in Thompson, introduction to Carleton, "*To the People of New Mexico*," 351; *Santa Fe New Mexican*, December 16, 1864, in Danziger, Jr., "The Steck-Carleton Controversy," 199.

23 Carleton, "*To the People of New Mexico*," 357.

24 Carleton, "*To the People of New Mexico*," 366.

25 Woolson to Carleton, January 18, 1865, in NARA RG 393, Part IV, Vol. 106, Entry

1218; *Santa Fe Weekly Gazette*, January 14, 1865, p. 2; Thompson, *The Army and the Navajo*, 72; Hunt, *Major General James Henry Carleton*, 288.

26   Crocker to Cutler, February 10, 1865, NARA RG 393, Part IV, Vol. 106, Entry 1218.

27   Carleton Statement, February 15, 1865, in Doolittle, *Condition of the Indian Tribes*, Appendix, 218; "Navajo Delegation," *Santa Fe Weekly Gazette*, February 18, 1865, p. 2.

28   Carleton to Henry Halleck, May 10, 1863, and Carleton to Thomas, August 2, 1863, in Doolittle, *Condition of the Indian Tribes*, Appendix, 110, 122; Carleton to his sister, August 2, 1863, as in Hunt, *Major General James Henry Carleton*, 339.

29   Carleton Report, March 21, 1865, in *Navajo Roundup*, ed. Kelly, 165–66; *Santa Fe Gazette*, April 1, 1865, p. 2.

30   Carleton to Julius Shaw, March 23, 1865, in Doolittle, *Condition of the Indian Tribes*, Appendix, 223.

31   James Carleton, General Orders No. 11, *Santa Fe Weekly Gazette*, April 29, 1865, p. 2.

32   *Santa Fe Weekly Gazette*, April 29, 1865, p. 2.

33   *Santa Fe Weekly Gazette*, April 29, 1865, p. 2.

34   *Santa Fe Weekly Gazette*, May 6, 1865, p. 2.

35   McCleave to Cutler, June 15, 1865, NARA RG 393, Part IV, Vol. 108, Entry 1217.

36   Donald Chaput, "Generals, Indian Agents, Politicians: The Doolittle Survey of 1865," *Western Historical Quarterly* 3, no. 3 (July 1972): 271.

37   Chaput, "Generals, Indian Agents, Politicians," 271–72; Gary L. Roberts, "Condition of the Tribes—1865: The McCook Report: A Military View," *Montana: The Magazine of Western History* 24, no. 1 (Winter 1974): 16.

38   *Santa Fe Weekly Gazette*, July 8, 1865, p. 2.

39   Alexander McCook to John Pope, August 12, 1865, in Roberts, "Condition of the Tribes—1865," 21–22.

40   Testimony of Herrera Grande, Bosque Redondo, June 26, 1865, in Doolittle, *Condition of the Indian Tribes*, 354–56.

41   Testimony of the Navajo Chiefs, Bosque Redondo, June 26, 1865, in Doolittle, *Condition of the Indian Tribes*, 355–56.

42   McCook to Pope, August 12, 1865, in Roberts, "Condition of the Tribes," 22, 23.

43   *Santa Fe Weekly Gazette*, July 8, 1865, p. 2; Clark Diary, July 2, 1865, FAC.

44   John Clark Diary, July 3–6, 1865, FAC; *Santa Fe Weekly Gazette*, July 15, 1865, p. 2.

45   Testimony of James Carleton, July 3, 1865, in Doolittle, *Condition of the Indian Tribes*, 323–25.

46   Testimony of James Carleton, July 3, 1865, in Doolittle, *Condition of the Indian Tribes*, 323–25.

47   Clark Diary, July 7, 1865, FAC; *Santa Fe Weekly Gazette*, July 15, 1865, p. 2.

Chapter 20: Juanita

1   Carleton Report, March 21, 1865, in Doolittle, *Condition of the Indian Tribes*, Appendix, 221–22.

2   Bighorse account, in Denetdale, *Reclaiming Diné History*, 73.

3   Report of Julius Shaw from Fort Wingate, March 24, 1865, *Santa Fe Weekly Gazette*, April 1, 1865, p. 2; Kelly, *Navajo Roundup*, 167.

4   Thompson, *The Army and the Navajo*, 91; Kelly, *Navajo Roundup*, 167; Captain E. Butler from Fort Wingate, September 2, 1866, in the *Santa Fe Weekly Gazette*, September 15, 1866.

5   Kelly, *Navajo Roundup*, 167; Trafzer, *The Kit Carson Campaign*, 221.

6 Bob Manuelito, "My Father's Day of the Long Walk," UNMD; Kelly, *Navajo Roundup*, 167; Trafzer, *The Kit Carson Campaign*, 221.

7 Iverson and Roessel, *Diné: A History of the Navajos*, 11.

8 McCleave to de Forrest, August 11, 1866, NARA RG 393, Part IV, Vol. 108, Entry 1217; Butler from Fort Wingate, *Santa Fe Weekly Gazette*, September 15, 1866.

9 Yasdesbah Silversmith and Betty Shorthair account, in *Navajo Stories of the Long Walk Period*, ed. Johnston, 113, 119; Denetdale, *The Long Walk*, 56.

10 Bob Manuelito, "My Father's Day of the Long Walk," UNMD.

11 Dugal Tsosie Begay, Howard W. Gorman, Curly Tso, Herbert Zahne, and Mose Denejolie accounts, in *Navajo Stories of the Long Walk Period*, ed. Johnston, 30–31, 103–4, 214, 234, 242.

12 Oakee James, "Kit Carson Rounding Up the Navajo" (1969), UNMD.

13 William Dute to his brother from Fort Bascom, NM, April 25, 1864, Folder 37, William Dute Papers, DPL; Oakee James, "Kit Carson Rounding Up the Navajo" (1969), UNMD.

14 Carleton Report, March 21, 1865, in *Navajo Roundup*, ed. Kelly, 165–66; Oakee James, "Kit Carson Rounding Up the Navajo" (1969), UNMD.

15 Bob Manuelito, "My Father's Day of the Long Walk," and Oakee James, "Kit Carson Rounding Up the Navajo" (1969), UNMD.

16 Oakee James, "Kit Carson Rounding Up the Navajo" (1969), UNMD.

17 *Long Walk National Historic Trail Feasibility and Environmental Impact Study*, January 2009, https://parkplanning.nps.gov/projectHome.cfm?projectID=12406.

18 Berney to Cutler, April 7, 1864, in *Navajo Roundup*, ed. Kelly, 115–16; McCleave to the Inspector General, June 14, [1866], NARA RG 393 Part IV, Vol. 108, Entry 1217.

19 Thompson, *The Army and the Navajo*, 99; Keleher, *Turmoil in New Mexico*, 323; Danziger, Jr., "The Steck-Carleton Controversy," 201.

20 George Sykes to Carleton, December 22, 1866 [marked "Personal"] and February 2, 1867, NARA RG 393 Part IV, Vol. 108, Entry 1217; Herbert Ration, "Grandparents' Story of the Long Walk" (1969), UNMD; Thompson, *The Army and the Navajo*, 120; Bailey, *The Long Walk*, 223.

21 McCleave to de Forrest, July 14, 1866, NARA RG 393 Part IV, Vol. 108, Entry 1217; Thompson, *The Army and the Navajo*, 120, 123, 135–36; Bailey, *The Long Walk*, 223.

22 Glen Sample Ely, "Gone from Texas and Trading with the Enemy: New Perspectives on Civil War West Texas," *Southwestern Historical Quarterly* 110, no. 4 (April 2007): 455; Thompson, *The Army and the Navajo*, 119.

23 McCleave to the Inspector General, June 14, [1866], in NARA RG 393 Part IV, Vol. 108, Entry 1217; Account of Charles T. Jennings, in Thompson, *The Army and the Navajo*, 109–10.

24 T.W. Woolson to Carleton, January 18, 1865, NARA RG 393 Part IV, Vol. 106, Entry 1218; Katherine Marie Birmingham Osburn, "The Navajos at the Bosque Redondo: Cooperation, Resistance, and Initiative, 1864–1868," *New Mexico Historical Review* (October 1985): 401, 403.

25 M.M. Crocker to Cutler, January 6, 1865, in NARA RG 393 Part IV, Vol. 106, Entry 1218; Osburn, "The Navajos at the Bosque Redondo," 401; Woolson to Carleton, January 18, 1865, NARA RG 393 Part IV, Vol. 106, Entry 1218; Thompson, *The Army and the Navajo*, 73; McCleave to Cutler, November 24, 1865, NARA RG 393 Part IV, Vol. 108, Entry 1217.

26 M.M. Crocker to Carleton, November 17, 1864, in NARA RG 393 Part IV, Vol. 106, Entry 1218; George Sykes to Carleton, December 22, 1866 [marked "Personal"], NARA RG 393, Part IV, Vol. 108, Entry 1217; Osburn, "The Navajos at the Bosque Redondo," 401.

27 Osburn, "The Navajos at the Bosque Redondo," 401.

28 George Guyther Testimony and Testimony of the Navajo chiefs, in Doolittle, *Condition of the Indian Tribes*, 340, 356; Osburn, "The Navajos at the Bosque Redondo," 403; Thompson, *The Army and the Navajo*, 48.

29 Charles J. Whiting to Lieut. Edward, AAAG, September 21, 1867, NARA RG 393 Part IV, Vol. 108, Entry 1217.

30 Sykes to Carleton, December 22, 1866 [marked "Personal"], NARA RG 393, Part IV, Vol. 108, Entry 1217; Hascon Benally account, in *Navajo Stories of the Long Walk Period*, ed. Johnston, 230.

31 Herrera Grande Testimony, in Doolittle, *Condition of the Indian Tribes*, 354; Thompson, *The Army and the Navajo*, 57; Dodd to the Indian Bureau, September 9, 1865, in Thompson, *The Army and the Navajo*, 96; Robert McDonald to McClure, July 6, 1867, NARA RG 92, Box 1093, Entry 225; Denetdale, *The Long Walk*, 79–80.

32 Roessel, *Women in Navajo Society*, 102–3.

33 Thompson, *The Army and the Navajo*, 140; Bailey, *The Long Walk*, 229–30.

34 Whiting to de Forrest, August 3, 1867, NARA RG 393 Part IV, Vol. 108, Entry 1217; Bailey, *The Long Walk*, 223.

35 Whiting to Edward Hunter, September 28, 1867, NARA RG 393 Part IV, Vol. 108, Entry 1217; Thompson, *The Army and the Navajo*, 145; Yasdesbah Silversmith account, in *Navajo Stories of the Long Walk Period*, ed. Johnston, 122.

36 Morning Report of the Navajos, October 1867, NARA RG 393 Part IV, Vol. 114, Entry 1234; Whiting to Hunter, October 2 and 5, 1867, NARA RG 393 Part IV, Vol. 108, Entry 1217; Whiting to Hunter, October 12 and 19, 1867, NARA RG 393 Part IV, Vol. 109, Entry 1217; Thompson, *The Army and the Navajo*, 146.

Chapter 21: Clark

1 John Ayers, "A Soldier's Experience in New Mexico," *New Mexico Historical Review* 24, no. 4 (October 1949): 260; Chris Wilson, *The Myth of Santa Fe: Creating a Modern Regional Tradition* (Albuquerque: University of New Mexico Press, 1997), 58, 60.

2 Clark Diary, April 25, May 1, and May 20, 1867, FAC; Andrew E. Masich, *Civil War in the Southwestern Borderlands, 1861–1867* (Norman: University of Oklahoma Press, 2017), 282.

3 Clark Diary, October [24], 1867, FAC; *Santa Fe Weekly Gazette*, June 13, 1868, p. 2, November 21, 1868, p. 1, March 14, 1868, p. 2, May 23, 1868, p. 2, and June 13, 1868, p. 2; Wilson, *The Myth of Santa Fe*, 58, 60.

4 Santa Fe Soldiers Monument, 1868; Wilson, *The Myth of Santa Fe*, 58, 60.

5 Clark Diary, October 29, 1867, and March 1, 1862, FAC.

6 Clark Diary, April 21, 1867, FAC.

7 Clark Diary, October 17–18, 1866, and March 5, 1867, FAC.

8 Clark Diary, September 21, 1866, May 13, 1867, October 1, 1867, FAC.

9 Clark Diary, October 19, 1866, FAC.

10 Clark Diary, January 23, 1867, February 11, 1867, March 27, 1867, April 19–20, 1867, May 7, 1867, June 11, 1867, FAC.

11 Clark Diary, March 24, 1867, April 12 and 21, 1867, July 21 and 31, 1867, FAC.

12 Clark Diary, August 2, 1867, FAC.

13 Clark Diary, September 28, 1866, FAC.

14 Clark Diary, September 28, 1866, FAC; Heather Cox Richardson, *West from Appomattox: The Reconstruction of America after the Civil War* (New Haven, Conn.: Yale

University Press, 2007), 40–42, 43; Eric Foner, *Reconstruction: America's Unfinished Revolution, 1863–1877* (New York: Harper & Row, 1988), 189, 200.

15 U.S. Constitution, 14th Amendment (1866; ratified, 1868), https://www.law.cornell .edu/constitution/amendmentxiv.

16 Clark Diary, December 18, 1866, October 11 and 15, 1867, FAC.

17 Clark Diary, March 5, 1867, FAC.

18 Clark Diary, March 25, 1867, FAC.

19 Clark Diary, March 14 and 25, 1867, April 12, 1867, FAC; Edward McPherson, *A Political Manual for 1868* (Washington, D.C.: Philip & Solomon, 1868), 267; Richardson, *West from Appomattox*, 58–59, 75; Eric Foner, *Reconstruction*, 333.

20 *Santa Fe Weekly Gazette*, June 27, 1868, p. 2; *Santa Fe New Mexican*, August 6, 1868, in Keleher, *Turmoil in New Mexico*, 472.

21 Clark Diary, December 10, 1867, FAC.

22 Clark Diary, January 1, 1868, FAC.

23 Clark Diary, February 23, August 2 and 27, September 13, 21, 25, 27, October 14, 19, 20, 1867, FAC.

24 Clark Diary, December 27, 1867, FAC.

25 Clark Diary, January 27, 1868, FAC.

26 Andrew Johnson to Edwin Stanton and Edwin Stanton to Ulysses S. Grant, August 12, 1867, and Thomas to Johnson, February 21, 1868, in McPherson, *A Political Manual for 1868*, 261, 263, 267; Richardson, *West from Appomattox*, 59; Foner, *Reconstruction*, 333–34; Clark Diary, January 18 and 21, August 21 and 28, September 11, 16, 29, 1867, January 20, 1868, FAC.

27 Clark Diary, September 2, 1867, FAC.

28 Clark Diary, August 9, 19, 21, October 23, and December 22, 1867, FAC; Joan Waugh, *U.S. Grant: American Hero, American Myth* (Chapel Hill: University of North Carolina Press, 2009), 1–4, 109; Foner, *Reconstruction*, 338–39.

29 Clark Diary, November 18, 1867, FAC.

Chapter 22: Juanita

1 Theodore Dodd to the Superintendent of Indian Affairs, October 31, 1867, in Bailey, *The Long Walk*, 231; Theodore Dodd to William Tecumseh Sherman and Samuel F. Tappan, May 30, 1868, in *The Navajo Treaty, 1868*, ed. Bernhard Michaelis (Native Child Dinetah, 2018), 25.

2 John L. Kessell, "General Sherman and the Navajo Treaty of 1868: A Basic and Expedient Misunderstanding," *Western Historical Quarterly* 12, no. 3 (July 1981): 257.

3 Thompson, *The Army and the Navajo*, 150.

4 Michaelis, *The Navajo Treaty, 1868*, 13.

5 Denetdale, *Reclaiming Diné History*, 83.

6 "Coyote," New Mexico Department of Game and Fish, Wildlife Notes, http://www .wildlife.state.nm.us/download/education/conservation/wildlife-notes/mammals /Coyotes.pdf; Guy H. Cooper, "Coyote in Navajo Religion and Cosmology," *Canadian Journal of Native Studies* 7, no. 2 (1987): 183.

7 Paul G. Zolbrod, *Diné Behané: The Navajo Creation Story* (Albuquerque: University of New Mexico Press, 1984), 87.

8 Denetdale, *The Long Walk*, 87–88; John Smith, George Littlesalt, John Tom, Fred Descheene, Friday Kinlicheenee, Mose Denejolie, and Curly Mustache accounts, in *Navajo Stories of the Long Walk Period*, ed. Johnston, 136–37, 167, 178–79, 212, 238, 244, 270.

9 Valentin Wolfenstein Diary, May [27], 1868, Valentin Wolfenstein Diaries Part II, 1868, Folder 23, Frank McNitt Collection, NMSR. Transcripts courtesy of C. P. "Kitty" Weaver, Manchester by the Sea, Massachusetts; Lt. Col. Cressey, May 26, 1868, NARA RG 393 Part IV, Vol. 109, Entry 1217.

10 HR 73, "Act for the relief of the Navajo Indians at the Bosque Redondo, to establish them on a reservation *and for other purposes*," March 9, 1868, as in, *The Navajo Treaty, 1868*, ed. Michaelis, 60–61; Martha A. Sandweiss, "Still Picture, Moving Stories: Reconstruction Comes to Indian Country," in *Civil War Wests: Testing the Limits of the United States*, ed. Adam Arenson and Andrew R. Graybill (Berkeley: University of California Press, 2015), 158–59; Elliott West, *The Last Indian War: The Nez Perce Story* (New York: Oxford University Press, 2009), xviii, 101.

11 Wolfenstein Diary, May 28, 1868, NMSR.

12 Transcript of Council Proceedings, May 28, 1868, in *The Navajo Treaty, 1868*, ed. Michaelis, 16; William T. Sherman to Ulysses S. Grant, June 1868, in Kessell, "General Sherman and the Navajo Treaty of 1868," 259.

13 Transcript of Council Proceedings, May 28, 1868, in *The Navajo Treaty, 1868*, ed. Michaelis, 16.

14 Transcript of Council Proceedings, May 28, 1868, in *The Navajo Treaty, 1868*, ed. Michaelis, 17.

15 Transcript of Council Proceedings, May 28, 1868, in *The Navajo Treaty, 1868*, ed. Michaelis, 17.

16 Transcript of Council Proceedings, May 28, 1868, in *The Navajo Treaty, 1868*, ed. Michaelis, 17.

17 Transcript of Council Proceedings, May 28, 1868, in *The Navajo Treaty, 1868*, ed. Michaelis, 18.

18 Transcript of Council Proceedings, May 28, 1868, in *The Navajo Treaty, 1868*, ed. Michaelis, 18; Sherman to the Commissioners, April 1, 1868, in Kessell, "General Sherman and the Navajo Treaty of 1868," 257; Prucha, *American Indian Treaties: A History of a Political Anomaly* (Berkeley: University of California Press, 1994), 266–67; Sherman to the Secretary of War, June 17, 1867, in Kerry R. Oman, "The Beginning of the End: The Indian Peace Commission of 1867–1868," *Great Plains Quarterly* (Winter 2002): 36.

19 Transcript of Council Proceedings, May 28, 1868, in *The Navajo Treaty, 1868*, ed. Michaelis, 18.

20 Transcript of Council Proceedings, May 28, 1868, in *The Navajo Treaty, 1868*, ed. Michaelis, 18.

21 Suzan Shown Harjo, "Introduction," *Nation to Nation: Treaties Between the United States & American Indian Nations*, ed. Suzan Shown Harjo (Washington, D.C.: Smithsonian Institution, 2014), 4; C. Joseph Genetin-Pilawa, "Ely Parker and the Contentious Peace Policy," *Western Historical Quarterly* 41, no. 2 (summer 2010): 198.

22 Transcript of Council Proceedings, May 29, 1868, in *The Navajo Treaty, 1868*, ed. Michaelis, 19.

23 Transcript of Council Proceedings, May 29, 1868, in *The Navajo Treaty, 1868*, ed. Michaelis, 19–20; Harjo, "Introduction," *Nation to Nation*, ed. Harjo, 3.

24 Transcript of Council Proceedings, May 29, 1868, in *The Navajo Treaty, 1868*, ed. Michaelis, 19–20.

25 Sandweiss, "Still Picture, Moving Stories," 162–63.

26 Transcript of Council Proceedings, May 29, 1868, in *The Navajo Treaty, 1868*, ed. Michaelis, 20–21.

27 Treaty with the Navaho, 1868, in *Indian Affairs: Laws and Treaties*, 1015–19; Transcript of Council Proceedings, May 30, 1868, in *The Navajo Treaty, 1868*, ed. Michaelis, 21.

28 Prucha, *American Indian Treaties*, 236; Sandweiss, "Still Picture, Moving Stories," 169.

29 Harjo, "Introduction," *Nation to Nation*, ed. Harjo, 4; Prucha, *American Indian Treaties*, 12–13.

30 Treaty with the Navaho, 1868, in *Indian Affairs*, 1015–19.

31 Law Creating the Peace Commission, July 20, 1867, in Prucha, *American Indian Treaties*, 280.

32 Treaty with the Navaho, 1868, in *Indian Affairs*, 1015–19.

33 Transcript of Council Proceedings, May 30, 1868, in *The Navajo Treaty, 1868*, ed. Michaelis, 21.

34 Valentin Wolfenstein Diary, June 1, 1868, NMSR.

35 Treaty with the Navaho, 1868, in *Indian Affairs*, 1015–19; Denetdale, "Naal Tsoos Saní: The Navajo Treaty of 1868, Nation Building, and Self-Determination," in *Nation to Nation*, ed. Harjo, 126.

36 Thompson, *The Army and the Navajo*, 155–56; *Santa Fe Weekly Gazette*, June 13, 1868, p. 2; Diné serape (c. 1868, New Mexico, Commercial wool yarn, dyes), National Museum of the American Indian 20/5235, as in Denetdale, "Naal Tsoos Saní," 118.

37 Bailey, *The Long Walk*, 233; Valentin Wolfenstein Diaries, NMSR; Albert James, *Navajo Times*, October 12, 2006, in *The Navajo Treaty, 1868*, ed. Michaelis, 11.

38 Manuelito's Account, in *The Navajo Treaty, 1868*, ed. Michaelis, 82.

39 Eli Gorman account, in *Navajo Stories of the Long Walk Period*, ed. Johnston, 205–6; An Occasional Correspondent, "Among the Indians," *New York Times*, August 1, 1868, p. 2.

40 "Among the Indians," *New York Times*, August 1, 1868, p. 2.

41 "Among the Indians," *New York Times*, August 1, 1868, p. 2; Bailey, *The Long Walk*, 233; *Santa Fe Weekly Gazette*, July 11, 1868, p. 2.

42 Denetdale, *The Long Walk*, 91–92; Manuelito's Account, in *The Navajo Treaty, 1868*, ed. Michaelis, 82.

43 Tezbah Mitchell and Notah Draper accounts, in *Navajo Stories of the Long Walk Period*, ed. Johnston, 227, 251.

Epilogue

1 "History and Culture," Golden Spike National Historic Site, https://www.nps.gov/gosp/learn/historyculture/index.htm; *Salt Lake Telegram*, May 10, 1869.

2 "History and Culture," Golden Spike National Historic Site, https://www.nps.gov/gosp/learn/historyculture/index.htm; *Salt Lake Telegram*, May 10, 1869.

3 John O'Sullivan, "Annexation," *United States Magazine and Democratic Review* 17 (New York, 1845): 5–6, 9–10.

4 *Salt Lake Telegram*, May 10, 1869.

5 Ickis, *Bloody Trails*, ed. Mumey, 37–39, 42.

6 Dunlay, *Kit Carson and the Indians*, 375–81, 387, 406–15; *New York Times*, June 8, 1868, p. 8; "The Carson Monument," *Santa Fe Weekly Gazette*, June 27, 1868, p. 2; Marc Simmons, "Santa Fe's Forgotten Monument to Kit Carson," *Santa Fe New Mexican*, February 26, 2016.

7 Thompson, "Introduction," *Civil War in the Southwest*, ed. Thompson, xxiii; Daniell, "William Lott Davidson," *Personnel of State Government, with Sketches of Distinguished Texans* (Austin, Texas: Smith, Hicks, & Jones, 1889), 421–22.

8 Thompson, *Colonel John Robert Baylor*, 86–87, 89–90, 94, 97; Martin Hardwick Hall, "Planter vs. Frontiersman: Conflict in Confederate Indian Policy," in *Essays on the American Civil War*, ed. William F. Holmes and Harold M. Hollingsworth (Austin: University of Texas Press, 1968), 71; "Incidents of Life on the Frontier in Olden Days," *El Paso Herald*, November 23, 1901, p. 5.

9 Clark Diary, July 18 and 28, 1867, FAC; Hunt, *Major James Henry Carleton*, 347–48; *Santa Fe New Mexican*, December 1, 1868, p. 1.

10 Report of Col. M.I. Ladington, February 26, 1870, "Complete List of Public Property at Fort Sumner, New Mexico, to be Sold at Las Vegas, New Mexico, on Monday, June 13th, 1870," NARA RG 92, Box 1093, Entry 225.

11 Denetdale, *Reclaiming Diné History*, 96–100, 147–48, 150; Charles M. Bell, "Juanita and Arny," 1874 [photograph], National Anthropological Archives, Smithsonian Institution.

12 Denetdale, *Reclaiming Diné History*, 8, 12, 88, 98, 183.

13 Clark Diary, November 23, 1867, and August 2, 8, 24, 26, and 28, 1868, FAC; Anna Jane Stone, "Biography of John Anderson Clark," 2004, John Clark Papers, FAC.

14 Heyman, *Prudent Soldier*, 189–90, 201–2, 222, 228–31, 234–35, 293, 295, 305–6, 335–36, 339; Wilhelmine Kiameche Crawford Bayless Diary, 1866–1868, Bayless-Crawford Family Papers, FHS; "Gen. Canby's Wife," *New York Times*, June 4, 1873, p. 5.

15 Louise J. Speed, "Personal Recollections of General Canby, with Letters Hitherto Unpublished," 7–8, Louise John Speed Papers, FHS; Heyman, *Prudent Soldier*, 349, 357, 363–64, 380–83; Richard Canby to Louisa Canby, February 15, 17, 18, 19, 1873, in Louise J. Speed, "Personal Recollections," 12, FHS; D.T., "In Memoriam," April 14, 1873, Folder 1, Canby Papers, FHS; H. Clay Wood, *Memorandum* [re: the death of Edward Canby], April 17, 1873, Louise John Speed Papers, FHS; Louisa Hawkins Canby Obituary, *Army and Navy Journal*, September 8, 1888, 940.

16 "'Tis Done: Junction of the Two Overland Roads," *Santa Fe Daily Gazette*, March 9, 1881, p. 2; *Vicksburg (Miss.) Herald*, March 12, 1881, p. 1; "Another 'Last Spike,'" *Sacramento (Calif.) Record-Union*, March 10, 1881, p. 2; "The Santa Fe and Southern Pacific Railroads Connect," *Topeka (Kans.) Daily Capital*, March 10, 1881, p. 8; Laura V. Krol, *Images of America: Deming* (Charleston, S.C.: Arcadia Publishing, 2012), 19.

17 "'Tis Done: Junction of the Two Overland Roads," *Santa Fe Daily Gazette*, March 9, 1881, p. 2; "Another 'Last Spike,'" *Sacramento (Calif.) Record-Union*, March 10, 1881, p. 2; Richardson, *West from Appomattox*, 80.

18 Geronimo, *Geronimo's Story of His Life*, 131–32; Robert M. Utley, *Geronimo* (New Haven, Conn.: Yale University Press, 2012), 88, 97, 103, 110–11.

Bibliography

ARCHIVES AND LIBRARIES

Archives and Special Collections, Branson Library, New Mexico State University. Las Cruces, New Mexico.

- Carl Schuchard Lithographs, 1856.
- George Courtright, *An expedition against the Indians in 1864; a true historical account of an Indian expedition under the command of Col. Christopher (Kit) Carson* (n.d., after 1886).
- *Mesilla Miner* (June 9, 1860).
- *The Mesilla Times*, vol. 1, no. 2 (October 25, 1860).
- *The Mesilla Times*, vol. 1, no. 3 (November 1, 1860).
- Philetus Morris Thompson Letters, 1851–1857.
- Reverend Horace S. Bishop Papers.

Arizona Historical Society. Tucson, Arizona.

- Alonzo Davis Reminiscences, c. 1916.
- Clarence Edmund Bennett Papers, 1851–1894.
- Edward Everett Ayer Papers, 1860–1918.
- Frederick G. Hughes Papers, 1872–1897.
- J. William ("Uncle Billy") Fourr Papers, 1864–1983.
- [James Henry] Tevis Papers, 1885.
- John R. Baylor Biographical File.
- William S. Grant Papers, 1862–1868.

C.L. Sonnichsen Special Collections, University of Texas, El Paso Library. El Paso, Texas.

- Gordon Family Papers, 1837–1873.
- H.P. Corbin, *Report of an Investigation in the Vicinity of Cook's Springs, N.M. Made in an Endeavor to Locate the Exact Spot Where Emmett Mills and Five Companions Lost Their Lives in a Battle with Apache Indians on July 23, 1861* (1920).
- Horace B. Stevens Papers.
- Mary Dowell Phillips Memoirs (1930s).

Center for Southwest Research and Special Collections, University of New Mexico. Albuquerque, New Mexico.

- Charles and Jacqueline Meketa Papers, 1792–1994.
  - Felix Robert Collard, "Reminiscences of a Private, Company 'G,' 7th Texas Cavalry, Sibley Brigade, C.S.A."
  - Louis Felsenthal Manuscripts.
  - Photographs Collection (Folders 4–12, Box 3).
  - Rafael Chacon Papers, 1863–1864.
- Charles Francis Clarke Papers, 1847–1914.
- Colonel John L. Gay Collection of Papers Pertaining to the Armijo Family, 1841–1902.
- Digital Collections: Navajo Oral Histories.
  - Bob Manuelito, "My Father's Day of the Long Walk" (1960).
  - Frank Apache, "Story of the Long Walk" (1969).
  - Herbert Ration, "Grandparents' Story of the Long Walk" (1969).
  - Oakee James, "Kit Carson Rounding Up the Navajo" (1969).
  - Rex Becenti, Jr., "Life in the Early Days" (1969).
- Felipe Chaves Family Papers, 1739–1937.
- U.S. Civil War Collection, 1858–1926.
- William A. Keleher Papers, 1714–1999.
  - Maps Collection (Oversize Folders).
  - W.G. Ritch Record Book.
    - Major Charles Emil Wesche, Account of Valverde.
- William A. Keleher Pictorial Collection.

Dolph Briscoe Center for American History, University of Texas at Austin. Austin, Texas.

- Baylor (John Robert) Family Papers, 1838, 1851–1869, 1906.
- James W. Freeman Family Papers, 1860–1911.
- John E. Campbell Papers, 1858–1861.

Filson Historical Society.
Louisville, Kentucky.

- Bullitt-Chenoweth Additional Papers, 1817–1949 [Correspondence, 1854–1859].
- Canby Family File.
- Carson Family File.
- Edward Richard Sprigg Canby Papers, 1819–1873.
- Elliott Warren Rice (1835–1877) Papers, 1861–1887.
- Hiram Wingate (1778–1875) Papers, 1831–1914.
- John Hawkins Ledger, 1832–1887.
- John Parker Hawkins, *Memoranda Concerning Some Branches of the Hawkins Family and Connections* Indianapolis, 1913.
- John Todd Roberts Papers, 1839–1869.
- Kit Carson Historical File.
- Louise John Speed Papers, 1863–1953.
- Mary Louise Speed Photograph Collection [boxed].
- R.S. Higgins Letter, 1861.
- Speed Family File.
- Thomas Speed, *Records and Memorials of the Speed Family* Louisville: Courier Journal Job Printing Company, 1892.
- United States Army. Military Post Order Book [Fort Fillmore], 1861, 1869–1870.
- Vault C. David Meriwether Memoirs, 1800–1855.
- Wilhelmine Kiameche Crawford Bayless Diary, 1866–1868, Bayless-Crawford Family Papers, 1770–1991.

Fray Angélico Chávez History Library, New Mexico History Museum.
Santa Fe, New Mexico.

- Arthur Olivas Collection.
- City File: Santa Fe.
- Diary of Edward L. Robb, Sibley's Brigade (1862).
- E. R. Boles Letters, 1862.
- Edward W. Wynkoop Collection.
- John A. Clark Papers, 1861–1868.
- Mauro Montoya Collection.
- Raymond McCoy Collection.
- Vertical File: Civil War.

Library of Congress, Manuscript Division.

- Abraham Lincoln Papers.

National Archives and Records Administration.
Washington, D.C.

- Record Group 49: Records of the Bureau of Land Management [General Land Office], Letters Received from the Surveyors General of Public Land States, 1826–1883 [New Mexico, 1862–1870], Box 92–93.
- Record Group 92: Records of the Office of the Quartermaster General, 1774–1985, Consolidated Correspondence File 1794–1915 [Packet: Fort Sumner, New Mexico, 1864], Box 1093, Entry 225.
- Record Group 393, Part IV: Records of the U.S. Army Continental Commands, 1817–1947.
    - Letters Sent [from Fort Sumner, New Mexico], 1862–1869, Vols. 107, 108, and 109, Entry 1217.
    - Lists, Registers, and Other Records, 1863–1865 [Fort Sumner, New Mexico], 1864–1868, Vol. 117, Entry 1235.
    - Morning Reports of Indians, 1866–1867 [Fort Sumner, New Mexico], Vol. 114, Entry 1234.
    - Records Relating to Indians [Fort Sumner, New Mexico], 1864–1868, Vol. 112, Entry 1228.
    - Supplemental Letters Sent [from Fort Sumner, New Mexico], 1864–1865, Vol. 106, Entry 1218.

New Mexico State Records Center and Archives.
Santa Fe, New Mexico.

- Albert H. Schroeder Collection.
- Fort Union National Monument Collection.
- Frank McNitt Collection.
    - Valentin Wolfenstein Diaries, 1868, Folder 23.
- Maps Collection.
- New Mexico Letters and Diaries Collection.
    - B.F. Powell Diary.
    - Diary of William Anderson Thornton, "Military Expedition to New Mexico, 1855–1856."
    - James E. Whitemore Diaries, 1852–1864, Miscellaneous Letters and Diaries Collection.
- Ward Allan Minge Collection of Historical Documents, Gonzalez Papers.

Photo Archives, Palace of the Governors.
Santa Fe, New Mexico.

- File: Individual Portraits.
- File: Santa Fe Plaza.
- *Souvenir of New Mexico.*

Stephen H. Hart Library, History Colorado.
Denver, Colorado.

- Alfred Cobb Correspondence, 1862: Letters from Camp near Fort Craig (1913).
- Augustus Vorhees Collection, 1858.
- Charles Porter, *Account of the Confederate Attempt to Seize Arizona and New Mexico.* Edited by Alwyn Barr, 1964.
- Civil War Collection.
- Colorado Volunteers: Civil War Collection.
- David Fletcher Spain Collection, 1859.
- Edward V. McCandless Collection, 1861.
- George Andrew Jackson Collection, 1859–1928.
- George Laird Shoup Diary, 1862–1863.
- James Marshall Paul Collection, 1859–1890.
- Jonah Girard Cisne Collection, 1860–1861.
- José Mariano Autobees Collection.
- *Map Of The Greater Portion Of The Gold-Mining Districts In The Vicinity Of Central City Colorado, As In The Period Of The Civil War (1864).*
- Pike's Peak Gold Rush Collection, 1859–1959.
- Samuel Forster Tappan Collection, 1861–1875.
- Silas Soule Collection, 1865.
- Zara C. Linder Collection, 1860–1862.

University Archives, University of Colorado, Boulder Libraries.
Boulder, Colorado.

- Hal Sayre Papers, 1859–1925.
- John K. Houston Papers, 1861–1866.

University of Arizona Special Collections.
Tucson, Arizona.

- Diary of Thomas Akers, 1861–1864.
- Richmond Jones Papers, 1859–1861.

Western History Collection, Denver Public Library.
Denver, Colorado.

- Alonzo Ferdinand Ickis Diary, 1861–1863.
- Calvin Perry Clark Diary, 1859–1860.
- Charlotte and Anna Ronk Papers, 1856–1866.
- D.M. Draper, *The Santa Fe Trail in '61.*
- James Henry Carleton Report to Philip St. George Cooke, June 5, 1854.

- John L. Lambert Papers, 1867.
- John Milton Chivington Papers.
- John Sedgwick Correspondence, 1860.
- Joseph Rodman West Papers.
- Kansas City, Santa Fe, and Cañon City Express Company Ledger, 1862–1870.
- Manning C. Hallowell Letters, 1856–1860.
- Morton C. Fisher Letter, July 29, 1859.
- Robert Rizer Papers, 1861–1912.
- Silas Soule Papers, 1861–1865.
- Territorial Letters, 1860–1878.
- William Baskerville Papers, 1852–1864.
- William Dute Papers, 1859–1864.
- William Kroenig Papers, 1849–1852.

GOVERNMENT DOCUMENTS

14th Amendment to the Constitution, 1866; ratified, 1868, https://www.law.cornell.edu/constitution/amendmentxiv.

Arizona Organic Act, February 24, 1863, Bills and Resolutions, House of Representatives, 37th Congress, 2nd Session.

Baird, Spencer F. *Report of the Assistant Secretary in Charge of the Natural History Department for the year, 1850*, in *Publications of Spencer Fullerton Baird*, in *Bulletin of the US National Museum*, vol. 20. Washington, D.C.: Department of the Interior, Government Printing Office, 1883.

Davis, Jefferson. *Report of the Secretary of War, December 4, 1854, in Message from the President of the United States to the Two Houses of Congress . . .* , Part II. Washington, D.C.: A.O.P. Nicholson, Printer, 1854.

Davis, Jefferson. *Report of the Secretary of War [. . . regarding] The Purchase of Camels for the Purposes of Military Transportation*. Washington, D.C.: A.O.P. Nicholson, 1857.

Doolittle, James R. *Condition of the Indian Tribes: Report of the Special Committee Appointed under Joint Resolution of March 3, 1865, with Appendix [Reports of the Committees of the Senate]*. Washington, D.C.: Government Printing Office, 1867.

Executive Documents of the Senate, 51st Congress, 1st Session. Washington, D.C.: Government Printing Office, 1890.

General Regulations for the Army, or Military Institutes. Washington, D.C.: Surgeon General's Office, 1821.

Indian Affairs: Laws and Treaties, vol. 2. Washington, D.C.: Government Printing Office, 1904.

Lincoln, Abraham. "Emancipation Proclamation," January 1, 1863. https://www.archives.gov/exhibits/featured-documents/emancipation-proclamation.

———. "Second Annual Message to Congress," December 1, 1862. https://www.americanantiquarian.org/Freedmen/Manuscripts/lincolnsecondannual.html.

Message from the President of the United States to the Two Houses of Congress . . . , Part II. Washington, D.C.: A.O.P. Nicholson, 1854.

Records of California Men in the War of the Rebellion, 1861 to 1867. Edited by Richard H. Orton. Sacramento, Calif.: J.D. Young, 1890.

Southern History of the War: Official Reports of Battles, as Published by Order of the Confederate Congress at Richmond. New York: Charles B. Richardson, 1864.

Treaty between the United States Government and the Navajo Indians Signed at Fort Sumner, New Mexico Territory on June 1, 1868 (Ratified Indian Treaty #372, 15 STAT 667). Record Group 11, General Records of the United States Government, Series: Indian Treaties, 1722–1869. National Archives, Washington, D.C.

Treaty Between the United States of America and the Arapahoe and Cheyenne Indians of the Upper Arkansas River, 1861. Stephen Hart Library, History Colorado, Denver.

United States Statutes at Large. https://memory.loc.gov/ammem/amlaw/lwsl.html.

United States War Department. *The War of Rebellion: A Compilation of the Official Records of the Union and Confederate Armies.* Washington, D.C.: Government Printing Office, 1880–1901.

Washington, George. "Farewell Address," 1796.

PRINTED PRIMARY SOURCES

Anderson, Gary Clayton and Alan Woolworth, eds. *Through Dakota Eyes: Narrative Accounts of the Minnesota Indian War of 1862.* Minneapolis: Minnesota Historical Society, 1988.

Anderson, Latham. "Canby's Services in the New Mexican Campaign." In *Battles and Leaders of the Civil War*, vol. 2, pp. 697–699. New York: The Century Co., 1887.

Audubon, John James. *The Missouri River Journals of John James Audubon.* Edited by Daniel Patterson. Lincoln: University of Nebraska Press, 2016.

Ayers, John. "A Soldier's Experience in New Mexico." *New Mexico Historical Review* 24, no. 4 (October 1949): 259–266.

Ball, Eve, ed. *In the Days of Victorio: Recollections of a Warm Springs Apache.* Tucson: University of Arizona Press, 1970.

———. *Indeh: An Apache Odyssey.* Reprint edition, Norman: University of Oklahoma Press, 1988.

Bartlett, John Russell. *Personal Narrative of Explorations and Incidents in Texas, New Mexico, California, Sonora, and Chihuahua, connected with the United States and Mexican Boundary Commission . . .*, vol. 2. New York: D. Appleton & Co., 1854.

Baylor, George Wythe. *Into the Far, Wild Country: True Tales of the Southwest.* Edited by Jerry D. Thompson. El Paso: Texas Western Press, 1996.

Brewer, William H. *Up and Down California in 1860–1864: The Journal of William H. Brewer.* Fourth Edition. Edited by Francis P. Farquhar. Berkeley: University of California Press, 2003.

Browne, John Ross. *Adventures in the Apache Country.* New York: Harper & Brothers, 1869.

Carleton, James H. " 'To the People of New Mexico': Gen. Carleton Defends the Bosque Redondo." Edited by Gerald E. Thompson. *Arizona and the West* 14, no. 4 (Winter 1972): 347–366.

Collins, Lewis. *Historical Sketches of Kentucky.* Maysville, Ky.: Lewis Collins, and Cincinnati, Ohio: J.A. & U.P. James, 1848.

Conner, Daniel Ellis. *Joseph Reddeford Walker and the Arizona Adventure.* Edited by Donald J. Berthrong and Odessa Davenport. Norman: University of Oklahoma Press, 1956.

Cremony, John C. *Life Among the Apaches.* San Francisco: A. Roman and Co., 1868.

Curtis, Charles A. *Ordered West: The Civil War Exploits of Charles A. Curtis.* Edited by Alan D. Gaff and Donald H. Gaff. Denton: University of North Texas Press, 2017.

Daniell, L.E. *Personnel of State Government, with Sketches of Distinguished Texans.* Austin, Texas: Smith, Hicks, & Jones, 1889.

Davis, Jefferson. *Jefferson Davis, Constitutionalist: His Letters, Papers, and Speeches.*
   Vol. 4. Edited by Dunbar Rowland. Jackson: Mississippi Department of Archives
   and History, 1923.
Du Bois, John Van Deusen. "Battle on the Gila: Lt. John Van Deusen Du Bois's Account
   of an Episode in the 1857 Gila-Apache Campaign." *Journal of Arizona History* 43,
   no. 2 (Summer 2002): 173–182.
Dunn, J.P. *Massacres of the Mountains: A History of the Indian Wars of the Far West.* New
   York: Harper and Bros., 1886.
Emory, William H. *Notes of a Military Reconnoissance [sic] from Fort Leavenworth, in Missouri,
   to San Diego, in California [. . .].* Washington, D.C.: Wendell and Van Benthuysen, 1848.
Evans, A.W. "Canby at Valverde." In *Battles and Leaders of the Civil War*, vol. 2, pp.
   699–700. New York: The Century Co., 1887.
Everett, Eben. "A Diary of Kit Carson's Navaho Campaign, 1863–4." Edited by Raymond
   E. Lindgren. *New Mexico Historical Review* 21, no. 3 (July 1946): 228–246.
Fowler, Orson Squire. *Human Science or Phrenology: Its Principles, Proofs, Facts, [etc.]* . . .
   Philadelphia: National Publishing Co., 1873.
Geronimo. *Geronimo's Story of His Life.* Edited by S.M. Barrett. New York: Duffield and
   Co., 1906.
Gienapp, William, ed. *The Civil War and Reconstruction: A Documentary Collection.*
   New York: W.W. Norton, 2001.
Gove, Jesse. *The Utah Expedition: Letters of Capt. Jesse A. Gove, 10th Inf., U.S.A. of
   Concord, N.H., to Mrs. Gove, and special correspondent of the New York Herald.*
   Concord: New Hampshire Historical Society, 1928.
Greeley, Horace. *An Overland Journey, from New York to San Francisco in the Summer of
   1859.* New York: C.M. Saxton, Barker & Co., 1860.
Hafen, Leroy R., ed. *Overland Routes to the Gold Fields, 1859, from Contemporary
   Diaries.* Glendale, Calif.: Arthur H. Clark, Co., 1942.
Hand, George. "The California Column Occupies Tucson: George O. Hand's Diary,
   August 8–Dec. 12, 1862." Edited by Neil B. Carmony. *Journal of Arizona History* 26,
   no. 1 (Spring 1985): 11–40.
Harding, Stephen S. *Oration, February 22, 1864.* Denver, Colo.: Byers & Dailey, Printers
   [Rocky Mountain News Office], 1864.
Hodge, Hiram C. *Arizona As It Is; or, the Coming Country.* New York: Hurd and
   Houghton, 1877.
Hollister, Ovando J. *Boldly They Rode: A History of the 1st Colorado Regiment of
   Volunteers.* Lakewood, Colo.: The Golden Press, 1949.
_____. *The Mines of Colorado.* Springfield, Mass.: Samuel Bowles & Co. 1867.
Howell, William Randolph. *Westward the Texans: The Civil War Journal of Private William
   Randolph Howell.* Edited by Jerry D. Thompson. El Paso: Texas Western Press, 1990.
Hughes, Sam, and James H. Carleton. "A Conversation between General James
   H. Carleton and Sam Hughes." *Arizoniana* 4, no. 3 (Fall 1963): 26–32.
Ickis, Alonzo Ferdinand. *Bloody Trails along the Rio Grande: The Diary of Alonzo Ferdinand
   Ickis.* Edited by Nolie Mumey. Denver, Colo.: Old West Publishing Company, 1958.
Johnston, Broderick H., ed. *Navajo Stories of the Long Walk Period.* Tsaile, Navajo Nation:
   Diné College Bookstore/Press, 1973.
Kelly, Lawrence, ed. *Navajo Roundup: Selected Correspondence of Kit Carson's Expedition
   Against the Navajo, 1863–1865.* Boulder, Colo.: The Pruett Publishing Company, 1970.
Lane, Lydia Spencer. *I Married a Soldier; or, Old Days in the Old Army.* Philadelphia:
   J.B. Lippincott Co., 1893.

"Major-General Canby." *Harper's Weekly* 433 (April 15, 1865): 1.

Matson, Sylvester W. "With the Third Infantry in New Mexico, 1851–1853: The Lost Diary of Private Sylvester W. Matson." Edited by Jerry D. Thompson. *Journal of Arizona History* 31, no. 4 (Winter 1990): 349–404.

McGee, W.J. "[The Phenomena of Desert Thirst]" (1906). In "Desert Thirst as a Disease." *American Medicine* 12 (May 1906): 51–52.

McPherson, Edward. *A Political Manual for 1868*. Washington, D.C.: Philip & Solomon, 1868.

Michaelis, Bernhard, ed. *The Navajo Treaty, 1868*. Native Child Dinetah, 2018.

Noel, Theophilus. *Autobiography and Reminiscences of Theophilus Noel*. Chicago: Theo. Noel Co., 1904.

———. *A Campaign from Santa Fe to the Mississippi: Being a History of the Old Sibley Brigade*. Shreveport, La.: Shreveport News Printing Establishment, 1865.

Ormsby, Waterman L. *The Butterfield Overland Mail*. Edited by Josephine M. Bynum and Lyle H. Wright. San Marino, Calif.: Huntington Library, 1942.

Ostrander, Romine H. *This Soldier Life: The Diaries of Romine H. Ostrander, 1863 and 1865 in Colorado Territory*. Edited by Paul A. Malkoski. Denver: Colorado Historical Society, 2007.

O'Sullivan, John. "Annexation." *United States Magazine and Democratic Review* 17 (1845): 5–6, 9–10.

Peticolas, Alfred B. *Rebels on the Rio Grande: The Civil War Journal of A.B. Peticolas*. Edited by Don E. Alberts. Albuquerque, N. Mex.: Bickerstaff's, 2013.

Pettis, George H. *The California Column: Its Campaigns and Services in New Mexico . . .* Santa Fe: Historical Society of New Mexico Circular No. 11, 1908.

———. "The Confederate Invasion of New Mexico and Arizona." In *Battles and Leaders of the Civil War*, vol. 2 pp. 103–111, New York: The Century Co., 1887.

Pruyn, John V.L. "The Impeachment of Andrew Johnson: A Contemporary View." Edited by Jerome Mushkat. *New York History* 48, no. 3 (July 1967): 275–286.

"Recent Deaths: Louisa Hawkins Canby." *Army and Navy Journal* (September 8, 1888): 940.

Rickard, T.A. *A History of American Mining*. New York: McGraw-Hill, 1932.

Robinson, Daniel. "Eyewitness to the Bascom Affair: An Account by Sergeant Daniel Robinson, Seventh Infantry." Edited by Douglas C. McChristian and Larry L. Ludwig. *Journal of Arizona History* 42, no. 3 (Autumn 2001): 277–300.

Roe, Lewis. *From Western Deserts to Carolina Swamps: A Civil War Soldier's Journals and Letters Home*. Edited by John P. Wilson. Albuquerque: University of New Mexico Press, 2012.

Seville, William. *Narrative of the March of Co. A, Engineers from Fort Leavenworth, Kansas to Fort Bridger, Utah, and Return (May 6 to October 3, 1858)*. Washington Barracks, D.C.: Press of the Engineer School, 1912.

Sherman, William Tecumseh. *The Sherman Letters*. Edited by Rachel Sherman Thorndike. New York: Scribner's, 1894.

Teal, John. "Soldier in the California Column: The Diary of John W. Teal." Edited by Henry P. Walker. *Arizona and the West* 13, no. 1 (Spring 1971): 33–82.

Teel, Trevanion T. "Sibley's New Mexican Campaign—Its Objects and the Causes of Its Failure." In *Battles and Leaders of the Civil War*, vol. 2, p. 700. New York: The Century Co., 1887.

Thompson, Gerald, ed. *The Army and the Navajo: The Bosque Redondo Reservation Experiment, 1863–1868*. Tucson: University of Arizona Press, 1976.

Thompson, Jerry D., ed. *Civil War in the Southwest: Recollections of the Sibley Brigade*. College Station: Texas A&M University Press, 2001.

———. *New Mexico Territory during the Civil War: Wallen and Evans Inspection Reports, 1862–1863*. Albuquerque: University of New Mexico Press, 2008.

Thompson, John. "The Destruction of Navajo Orchards in 1864: Captain John
    Thompson's Report." Edited by Stephen C. Jett. *Arizona and the West* 16, no. 4
    (Winter 1974): 365–378.
Tracy, Albert. "The Utah War: Journal of Albert Tracy, March–April 1858." *Utah
    Historical Quarterly* 13 (1945): 1–119.
Way, Phocion R. "Overland via 'Jackass Mail' in 1858: The Diary of Phocion. R. Way."
    Edited by William A. Duffen. *Arizona and the West* 2, no. 2 (Summer 1960): 147–164.
Whitney, J.D. *The Metallic Wealth of the United States, Described and Compared with that
    of Other Countries.* Philadelphia: Lippincott, Grambo & Co., 1854.
_____. *Notice of the Two Masses of Meteoric Iron brought from Tucson to San Francisco,
    1862 and 1863.* San Francisco: Town & Bacon, 1863.
Williams, Ellen. *Three Years and a Half in the Army; or, a History of the Second Colorados.*
    New York: Fowler & Wells Co., 1885.
Wilson, John P., ed. *When the Texans Came: Missing Records from the Civil War in the
    Southwest.* Albuquerque: University of New Mexico Press, 2001.
Wright, Henry C. "A Johnny Reb in Sibley's New Mexico Campaign: Reminiscences of
    Pvt. Henry C. Wright, 1861–1862, Part II." Edited by Michael L. Tate. *East Texas
    Historical Journal* 26, no. 1 (1988): 23–35.

NEWSPAPERS AND MAGAZINES

The American Mining Gazette and Geological Magazine
Arizona Miner
Chicago Tribune
The Deseret News
El Paso Herald
Harper's Weekly
Houston (Texas) Tri-Weekly Telegraph
(Lawrence) Daily Kansas Tribune
Leavenworth (Kansas) Times
Los Angeles Star
Mesilla Times
New York Daily Herald
New York Times
Richmond Enquirer
Sacramento Record-Union
Salt Lake [City] Telegram
Santa Fe [Weekly] Gazette
Santa Fe Weekly New Mexican

PHOTOGRAPHS AND MAPS

Bell, Charles M. "Juanita and Arny." 1874. National Anthropological Archives.
    Smithsonian Institution, Washington, D.C.
Griffith, G.E., J.M. Omernik, M.M. McGraw, G.Z. Jacobi, C.M. Canavan, T.S. Schrader,

D. Mercer, R. Hill, and B.C. Moran. *Ecoregions of New Mexico*. Reston, Va.: U.S. Geological Survey, 2006.

Griffith, G.E., S.A. Bryce, J.M. Omernik, J.A. Comstock, A.C. Rogers, B. Harrison, S.L. Hatch, and D. Bezanson. *Ecoregions of Texas*. Reston, Va.: U.S. Geological Survey, 2004.

Hillers, John K. "Cliff Ruins near Fort Wingate, New Mexico." c. 1873–1879. Library of Congress Prints and Photographs Division, Washington, D.C.

Hillyer, John K. "Ruins near Fort Wingate, New Mexico." c. 1870s. J. Paul Getty Museum, Los Angeles, California.

Russell, Andrew Joseph. "East and West Shaking Hands at the Laying of the Last Rail," 1869. Golden Spike National Historical Park, Brigham City, Utah.

Watkins, Carleton. "The Carleton Aerolite." 1863. In *Complete Mammoth Photographs*. Ed. Weston Naef and Christine Hult-Lewis. Los Angeles: J. Paul Getty Museum, 2011.

ONLINE AND PUBLIC HISTORY SECONDARY SOURCES

"The Alamo." *Texas Almanac Online*. http://texasalmanac.com/topics/history/alamo.

Bessin, Ric. "Armyworms in Corn" (2004). https://entomology.ca.uky.edu/ef109.

Bowden, J.J. "Jornada del Muerto Grant." *New Mexico History*. http://newmexicohistory .org/2015/07/20/jornada-del-muerto-grant/

"Coyote." New Mexico Department of Game and Fish Wildlife Notes. http://www .wildlife.state.nm.us/download/education/conservation/wildlife-notes/mammals /Coyotes.pdf.

Cutrer, Thomas W. "Reily, James." *Handbook of Texas Online*. http://www.tshaonline.org /handbook/online/articles/fre26.

"Geology of the Taos Area: *The Taos Landscape*." Astronaut Geophysical Training Manual (Summer 1999). https://geoinfo.nmt.edu/geoscience/projects/astronauts/taos _geology.html.

"History and Culture." Golden Spike National Historic Site. https://www.nps.gov/gosp /learn/historyculture/index.htm.

Ingram, Lynn. "California Megaflood: Lessons from a Forgotten Catastrophe." *Scientific American* (January 1, 2013). http://www.scientificamerican.com/article/atmospheric -rivers-california-megaflood-lessons-from-forgotten-catastrophe/.

Ivey, James. "An Uncertain Founding: Santa Fe." *Common-place* 3, no. 4 (July 2003).

"John Henry Moore." *Handbook of Texas Online*. https://tshaonline.org/handbook /online/articles/fmo30.

Lindsey, David A. *The Geologic Story of Colorado's Sangre de Cristo Range*. Circular 1349. United States Geological Survey. 2010. https://pubs.usgs.gov/circ/1349/pdf/C1349.pdf.

Long Walk National Historic Trail Feasibility and Environmental Impact Study. January 2009. https://parkplanning.nps.gov/projectHome.cfm?projectID=12406.

Magnum, Neil C. "In the Land of Frozen Fires: A History of Occupation in El Malpais County." 1990. https://www.nps.gov/elma/learn/historyculture/upload/ELMA_hist.pdf.

McLarey, Myra. "Coons, Benjamin Franklin." *Handbook of Texas Online*. http://www .tshaonline.org/handbook/online/articles/fcodb.

Myers, Lee. "The Enigma of Mangas Coloradas's Death." *New Mexico History*. http:// newmexicohistory.org/people/the-enigma-of-mangas-coloradas.

"Native Arrow Technology." Bosque Redondo Memorial Museum, Fort Sumner National Monument. Fort Sumner, New Mexico.

Ramos, Donna G. "Utah War." *HistoryNet*. http://www.historynet.com/utah-war-us
    -government-versus-mormon-settlers.htm.
Ramsay, John B. "John A. Clark." *New Mexico History*. http://newmexicohistory.org
    /people/john-a-clark.
Rasby, Rick. "Daily Water Intake." *UNL Beef*. http://beef.unl.edu.
"Republican Party Platforms of 1856 and 1860." *The American Presidency Project*. https://
    www.presidency.ucsb.edu/documents/presidential-documents-archive-guidebook
    /national-political-party-platforms.
Roeder, Fred. "The Journals of John A. Clark." *The American Surveyor* (April 5, 2009).
    http://www.amerisurv.com/content/view/6018/136/.
Ruge, Justin. "Fort Yuma." http://www.militarymuseum.org.
Ruleman, Cal, and Michael Machette. "An Overview of the Sangre de Cristo Fault System
    and New Insights to Interactions Between Quaternary Faults in the Northern Rio
    Grande Rift." U.S. Geological Survey. http://pubs.usgs.gov/of/2007/1193/pdf/OF07
    -1193_ChJ.pdf.
"Second Fort Union." Fort Union National Monument. https://www.nps.gov/foun/learn
    /historyculture/the-star-fort.htm.
Sharpe, Tom. "Confederate Army in Santa Fe." *New Mexico History* http://www
    .newmexicohistory.org.
Simmons, Marc. "Bishop Lamy's Garden." *Santa Fe Online* http://sfol.com/history
    /bishop.html.
_____. "Santa Fe's Forgotten Monument to Kit Carson." *Santa Fe New Mexican*
    (February 26, 2016). http://www.santafenewmexican.com/news/local_news
    /santa-fe-s-forgotten-monument-to-kit-carson/article_ec773aab-cc9c-51f0
    -bc3e-77582816c608.html.
Stammerjohn, George. "The Mythical Fort Tejon 'Camel Corps.' " Fort Tejon Historical
    Association. http://www.forttejon.org/camel.html.
U.S. Geological Survey. *Overview of the Arkstorm Scenario*. U.S. Geological Survey Open-
    File Report 2010-1312, 2–3. http://pubs.usgs.gov/of/2010/1312/.
U.S. Treaty with the Navajos, 1861, http:///www.lapahie.com/Dine_Treaty_1861.cfm.
Utley, Robert M. "Victorio's War." *HistoryNet*. http://www.historynet.com.
"Valverde." *New Mexico History*. http://newmexicohistory.org/places/valverde.

PRINTED SECONDARY SOURCES

Abbott, Carl, Stephen J. Leonard, and Thomas J. Noel. *Colorado: A History of the
    Centennial State*. Fifth edition. Boulder: University Press of Colorado, 2013.
Ackerly, Neal W. "Mimbreno and Gileno Apache Irrigation Systems, 1853–1859." *Kiva*
    62, no. 4 (Summer 1997): 349–363.
Agnew, Dwight L. "The Government Land Surveyor as a Pioneer." *Mississippi Valley
    Historical Review* 28, no. 3 (December 1941): 369–382.
Alberts, Don E. *The Battle of Glorieta: Union Victory in the West*. College Station: Texas
    A&M Press, 1998.
Altshuler, Constance Wynn. "The Case of Sylvester Mowry: The Mowry Mine." *Arizona
    and the West* 15, no. 2 (Summer 1973): 149–174.
Altshuler, Constance Wynn and Ben C. Cutler. "Military Administration in Arizona,
    1854–1865." *Journal of Arizona History* 10, no. 4 (Winter 1969): 215–238.

Alward, Dennis M. and Andrew F. Rolle. "The Surveyor-General Edward Fitzgerald Beale's Administration of California Lands." *Southern California Quarterly* 53, no. 2 (June 1971): 113–122.

Apostal, Jane. "An Army Bride Goes West." *Southern California Quarterly* 72, no. 4 (Winter 1990): 303–320.

Apple, Lindsey, Frederick A. Johnstone, and Ann Bolton Bevins. *Scott County, Kentucky: A History*. Georgetown, Ky.: Scott County Historical Society, 1993.

Austerman, Wayne R. " 'Sick, Dead and Discharged': Disease and the Defeat of the Confederate Campaign into New Mexico, 1862." *U.S. Army Medical Department Journal* (April–June 2007): 5–12.

Bailey, Anne. *Invisible Southerners: Ethnicity in the Civil War*. Athens: University of Georgia Press, 2006.

Bailey, L.R. *The Long Walk: A History of the Navajo Wars, 1846–68*. Los Angeles: Westernlore Press, 1964.

Ball, Durwood. *Army Regulars on the Western Frontier, 1848–1861*. Norman: University of Oklahoma Press, 2001.

Barr, Juliana. "Geographies of Power: Mapping Indian Borders in the 'Borderlands' of the Early Southwest." *William and Mary Quarterly* 68, no. 1 (January 2011): 5–46.

Billings, Elden E. "Social and Economic Conditions in Washington during the Civil War." *Records of the Columbia Historical Society, Washington, D.C.* 63/65 (1963/1965): 191–209.

Blount, Bertha. "The Apache in the Southwest, 1846–1886." *Southwestern Historical Quarterly* 23, no. 1 (July 1919): 20–38.

Blyth, Lance R. *Chiricahua and Janos: Communities of Violence in the Southwestern Borderlands*. Lincoln: University of Nebraska Press, 2012.

_____. "The Navajo–New Mexico War, 1800–1880: Struggle for a Pastoral Borderland." Unpublished manuscript.

Bourke, John G. "Notes on Apache Mythology." *Journal of American Folklore* 3, no. 10 (July–September 1890): 209–212.

_____. "Notes upon the Religion of the Apache Indians." *Folklore* 2, no. 4 (December 1891): 419–454.

Bowers, Janice Emily, and Brian Wignall. *Shrubs and Trees of the Southwest Deserts*. Tucson, Ariz.: Western National Parks Association, 1993.

Brandes, Ray. "A Guide to the History of the U.S. Army Installations in Arizona, 1849–1886." *Arizona and the West* 1, no. 1 (Spring 1959): 42–65.

Brands, H.W. *The Age of Gold: The California Gold Rush and the New American Dream*. New York: Doubleday, 2002.

Brooks, James F. *Captives and Cousins: Slavery, Kinship, and Community in the Southwest Borderlands*. Chapel Hill: University of North Carolina Press, 2002.

Bryan, Howard. *Albuquerque Remembered*. Albuquerque: University of New Mexico Press, 2006.

Byars, Charles. "The First Map of Tucson." *Journal of Arizona History* 7, no. 4 (Winter 1966): 188–195.

Campbell, Randolph B. *Gone to Texas: A History of the Lone Star State*. Second edition. New York: Oxford University Press, 2012.

Carrell, J. Lee. *Through White Men's Eyes: A Contribution to Navajo History*. Vol. 1. Window Rock, Ariz.: Navajo Heritage Center, 1976.

Cashin, Joan E. "Trophies of War: Material Culture in the Civil War Era." *Journal of the Civil War Era* 1, no. 3 (September 2011): 339–367.

Cazier, Lola. *Surveys and Surveyors of the Public Domain, 1785–1975*. Washington, D.C.:
    U.S. Department of the Interior, Bureau of Land Management, 1976.
Chapin, David. "The Fox Sisters and the Performance of Mystery." *New York History* 81,
    no. 2 (April 2000): 157–188.
Chaput, Donald. "Generals, Indian Agents, Politicians: The Doolittle Survey of 1865."
    Western Historical Quarterly 3, no. 3 (July 1972): 269–282.
Clarke, Laverne Harrell. "Early Horse Trappings of the Navajo and Apache Indians."
    Arizona and the West 5, no. 3 (Autumn 1963): 233–248.
Clarke, Roy S., Howard Plotkin, and Timothy J. McCoy. "Meteorites at the Smithsonian
    Institution." In *The History of Meteoritics and Key Meteorite Collections: Fireballs,
    Falls and Finds*, ed. G.J.H. McCall, A.J. Bowden, and R.J. Howarth pp. 237–265.
    London: Geological Society Special Publication No. 256, 2006.
Clinton, Robert N. "Treaties with Native Nations: Iconic Historical Relics or Modern
    Necessity?" In *Nation to Nation: Treaties Between the United States & American
    Indian Nations*, ed. Suzan Shown Harjo, pp. 15–33. Washington, D.C.: Smithsonian
    Institution, 2014.
Clodfelter, Micheal. *The Dakota War: The United States Army and the Sioux*. Jefferson,
    N.C.: McFarland & Co., 2006.
Colton, Ray C. *The Civil War in the Western Territories: Arizona, Colorado, New Mexico,
    and Utah*. Norman: University of Oklahoma Press, 1959.
Colwell-Chanthaphonh, Chip. "Western Apache Oral Histories and Traditions of the
    Camp Grant Massacre." *American Indian Quarterly* 2, no. 3–4 (Summer–Autumn
    2003): 639–666.
Confer, Clarissa W. *The Cherokee Nation in the Civil War*. Norman: University of
    Oklahoma Press, 2007.
Connelly, Thomas L. "The American Camel Experiment: A Reappraisal." *Southwestern
    Historical Quarterly* 69, no. 4 (April 1966): 442–462.
Cooper, Guy H. "Coyote in Navajo Religion and Cosmology." *Canadian Journal of Native
    Studies* 7, no. 2 (1987): 181–193.
Cooper, William J., Jr. *Jefferson Davis, American*. New York: Vintage, 2001.
Cullimore, Clarence. "Fort Tejon's Centennial." *Historical Society of Southern California
    Quarterly* 36, no. 3 (September 1954): 249–254.
Cureton, Gilbert. "The Cattle Trail to California, 1840–1860." *Historical Society of
    Southern California Quarterly* 35, no. 2 (June 1953): 99–109.
Daniel, Lewis E., ed. *Personnel of State Government, with Sketches of Distinguished
    Texans*. Austin, Tex.: Smith, Hicks, & Jones, 1889.
Danziger, Edmund J., Jr. "The Steck-Carleton Controversy in Civil War New Mexico."
    Southwestern Historical Quarterly 74, no. 2 (October 1970): 189–203.
Davis, W.N., Jr. "The Sutler at Fort Bridger." *Western Historical Quarterly* 2, no. 1
    (January 1971): 37–54.
DeJong, David. " 'The Granary of Arizona': The Civil War, Settlers, and Pima-Maricopa
    Agriculture, 1860–1869." *Journal of Arizona History* 48, no. 3 (Autumn 2007):
    221–256.
DeLay, Brian. *War of a Thousand Deserts: Indian Raids and the U.S.-Mexican War*. New
    Haven, Conn.: Yale University Press, 2009.
Denetdale, Jennifer Nez. "Chairmen, Presidents, and Princesses: The Navajo Nation,
    Gender, and the Politics of Tradition." *Wicazo Sa Review* 21, no. 1 (Spring 2006): 9–28.
_____. *The Long Walk: The Forced Navajo Exile*. New York: Chelsea House, 2008.
_____. "Naal Tsoos Sani: The Navajo Treaty of 1868, Nation Building, and Self-

Determination." In *Nation to Nation: Treaties Between the United States &*
American Indian Nations, ed. Suzan Shown Harjo, pp. 117–131. Washington, D.C.:
Smithsonian Institution, 2014.

———. *Reclaiming Diné History: The Legacies of Navajo Chief Manuelito and Juanita.*
Tucson: University of Arizona Press, 2007.

———. " 'You Brought History Alive for Us': Reflections on the Lives of Nineteenth-
Century Diné Women." In *Empire and Liberty: The Civil War and the West*,
ed. Virginia Scharff, pp. 190–206. Oakland: University of California Press, 2015.

Doyle, Don H. *The Cause of All Nations: An International History of the American Civil
War*. New York: Basic Books, 2015.

Dunlay, Tom. *Kit Carson and the Indians*. Lincoln: University of Nebraska Press, 2000.

Ehrenberg, Ralph E. "Mapping the Nation's Capital: The Surveyor's Office, 1791–1818."
Quarterly Journal of the Library of Congress 38, no. 3 (Summer 1979): 279–319.

Ely, Glen Sample. "Gone from Texas and Trading with the Enemy: New Perspectives on
Civil War West Texas." *Southwestern Historical Quarterly* 110, no. 4 (April 2007):
438–463.

Etulain, Richard W. "Abraham Lincoln and the Trans-Mississippi American West: An
Introductory Overview." In *Lincoln Looks West: From the Mississippi to the Pacific*,
ed. Richard W. Etulain, pp. 1–67. Carbondale: Southern Illinois University Press, 2010.

Evans, William McKee. "Native Americans in the Civil War." In *Civil War Citizens:
Race, Ethnicity, and Identity in America's Bloodiest Conflict*, ed. Susannah J. Ural,
pp. 187–212. New York: New York University Press, 2010.

Fabian, Ann. *The Skull Collectors: Race, Science, and America's Unburied Dead*. Chicago:
University of Chicago Press, 2010.

Farish, Thomas Edwin. *History of Arizona*. 8 vols. San Francisco: Filmer Brothers, 1915–1918.

Farwell, Byron. *Encyclopedia of Nineteenth-Century Land Warfare: An Illustrated World
View*. New York: W.W. Norton, 2001.

Finch, L. Boyd. *Confederate Pathway to the Pacific: Major Sherod Hunter and Arizona
Territory, C.S.A.* Tucson: Arizona Historical Society, 1996.

Foner, Eric. *Reconstruction: America's Unfinished Revolution, 1863–1877*. New York:
Harper & Row, 1988.

Francaviglia, Richard V. *Over the Range: A History of the Promontory Summit Route of the
Pacific Railroad*. Boulder: University Press of Colorado, 2008.

Frantz, Klaus. *Indian Reservations in the United States: Territory, Sovereignty, and
Socioeconomic Change*. Chicago: University of Chicago Press, 1999.

Frazier, Donald. *Blood and Treasure: Confederate Empire in the Southwest*. Reprint,
College Station: Texas A&M Press, 1995.

Genetin-Pilawa, C. Joseph. "Ely Parker and the Contentious Peace Policy." *Western
Historical Quarterly* 41, no. 2 (Summer 2010): 196–217.

Goetzmann, William H. *Army Exploration in the American West, 1803–1863*. Austin:
Texas State Historical Association, 1991.

———. *Exploration and Empire: The Explorer and the Scientist in the Winning of the
American West*. Austin: Texas State Historical Association, 2000.

Gonzales, Manuel G. "Mariano G. Samaniego." *Journal of Arizona History* 31, no. 2
(Summer 1990): 141–160.

Goodwin, Doris Kearns. *Team of Rivals: The Political Genius of Abraham Lincoln*. New
York: Simon & Schuster, 2005.

Graybill, Andrew R. "Rangers, Mounties, and the Subjugation of Indigenous Peoples,
1870–1885." *Great Plains Quarterly* 24 (Spring 2004): 83–100.

Green, Michael S. "Lincoln, the West, and Antislavery Politics of the 1850s." In *Lincoln Looks West: From the Mississippi to the Pacific*, ed. Richard W. Etulain, pp. 90–112. Carbondale: Southern Illinois University Press, 2010.

Greenberg, Amy S. *A Wicked War: Polk, Clay, Lincoln, and the 1846 U.S. Invasion of Mexico*. New York: Alfred A. Knopf, 2012.

Greenleaf, Cameron and Andrew Wallace. "Tucson: Pueblo, Presidio, and American City: A Synopsis of Its History." *Arizoniana* 3, no. 2 (Summer 1962): 18–27.

Griffen, William B. "The Chiricahua Apache Population Resident at the Janos Presidio, 1792 to 1858." *Journal of the Southwest* 33, no. 2 (Summer 1991): 151–199.

Grimsley, Mark. *The Hard Hand of War: Union Military Policy toward Southern Civilians, 1861–1865*. New York: Oxford University Press, 1995.

Grinnell, Joseph. "Old Fort Tejon." *The Condor* 7, no. 1 (January–February 1905): 9–13.

Guinn, J.M. "Exceptional Years: A History of California Floods and Drought." *Historical Society of Southern California, Los Angeles* 1, no. 5 (1890): 33–39.

Haines, Helen. *History of New Mexico from the Spanish Conquest to the Present Day, 1530–1890*. New York: New Mexico Historical Publishing Co., 1891.

Hall, Martin Hardwick. "Colonel James Reily's Diplomatic Missions to Chihuahua and Sonora." *New Mexico Historical Review* 31, no. 3 (July 1956): 232–243.

_____. *The Confederate Army of New Mexico*. Austin, Tex.: Presidial Press, 1978.

_____. "Planter vs. Frontiersman: Conflict in Confederate Indian Policy." In *Essays on the American Civil War*, ed. William F. Holmes and Harold M. Hollingsworth, pp. 45–72. Austin: University of Texas Press, 1968.

_____. *Sibley's New Mexico Campaign*. 1960; reprint, Albuquerque: University of New Mexico Press, 2000.

_____. "The Skirmish at Mesilla." *Arizona and the West* 1, no. 4 (Winter 1959): 343–351.

Hämäläinen, Pekka. *The Comanche Empire*. New Haven, Conn.: Yale University Press, 2008.

Harjo, Suzan Shown, ed. *Nation to Nation: Treaties Between the United States & American Indian Nations*. Washington, D.C.: Smithsonian Institution, 2014.

Harmon, George D. "The United States Indian Policy in Texas, 1845–1860." *Mississippi Valley Historical Review* 17, no. 3 (December 1930): 377–403.

Hauptman, Laurence M. *Between Two Fires: American Indians in the Civil War*. New York: The Free Press, 1995.

Henderson, Martha L. "Duality in Modern Chiricahua Apache Settlement Patterns." *Traditional Dwellings and Settlements Review* 2, no. 2 (Spring 1991): 7–16.

Heyman, Max L., Jr. *Prudent Soldier: Biography of Major General E.R.S. Canby, 1817–1873*. Glendale, Calif.: Arthur H. Clark Co., 1959.

Hilde, Libra R. *Worth a Dozen Men: Women and Nursing in the Civil War South*. Charlottesville: University of Virginia Press, 2013.

Hoagland, Allison K. "Village Constructions: Army Forts on the Plains, 1848–1890." *Winterthur Portfolio* 34, no. 4 (Winter 1999): 215–237.

Hoffman, Virginia. *Navajo Biographies*. 2 vols. Phoenix, Ariz.: Navajo Curriculum Center Press, 1974.

Houston, Alan Fraser. "Cadwalader Ringgold, U.S. Navy: Gold Rush Surveyor of San Francisco Bay and Waters to Sacramento, 1849–1850." *California History* 79, no. 4 (Winter 2000/2001): 208–221.

Hume, Brad D. "The Romantic and the Technical in Early Nineteenth-Century American Exploration." In *Surveying the Record: North American Scientific Exploration to 1930*, ed. Edward C. Carter II, pp. 301–316. Philadelphia: American Philosophical Society, 1999.

Hunt, Aurora. *The Army of the Pacific.* Glendale, Calif.: The Arthur Clark Co., 1951.
_____. *Major James Henry Carleton, 1814–1873: Western Frontier Dragoon.* Glendale, Calif.: The Arthur H. Clark Co., 1958.
Hutton, Paul Andrew. *The Apache Wars.* New York: Crown, 2016.
Iverson, Peter and Monty Roessel. *Diné: A History of the Navajos.* Albuquerque: University of New Mexico Press, 2002.
Jacoby, Karl. *Shadows at Dawn: A Borderlands Massacre and the Violence of History.* New York: Penguin, 2008.
Jastrzembski, Joseph C. "Treacherous Towns in Mexico: Chiricahua Apache Personal Narratives of Horrors." *Western Folklore* 54, no. 3 (July 1995): 169–196.
Johnston, William Preston. *The Life of General Albert Sidney Johnston.* New York: D. Appleton & Co., 1879.
Josephy, Alvin M., Jr. *The Civil War in the American West.* New York: Vintage, 1993.
Keleher, William A. *Turmoil in New Mexico, 1846–1868.* Santa Fe: The Rydal Press, 1952.
Kellogg, Daren Earl. "Lincoln's New Mexico Patronage: Saving the Far Southwest for the Union." In *Lincoln Looks West: From the Mississippi to the Pacific,* ed. Richard W. Etulain, pp. 134–152. Carbondale: Southern Illinois University, 2010.
Kelman, Ari. *A Misplaced Massacre: Struggling over the Memory of Sand Creek.* Cambridge, Mass.: Harvard University Press, 2013.
Kent, Susan. "The Differentiation of Navajo Culture, Behavior, and Material Culture: A Comparative Study in Culture Change." *Ethnology* 22, no. 1 (January 1983): 81–91.
Kessell, John L. "General Sherman and the Navajo Treaty of 1868: A Basic and Expedient Misunderstanding." *Western Historical Quarterly* 12, no. 3 (July 1981): 251–272.
Kibby, Leo P. "With Colonel Carleton and the California Column." *Historical Society of Southern California Quarterly* 41, no. 4 (December 1959): 337–344.
Kieta, Emily E. "The New Mexico Fandango." *Wagon Tracks* 19, no. 3 (2004–2005): 11–15.
Kiser, William S. *Coast-to-Coast Empire: Manifest Destiny and the New Mexico Borderlands.* Norman: University of Oklahoma Press, 2018.
_____. *Turmoil on the Rio Grande: The Territorial History of the Mesilla Valley, 1846–1865.* College Station: Texas A&M Press, 2011.
Klein, Robert F. *Dubuque during the California Gold Rush: When the Midwest Went West.* Charleston, S.C.: The History Press, 2011.
Klos, George. " 'Our People Could Not Distinguish One Tribe from Another': The 1859 Expulsion of the Reserve Indians from Texas." *Southwestern Historical Quarterly* 97, no. 4 (April 1994): 598–619.
Koch, Lena Clara. "The Federal Indian Policy in Texas, 1845–1860: Chapter III. The Rangers and Frontier Protection." *Southwestern Historical Quarterly* 29, no. 1 (July 1925): 19–35.
Krol, Laura V. *Images of America: Deming.* Charleston, S.C.: Arcadia Publishing, 2012.
Kühn, Bernd. "Siege in Cooke's Canyon: The Freeman Thomas Fight of 1861." *Journal of Arizona History* 38, no. 2 (Summer 1997): 155–176.
Lahti, Janne. *Cultural Construction of Empire: The U.S. Army in Arizona and New Mexico.* Lincoln: University of Nebraska Press, 2012.
Lamberton, Ken. *Chasing Arizona: One Man's Yearlong Obsession with the Grand Canyon State.* Tucson: University of Arizona Press, 2015.
Lamphere, Louise. "Historical and Regional Variability in Navajo Women's Roles." *Journal of Anthropological Research* 45, no. 4 (Winter 1989): 431–456.
Lawlor, Mary. *Public Native America: Tribal Self-Representation in Museums, Powwows, and Casinos.* New Brunswick, N.J.: Rutgers University Press, 2006.

Levin, Kevin M. *Searching for Black Confederates: The Civil War's Most Persistent Myth.* Chapel Hill: University of North Carolina Press, 2019.

Limerick, Patricia Nelson. *Desert Passages: Encounters with American Deserts.* Albuquerque: University of New Mexico Press, 1985.

MacKinnon, William P. "Epilogue to the Utah War: Impact and Legacy." *Journal of Mormon History* 29, no. 2 (Fall 2003): 186–248.

Mahan, Don M. "John W. Jones: The Southwest's Unsung Civil War Hero." *Journal of Arizona History* 51, no. 3 (Autumn 2010): 223–240.

Malm, Norman R. "Climate Guide, Las Cruces, 1892–2000." Las Cruces: New Mexico State University, 2003.

Masich, Andrew E. *The Civil War in Arizona: The Story of the California Volunteers, 1861–1865.* Norman: University of Oklahoma Press, 2006.

_____. *Civil War in the Southwestern Borderlands, 1861–1867.* Norman: University of Oklahoma Press, 2017.

McClintock, James H. *Arizona: Prehistoric-Aboriginal-Pioneer-Modern*, vol. 2. Chicago: The S.J. Clarke Publishing Co., 1916.

McDonough, James Lee, and William T. Alderson. "Republican Politics and the Impeachment of Andrew Johnson." *Tennessee Historical Quarterly* 26, no. 2 (Summer 1967): 177–183.

McGinnis, Verity G. "Agents of Empire: Officers' Wives in British India and the American West, 1830–1875." *Pacific Historical Review* 83, no. 3 (August 2014): 378–409.

McNitt, Frank. *Navajo Wars: Military Campaigns, Slave Raids, and Reprisals.* Albuquerque: University of New Mexico Press, 1972.

McPherson, Robert S. *Northern Navajo Frontier, 1860–1900.* Boulder: University Press of Colorado, 2001.

Miller, Angela. "Albert Bierstadt, Landscape Aesthetics, and the Meanings of the West in the Civil War Era." *Art Institute of Chicago Museum Studies* 27, no. 1 (2001): 40–59, 101–102.

Miller, Darlis A. *The California Column in New Mexico.* Albuquerque: University of New Mexico Press, 1982.

Monroe, John. "Making the Séance 'Serious': 'Tables Tournantes' and Second Empire Bourgeois Culture, 1853–1861." *History of Religions* 38, no. 3 (February 1999): 219–246.

Muckleroy, Anna. "The Indian Policy of the Republic of Texas, III." *Southwestern Historical Quarterly* 26, no. 2 (October 1922): 128–148.

Mulligan, Raymond A. "Sixteen Days in Apache Pass." *Kiva* 24, no. 2 (December 1958): 1–13.

Muntz, A. Philip. "Union Mapping in the American Civil War." *Imago Mundi* 17 (1963): 90–94.

Myres, Sandra L. "Romance and Reality on the American Frontier: Views of Army Wives." *Western Historical Quarterly* 13, no. 4 (October 1982): 409–427.

Myrick, David F. *New Mexico's Railroads: A Historical Survey.* Revised edition. Albuquerque: University of New Mexico Press, 1990.

Nackman, Mark E. "The Making of the Texan Citizen Soldier, 1835–1860." *Southwestern Historical Quarterly* 78, no. 3 (January 1975): 231–253.

Nartonis, David K. "The Rise of Nineteenth-Century American Spiritualism, 1854–1873." *Journal for the Scientific Study of Religion* 49, no. 2 (June 2010): 361–373.

Neely, Mark E., Jr. *The Civil War and the Limits of Destruction.* Cambridge, Mass.: Harvard University Press, 2007.

Nelson, Megan Kate. "Alonzo Ickis." In *Soldiers in the Southwest Borderlands, 1848–1886*, ed. Janne Lahti, pp. 77–94. Norman: University of Oklahoma Press, 2017.

———. "The Civil War from Apache Pass." *Journal of the Civil War Era* 6, no. 4 (December 2016): 510–535.

———. "Death in the Distance: The Confederate Campaign for New Mexico, 1861–1862." In *Civil War Wests: Testing the Limits of the United States*, ed. Adam Arenson and Andrew R. Graybill, pp. 33–52. Berkeley: University of California Press, 2015.

———. " 'The Difficulties and Seductions of the Desert': Landscapes of War in 1861 New Mexico." In *The Blue, the Gray, and the Green: Toward an Environmental History of the Civil War*, ed. Brian Allen Drake, pp. 34–51. Athens: University of Georgia Press, 2015.

———. "Indian America." In *Blackwell Companion to the U.S. Civil War*, vol. 1, ed. Aaron Sheehan-Dean, pp. 365–385. Oxford, Eng.: Blackwell, 2014.

———. "Indians Make the Best Guerrillas: Native Americans and the War for the Desert Southwest, 1861–1862." In *The Civil War Guerrilla: Unfolding the Black Flag in History, Memory, and Myth*, ed. Joseph M. Beilein, Jr. and Matthew C. Hulbert, pp. 99–122. Lexington: University Press of Kentucky, 2015.

———. *Ruin Nation: Destruction and the American Civil War*. Athens: University of Georgia Press, 2012.

Noe, Kenneth. *The Howling Storm: Climate, Weather, and the American Civil War*. Baton Rouge: Louisiana State University Press, forthcoming, 2021.

Noel, Thomas J. *The City and the Saloon: Denver, 1858–1916*. Second edition. Lincoln: University of Nebraska Press, 1982.

Oman, Kerry R. "The Beginning of the End: The Indian Peace Commission of 1867–1868." *Great Plains Quarterly* 22, no. 1 (Winter 2002): 35–51.

Osburn, Katherine Marie Birmingham. "The Navajos at the Bosque Redondo: Cooperation, Resistance, and Initiative, 1864–1868." *New Mexico Historical Review* 60, no. 4 (October 1985): 399–413.

Park, Joseph F. "The Apaches in Mexican-American Relations, 1848–1861: A Footnote to the Gadsden Treaty." *Arizona and the West* 3, no. 2 (Summer 1961): 129–146.

Perdue, Theda. "The Legacy of Indian Removal." *Journal of Southern History* 78, no. 1 (February 2012): 3–36.

Perrine, Fred S. "Uncle Sam's Camel Corps." *New Mexico Historical Review* 1, no. 4 (October 1926): 434–444.

Phillips, George Harwood. *Bringing Them Under Subjection: California's Tejón Reservation and Beyond, 1852–1864*. Lincoln: University of Nebraska Press, 2004.

Pittman, Walter. *Rebels in the Rockies: Confederate Irregulars in the Western Territories*. Jefferson, N.C.: McFarland and Co., 2014.

Prucha, Frances Paul. *American Indian Treaties: A History of a Political Anomaly*. Berkeley: University of California Press, 1994.

———. "Indian Removal and the Great American Desert." *Indiana Magazine of History* 59, no. 4 (December 1963): 299–322.

Rebert, Paula. "A Civilian Surveyor in the United States–Mexico Boundary: The Case of Arthur Schott." *Proceedings of the American Philosophical Society* 155, no. 4 (December 2011): 433–462.

Reger, Gary. "Making the Desert American." *Cultural History* 2, no. 2 (2013): 165–181.

Remley, David. *Kit Carson: The Life of an American Border Man*. Norman: University of Oklahoma Press, 2011.

Reséndez, Andrés. *The Other Slavery: The Uncovered Story of Indian Enslavement in America*. Boston: Houghton Mifflin, 2016.

Richardson, Heather Cox. *West from Appomattox: The Reconstruction of America after the Civil War*. New Haven, Conn.: Yale University Press, 2007.

Rickard, T.A. *A History of American Mining*. New York: McGraw-Hill, 1932.

Rippy, J. Fred. "Mexican Projects of the Confederates." *Southwestern Historical Quarterly* 22, no. 4 (April 1919): 291–317.

Roberts, Gary L. "Condition of the Tribes—1865: The McCook Report: A Military View." *Montana: Magazine of Western History* 24, no. 1 (Winter 1974): 14–25.

Roberts, Virginia Culin. "Heroines on the Arizona Frontier: The First Anglo-American Women." *Journal of Arizona History* 23, no. 1 (Spring 1982): 11–34.

Robinson, John W. *Los Angeles in Civil War Days, 1860–1865*. Norman: University of Oklahoma Press, 1977.

Roessel, Ruth. *Women in Navajo Society*. Rough Rock, Ariz.: Navajo Resource Center, 1981.

Romero de Terreros, Juan M. "The Destruction of the San Sabá Apache Mission: A Discussion of the Casualties." *The Americas* 60, no. 4 (April 2004): 617–627.

Rubin, Anne Sarah. " 'Seventy-Six and Sixty-One': Confederates Remember the American Revolution." In *Where These Memories Grow: History, Memory, and Southern Identity*, ed. W. Fitzhugh Brundage, pp. 85–106. Chapel Hill: University of North Carolina Press, 2000.

Sabin, Edwin Legrand. *Kit Carson Days: Adventures in the Path of Empire*. New York: The Press of the Pioneers, 1935.

Sandweiss, Martha A. "Still Picture, Moving Stories: Reconstruction Comes to Indian Country." In *Civil War Wests: Testing the Limits of the United States*, ed. Adam Arenson and Andrew R. Graybill, pp. 158–180. Berkeley: University of California Press, 2015.

Scalet, Charles G., Lester D. Flake, and David W. Willis. *Introduction to Wildlife and Fisheries: An Integrated Approach*. Second edition. New York: W.H. Freeman, 2008.

Scharff, Virginia, ed. *Empire and Liberty: The Civil War and the West*. Oakland: University of California Press, 2015, pp. 1–8.

Schulten, Susan. "The Civil War and the Origins of Colorado Territory." *Western Historical Quarterly* 44, no. 1 (Spring 2013): 21–46.

———. *The Geographical Imagination in America, 1880–1950*. Chicago: University of Chicago Press, 2001.

———. *Mapping the Nation: History and Cartography in Nineteenth-Century America*. Chicago: University of Chicago Press, 2012.

Schultz, Jane E. *Women at the Front: Hospital Workers in Civil War America*. Chapel Hill: University of North Carolina Press, 2004.

Schwarz, Maureen Trudelle. *Molded in the Image of Changing Woman: Navajo Views on the Human Body and Personhood*. Tucson: University of Arizona Press, 1997.

Shaw, Duane. *Civil War West*. Bloomington, Ind.: Authorhouse, 2011.

Sides, Hampton. *Blood and Thunder: The Epic Story of Kit Carson and the Conquest of the American West*. New York: Random House, 2006.

Silver, Timothy and Judkin Browning. *The Civil War: An Environmental History*. Chapel Hill: University of North Carolina Press, forthcoming 2020.

Smith, Duane A. *The Trail of Gold and Silver: Mining in Colorado, 1859–2009*. Boulder: University Press of Colorado, 2011.

Smith, Ralph A. "The Scalp Hunter in the Borderlands 1835–1850." *Arizona and the West* 6, no. 1 (Spring 1964): 5–22.

Smith, Stacey L. "Beyond North and South: Putting the West in the Civil War and Reconstruction." *Journal of the Civil War Era* 6, no. 4 (December 2016): 566–591.

Smith, Thomas T. "U.S. Army Combat Operations in the Indian Wars of Texas, 1849–1881." *Southwestern Historical Quarterly* 99, no. 4 (April 1996): 501–531.

Spencer, Emma Dill Russell. *Green Russell and Gold.* Austin: University of Texas Press, 1966.

Stark, Peter. *Last Breath: The Limits of Adventure.* New York: Penguin Books, 2002.

Sternhell, Yael A. *Routes of War: The World of Movement in the Confederate South.* Cambridge, Mass.: Harvard University Press, 2012.

Stoddard, William O. *Inside the White House in War Times.* New York: Charles L. Webster & Co., 1890.

Storey, Margaret M. "A Conquest of Manners: Gender, Sociability, and Northern Wives' Occupation of Memphis, 1862–1865." *Ohio Valley History* 15, no. 1 (Spring 2015): 4–20.

Sutherland, Daniel E. *A Savage Conflict: The Decisive Role of Guerrillas in the American Civil War.* Chapel Hill: University of North Carolina Press, 2009.

Sweeney, Edwin R. *Cochise: Chiricahua Apache Chief.* Norman: University of Oklahoma Press, 1991.

_____. *Mangas Coloradas: Chief of the Chiricahua Apaches.* Norman: University of Oklahoma Press, 1998.

_____. "Mangas Coloradas and Apache Diplomacy: Treaty-Making with Chihuahua and Sonora, 1842–43." *Journal of Arizona History* 39, no. 1 (Spring 1998): 1–22.

_____. " 'One of Heaven's Heroes': A Mexican General Pays Tribute to the Honor of a Chiricahua Apache." *Journal of Arizona History* 36, no. 3 (Autumn 1995): 209–232.

Taylor, John. *Bloody Valverde: A Civil War Battle on the Rio Grande, February 21, 1862.* Albuquerque: University of New Mexico Press, 1995.

Tegeder, Vincent G. "Lincoln and the Territorial Patronage: The Ascendancy of the Radicals in the West." In *Lincoln Looks West: From the Mississippi to the Pacific,* ed. Richard W. Etulain, pp. 121–133. Carbondale: Southern Illinois University Press, 2010.

Thompson, Jerry D. *A Civil War History of the New Mexico Volunteers and Militia.* Albuquerque: University of New Mexico Press, 2015.

_____. *Colonel John Robert Baylor: Texas Indian Fighter and Confederate Soldier.* Hillsboro, Tex.: Hill Junior College, 1971.

_____. *Desert Tiger: Captain Paddy Graydon and the Civil War in the Fur Southwest.* El Paso: Texas Western Press, 1992.

_____. *Henry Hopkins Sibley: Confederate General of the West.* College Station: Texas A&M University Press, 1996.

_____. "The Vulture over the Carrion: Captain James 'Paddy' Graydon and the Civil War in the Territory of New Mexico." *Journal of Arizona History* 24, no. 4 (Winter 1983): 381–404.

Thrapp, Dan L. *The Conquest of Apacheria.* Norman: University of Oklahoma Press, 1967.

Tilden, M.H., comp. *History of Stephenson County, Illinois.* Chicago: Western Historical Company, 1880.

Tohe, Laura. "Hwéeldi Bééháániih: Remembering the Long Walk." *Wicazo Sa Review* 22, no. 1 (Spring 2007): 77–82.

Trafzer, Clifford E. *The Kit Carson Campaign: The Last Great Navajo War.* Norman: University of Oklahoma Press, 1982.

Truett, Samuel. *Fugitive Landscapes: The Forgotten History of the U.S.-Mexico Borderlands.* New Haven, Conn.: Yale University Press, 2008.

_____. "The Ghosts of Frontiers Past: Making and Unmaking Space in the Borderlands." *Journal of the Southwest* 46, no. 2 (Summer 2004): 309–350.

Tweedie, M. Jean. "Notes on the History and Adaptation of the Apache Tribes." *American Anthropologist* 70, no. 6 (December 1968): 1132–1142.

Tyler, Barbara Ann. "Cochise: Apache War Leader, 1858–1861." *Journal of Arizona History* 6, no. 1 (Spring 1965): 1–10.

Tyler, Ron. "Illustrated Government Publications Related to the American West, 1843–1863." In *Surveying the Record: North American Scientific Exploration to 1930*, ed. Edward C. Carter II, pp. 147–172. Philadelphia: American Philosophical Society, 1999.

Utley, Robert M. *Frontiersmen in Blue: The United States Army and the Indian, 1848–1865*. Lincoln: University of Nebraska Press, 1967.

_____. *Geronimo*. New Haven, Conn.: Yale University Press, 2012.

_____. "The Past and Future of Old Fort Bowie." *Arizoniana* 5, no. 4 (Winter 1964): 55–60.

Veregge, Nina. "Transformations of Spanish Urban Landscapes in the American Southwest, 1821–1900." *Journal of the Southwest* 35, no. 4 (Winter 1993): 371–459.

Vrtis, George. "A World of Mines and Mills: Precious-Metals Mining, Industrialization, and the Nature of the Colorado Front Range." In *Mining North America: An Environmental History since 1522*, ed. J.R. McNeill and George Vrtis, pp. 73–107. Berkeley: University of California Press, 2017.

Waite, Kevin. "Jefferson Davis and Proslavery Visions of Empire in the Far West." *Journal of the Civil War Era* 6, no. 4 (December 2016): 536–565.

Wallace, Andrew. "John W. Swilling." *Arizoniana* 2, no. 1 (Spring 1961): 16–19.

Waugh, Joan. *U.S. Grant: American Hero, American Myth*. Chapel Hill: University of North Carolina Press, 2009.

Welch, John R., and Ramon Riley. "Reclaiming Land and Spirit in the Western Apache Homeland." *American Indian Quarterly* 25, no. 1 (Winter 2001): 5–12.

West, Elliott. *The Contested Plains: Indians, Goldseekers, and the Rush to Colorado*. Lawrence: University Press of Kansas, 1998.

_____. *The Last Indian War: The Nez Perce Story*. New York: Oxford University Press, 2009.

Whites, LeeAnn and Alecia P. Long, eds. *Occupied Women: Gender, Military Occupation, and the American Civil War*. Baton Rouge: Louisiana State University Press, 2009.

Whitford, William Clarke. *Colorado Volunteers in the Civil War: The New Mexico Campaign in 1862*. Denver, Colo.: The State Historical and Natural History Society, 1906.

Whitlock, Flint. *Distant Bugles, Distant Drums: The Union Response to the Confederate Invasion of New Mexico*. Boulder: University Press of Colorado, 2006.

Wiley, Richard R. "Fallen Anvils: The Tucson Meteorite." *Archaeology in Tucson Newsletter* 12, no. 3 (Summer 1998): 5.

Wilkins, David E. *The Navajo Political Experience*. Revised Edition. New York: Rowman and Littlefield, 2003.

Wilson, Chris. *The Myth of Santa Fe: Creating a Modern Regional Tradition*. Albuquerque: University of New Mexico Press, 1997.

Woodward, Arthur. "Side Lights on Fifty Years of Apache Warfare, 1836–1886." *Arizoniana* 2, no. 3 (Fall 1961): 3–14.

Worcester, Donald E. "Early Spanish Accounts of the Apache Indians." *American Anthropologist* 43, no. 2, Part 1 (April-June 1941): 308–312.

Wyatt, Robert N. "Victorio's Military and Political Leadership of the Warm Springs Apache." *War in History* 18, no. 4 (November 2011): 457–494.

Zolbrod, Paul G. *Diné Behané: The Navajo Creation Story*. Albuquerque: University of New Mexico Press, 1984.

Index

Adobe Walls, Battle of (1864), 204, 248

Ake party, 22–23

Alamo, Texas, 33–34

Albuquerque, New Mexico Territory
  Canby's departure from Fort Craig on march to, 114, 115
  Canby's reluctance to attack because of resident women and children, 115
  Confederates' arrival at, after Valverde battle, 99
  defensive burning of supplies in, 99
  Sibley Brigade's retreat to, from Santa Fe, 114, 115
  Sibley's base in, before and after occupation of Santa Fe, 99, 114, 118
  Union departure from and Texan occupation of, 93
  Union loss at Valverde and Canby's warning to, 74

Apache Canyon, Battle of (1862)
  Davidson's company in, 103–6
  Sibley's dispatches received on, 114

Apache Pass
  Californians' control over, 148
  Cochise's capture, 20–22
  Eyre's reconnaissance mission's meeting with Cochise at, 137–38
  killing of Carleton's emissaries Wheeling and Chavez at, 136–37, 167
  Mangas Coloradas and, 140–42, 165, 169

Apachería (Chiricahuas homeland)
  Americans' decision to colonize with forts in, 19, 20
  attacks on American travelers through, 134–35
  Butterfield overland mail route through, 16–17

Carleton's war campaign strategy for, 167

Chiricahuas; defense of, against Americans, 143

first appearance of U.S. soldiers on edge of, 17

Geronimo's claiming of, 252

Mangas Coloradas's desire for peace negotiations to protect, 169

Mexican attacks on, 17–18

mining in, 20, 139

size of territory of, 16

Union soldiers' presence in, during absence of Mangas Coloradas, 166

Apaches. See also Chiricahua Apaches; Mescalero Apaches
  attacks on Mexican settlements by, 84, 85, 165
  enslavement of, in New Mexico Territory, 92
  raids on Sibley Brigade by, 38–39, 121

Apache Spring, New Mexico Territory
  American preparations to build a fort near, 166
  Chiricahuas' loss of control (1862) over, 143
  Cochise's shooting of men in Eyre's reconnaissance mission near, 137–38, 144
  Cut the Tent incident (1861) with Bascom and Mangas Coloradas at, 21–22, 139, 168, 169
  Mangas Coloradas's ambush of Carleton's emissary Roberts and soldiers at, 140–43

Arizona Guards, 23, 24, 139–40

Arizona Rangers
  Baylor's formation of, 82

315

Arizona Rangers (*cont.*)
   Hunter's command of, 82, 88
   Hunter's occupation of Tucson with, 127
   march to Arizona by, 82, 83, 85
Arizona, Confederate Territory of
   Arizona Rangers' march to 82, 83, 85
   Baylor as governor of, 12, 83, 85, 87,
      88–89
   Baylor's campaign against Chiricahua
      Apaches in, 14, 80, 81–82
   Baylor's creation and 2nd Texas's seizure
      of, 11–12, 13, 24–25
   Baylor's departure from, 89
   Confederate soldiers' desire to return to
      Texas from, 120
   Davis's proclamation recognizing,
      82–83
   Sibley's military command over, 40
   Sibley's planned defense of, 116
   Sibley's retreat from and return to
      Texas, 122, 124
Arizona, Union Territory of
   Carleton as military governor of, 133
   Carleton's arrival in, 128–34, 148
   Carleton's plans to retake, 124, 126
   Chiricahua Apaches' control of, 24–25
   Civil War and large number of soldiers
      in, 175
   Clark's expeditions for gold in, 179–82
   secessionist sentiment in, 131
   Union Army control over, for
      settlement, 178
   Walker's gold discovery in, 178–82
Armijo, Rafaél and Manuel, 99, 118, 152
A'ts'ina ("Place of Writing on the Rock"),
   215
Audubon, John James, 132

Barboncito, 222, 233–34, 235, 236–38, 239,
   241–43
Bartlett, John Russell, 18–19, 132
Bascom, George, 21–22, 73, 137
Baylor, Emy, 5, 79, 80, 81, 86, 88, 89, 249
Baylor, Fanny, 5, 13, 86, 87
Baylor, George, 81, 85
Baylor, John R., xix, xx, 5–14, 79–89, 249
   Arizona Territory creation and
      occupation by, 11–12, 13, 25
   background of, 5–6
   campaign against Chiricahua Apaches
      by, 14, 80, 81–82, 87–89

campaign for California and, 79–80,
   82, 85
Comanche camp attacked by, 81
Comanche raids on ranch of, 81
criticism of leadership of, 85
departure from Arizona Territory by, 89
early Confederate Army service in
   Texas by, 5–6, 37
extermination order to murder
   Chiricahua Apaches in Mexico by,
   88–89, 120–21
as first Confederate to lead a successful
   invasion of Union territory, 7
Fort Fillmore planned attack of, 6, 8–9
as governor of Confederate Territory of
   Arizona, 83, 85, 87, 88–89
Hunter's capture of McCleave and, 128
Hunter's occupation of Tucson and, 127
Indian agent appointment of, 80
Kelley's dispute with and assault by,
   85–86
letter of resignation to Sibley from, 89,
   120–21
Lynde's surrender to, 10, 154
Mangas Coloradas and the
   extermination order issued by, 139,
   140
Mangas Coloradas's desire for treaty
   negotiations with, 88–89
Mangas Coloradas's proposed meeting
   with Arizona Guards and, 139
Mesilla, New Mexico Territory,
   occupation and battle of, 7–8,
   11–12, 13, 82, 124
need for reinforcements by, 13–14
news of Valverde battle victory and, 79
plan to move family to Arizona, 86–87
praise for successes of, 12–13
raid on Corralitos, in Chihuahua,
   Mexico, by, 87–88, 120–21
San Augustin Springs defeat of Union
   soldiers by, 9–11, 82
Sibley Brigade's absorption of troops of,
   39–40, 79
Sibley's apology for raid into Mexico by,
   120–21
Sibley's command supported by, 33, 35,
   39–40
Texas Rangers' raid against Comanches
   and, 80
Union prisoners freed by, 11

West Texas ranching by, 80–81, 89
Bedonkohe Apaches, 15, 138, 168–69, 170, 174
Benedict, A. C., 181, 182
Benjamin, Judah, 12–13
Bosque Redondo reservation, New Mexico Territory, 177
    agricultural produce from, 200–2
    breakout of runaways from, 209
    Carleton's policy on, 188, 192, 198, 201–3, 205–13, 232
    Doolittle Commission's review of, 210–13, 215, 227, 234
    Juanita and Manuelito's escape from, 222–23
    Juanita and Manuelito's life at, 218–22
    Juanita and Manuelito's removal to, 216–18
    Mescalero Apaches and, 157, 200, 201, 204, 218
    Navajos and, 188, 192, 195, 196, 197–99, 201–3, 205, 205–12
    newspaper editorials on, 205
    problems with, 200–2
    vision and selection of site for, 202–3
Breckinridge, John C., xvi, 7
Brigands, 99, 100, 103
Bristol, Henry, 200, 201–2
Buchanan, James, 27, 29

California
    admission to Union as free state, xiv
    Baylor's planned campaign against, 79–80, 82
    Confederate plans to reach, xv–xvi, 12, 79–80, 84
    New Mexico Territory as gateway to, xiv
    secessionist sentiment in, xv, 82
California Column. See 1st California Volunteers
California Volunteers. See 1st California Volunteers
Canby, Edward Richard Sprigg, 144–51
    assignment of soldiers to various locations as defense, 146–47
    Carleton's letter about Tucson occupation sent to, 133
    Carleton's pursuit of Sibley Brigade and, 148–49
    Clark's concerns about military leadership of, 95
Clark's return to Santa Fe and, 147
clashes between Navajos and Fort Defiance soldiers and, 46
Confederate retreat from Santa Fe to Mesilla avoiding confrontation with, 116, 118, 146
defense of New Mexico Territory by, 31, 32, 97–98
departure from Santa Fe by, 150–51
dispatches from Carleton in Tucson to, 133, 134–35, 136
Eyre's dispatch from Fort Thorn to, 144
federal control of the West's lands and, 148
federal troops amassing near base of Sandia Mountains with, 115
Fort Craig encampment of, 116
Fort Defiance renamed in honor of, 187
hidden supply of blankets promised to Navajos and, 113, 146
Ickis and Dodd's Independents' move to join, 55–56, 58
July 4 celebration at Santa Fe with, 144–45
march to Albuquerque after leaving Fort Craig by, 114, 115
military background and marriage of, 25, 26–30
move to New Mexico Territory by, 29–30
Navajo campaign of, 30, 191
New Mexico Territory controlled by, 148
orders to Carson to come to Fort Craig, 57
position of soldiers of, after Valverde loss, 74
promotion as military advisor to Stanton, 149, 150
return from Fort Craig by, 146
Sibley's desire to avoid battles with, 122
Sibley's plan for fighting, 61
training of militias under, 58
treaty negotiations with Manuelito, 113
Tséyi' campaign (1861) and, 46
Union-Confederate meeting without battle outside Fort Craig and, 59, 60–61
Union soldiers' abandonment of Santa Fe and move to Fort Union and, 95, 96

Canby, Edward Richard Sprigg (*cont.*)
    Utah Expedition and, 27–29
    Valverde battle loss and, 62, 63, 64–65,
        68–69, 71, 72, 91, 92, 95, 147
    warning to Santa Fe and Albuquerque
        after Valverde loss, 74
    wife Louisa's decision to stay in Santa Fe
        and, 93, 100, 114
Canby, Louisa Hawkins, xiv, xx, 24–32,
        144–51, 250
    Clark's friendship with, 91, 93, 147, 150,
        151
    concerns about impending threats to
        New Mexico Territory and, 31–32
    Confederate occupation of Santa Fe
        and, 100–2
    decision to stay in Santa Fe before
        Texans' march on, 93, 99–100
    departure from Santa Fe by, 151
    frontier nursing experience of, 102
    Glorieta Pass battle wounded and, 111,
        112–13
    hidden supply of blankets for Navajos
        and, 113, 146
    husband's promotion to Washington,
        D.C., and, 149, 150
    impact of Civil War on, 30–31
    July 4 celebration at Santa Fe with,
        144–45
    military life background and marriage
        of, 25–29
    nursing of Confederate wounded by,
        113, 114, 145–46, 149–50
    organizing women to prepare supplies
        for nursing wounded soldiers by,
        102–3
    Santa Fe life and, 29–32, 91, 148, 149
    Sibley and, 61, 113, 146
    Sibley Brigade's taking of ambulance
        wagons of, 114
    Utah Expedition and, 27–29
    waiting for husband's return to Santa
        Fe, 100, 114
Canby, Mary, xiv, 26, 27, 29, 91
Canyon de Chelly, Battle of. *See* Tséyi'
    (Canyon de Chelly) Battle of
Carey, Asa B., 195, 197–98
Carleton, James, xv-xvi, xx, 124–35,
        200–13, 249
    Apache Spring ambush of emissary
        Roberts and soldiers and, 140–43

    as Arizona Territory military governor,
        133
    arrival and encampment in Tucson by,
        131–35
    arrival in Arizona Territory by, 128–30
    Audubon's meeting with, 132
    Bosque Redondo reservation policy for
        Navajos and, 188, 192, 198, 201–3,
        205–13, 232
    Canby's departure from Santa Fe and,
        150, 151
    Carson's Navajo campaign and, 187–88,
        190, 195
    Carson's pursuit of Jicarilla Apaches
        and, 155
    Carson's request for leave denied by,
        190, 191
    Chiricahua Apache campaign of,
        171–72
    Clark's gold expeditions and, 179, 181,
        182, 183
    Cochise's killing of emissaries Wheeling
        and Chavez sent to Canby by,
        136–37
    Cochise's knowledge of Tucson position
        of, 137–38
    confiscation of meteorite by, 132–33
    dispatches to Canby from, 133, 134–35,
        136
    Dodd's Independents' punishment by,
        157, 159–60
    Doolittle Commission's review of
        Bosque Redondo and, 210–13
    Eyre's reconnaissance mission for, 135,
        137–38
    Fort Bliss retaken by, 148
    Fort Stanton rebuilding by, 154–55
    Fort Wingate establishment by, 153–54
    Fort Yuma encampment of, 124
    Mangas Coloradas's message to, 166–67
    march across desert from Los Angeles
        to Tucson by, 124–31
    Mescalero Apache campaign of, 155,
        167, 171, 172
    Mescalero Apache defeat and, 156–57
    military background of, 124–25
    Navajo campaigns of, 155, 183, 187–88,
        190, 195, 200–1, 205
    as New Mexico Territory commander,
        149, 150
    newspaper editorials on, 205

Picacho Peak battle casualties and, 127–28
planned march on Tucson by, 128, 129
refusal of peace negotiations with Mangas Coloradas, 167
Sibley Brigade pursuit by, 148–49
strategy of staggering troops by, 126, 128, 130
supply trains organized and stocked by, 125
survey of arable land by, 177
three-step method for dealing with "Indian problem" used by, 188
Union Indian Policy and, 156
vigorous warfare strategy of, 187–88
winter campaign strategy of, 190–91, 199
Carson, Kit, xvi, xx, 248
Battle of Adobe Walls and, 204
Carleton and pursuit of Jicarilla Apaches by, 155
Carleton's denial of request for leave by, 190, 191
fame and reputation of, 57–58
Fort Craig encampment of, 57, 116, 146
Fort Stanton assignment of, 154–55
Hispano soldiers under, 32, 58, 71
Ickis's excitement at joining, 58
Mescalero Apache campaign by, 154–57
Navajo campaign of, 183–84, 186–88, 190–92
Navajo surrenders during Tséyi' campaign, 192, 195–96
training of militias under, 58
Tséyi' campaign and, 190, 191–92, 195
Union-Confederate meeting without battle outside Fort Craig and, 60
Union troops in Albuquerque under, 32, 36
Valverde battle and, 62, 63, 64–65, 68–69, 71, 74
vigorous warfare strategy and, 188
Zuñi allies of, 186
Cayetanito, 207
Chaves, José Francisco, 227
Chaves, Manuel Antonio, 108, 109
Chávez (guide), 135, 136–37, 167
Chihenne Apaches, 15, 138, 168, 170
Chiricahua Apaches
ambush of Carleton's emissary Roberts and soldiers by, 140–43
Arizona Guards' attack on, 23

Arizona Territory held by, 24–25
attacks on travelers by, 134
Bartlett's surveying party and, 18–19
Baylor's campaign against, 14, 80, 81–82, 87–89
Baylor's extermination order against, 88–89, 120–21
Carleton's campaign against, 171–72, 174
Carleton's emissaries Wheeling and Chávez caught and killed by, 136–37, 167, 172
Cut the Tent incident (1861) and, 20–22
Eyre's reconnaissance mission for Carleton and, 137–38, 144
Hunter's farm along Mimbres River raided by, 82
Janos, Mexico, visit for medical care by, 165–66
Kearny's passage through lands of, xvii, 17, 18
Mangas Coloradas's death and beheading and, 174–75
Mexican raids by, 17–18, 19, 139
mining camp raids by, 14, 20, 167
mountain camp life of, 16
Pinos Altos mining town attack by, 20, 23, 24, 88
size of homeland of, 16, 17
Sumner's treaty and jurisdiction of, 19–20
Union Army campaign against, 175, 176, 178
U.S. forts built in lands of, 19, 20
U.S. treaty negotiations with, 17–18, 44
U.S. treaty with Mexico and protection against raids by, 18, 19
wagon train raids by, 14, 18, 22–23, 167, 172, 180
war dance with Mangas Coloradas and Cochise, 15–16
war of revenge for Mangas Coloradas's death and, 175, 180
Chivington, John, 108, 109, 210
Civil War See also Confederacy; Union
California Column's desire to fight in, 135
Confederate view about long marches as epic achievements in, 118
disease in camps during, 59
importance of controlling New Mexico Territory during, xv

Civil War (*cont.*)
   large number of soldiers in New Mexico
      and Arizona during, 175
   need to retain control of the West in
      order to win, xiv
   New Mexico Territory affected by, 30–31
   New Mexico Territory land sales to
      support Union effort in, 90
   news reaching New Mexico Territory
      about progress of, 30–31, 51, 52, 94,
      119, 182, 204–5, 208
   work of civilian women during, 146
Clark, John, xviii, xx, 90–98, 176–84,
     224–31, 250
   arrival in Santa Fe, 31
   background in surveying and real estate
      of, 92
   Canby's military leadership questioned
      by, 95
   Carson's fame and, 57–58
   Carson's Navajo campaign and, 183, 184
   Chiricahua Apache campaign and, 176
   Colorado Volunteers' arrival at Fort
      Union and, 96
   concerns about impending war threats
      to Santa Fe and, 90–91, 92
   Confederate occupiers of Santa Fe in
      former office of, 101
   decision to leave New Mexico Territory
      until end of Civil War, 96–97
   departure from Santa Fe before Texans'
      march on, 93–94
   federal control of the West's lands and,
      148
   gold country expeditions of, 179–84
   Louisa Canby's friendship with, 91, 93,
      147, 150, 151
   news about Valverde loss and, 91–92
   opinion of Hispano soldiers held by,
      95–96
   reasons for Lincoln's appointment to
      New Mexico Territory of, 92–93
   return to Santa Fe by, 147
   séance attendance by, 91
   surveys of arable land and mineral
      resources by, 176–78
   as surveyor general of New Mexico
      Territory, xviii, 31, 90, 92, 93, 101,
      179, 227, 229
   Texans' plan to march on Santa Fe and,
      93
   trip to Washington, D.C., to meet with
      Edmunds and Lincoln by, 97–98,
      147
   Union soldiers' abandonment of Santa
      Fe and move to Fort Union by,
      94–95
   Valverde battle notes of, 225
Clever, Charles, 224, 227, 229
Cochise
   Ake party attack by, 22–23
   alliance between Mangas Coloradas
      and, 16, 20
   ambush of Carleton's emissary Roberts
      and soldiers by, 140–43
   Arizona Guards' attack on, 23
   Carleton's emissaries Wheeling and
      Chávez caught and killed by,
      136–37, 167
   Cut the Tent incident (1861) and, 20–22
   Eyre's reconnaissance mission for
      Carleton and, 137–38, 144
   Pinos Altos mining town attack by, 23,
      24, 139
   request to Mangas Coloradas for
      assistance against Carleton, 138, 140
   war dance with Mangas Coloradas,
      15–16
Colorado Territory
   gold discovery and mines in, xvi, 50,
      159
   recruitment of soldiers in, 51
Colorado Volunteers. *See* 1st Colorado
     Volunteers
Comanches
   Adobe Walls battle and, 204, 248
   Apache slaves and, 88
   attacks on Mexican settlements by, 84
   attacks on Navajo at Bosque Redondo
      by, 218, 236
   Baylor party's attack on camp of, 81
   Baylor's appointment as Indian agent
      for, 80, 81
   Baylor's ranch raided by, 81
   Clear Fork reservation of, 80
   Confederate military attacks on, 84
   1st New Mexico attacks on, 248
   rebel yell used during wars with, 62
   Texas Rangers' attack on, 80
   towns and wagon trains attacked by,
      202, 203
   Union army attacks on, 223

Confederacy
  areas of the South under Union control
    in 1862, as threat to, 119–20
  Arizona Territory creation and
    occupation of, 11–12, 13
  camp slave escapes and, 40–41
  conflict in New Mexico as "three-
    cornered war" involving, xx
  Davis's proclamation recognizing
    Arizona as a Confederate Territory
    in, 82–83
  Hispanos' fluctuating loyalties to, 121
  long marches seen as epic achievements
    of Civil War in, 118
  New Mexico Territory's importance
    to, 40
  plans to reach California by, xv–xvi, 12
  Reily's mission to Mexico seeking
    recognition for, 83–85
  Sibley Brigade march through Texas to
    New Mexico as longest march in, 41
  Union occupation of Nashville and, 112
  Union states and territories
    surrounding on all sides, 123
  U.S. Army officers resigning
    commissions to join, 30
Confederate soldiers
  Apache Canyon battle and, 103–6
  Glorieta Pass battle and, 106–13
  Louisa Canby's nursing of wounded
    among, 102–3, 113, 114, 145–46,
    149–50
  Peralta skirmish and, 115–16
  possible Union threat to Texas and, 120
  retreat from Santa Fe along Coopwood's
    Trail to Mesilla by, 116–18, 119, 120
  Shiloh battle and, 119
  Valverde battle and, xx, 62–74, 147
Confederate War Department
  Baylor's desire for more troops and, 88
  Baylor's Mesilla battle victory praised
    in, 12
  Sibley on meeting Union soldiers
    without battle outside Fort Craig
    and, 61
  Sibley's campaign for New Mexico and,
    34, 121–22
  Sibley's forwarding of Baylor's Apache
    extermination letter to, 121
Confiscation Act (1861), 132–33
Connelly, Henry, 94, 95, 96, 224

July 4 celebration at Santa Fe with,
    144–45
  letter to Santa Fe about Valverde loss, 91
Coopwood, Bethel, 116, 118
Corralitos, Chihuahua, Mexico, Baylor's
    raid on, 87–88, 120–21
Coyuntera, 21, 22
Cut the Tent incident (1861), with Bascom,
    21–22, 139, 168, 169

Dakota Sioux, 155
Davidson, William Lott "Bill," xix, xx,
    33–41, 249
  Apache Canyon battle and, 103–6
  Camp Manassas, Texas, waiting period
    of, 33–34, 35
  Fort Bliss, Texas, conditions and, 39–41
  Glorieta Pass battle wounding of,
    106–7, 109, 110, 112, 114
  hidden supply of blankets for Navajos
    and, 113
  Louisa Canby's nursing of wounded
    and, 112, 113
  march from Santa Fe along Santa Fe
    Trail toward Fort Union by, 101–2,
    103
  march through Texas to New Mexico
    by, 35–39, 41
  military background of, 33
  Peralta skirmish and, 115
  possible Union threat to Texas and, 120
  raids into Mexico for supplies and
    retaliatory Mexican raids on, 122–23
  rebel yell used by company of, 62
  retreat from Fort Bliss to Fort Quitman
    by, 123
  retreat from Santa Fe to Mesilla by,
    116–17, 118, 119, 120
  retreat to Albuquerque as wagon
    master, 114
  retreat to Fort Bliss by, 122–23
  Santa Fe occupation by, 100, 101
  Sibley Brigade enthusiasm of, 35
  Union-Confederate meeting without
    battle outside Fort Craig and, 59–60,
    61
  Valverde battle and, 62, 63, 64, 68,
    69–72
Davis, Jefferson, xviii, xix, 34, 35, 212
  allegiance of Native groups sought by, 121
  Baylor's appeal to, 89

Davis, Jefferson (*cont.*)
  Baylor's creation of Arizona Territory
    and, 12
  European and Mexican support sought
    by, 83–84
  proclamation recognizing Arizona as a
    Confederate Territory and, 82–83
  proposed Mexican alliance and, 84
Denver, Colorado Territory
  Canby's recruitment of miners from, 51
  Colorado Volunteers' departure for Fort
    Union from, 96
  fight between northerners and
    southerners for control of, xvi
  gold strikes in gullies west of, 50
  Sibley Brigade's plan to take, 114
Diné. *See* Navajos
Diné Bikéyah (Navajo homeland)
  clashes between Fort Defiance soldiers
    and Navajos in, 45–46, 47
  daily life in, 42–43
  Manuelito's leadership and, 45
  narrating Diné history during winter
    gatherings and, 48–49
  U.S. treaty negotiations and, 44–45,
    46–47
  women's weaving in, 47–48
Dodd, Theodore, 52, 55, 153, 157
  as Navajo Indian agent, 232–35
  Valverde battle and, 66–67
Dodd's Independents
  Camp Carson at Fort Craig
    encampment by, 58
  disagreement between Wallen and,
    157–58
  federal troops amassing near base of
    Sandia Mountains with, 115
  1st Colorado on reputation of, 158
  Fort Garland training period and, 50,
    52–53, 55
  Ickis's volunteering for, 51–53
  march to Santa Fe by, 53–55
  miners recruited for, 50–51, 60, 159
  move to Fort Union by, 158–60
  move to join Canby and Union Army at
    Fort Craig, 55–56, 58
  Santa Fe assignment of, 152–53, 156,
    157–58
  Union-Confederate meeting without
    battle outside Fort Craig and, 59,
    60, 61

  Valverde battle and, 62, 63, 65–67, 69,
    70, 71, 73
Donaldson, James, 93, 94–95, 96, 100
Doniphan, Alexander, 44–45
Doolittle, James, 210, 212–13
Doolittle Commission, 210–11, 215, 227, 234
Douglas, Stephen, 7
Dziltanatal ("Mountain Holds Up Its Head
    Proudly"), 16, 18, 22–23

Edmunds, James, 97, 147, 176–77, 178, 180
Evans, John, 203–4, 224
Explorations (Bartlett), 132
Eyre, Edward, 135, 137–38, 140, 144

5th Texas Mounted Volunteers (5th Texas),
    33, 34, 36
  Santa Fe occupation by, 99, 101
  Valverde battle and, 64, 65, 67, 68
1st California Volunteers (1st California,
    "California Column")
  arrival in Arizona Territory by, 128,
    131, 148
  Canby's praise for, 151
  Carleton's confiscated meteorite
    planned as monument to, 133
  Carleton's training of, 124–25
  Clark's gold expeditions with, 179
  Eyre's reconnaissance mission and, 135
  Fort Yuma encampment of, 124
  Mangas Coloradas's death and, 174
  Mangas Coloradas's peace negotiations
    with Pinos Altos mining town and,
    167–68
  march across desert from Los Angeles
    to Tucson by, 124–31
  Picacho Peak battle casualties of,
    127–28
  recruitment of miners for, 125
  Swilling's betrayal and capture of
    Mangas Coloradas and, 171
  Tucson encampment of, 134–35
1st Colorado Volunteers (1st Colorado),
    234, 235
  Apache Canyon battle and, 104
  arrival at Fort Union and, 96
  Canby's recruitment of miners for, 51
  Dodd's Independents at Fort Union
    and, 158
  federal troops amassing near base of
    Sandia Mountains with, 115

Fort Union and, 96, 101, 153
Glorieta Pass battle and, 108, 109, 115
1st New Mexico Volunteers (1st New
  Mexico), xvi, 32
  Carson's Mescalero Apache campaign
    and, 154–57
  Carson's Navajo campaign and, 186–87
  Clark's concerns about military ability
    of, 95
  Fort Craig defense by, 116
  Fort Stanton assignment of, 154–55
  Fort Wingate establishment by, 153–54
  Glorieta Pass battle and, 108
  re-formation of, in Santa Fe, 153
  Valverde battle and, 62, 63, 65, 68, 71
Fort Bliss, Texas
  Carleton's retaking of, 148
  Davidson and Company A's retreat to,
    122–23
  Davidson and Sibley Brigade at, 40–41
Fort Burgwin, New Mexico Territory, 36
Fort Canby, Arizona Territory
  Fort Defiance's renaming to, 187
  Navajo campaign and, 189, 191
  Navajo surrenders during Tséyi'
    campaign living at, 195–96
  Tséyi' campaign preparations at, 191
Fort Craig, New Mexico Territory
  background and description of, 59
  Canby's establishment of Camp Carson
    at, 57
  Canby's march to Albuquerque after
    leaving, 114
  Carson and 1st New Mexico Volunteers'
    defense of, 116
  Carson's training of his militias at, 58
  Ickis and Dodd's Independents' arrival
    at, 58
  Ickis on life at, 58
  Sibley's plan to capture, 72
  Union-Confederate meeting without
    battle outside, 59–61
  Valverde and importance of protecting, 63
Fort Davis, Texas, 39, 148
Fort Defiance, New Mexico/Arizona Territory
  Carson's Navajo campaign and, 184, 187
  clashes between Navajos and soldiers
    from, 45–46, 47
  rebuilding of, 185
  renaming to Fort Canby of, 187
Fort Garland, New Mexico Territory

Carson's command of, 248
Ickis and Dodd's Independents at, 50,
  52–53
Fort Lyon, Colorado Territory, 160, 248
Fort Marcy, New Mexico Territory, 32, 55,
  112, 152
Fort McLane
  Chiricahua Apache campaign based at,
    171–72, 174
  Mangas Coloradas's imprisonment and
    shooting at, 172–73
Fort Quitman, Texas, 123
  Carleton's retaking of, 148, 149
  Davidson and Company A's retreat from
    Fort Bliss to, 39, 123
Fort Stanton, New Mexico Territory, 9
  Carson and 1st New Mexico's rebuilding
    of, 154–55
  Mescalero Apaches' attack on, 13, 154
Fort Thorn, New Mexico Territory, 59, 116,
  124, 144
Fort Union, New Mexico Territory, 196
  Clark's arrival at, 94
  Colorado Volunteers at, 96, 101, 153
  Confederate plans to lay siege to, 99
  Dodd's Independents' move to, 158–60
  Glorieta Pass battle's impact on
    Confederate plans for, 112
  Santa Fe occupation and Confederate
    preparations for march to, 101
  Santa Fe residents' wagon trains to,
    ahead of Texans' arrival in Santa Fe,
    93–94
  Sibley Brigade's plan to take, 114
  as temporary seat of New Mexico
    Territory's government, 94
  Union Army abandonment of Santa Fe
    and withdrawal to, 93, 99
Fort West, New Mexico Territory
  Clark's survey stop at, 178
  Union Army campaign against
    Chiricahua Apaches and, 176
Fort Wingate, New Mexico Territory,
  153–54, 180, 183, 185, 196
Fort Yuma, California
  Carleton and California Volunteers'
    encampment at, 124, 126–27
  Pimas' and Maricopas' agricultural
    support for, 82
4th Texas Mounted Volunteers (4th Texas),
  35, 65–66, 67, 71–72, 104–5

Fox, Margaret and Kate, 91
Frémont, John C., 52, 57

Gadsden Purchase (1854), 13, 131
Geronimo
    Mangas Coloradas's death and
        beheading and, 174–75
    Mangas Coloradas's peace negotiations
        with Pinos Altos mining town and,
        168–70
    as war leader of Bedonkohe Apaches, 168
Getty, George, 224, 233, 234, 235, 238,
    244–45
Glorieta Pass, Battle of (1862), New Mexico
    Territory, xx, 106–14
    Davidson's wounding in 106–7
    description of pass, 106
    field hospitals in, 107, 108, 111
    initial engagement with Texan advance
        guard in, 106
    Louisa Canby's nursing of wounded
        from, 111, 112–13
    Scurry's address to his men after, 111–12
    Sibley's dispatches received on, 114
    Union soldiers' rifling through and
        burning of Texans' wagons during,
        108–10, 114
gold miners, as soldiers, 50–51, 60, 125, 159
gold mining, 159, 168, 178–79
    Arizona Territory and, 130–31, 179–84
    Clark's expeditions for gold and, 179–84
    Confederacy and, 123
    Ickis's background in, 50–51
Gove, Jesse, 27
Grant, Ulysses S., 94, 149, 182, 195, 231, 250
Green, Tom, 36, 40–41, 62, 68, 69, 72
Guadalupe Hidalgo, Treaty of, 18, 84, 85

Herrera Grande, 198, 206, 207–8, 210, 214,
    222
Hispanos
    federal control of the West's lands and,
        148
    fluctuating loyalties of, 121
    Ickis's opinion of, in Santa Fe, 55
    Juanita and Manuelito attacked by,
        214–15
    land ownership disputes between
        United States and, 90
    Navajo raids by, 185, 196
    Sibley's lack of help from, 121

Hispano soldiers
    Carson's unit with, 32, 58, 71
    Clark's concerns about ability of, 95–96
    1st New Mexico re-formation with, 153
    Ickis's opinion of, 58
    Valverde battle and, 95
Homestead Act (1862), 97, 147, 176
Hopis, 185, 189, 215
Hunter, Sherod, 85, 132, 133
    Arizona Rangers command of, 82, 88
    Chiricahua Apaches' attack on farm
        of, 82
    groundwork for invasion of California
        and, 82
    McCleave's capture by, 127
    Pima and Maricopa chiefs and, 130
    Tucson capture and later abandonment
        by, 127, 129, 131, 132

Ickis, Alonzo, xvi, xx, 50–56, 152–60, 248
    Camp Carson at Fort Craig
        encampment by, 58
    Carson and his New Mexico Volunteers
        and, 58
    Colorado gold mining background of,
        50–51, 53
    disagreement between Wallen and
        Dodd's Independents and, 157–58
    Dodd's Independents and, 52–53
    Fort Garland training period and, 50,
        52–53
    march to Santa Fe by, 53–55
    move to Fort Lyon by, 160
    move to Fort Union by, 158–60
    move to join Canby and Union Army at
        Fort Craig, 55–56, 58
    opinion of Hispano soldiers held by, 58
    Santa Fe assignment of, 152, 153, 156,
        157–58
    Union-Confederate meeting without
        battle outside Fort Craig and, 59,
        60, 61
    Valverde battle and, 62, 63, 64, 65–67,
        70, 72–73
    visit to Fort Craig's dead room after
        Valverde battle and, 73–74
    volunteering for Colorado company by,
        51–52

Jackson, Andrew, 188
Janos, Mexico, 167

Geronimo's visit to, 169
Mangas Coloradas's medical care at,
    143, 165–66
Jicarilla Apaches, 155
Johnson, Andrew, 227, 228, 230, 231, 234,
    235
Johnston, Joseph, 97, 150
Jones, John W., 134–35, 136
Juanita, 214–23, 232–46
    Bosque Redondo escape by, 222–23
    Bosque Redondo life of, 218–22
    Bosque Redondo removal to, 216–18
    daily life for, 42, 43, 46, 47–48
    decision not to surrender and move to
        Bosque Redondo by, 196–98, 214
    Hispano raiders and, 214–15
    Manuelito's marriage to, 45
    moving for safety by, 214, 215
    narrating Diné history during winter
        gatherings and, 48–49
    return to Diné Bikéyah by, 245–46
    San Francisco Mountains home of, 185,
        186, 188, 189, 196–97
    surrender to U.S. Army by, 215
    weaving by, 47–48

Kearny, Stephen Watts, xvii, 17–18, 44, 191
Kelley, Robert P., 13, 85–86
Kiowas, 153, 159, 202, 203, 218, 236, 248

land claims
    disputes between United States and
        Hispano New Mexicans over, 90
    Homestead Act and, 97, 147, 148
Lang's Lancers, 34–35, 65, 66–67, 68
Lee, Robert E., 150, 156, 182
Lincoln, Abraham, 31, 228
    assassination of, 209, 227
    Clark's mission and, 92, 97–98, 147
    Confiscation Act and, 132–33
    control of the West and, xiv, xviii, 123, 177
    desire to hold West as Union territory
        and, 98
    European and Mexican support sought
        by, 83–84
    fall of Savannah and, 207
    Frémont relieved of command by, 52
    New Mexico's loyalty to, 7, 92–93, 209
    reelection to presidency (1864), 205
    reservation system and, 201, 203
    slavery in Arizona Territory and, 213

Lipan Apaches, 39
Long Walk, 196, 197, 198, 216, 236, 249–50
Loring, William, 30
Lynde, Isaac, 8, 10, 31, 95, 154

Mangas Coloradas, xvii, xx, 15–23, 45,
    165–75, 136–43, 252
    alliance between Cochise and, 16, 20
    ambush of Carleton's emissary Roberts
        and soldiers by, 140–43
    American presence in Apachería during
        absence of, 166
    Apache Pass battle and wounding of,
        142, 143, 165–66, 169
    background as fighter, 15
    Bartlett's surveying party and, 18–19,
        132
    Carleton's refusal of peace negotiations
        with, 167
    Chihenne war leader Victorio and
        peace negotiations with Pinos Altos
        mining town by, 170
    Chiricahuas' war of revenge for death
        of, 175, 180
    Cochise's request for assistance against
        Carleton from, 138, 140
    Cut the Tent incident (1861) and,
        20–22, 139, 168, 169
    declaration of war against Americans
        by, 22
    desire for treaty negotiations with
        Baylor, 88–89
    Geronimo and peace negotiations with
        Pinos Altos mining town by, 168–70
    Geronimo's reaction to death and
        beheading and, 174–75
    horses stolen from military camps by, 139
    Janos, Mexico, visit for medical care by,
        165–66
    Kearny's passage through lands of, 17, 18
    message to Carleton from, 166–67
    Mexican settlement raids by, 17–18,
        19, 139
    mining camp raids by, 14, 20
    mountain camp life of, 16
    Pinos Altos mining town attack by, 23,
        24, 31, 138–39
    Pinos Altos mining town peace
        negotiations of, 167–70, 172
    pragmatist approach to warfare and
        diplomacy by, 166

Mangas Coloradas (*cont.*)
   preservation of skull of, 174
   as prisoner of Joseph West at Fort
      McLane, 172–73
   proposed meeting with Arizona
      Guards, 139–40
   shooting and death of, 173–74
   Sumner's treaty and jurisdiction of,
      19–20
   Swilling's betrayal and capture of,
      170–71, 172
   U.S. forts built in lands of, 19, 20
   U.S. treaty with Mexico and protection
      against raids by, 18, 19
   wagon train raids by, 14, 18, 22–23, 172
   war dance with Cochise, 15–16
Manuelito, xvii, 30, 42, 250
   Bosque Redondo escape by, 222–23
   Bosque Redondo life of, 218–22
   Bosque Redondo removal to, 216–18
   Canby's promise of blankets to, 113
   Carleton's campaign against, 183
   Carleton's negotiations with, 199–200,
      206, 207–8
   clashes between Fort Defiance soldiers
      and, 45–46, 47
   confrontation with soldiers and loss of
      rifles by, 188–89
   decision not to surrender and move to
      Bosque Redondo by, 196–99, 214
   Fort Defiance rebuilding and, 185
   Indian agent Dodd's meeting with,
      232–33
   return to Diné Bikéyah, 245–46
   San Francisco Mountains home of,
      196–97
   surrender to U.S. Army by, 215
   Union raids and, 189–90
   U.S.-Navajo Treaty negotiations and
      signing of, 235–44
   U.S. treaty negotiations (1846; 1861)
      with, 45, 46–47, 113
maps
   United States in 1861, x–xi
   Southwestern theater, Summer 1861–
      Winter 1862, 2–3
   Southwestern theater, Winter–Summer
      1862, 76–77
   Southwestern theater, Summer 1862–
      Summer 1868, 162–63
Maricopas, 82, 129–30, 131

McCleave, William, 127–28
McClellan, George, 97, 149, 205
McGee brothers, 225
McRae, Alexander, 67, 69–70, 71, 73, 74,
   147
Meade, George, 182
Mescalero Apaches
   Bosque Redondo reservation and, 157,
      200, 201, 204, 218
   Carleton's campaign against, 167, 171,
      172
   Carson's campaign against, 154–57
   Fort Stanton attack by, 13, 154
   Fort Sumner agricultural work of,
      200–2
   Sibley Brigade's march through Texas
      and, 38–39
Mesilla, New Mexico Territory
   Baylor's occupation of as capital of
      Confederate Territory of Arizona,
      7–8, 11–12, 13, 82–83
   Confederate campaign for the West
      based in, 11
   Confederate encampment around, after
      retreat march, 119
   Davis's proclamation recognizing
      Arizona as a Confederate Territory,
      82–83
   mining activity around, 6–7
   retreat from Santa Fe along Coopwood's
      Trail to, 115, 116–18, 119, 120
   secessionist sentiment in, 7, 30
   Sibley's desire to leave, 122
Mesilla Times, 12, 13, 24, 79, 82, 85
Mexican–American War (1846), 26
Mexico
   Baylor's raid against Chiricahua
      Apaches in, 87–88, 120–21
   Chiricahua Apache raids into, 17–18,
      84, 139
   Davidson and Company A's raids for
      supplies in and retaliatory raids
      from, 122–23
   Navajo wars with, 45
   Reily's mission to, seeking Confederacy
      recognition, 83–85
   U.S. treaty with, and promise of
      protection against Apache raids,
      18, 19
miners
   Arizona Territory and, 130–31

Cochise's attack on Ake party of, 22–23
Pinos Altos and other makeshift towns
    built by, 20, 23, 24, 139
as soldiers, 50–51, 60, 96, 125, 159
mining camps
    Chiricahua Apache raids on, 14, 20
    Mangas Coloradas's attack on Pinos
        Altos mining town, 23, 24, 31,
        138–39
    Union soldiers' protection of, 166
Missouri
    Civil War in, 94
    as key state for Union, 52–53, 119
    transportation disruption from armed
        struggles in, 30
Mormons, 27, 28–29

Nashville, Union occupation of, 112
Native peoples. *See also specific peoples*
    Army conflicts in the West with, 190
    Canby's campaigns against, in Pacific
        Northwest, 250
    Civil War and larger struggle for future
        of, xx
    conflict in New Mexico as "three-
        cornered war" involving, xx
    Davis's desire for allegiance of, 121
    emancipation from slavery as a
        civilizing process for, 213
    federal control of the West's lands and,
        148
    Jackson's removal policy and, 188
    Peace Commission and, 234–35, 243
    power for negotiating treaties with, 84,
        234
    three-step method for dealing with, 188
    Union Army's campaign against, 188
    Union Indian Policy on, 155
    vigorous warfare strategy against, 188
    winter campaigns against, 190–91
Navajos, 42–45
    Bosque Redondo reservation and,
        188, 192, 195, 196, 197–99, 200–3,
        205–12
    Canby's campaign against, 30, 191
    Carleton's campaigns against, 155, 183,
        200–1, 205
    Carson's campaign against, 183–84,
        186–88, 190–92, 195–96
    clashes between Fort Defiance soldiers
        and, 45–46, 47
    daily life for, 42–43
    enslavement of, in New Mexico
        Territory, 92, 213, 245
    Fort Sumner agricultural work of,
        200–1
    hidden Santa Fe supply of blankets
        promised to, 113, 146
    Long Walk and forced removals of, 196,
        197, 198, 216, 236, 249–50
    Manuelito's leadership of, 45
    narrating Diné history during winter
        gatherings and, 48–49
    New Mexico Territory raids by, 44
    raids on Sibley Brigade by, 121
    skirmishes between Canby and, 30
    Tséyi' campaign and, xx, 190–99
    Union Army campaign against, 178,
        189–90
    U.S. treaty negotiations with, 44–45,
        46–47
    vigorous warfare strategy against,
        187–88
    women's weaving and, 47–48
New Mexico Territory
    adobe towns and pueblos in, 54
    Baylor and 2nd Texas's occupation of,
        6–8, 12–13, 25, 124
    Canby's control over, 148
    Canbys' stay in, 29–32
    Carleton as commander of, 149, 150
    Civil War and large number of soldiers
        in, 175
    Clark as surveyor general of, xviii, 31,
        90, 92, 93, 101, 176, 179, 227, 229
    Confederate interest in, 89
    desert landscape as problem for military
        operations in, 121–22
    Fort Union as temporary seat of
        government of, 94
    as gateway to California and the larger
        West, xiv
    impact of Civil War on, 30–31
    land covered by, xiv
    land ownership disputes between
        United States and Hispano residents
        of, 90
    Lincoln's assassination proclamation
        in, 209
    Lincoln's concerns about loyalty of,
        92–93
    Navajo raids against Americans in, 44

New Mexico Territory (*cont.*)
  peonage and Indian slavery abolished
    in, 229
  political scene in, 226–27
  secessionist sentiment in, xiv, 7, 23, 30,
    92, 95, 99, 100, 121, 149, 206
  Sibley's command over, 40, 72, 84, 97,
    123
  Sibley's letter to War Department about
    failure in, 121
  survey of arable land in, 176–77
  survival strategies of people in, xv
  Union Army control over settlement
    of, 178
  Union Indian Policy in, 155
New Mexico Volunteers. *See* 1st New
  Mexico Volunteers
Norton, A. B., 222, 224

Pacheco, Ramón, 132–33
Pacific Railway Act (1862), 147–48
Penateka Comanches, 80
*Personal Narrative of Explorations and
  Incidents* (Bartlett), 132
Pesqueira, Ignacio, 84
Pfeiffer, Albert, 191, 192–94
Picacho Peak, Battle of (1862), 127–28
Pimas, 82, 129–30, 131
Pima Villages, Arizona, Carleton's
  encampment at, 127, 129–30, 178,
  180, 182
Pinos Altos mining town, New Mexico
  Territory
  Chiricahua Apaches' attacks on, 23, 24,
    31, 138–39
  Mangas Coloradas's peace negotiations
    with, 167–70, 172
Polk, James, 26
Pyron, Charles
  Apache Canyon battle and, 103, 104,
    105
  march from Santa Fe along Santa Fe
    Trail toward Fort Union by, 101–2,
    103
  Santa Fe occupation by, 99, 100
  Valverde battle and, 64, 101

Reconstruction, 228, 230, 231, 234
Reily, James, 83–85, 88
reservations. *See also* Bosque Redondo
  reservation

Carleton and Union Indian Policy and,
  156
Comanche, at Clear Fork, 80
Dakota Sioux, 155
Jackson's removal policy and, 188
Rigg, Edwin, 125, 127
Roberts, Benjamin, 63, 68, 145–46, 235,
  238, 244
Roberts, Thomas L., 140–42, 143
Russell, Green, 159

San Antonio–El Paso Road
  Baylor and 2nd Texas' march along, xix,
    5–6, 37
  Davidson and Sibley Brigade's march
    along, 35–39
San Francisco, Carleton's confiscated
  meteorite planned for, 132–33
Santa Fe
  Canbys' life in, 29–32, 148, 149
  Canby's reassurances about departure of
    Texans from, 146–47
  Carleton's martial law in, 153
  Civil War eastern theater news and, 149,
    150, 156
  Confederate occupation of, 99, 100–1
  Confederate retreat from, 114, 115, 116,
    118, 146
  defensive burning of supplies in, before
    Texans' march on, 94–95
  gold fever from discovery in Arizona
    Territory and, 179
  hidden supply of blankets for Navajos
    in, 113, 146
  Ickis's opinion of residents of, 55
  impact of Civil War on, 30–31
  July 4 celebration in, 144–45
  Lincoln's assassination and, 209
  Louisa Canby's nursing of Confederate
    wounded in, 102–3, 111, 113, 114,
    145–46, 149–50
  news of Texans' plan to march on, 93
  problems housing large Confederate
    army in, 101
  residents' concerns about impending
    war threats to, 31–32, 90–91, 92
  residents' decision to stay and activities
    after Union Army departure, 100
  Richard Canby's warning to, about
    dangers after Valverde's loss, 74
  secessionist sentiment in, 30

Sibley's broadside to citizens of, after
  Confederate occupation, 100–1
Sibley's visit to, after Glorieta Pass
  battle, 113–14
soldiers passing through or residing
  in, 32
transcontinental railroad construction
  bypassing, 148
Union Army abandonment of and
  withdrawal to Fort Union, 93, 99
Union Army loss at Valverde and, 74, 91
Santa Fe Gazette, 111, 113, 146, 150–51
Santa Fe Mining Company, 179, 182, 183
Santa Fe Weekly Gazette, 156, 206, 209
Scott, Winfield, 28
Scurry, William, 65
  address to his men after Glorieta Pass
    battle, 111–12
  advance guard in Glorieta Pass and, 106
  Apache Canyon battle and, 104–6
  Glorieta Pass battle and, 106, 108, 110
  Louisa Canby's nursing of wounded
    and, 113
  retreat along Coopwood's Trail to
    Mesilla by, 117
séances, 91
2nd Texas Mounted Rifles (2nd Texas), xix,
  5, 11, 37, 64, 89, 110
Sethmooda, 170, 171, 174
7th Texas Mounted Volunteers (7th Texas),
  34, 36, 37, 79, 104, 105, 107, 117
Shash Bitoh ("Bear Spring"), 43–44, 46, 254
Sheridan, Philip, 204
Sherman, William Tecumseh, 194–95,
  204–5, 234, 235–45
Shiloh, Battle of (1862), 119, 149
Shirland, Edmund, 171, 172, 174
Shropshire, John, 33, 72, 103, 110
Sibley, Henry Hopkins, xix
  Albuquerque base of, after occupation
    of Santa Fe, 99, 113, 118
  Albuquerque return of, to defend
    against Canby, 114, 115
  Arizona Territory defense and, 116
  Baylor and his soldiers providing
    support for, 33, 35, 40
  Baylor's letter of resignation to, 89,
    120–21
  Baylor's raid on Corralitos, Chihuahua,
    Mexico, by, 87–88, 120–21
  Baylor's soldiers absorbed into

command of, 39–40, 79
brigade preparations by, 34–35
campaign against Chiricahua Apaches
  and, 80
campaign for the West by, 33, 99, 123
Canby known by, 61
Canby on departure from New Mexico
  Territory of, 147
decision to cross Rio Grande at
  Valverde by, 61–62
Fort Bliss, Texas, headquarters of, 40–41
Louisa Canby's nursing of Confederate
  wounded and, 113, 146
march through Texas to New Mexico
  and, 36, 37, 38, 41
New Mexico campaign planning by,
  34, 35
Peralta skirmish and, 115
plan for fighting Canby by, 61
plan to leave Mesilla and return to San
  Antonio by, 122
praise for his troops in address by, 120
protests against Baylor's killing of
  Chiricahua Apaches and, 87–88
Reily's mission to Mexico seeking
  Confederacy recognition and, 83–85
retreat from Santa Fe along
  Coopwood's Trail to Mesilla by,
  115, 116–18, 119, 120
rumors about Union army on move
  toward Mesilla, 122, 124
Santa Fe occupation and, 99, 100–1
Santa Fe visit of, after Glorieta Pass
  battle, 113–14
strategy of staggering troops by, 36
Terrazas's letter to and later apology
  from, about Baylor's raid in Mexico,
  87–88, 120–21
troop's opinion of, 118, 149–50
Union-Confederate meeting without
  battle outside Fort Craig and, 60–61
Valverde battle and, 62, 68, 72
War Department letter on New Mexico
  Territory campaign from, 121–22
Sibley Brigade, 60
  Apache and Navajo raiders' attacks on,
    121
  Baylor's soldiers absorbed into, 39–40,
    79
  Camp Manassas, Texas, waiting period
    of, 33–34, 35

Sibley Brigade (*cont.*)
  Davidson's enthusiasm for, 35
  Fort Bliss, Texas, conditions and, 39–41
  Glorieta Pass defeat and, 110, 111–12
  march through Texas to New Mexico by, 35–39, 41, 97
  march to Albuquerque, to defend against Canby, 114, 115
  Mescalero Apaches and, 154
  Peralta skirmish and, 115
  planned return to San Antonio by, 122
  possible Union threat to Texas and, 120
  retreat from Santa Fe along Coopwood's Trail to Mesilla by, 115, 116–18, 119, 120
  Santa Fe occupation by, 99, 100–1
  Sibley's leadership criticized within, 118
  Sibley's praiseful address to, 120
  slaves of officers in, 40–41, 83
  Union-Confederate meeting without battle outside Fort Craig and, 60–61
  Valverde battle and, 63, 68, 72, 73, 79
slaves
  Apaches and Navajos in New Mexico Territory as, 92
  Apaches in Mexico as, 87–88
  Confederate Territory of Arizona and, 83
  Hispanos as, 17, 46
  Navajos and, 43, 44, 46
  Sibley Brigade officers and, 40–41, 83
Slough, John, 108, 109
Snow, Miss (Eliza), 28–29
Stanton, Edwin, 97, 147, 149, 230
Steck, Michael, 201
Steele, William, 79
Sumner, Edwin Vose, 19–20
Swilling, Jack, 168
  gold mining by, 182
  Mangas Coloradas's betrayal by, 170–71, 172

Tappan, Samuel F., 234, 235, 240–41, 244
Taylor, Zachary, 17
Teal, John, 142
Tennessee
  Battle of Shiloh in, 119
  Grant's army clearing way for invasion of, 94
Terrazas, Luis, 84, 85, 87–88, 120

Texas
  Alamo battle and, 33–34
  areas of the South under Union control in 1862 as threat to, 119–20
  Baylor's early Confederate Army service in, 5–6, 37
  Comanche raids in, 80
  Indian removal policy of, 80
  Sibley Brigade's march to New Mexico through, 35–39
  Sibley's retreat from Arizona Territory and return to, 122-3, 124
  Union Army's planned invasion of, 112
Texas Mounted Volunteers. *See* 5th Texas Mounted Volunteers; 4th Texas Mounted Volunteers; 7th Texas Mounted Volunteers
Texas Rangers, 80, 158
Tséhootsoh ("Meadow in the Rocks"), 42, 45, 185, 197–98, 250
Tséyi' (Canyon de Chelly), campaign for (1864), Arizona Territory, xx, 190–96
  Carson in, 190, 191–92, 195
  description of, 190
  early campaigns in, 191–92
  first skirmish in, 192
  Navajo surrenders to Carson as result of, 192, 195–96
  Pfeiffer's detachment in, 192–94
  winter campaign strategy in, 190–91, 199
Tsoodzil ("Blue Bead"), 47, 49, 154, 185, 215, 246
Tucson, Arizona Territory
  Carleton's advance group's occupation of, 129, 130
  Carleton's arrival and setting up headquarters in, 131
  Carleton's confiscation of meteorite in, 132–33
  Carleton's plan to march on, 128, 129
  Hunter's occupation and later abandonment of, 127, 129
  Union troops' reoccupying forts near, 166

Union
  areas of the South controlled by, in 1862, 119–20
  Confederacy surrounded on all sides by states and territories of, 123
  conflict in New Mexico as "three-cornered war" involving, xx

conquest and Anglo settlement of the
    West by, 177, 184
Hispanos' fluctuating loyalties to, 121
Lincoln's desire to hold West for, 98
Missouri as key state for, 52–53, 119
New Mexico Territory land sales to
    support war effort of, 90
Union soldiers
    Apache Canyon battle and, 103–6
    burial in Fort Craig's graveyard after
        Valverde battle, 74
    Chiricahua Apache campaign of, 175,
        176
    Confederate gold miners arrested by, 159
    Confiscation Act used by, 132–33
    defensive burning of supplies by, 94–95,
        99
    Fort Craig expansion for, 59
    Glorieta Pass battle and, 106–13
    Nashville occupation by, 112
    Peralta skirmish and, 115
    planned invasion of Texas by, 112
    Shiloh battle and, 119
    Valverde battle and, xx, 62–74, 91, 95,
        147
    vigorous warfare strategy of, 187–88
Utah Territory
    campaign against Mormons in, 27,
        28–29
    Canbys' stay in, 27–29
Utes, 46, 53, 58, 185, 196, 204, 206, 215, 237

Valverde, Battle of (1862), New Mexico
    Territory, xx, 61–74, 147
    Baylor on news of victory in, 79
    Clark's concerns about Canby's
        leadership at, 95
    Clark's notes on, 225
    description of, 61–62
    federal government's delay in receiving
        news of, 97
    Ickis's visit to Fort Craig's dead room
        after, 73–74
    Lang's Lancers in, 66–67
    letter to Santa Fe about loss in, 91
    Santa Fe residents and impact of Union
        loss at, 91

Sibley Brigade's field funeral service
    after, 73
Sibley's decision to cross Rio Grande at,
    61–62
Union burials in Fort Craig's graveyard
    after, 74
Union casualties at, 73
Van Dorn, Earl, 12, 13, 34, 119
Victorio (Chihenne Apache war leader),
    170, 171, 172, 174

Walker, Joseph Reddeford, 171, 172, 174,
    178–81
Wallen, Henry, 157–58
West
    Confederate plans for taking, xix, 8, 33,
        99, 120, 123
    Lincoln's desire to hold West as Union
        territory, 98
    network of Republican officials sent
        to, to establish political and civil
        control, 92
    New Mexico conflict in Civil War and
        larger struggle for future of, xx
    Sibley's campaign for, 99
    Union Congress's encouragement of
        colonization of, 147–48
    Union conquest and Anglo settlement
        of, 177, 184
    Union Indian Policy in, 155
West, Joseph Rodman, 173
    Chiricahua Apache campaign and,
        171–72, 178
    Mangas Coloradas as prisoner of,
        172–73
    Mangas Coloradas's shooting and death
        and, 173–74
    march across desert from Los Angeles
        to Tucson and, 125
    Tucson capture by, 129, 131
Wheeling, Lieutenant, 135, 136–37, 167
White, Ammi, 127, 129
Wright, George, 124, 125, 127, 133

Young, Brigham, 27, 28, 29

Zuñis, 180, 183, 185, 186, 189, 196, 215

About the Author

Megan Kate Nelson is a writer and historian. She has written about the Civil War, US Western history, and American culture for *The New York Times*, *The Washington Post*, *Smithsonian* magazine, *Preservation* magazine, and *The Civil War Monitor*. Nelson is the author of *Ruin Nation* and *Trembling Earth*.